THE CHAINS OF OLYMPUS

COLLECTED COMIC STRIPS
from the pages of

BBC
DOCTOR WHO
MAGAZINE™

panini COMICS

CONTENTS

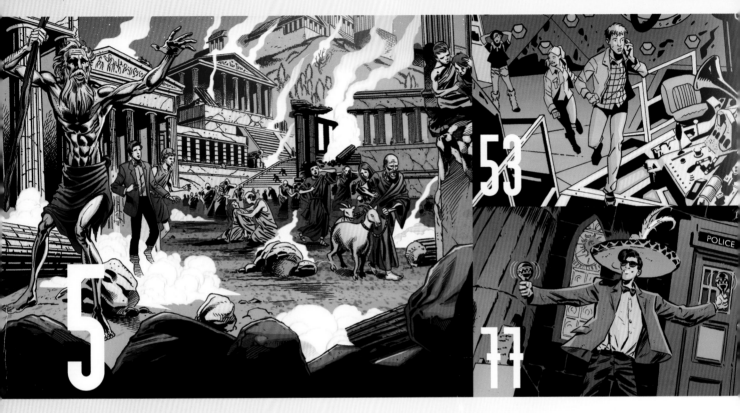

53
POLICE
5
77

Project Editors **TOM SPILSBURY & SCOTT GRAY** Designer **PERI GODBOLD**
Cover pencils and inks by **DAVID A ROACH** Cover colours by **JAMES OFFREDI**

Head of Production **MARK IRVINE** Managing Editor **ALAN O'KEEFE** Managing Director **MIKE RIDDELL**

Special thanks to **STEVEN MOFFAT, MATT SMITH, KAREN GILLAN, ARTHUR DARVILL, GARY RUSSELL, RICHARD ATKINSON, PETER WARE, JOHN AINSWORTH and all the writers and artists whose work is presented herein.**

MIX
Paper from responsible sources
FSC www.fsc.org FSC® C002386

Doctor Who Graphic Novel #16: *The Chains of Olympus*. Published in 2013 by Panini Publishing Ltd. Office of publication: Brockbourne House, 77 Mount Ephraim, Tunbridge Wells, Kent TN4 8BS.

ISBN 978-1-84653-558-1

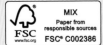

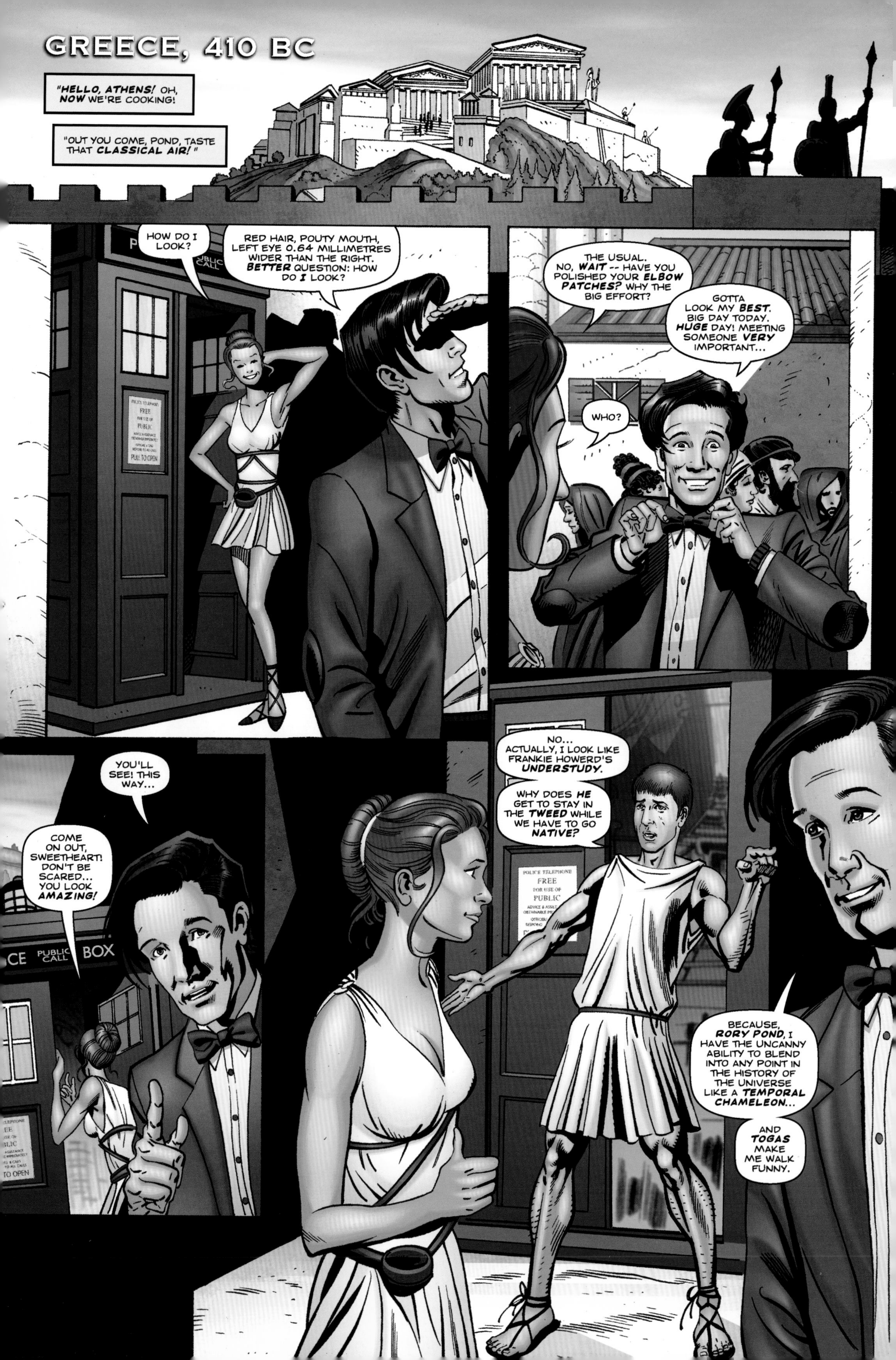
GREECE, 410 BC
"HELLO, ATHENS! OH, NOW WE'RE COOKING!
"OUT YOU COME, POND, TASTE THAT CLASSICAL AIR!"
HOW DO I LOOK?
RED HAIR, POUTY MOUTH, LEFT EYE 0.64 MILLIMETRES WIDER THAN THE RIGHT. BETTER QUESTION: HOW DO I LOOK?
THE USUAL. NO, WAIT -- HAVE YOU POLISHED YOUR ELBOW PATCHES? WHY THE BIG EFFORT?
GOTTA LOOK MY BEST. BIG DAY TODAY. HUGE DAY! MEETING SOMEONE VERY IMPORTANT...
WHO?
YOU'LL SEE! THIS WAY...
COME ON OUT, SWEETHEART! DON'T BE SCARED... YOU LOOK AMAZING!
NO... ACTUALLY, I LOOK LIKE FRANKIE HOWERD'S UNDERSTUDY.
WHY DOES HE GET TO STAY IN THE TWEED WHILE WE HAVE TO GO NATIVE?
BECAUSE, RORY POND, I HAVE THE UNCANNY ABILITY TO BLEND INTO ANY POINT IN THE HISTORY OF THE UNIVERSE LIKE A TEMPORAL CHAMELEON...
AND TOGAS MAKE ME WALK FUNNY.

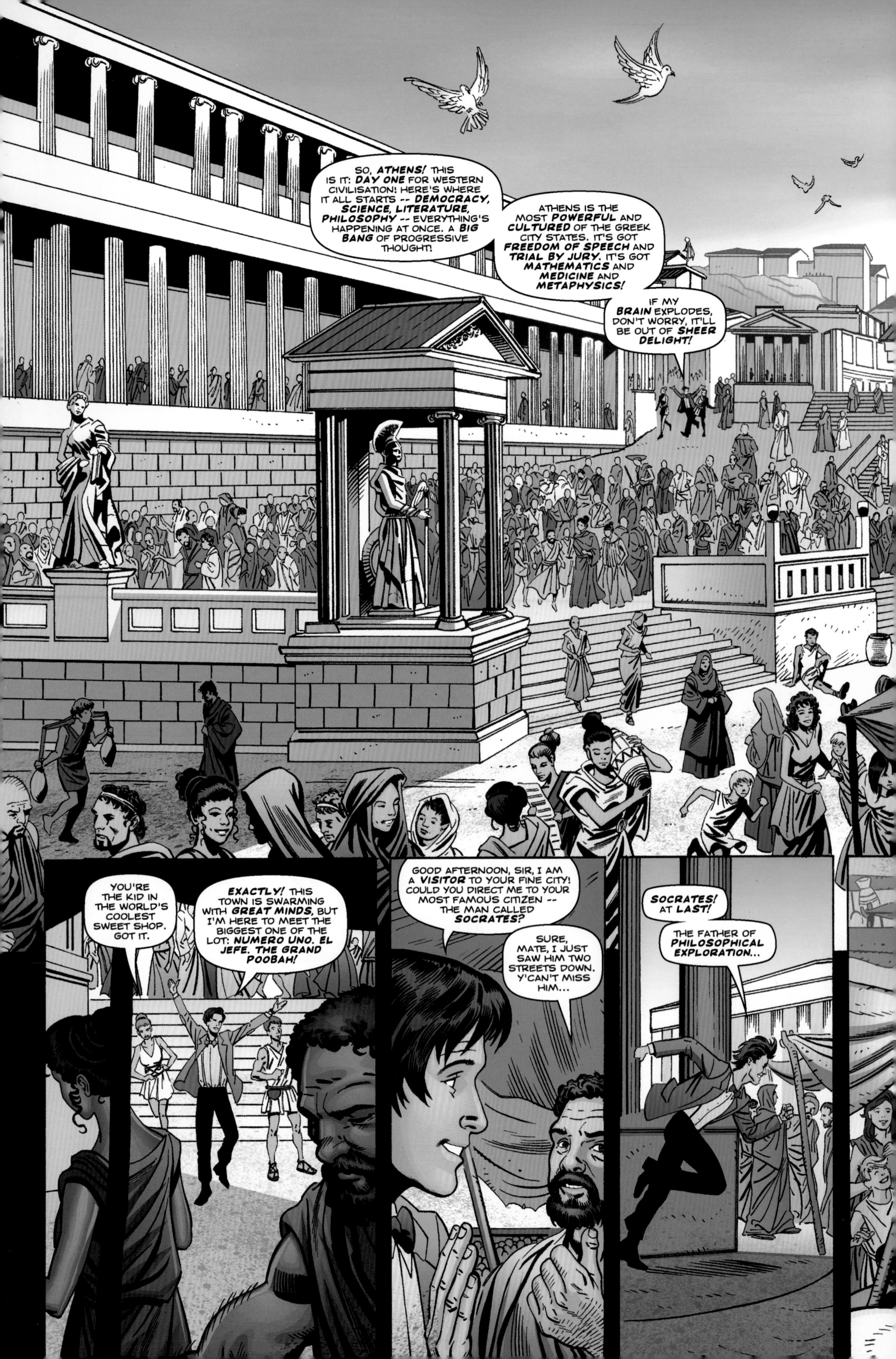
SO, ATHENS! THIS IS IT: DAY ONE FOR WESTERN CIVILISATION! HERE'S WHERE IT ALL STARTS -- DEMOCRACY, SCIENCE, LITERATURE, PHILOSOPHY -- EVERYTHING'S HAPPENING AT ONCE. A BIG BANG OF PROGRESSIVE THOUGHT!
ATHENS IS THE MOST POWERFUL AND CULTURED OF THE GREEK CITY STATES. IT'S GOT FREEDOM OF SPEECH AND TRIAL BY JURY. IT'S GOT MATHEMATICS AND MEDICINE AND METAPHYSICS!
IF MY BRAIN EXPLODES, DON'T WORRY, IT'LL BE OUT OF SHEER DELIGHT!
YOU'RE THE KID IN THE WORLD'S COOLEST SWEET SHOP. GOT IT.
EXACTLY! THIS TOWN IS SWARMING WITH GREAT MINDS, BUT I'M HERE TO MEET THE BIGGEST ONE OF THE LOT: NUMERO UNO. EL JEFE. THE GRAND POOBAH!
GOOD AFTERNOON, SIR, I AM A VISITOR TO YOUR FINE CITY! COULD YOU DIRECT ME TO YOUR MOST FAMOUS CITIZEN -- THE MAN CALLED SOCRATES?
SURE, MATE, I JUST SAW HIM TWO STREETS DOWN. Y'CAN'T MISS HIM...
SOCRATES! AT LAST!
THE FATHER OF PHILOSOPHICAL EXPLORATION...

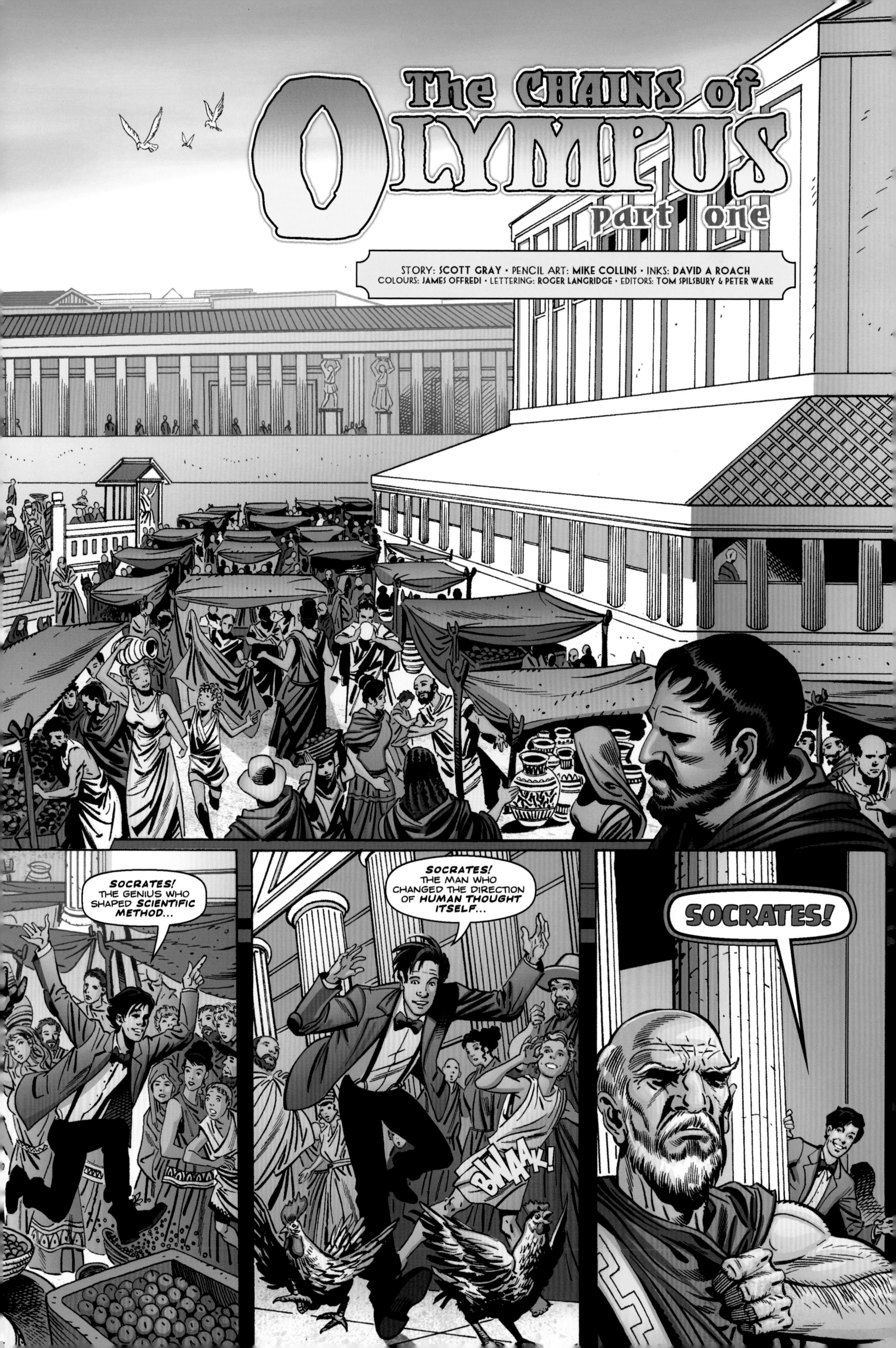
The CHAINS of OLYMPUS
part one
STORY: SCOTT GRAY • PENCIL ART: MIKE COLLINS • INKS: DAVID A ROACH
COLOURS: JAMES OFFREDI • LETTERING: ROGER LANGRIDGE • EDITORS: TOM SPILSBURY & PETER WARE
SOCRATES! THE GENIUS WHO SHAPED SCIENTIFIC METHOD...
SOCRATES! THE MAN WHO CHANGED THE DIRECTION OF HUMAN THOUGHT ITSELF...
BWAAK!
SOCRATES!

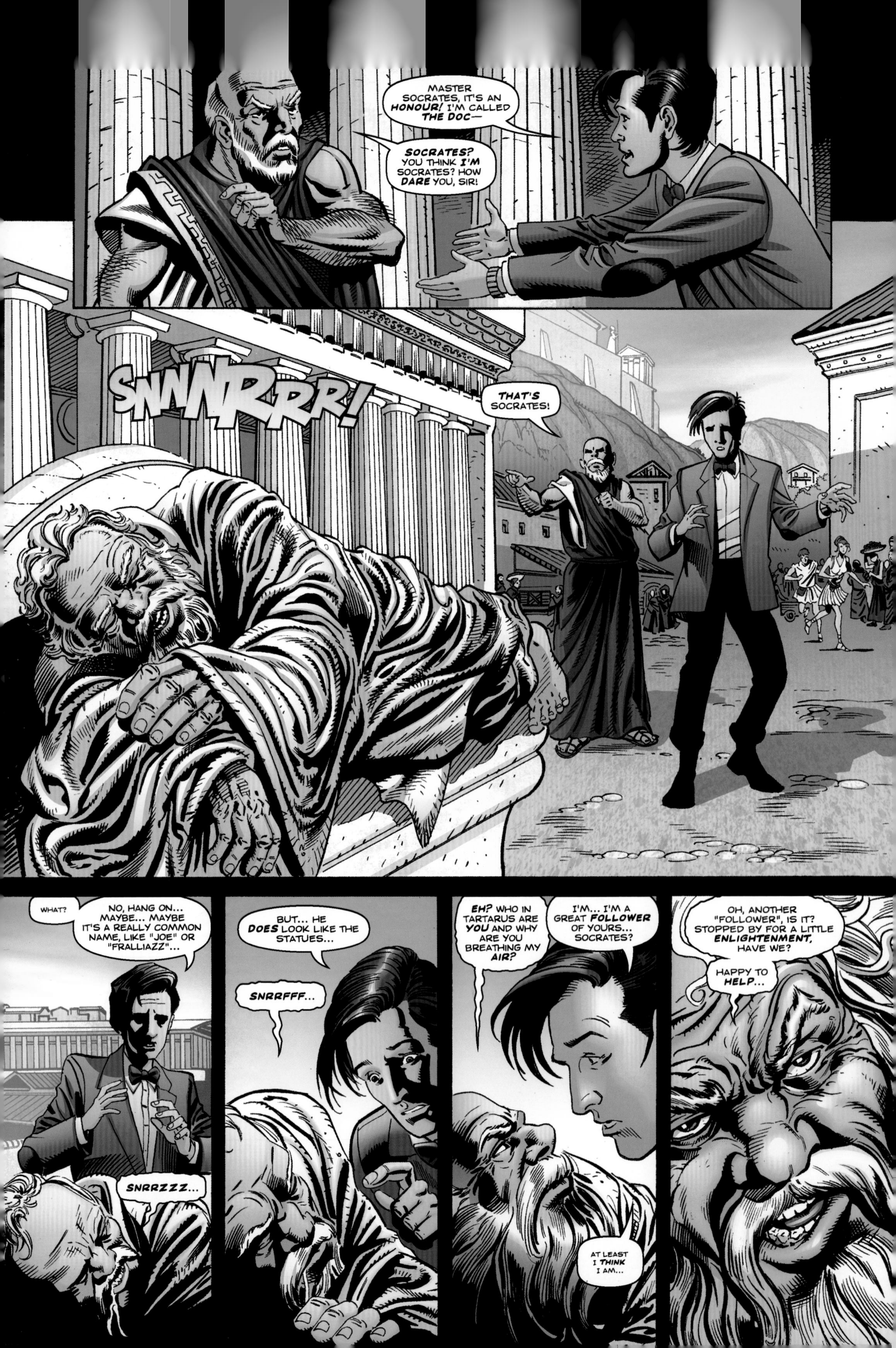

MASTER SOCRATES, IT'S AN HONOUR! I'M CALLED THE DOC—
SOCRATES? YOU THINK I'M SOCRATES? HOW DARE YOU, SIR!
SNNNRRR!
THAT'S SOCRATES!
WHAT?
NO, HANG ON... MAYBE... MAYBE IT'S A REALLY COMMON NAME, LIKE "JOE" OR "FRALLIAZZ"...
SNRRZZZ...
BUT... HE DOES LOOK LIKE THE STATUES...
SNRRFFF...
EH? WHO IN TARTARUS ARE YOU AND WHY ARE YOU BREATHING MY AIR?
I'M... I'M A GREAT FOLLOWER OF YOURS... SOCRATES?
AT LEAST I THINK I AM...
OH, ANOTHER "FOLLOWER", IS IT? STOPPED BY FOR A LITTLE ENLIGHTENMENT, HAVE WE?
HAPPY TO HELP...

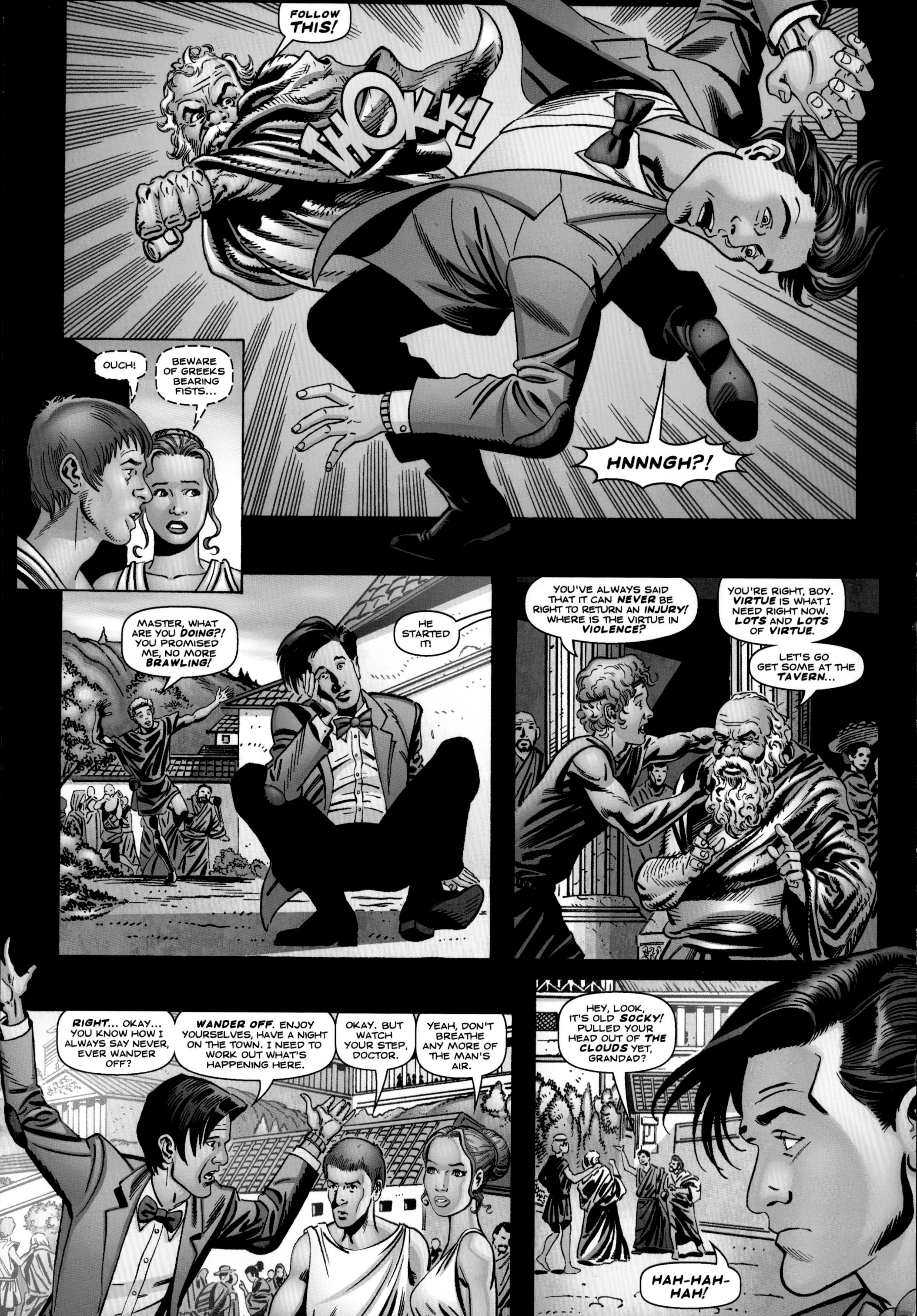
FOLLOW THIS!
THOKK!
HNNNGH?!
OUCH!
BEWARE OF GREEKS BEARING FISTS...
MASTER, WHAT ARE YOU DOING?! YOU PROMISED ME, NO MORE BRAWLING!
HE STARTED IT!
YOU'VE ALWAYS SAID THAT IT CAN NEVER BE RIGHT TO RETURN AN INJURY! WHERE IS THE VIRTUE IN VIOLENCE?
YOU'RE RIGHT, BOY. VIRTUE IS WHAT I NEED RIGHT NOW. LOTS AND LOTS OF VIRTUE.
LET'S GO GET SOME AT THE TAVERN...
RIGHT... OKAY... YOU KNOW HOW I ALWAYS SAY NEVER, EVER WANDER OFF?
WANDER OFF. ENJOY YOURSELVES, HAVE A NIGHT ON THE TOWN. I NEED TO WORK OUT WHAT'S HAPPENING HERE.
OKAY. BUT WATCH YOUR STEP, DOCTOR.
YEAH, DON'T BREATHE ANY MORE OF THE MAN'S AIR.
HEY, LOOK, IT'S OLD SOCKY! PULLED YOUR HEAD OUT OF THE CLOUDS YET, GRANDAD?
HAH-HAH-HAH!

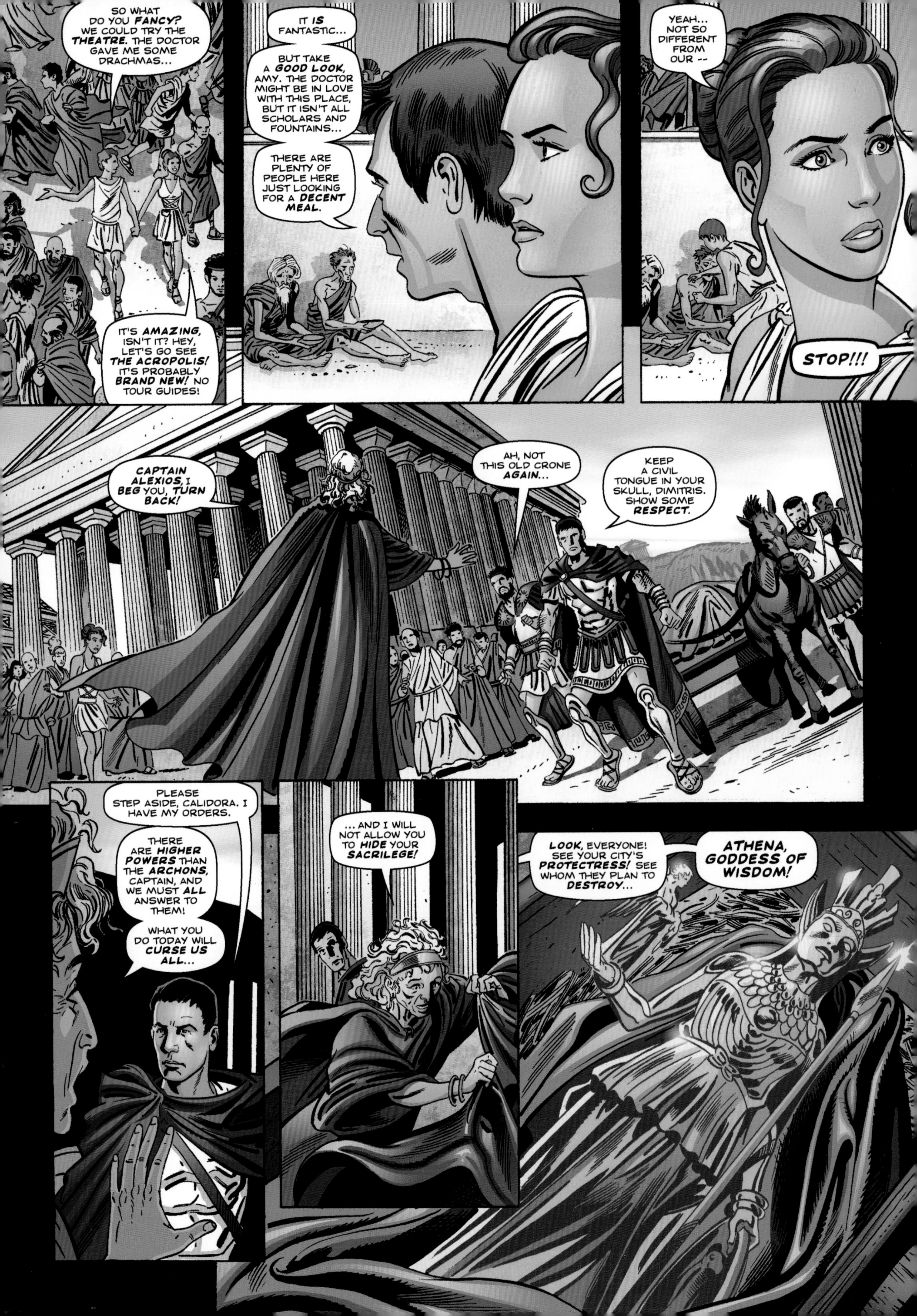
SO WHAT DO YOU FANCY? WE COULD TRY THE THEATRE. THE DOCTOR GAVE ME SOME DRACHMAS...
IT'S AMAZING, ISN'T IT? HEY, LET'S GO SEE THE ACROPOLIS! IT'S PROBABLY BRAND NEW! NO TOUR GUIDES!
IT IS FANTASTIC...
BUT TAKE A GOOD LOOK, AMY. THE DOCTOR MIGHT BE IN LOVE WITH THIS PLACE, BUT IT ISN'T ALL SCHOLARS AND FOUNTAINS...
THERE ARE PLENTY OF PEOPLE HERE JUST LOOKING FOR A DECENT MEAL.
YEAH... NOT SO DIFFERENT FROM OUR --
STOP!!!
CAPTAIN ALEXIOS, I BEG YOU, TURN BACK!
AH, NOT THIS OLD CRONE AGAIN...
KEEP A CIVIL TONGUE IN YOUR SKULL, DIMITRIS. SHOW SOME RESPECT.
PLEASE STEP ASIDE, CALIDORA. I HAVE MY ORDERS.
THERE ARE HIGHER POWERS THAN THE ARCHONS, CAPTAIN, AND WE MUST ALL ANSWER TO THEM!
WHAT YOU DO TODAY WILL CURSE US ALL...
... AND I WILL NOT ALLOW YOU TO HIDE YOUR SACRILEGE!
LOOK, EVERYONE! SEE YOUR CITY'S PROTECTRESS! SEE WHOM THEY PLAN TO DESTROY...
ATHENA, GODDESS OF WISDOM!

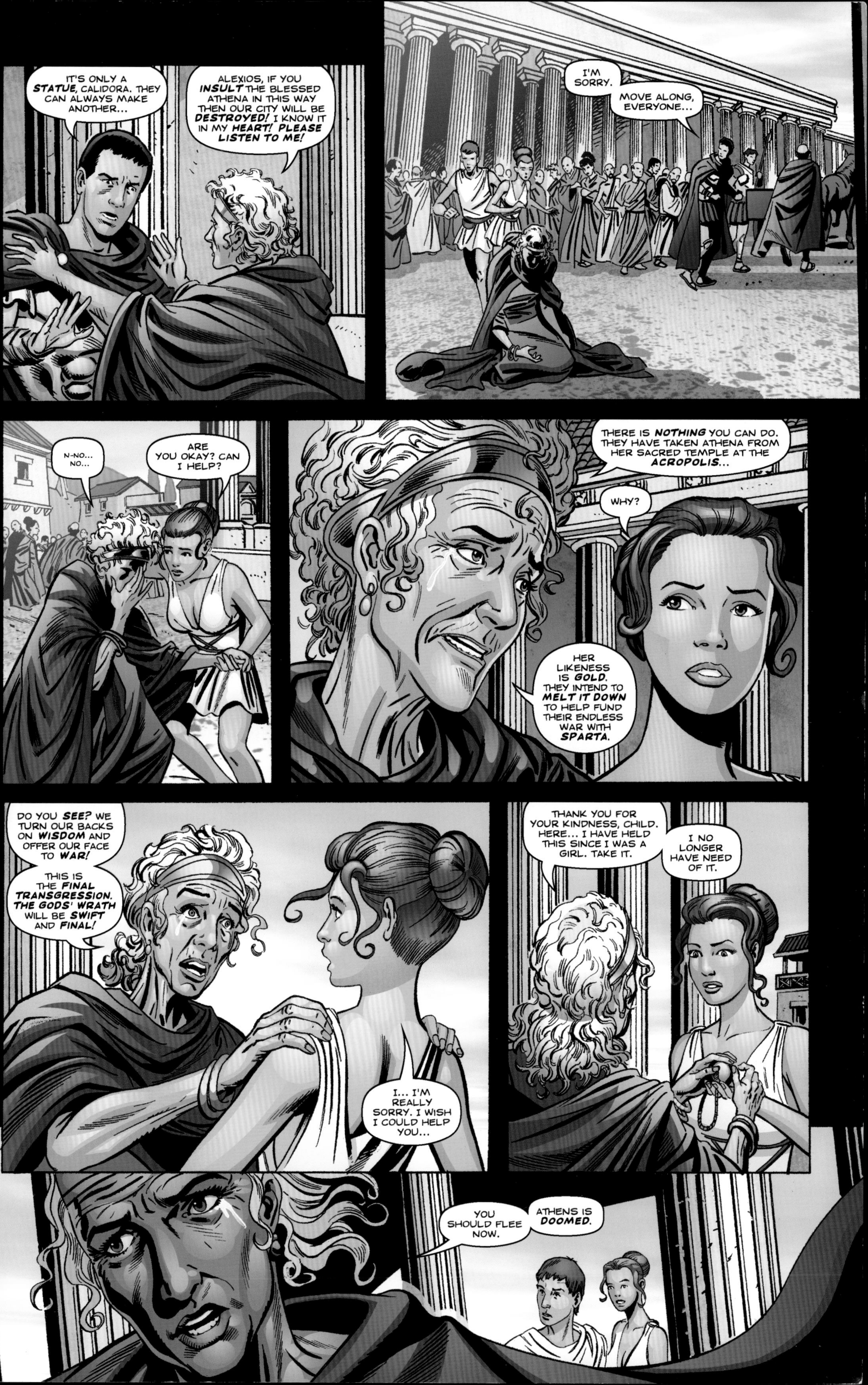
IT'S ONLY A STATUE, CALIDORA. THEY CAN ALWAYS MAKE ANOTHER...
ALEXIOS, IF YOU INSULT THE BLESSED ATHENA IN THIS WAY THEN OUR CITY WILL BE DESTROYED! I KNOW IT IN MY HEART! PLEASE LISTEN TO ME!
I'M SORRY.
MOVE ALONG, EVERYONE...
ARE YOU OKAY? CAN I HELP?
N-NO... NO...
THERE IS NOTHING YOU CAN DO. THEY HAVE TAKEN ATHENA FROM HER SACRED TEMPLE AT THE ACROPOLIS...
WHY?
HER LIKENESS IS GOLD. THEY INTEND TO MELT IT DOWN TO HELP FUND THEIR ENDLESS WAR WITH SPARTA.
DO YOU SEE? WE TURN OUR BACKS ON WISDOM AND OFFER OUR FACE TO WAR!
THIS IS THE FINAL TRANSGRESSION. THE GODS' WRATH WILL BE SWIFT AND FINAL!
I... I'M REALLY SORRY. I WISH I COULD HELP YOU...
THANK YOU FOR YOUR KINDNESS, CHILD. HERE... I HAVE HELD THIS SINCE I WAS A GIRL. TAKE IT.
I NO LONGER HAVE NEED OF IT.
YOU SHOULD FLEE NOW.
ATHENS IS DOOMED.

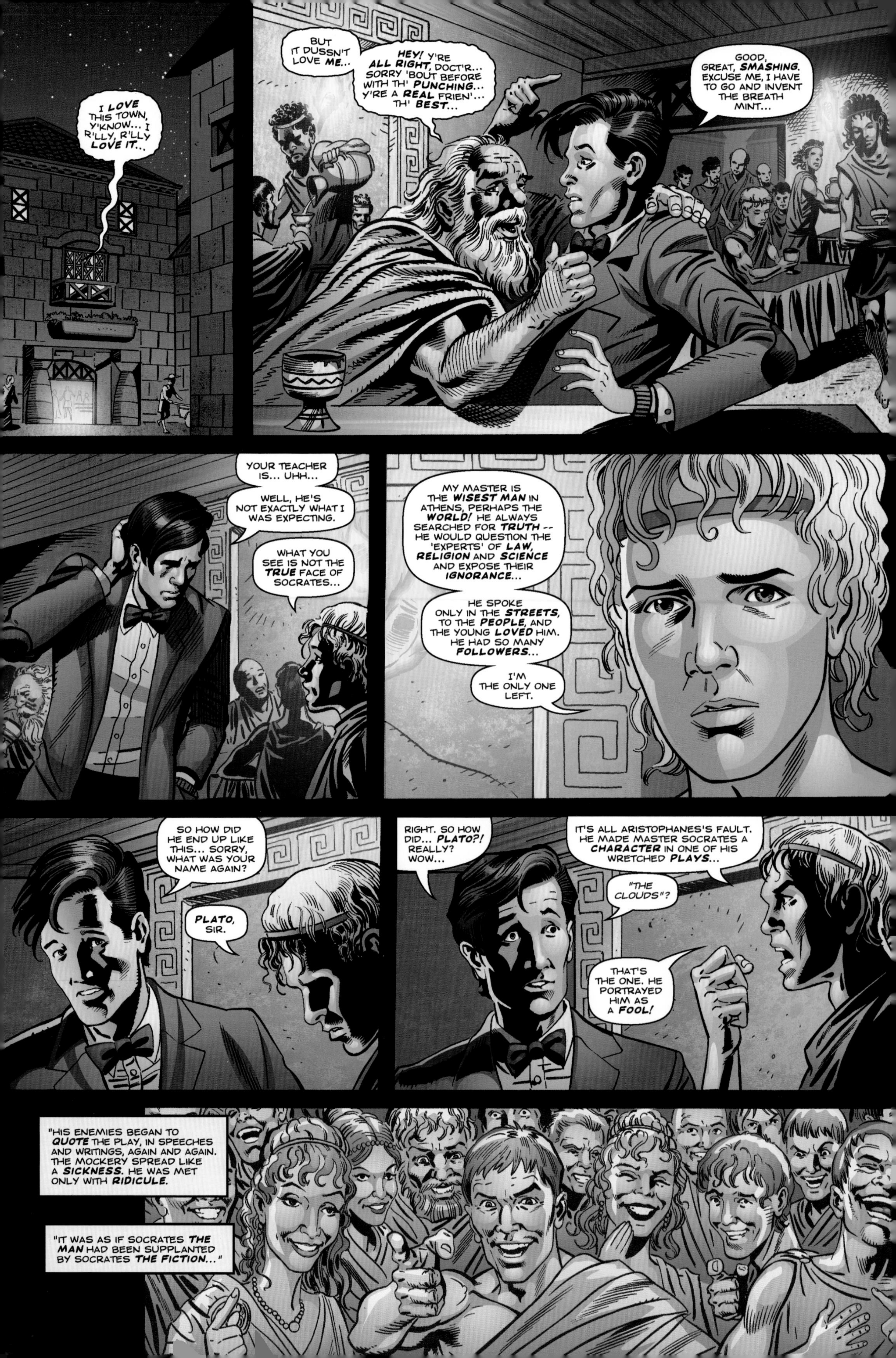
I LOVE THIS TOWN, Y'KNOW... I R'LLY, R'LLY LOVE IT...
BUT IT DUSSN'T LOVE ME...
HEY! Y'RE ALL RIGHT, DOCT'R... SORRY 'BOUT BEFORE WITH TH' PUNCHING... Y'RE A REAL FRIEN'... TH' BEST...
GOOD, GREAT, SMASHING. EXCUSE ME, I HAVE TO GO AND INVENT THE BREATH MINT...
YOUR TEACHER IS... UHH...
WELL, HE'S NOT EXACTLY WHAT I WAS EXPECTING.
WHAT YOU SEE IS NOT THE TRUE FACE OF SOCRATES...
MY MASTER IS THE WISEST MAN IN ATHENS, PERHAPS THE WORLD! HE ALWAYS SEARCHED FOR TRUTH -- HE WOULD QUESTION THE 'EXPERTS' OF LAW, RELIGION AND SCIENCE AND EXPOSE THEIR IGNORANCE...
HE SPOKE ONLY IN THE STREETS, TO THE PEOPLE, AND THE YOUNG LOVED HIM. HE HAD SO MANY FOLLOWERS...
I'M THE ONLY ONE LEFT.
SO HOW DID HE END UP LIKE THIS... SORRY, WHAT WAS YOUR NAME AGAIN?
PLATO, SIR.
RIGHT. SO HOW DID... PLATO?! REALLY? WOW...
IT'S ALL ARISTOPHANES'S FAULT. HE MADE MASTER SOCRATES A CHARACTER IN ONE OF HIS WRETCHED PLAYS...
"THE CLOUDS"?
THAT'S THE ONE. HE PORTRAYED HIM AS A FOOL!
"HIS ENEMIES BEGAN TO QUOTE THE PLAY, IN SPEECHES AND WRITINGS, AGAIN AND AGAIN. THE MOCKERY SPREAD LIKE A SICKNESS. HE WAS MET ONLY WITH RIDICULE.
"IT WAS AS IF SOCRATES THE MAN HAD BEEN SUPPLANTED BY SOCRATES THE FICTION..."

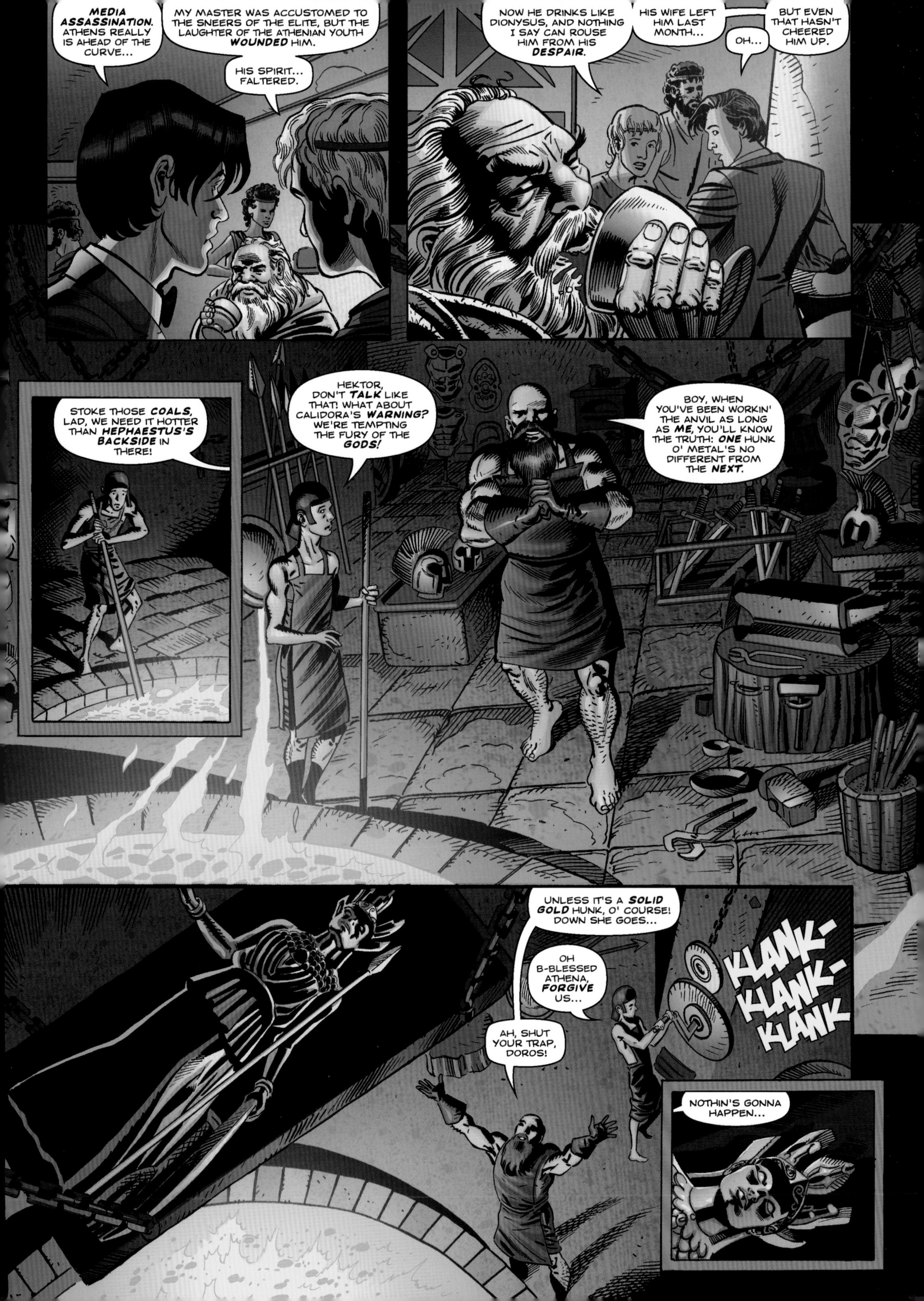
MEDIA ASSASSINATION. ATHENS REALLY IS AHEAD OF THE CURVE...
MY MASTER WAS ACCUSTOMED TO THE SNEERS OF THE ELITE, BUT THE LAUGHTER OF THE ATHENIAN YOUTH WOUNDED HIM.
HIS SPIRIT... FALTERED.
NOW HE DRINKS LIKE DIONYSUS, AND NOTHING I SAY CAN ROUSE HIM FROM HIS DESPAIR.
HIS WIFE LEFT HIM LAST MONTH...
OH...
BUT EVEN THAT HASN'T CHEERED HIM UP.
STOKE THOSE COALS, LAD, WE NEED IT HOTTER THAN HEPHAESTUS'S BACKSIDE IN THERE!
HEKTOR, DON'T TALK LIKE THAT! WHAT ABOUT CALIDORA'S WARNING? WE'RE TEMPTING THE FURY OF THE GODS!
BOY, WHEN YOU'VE BEEN WORKIN' THE ANVIL AS LONG AS ME, YOU'LL KNOW THE TRUTH: ONE HUNK O' METAL'S NO DIFFERENT FROM THE NEXT.
UNLESS IT'S A SOLID GOLD HUNK, O' COURSE! DOWN SHE GOES...
OH B-BLESSED ATHENA, FORGIVE US...
AH, SHUT YOUR TRAP, DOROS!
KLANK-KLANK-KLANK
NOTHIN'S GONNA HAPPEN...

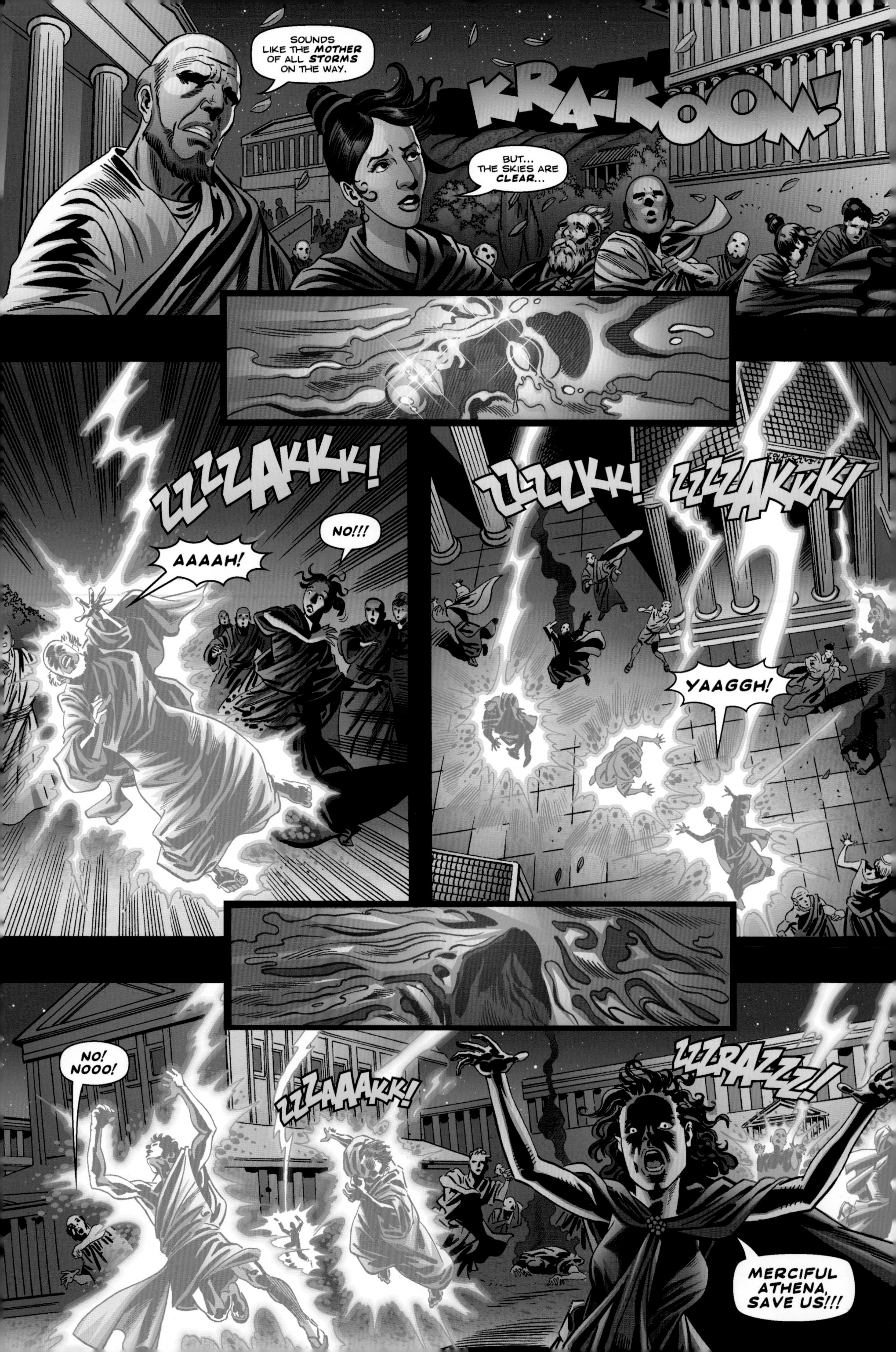
SOUNDS LIKE THE MOTHER OF ALL STORMS ON THE WAY.
KRA-KOOOM!
BUT... THE SKIES ARE CLEAR...
ZZZZAKKK!
NO!!!
AAAAH!
ZZZZKK!
ZZZZAKKK!
YAAGGH!
NO! NOOO!
ZZZAAAKK!
ZZZRAZZZ!
MERCIFUL ATHENA, SAVE US!!!

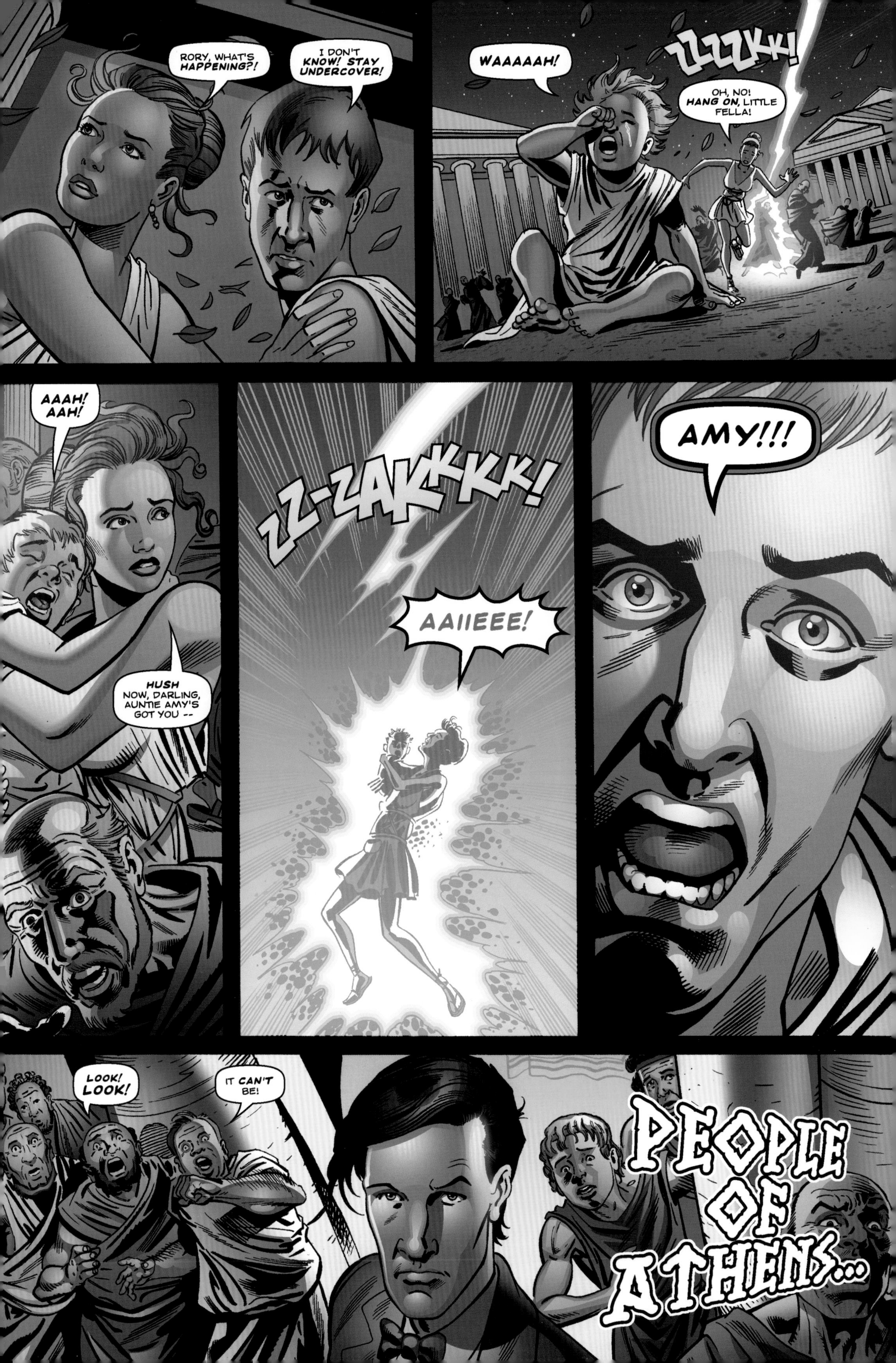
RORY, WHAT'S HAPPENING?!
I DON'T KNOW! STAY UNDERCOVER!
WAAAAAH!
ZZZZKK!
OH, NO! HANG ON, LITTLE FELLA!
AAAH! AAH!
HUSH NOW, DARLING, AUNTIE AMY'S GOT YOU --
ZZ-ZAKKKKK!
AAIIEEE!
AMY!!!
LOOK! LOOK!
IT CAN'T BE!
PEOPLE OF ATHENS...

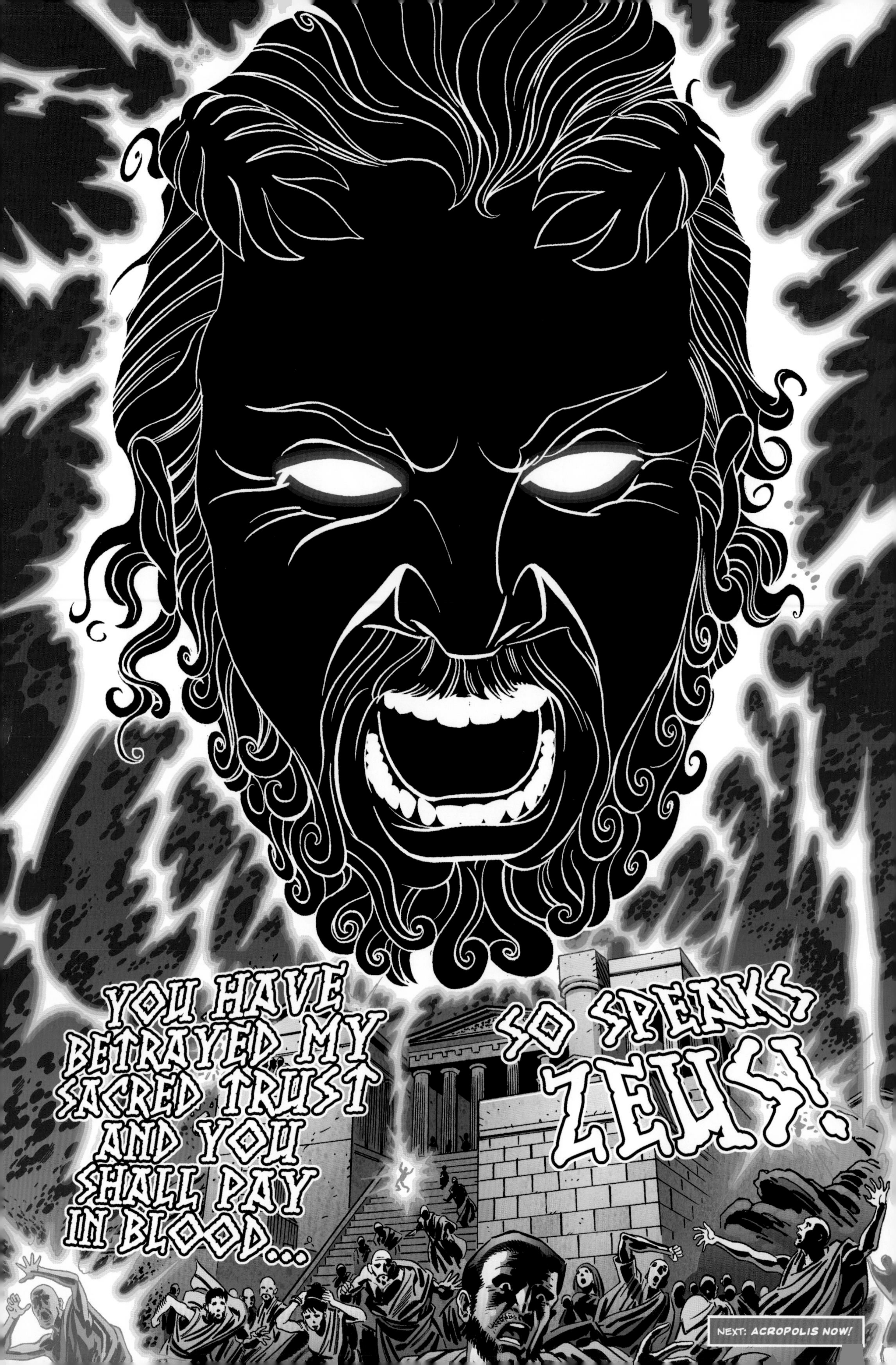
YOU HAVE BETRAYED MY SACRED TRUST AND YOU SHALL PAY IN BLOOD...
SO SPEAKS ZEUS!
NEXT: ACROPOLIS NOW!

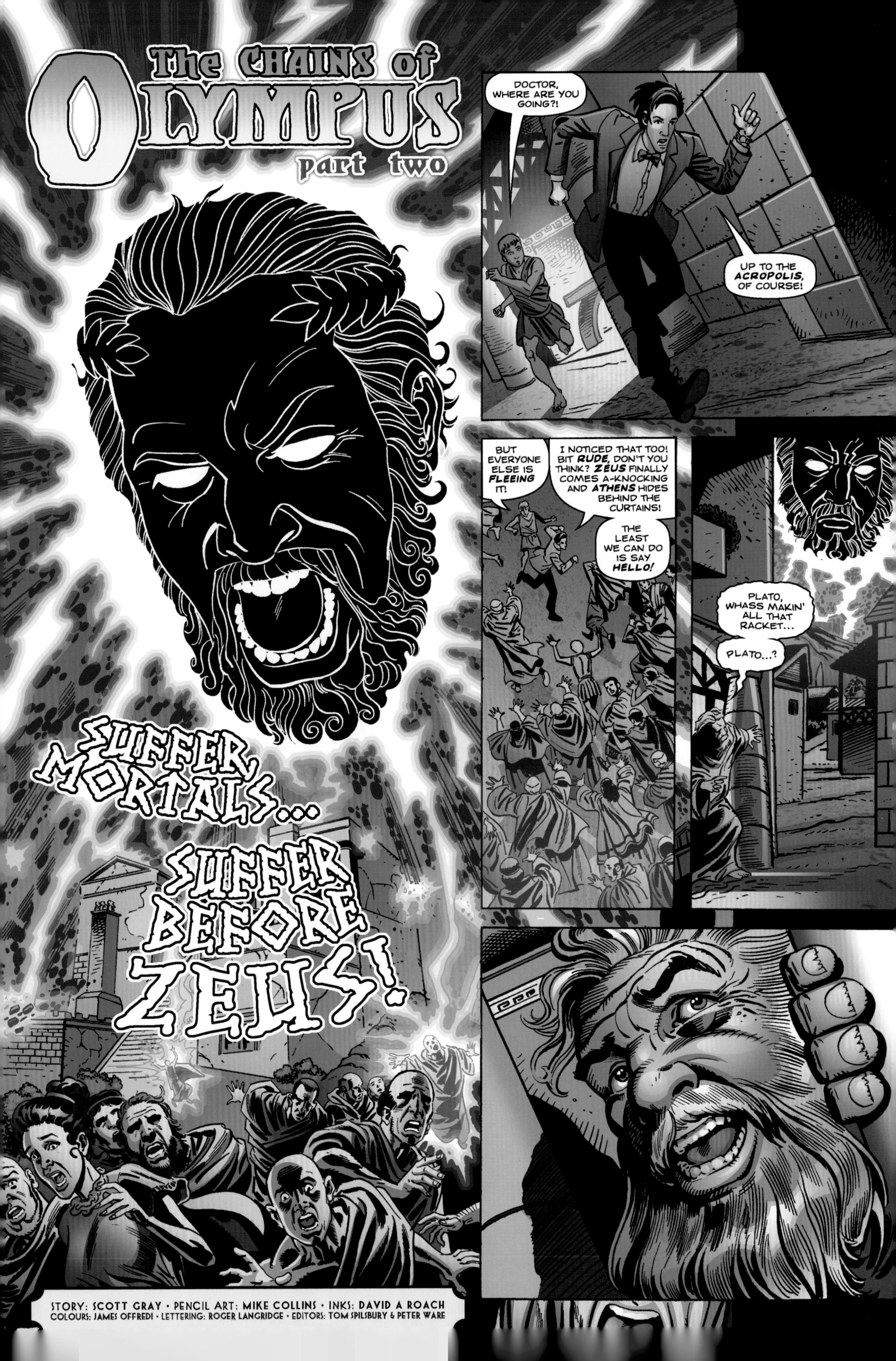
The CHAINS of OLYMPUS
part two
SUFFER, MORTALS... SUFFER BEFORE ZEUS!
DOCTOR, WHERE ARE YOU GOING?!
UP TO THE ACROPOLIS, OF COURSE!
BUT EVERYONE ELSE IS FLEEING IT!
I NOTICED THAT TOO! BIT RUDE, DON'T YOU THINK? ZEUS FINALLY COMES A-KNOCKING AND ATHENS HIDES BEHIND THE CURTAINS!
THE LEAST WE CAN DO IS SAY HELLO!
PLATO, WHASS MAKIN' ALL THAT RACKET...
PLATO...?
STORY: SCOTT GRAY • PENCIL ART: MIKE COLLINS • INKS: DAVID A ROACH
COLOURS: JAMES OFFREDI • LETTERING: ROGER LANGRIDGE • EDITORS: TOM SPILSBURY & PETER WARE

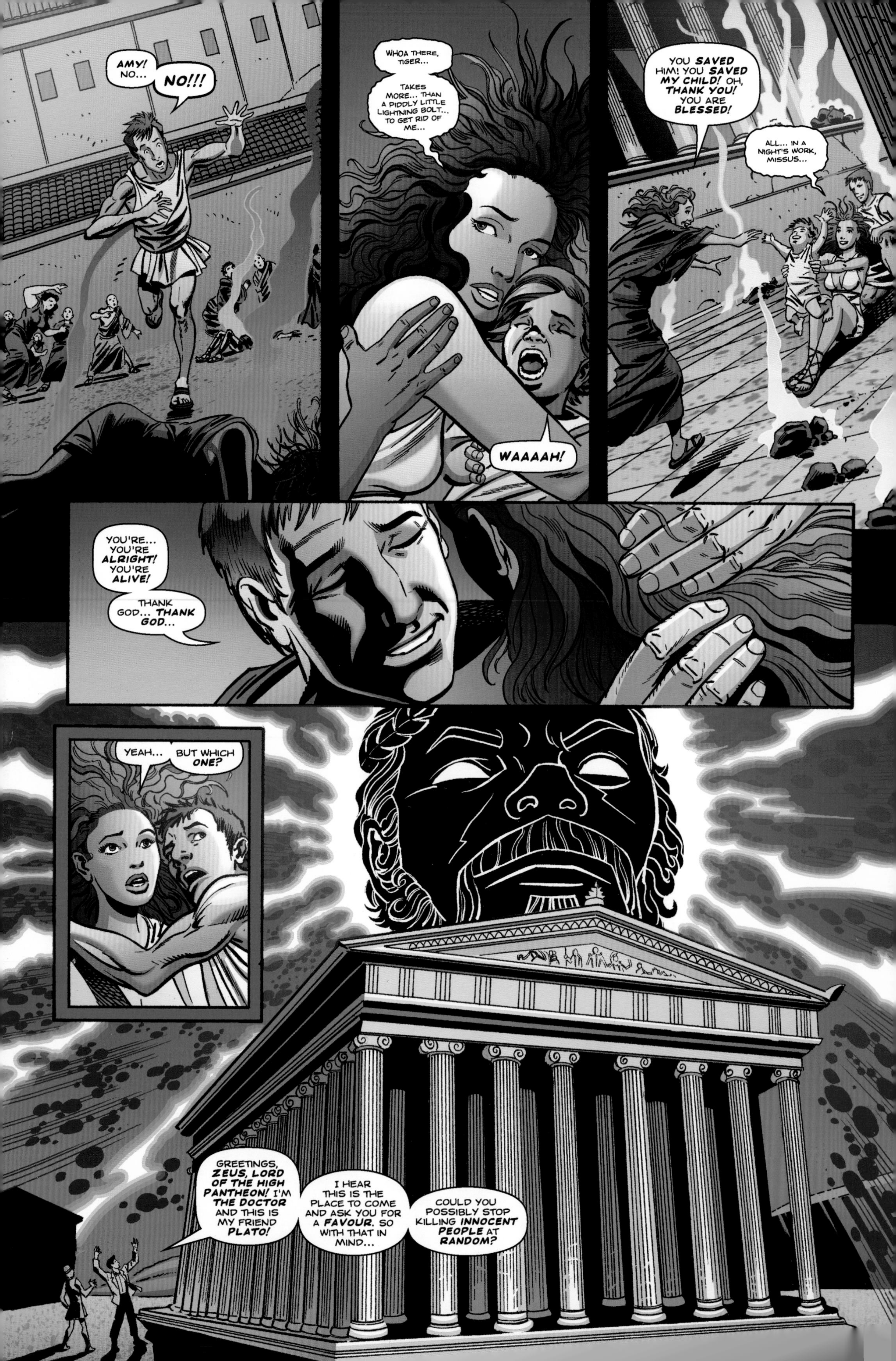
AMY! NO...
NO!!!
WHOA THERE, TIGER...
TAKES MORE... THAN A PIDDLY LITTLE LIGHTNING BOLT... TO GET RID OF ME...
WAAAAH!
YOU SAVED HIM! YOU SAVED MY CHILD! OH, THANK YOU! YOU ARE BLESSED!
ALL... IN A NIGHT'S WORK, MISSUS...
YOU'RE... YOU'RE ALRIGHT! YOU'RE ALIVE!
THANK GOD... THANK GOD...
YEAH...
BUT WHICH ONE?
GREETINGS, ZEUS, LORD OF THE HIGH PANTHEON! I'M THE DOCTOR AND THIS IS MY FRIEND PLATO!
I HEAR THIS IS THE PLACE TO COME AND ASK YOU FOR A FAVOUR, SO WITH THAT IN MIND...
COULD YOU POSSIBLY STOP KILLING INNOCENT PEOPLE AT RANDOM?

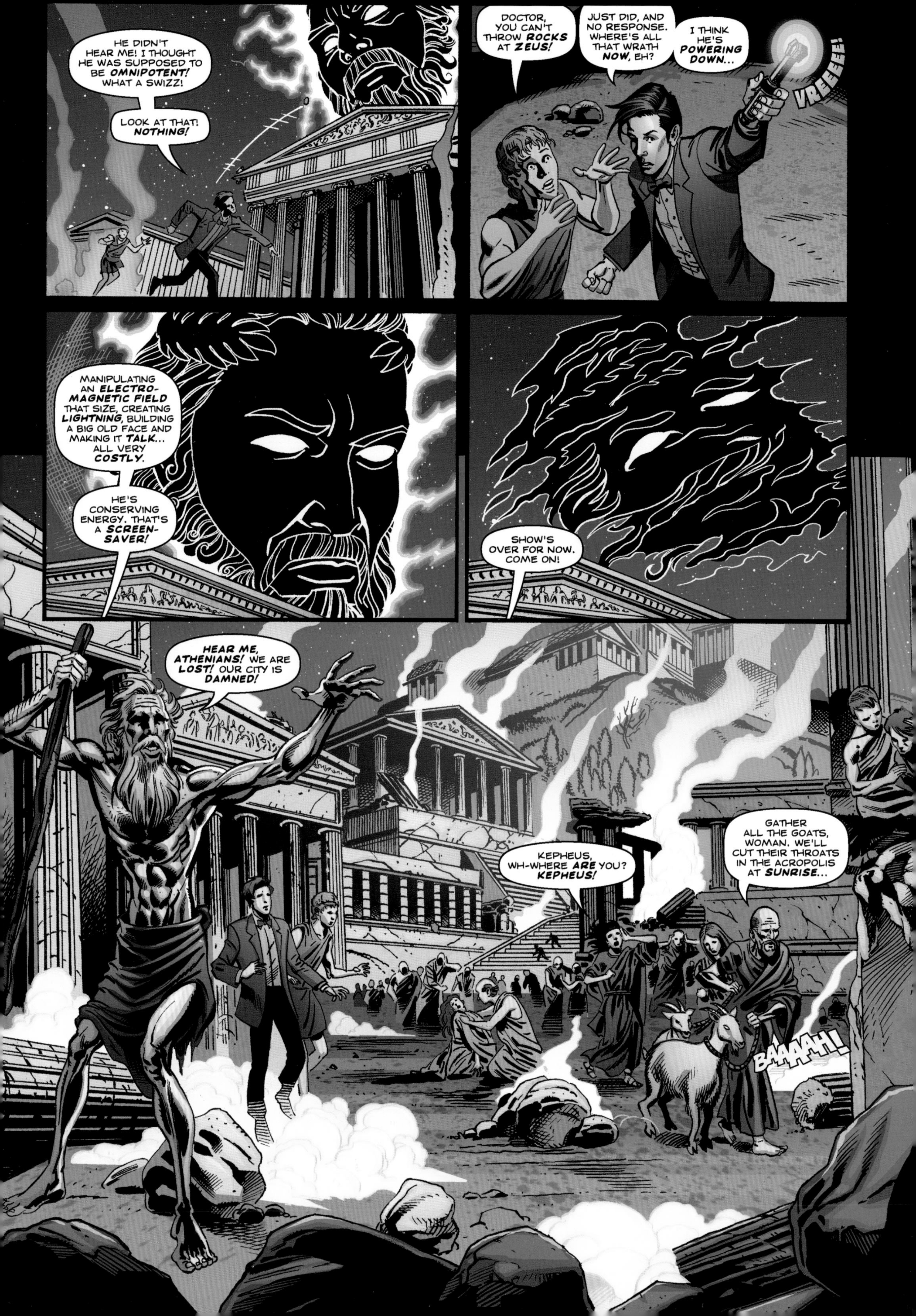

HE DIDN'T HEAR ME! I THOUGHT HE WAS SUPPOSED TO BE OMNIPOTENT! WHAT A SWIZZ!
LOOK AT THAT! NOTHING!
DOCTOR, YOU CAN'T THROW ROCKS AT ZEUS!
JUST DID, AND NO RESPONSE. WHERE'S ALL THAT WRATH NOW, EH?
I THINK HE'S POWERING DOWN...
VREEEEE!
MANIPULATING AN ELECTRO-MAGNETIC FIELD THAT SIZE, CREATING LIGHTNING, BUILDING A BIG OLD FACE AND MAKING IT TALK... ALL VERY COSTLY.
HE'S CONSERVING ENERGY. THAT'S A SCREEN-SAVER!
SHOW'S OVER FOR NOW. COME ON!
HEAR ME, ATHENIANS! WE ARE LOST! OUR CITY IS DAMNED!
KEPHEUS, WH-WHERE ARE YOU? KEPHEUS!
GATHER ALL THE GOATS, WOMAN. WE'LL CUT THEIR THROATS IN THE ACROPOLIS AT SUNRISE...
BAAAAH!

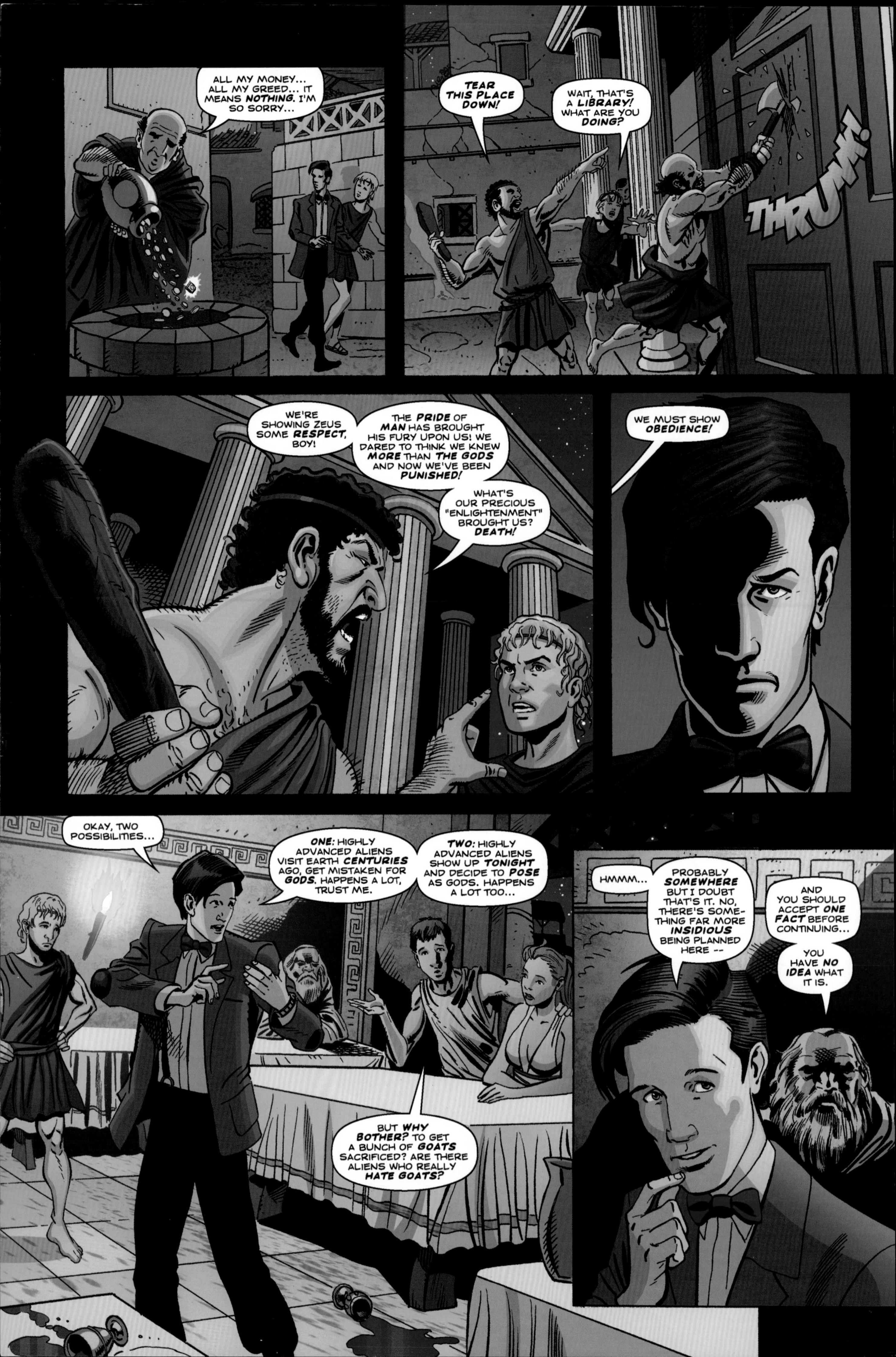

ALL MY MONEY... ALL MY GREED... IT MEANS NOTHING. I'M SO SORRY...
TEAR THIS PLACE DOWN!
WAIT, THAT'S A LIBRARY! WHAT ARE YOU DOING?
THRUM!
WE'RE SHOWING ZEUS SOME RESPECT, BOY!
THE PRIDE OF MAN HAS BROUGHT HIS FURY UPON US! WE DARED TO THINK WE KNEW MORE THAN THE GODS AND NOW WE'VE BEEN PUNISHED!
WHAT'S OUR PRECIOUS "ENLIGHTENMENT" BROUGHT US? DEATH!
WE MUST SHOW OBEDIENCE!
OKAY, TWO POSSIBILITIES...
ONE: HIGHLY ADVANCED ALIENS VISIT EARTH CENTURIES AGO, GET MISTAKEN FOR GODS. HAPPENS A LOT, TRUST ME.
TWO: HIGHLY ADVANCED ALIENS SHOW UP TONIGHT AND DECIDE TO POSE AS GODS. HAPPENS A LOT TOO...
BUT WHY BOTHER? TO GET A BUNCH OF GOATS SACRIFICED? ARE THERE ALIENS WHO REALLY HATE GOATS?
HMMM...
PROBABLY SOMEWHERE BUT I DOUBT THAT'S IT. NO, THERE'S SOME-THING FAR MORE INSIDIOUS BEING PLANNED HERE --
AND YOU SHOULD ACCEPT ONE FACT BEFORE CONTINUING...
YOU HAVE NO IDEA WHAT IT IS.

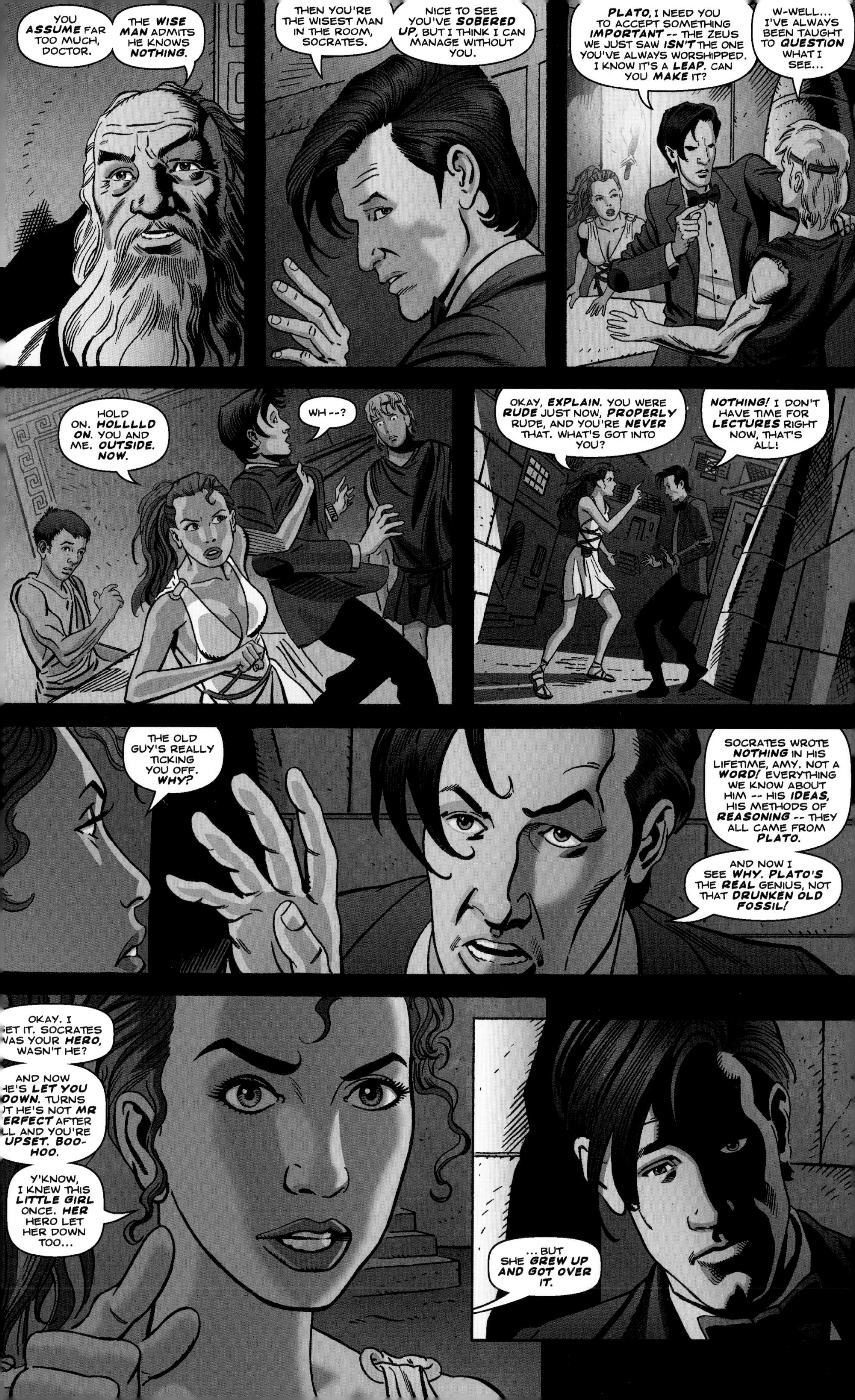

YOU ASSUME FAR TOO MUCH, DOCTOR.
THE WISE MAN ADMITS HE KNOWS NOTHING.
THEN YOU'RE THE WISEST MAN IN THE ROOM, SOCRATES.
NICE TO SEE YOU'VE SOBERED UP, BUT I THINK I CAN MANAGE WITHOUT YOU.
PLATO, I NEED YOU TO ACCEPT SOMETHING IMPORTANT -- THE ZEUS WE JUST SAW ISN'T THE ONE YOU'VE ALWAYS WORSHIPPED. I KNOW IT'S A LEAP. CAN YOU MAKE IT?
W-WELL... I'VE ALWAYS BEEN TAUGHT TO QUESTION WHAT I SEE...
HOLD ON. HOLLLLD ON. YOU AND ME. OUTSIDE. NOW.
WH--?
OKAY, EXPLAIN. YOU WERE RUDE JUST NOW, PROPERLY RUDE, AND YOU'RE NEVER THAT. WHAT'S GOT INTO YOU?
NOTHING! I DON'T HAVE TIME FOR LECTURES RIGHT NOW, THAT'S ALL!
THE OLD GUY'S REALLY TICKING YOU OFF. WHY?
SOCRATES WROTE NOTHING IN HIS LIFETIME, AMY. NOT A WORD! EVERYTHING WE KNOW ABOUT HIM -- HIS IDEAS, HIS METHODS OF REASONING -- THEY ALL CAME FROM PLATO.
AND NOW I SEE WHY. PLATO'S THE REAL GENIUS, NOT THAT DRUNKEN OLD FOSSIL!
OKAY. I ET IT. SOCRATES AS YOUR HERO, WASN'T HE?
AND NOW HE'S LET YOU DOWN. TURNS UT HE'S NOT MR ERFECT AFTER LL AND YOU'RE UPSET. BOO-HOO.
Y'KNOW, I KNEW THIS LITTLE GIRL ONCE. HER HERO LET HER DOWN TOO...
...BUT SHE GREW UP AND GOT OVER IT.

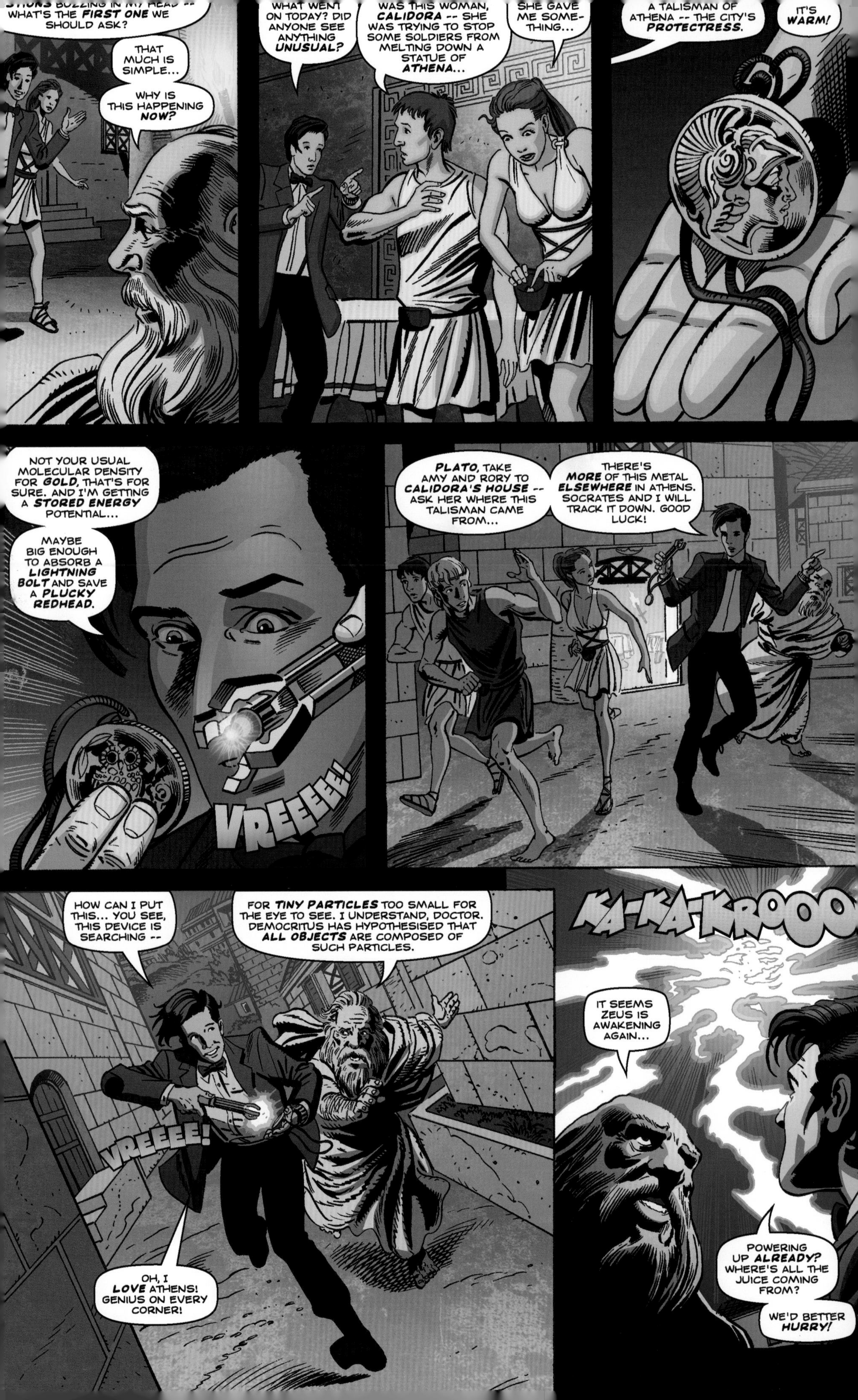
WHAT'S THE FIRST ONE WE SHOULD ASK?
THAT MUCH IS SIMPLE...
WHY IS THIS HAPPENING NOW?
WHAT WENT ON TODAY? DID ANYONE SEE ANYTHING UNUSUAL?
WAS THIS WOMAN, CALIDORA -- SHE WAS TRYING TO STOP SOME SOLDIERS FROM MELTING DOWN A STATUE OF ATHENA...
SHE GAVE ME SOMETHING...
A TALISMAN OF ATHENA -- THE CITY'S PROTECTRESS.
IT'S WARM!
NOT YOUR USUAL MOLECULAR DENSITY FOR GOLD, THAT'S FOR SURE. AND I'M GETTING A STORED ENERGY POTENTIAL...
MAYBE BIG ENOUGH TO ABSORB A LIGHTNING BOLT AND SAVE A PLUCKY REDHEAD.
VREEEEE!
PLATO, TAKE AMY AND RORY TO CALIDORA'S HOUSE -- ASK HER WHERE THIS TALISMAN CAME FROM...
THERE'S MORE OF THIS METAL ELSEWHERE IN ATHENS. SOCRATES AND I WILL TRACK IT DOWN. GOOD LUCK!
HOW CAN I PUT THIS... YOU SEE, THIS DEVICE IS SEARCHING --
FOR TINY PARTICLES TOO SMALL FOR THE EYE TO SEE. I UNDERSTAND, DOCTOR. DEMOCRITUS HAS HYPOTHESISED THAT ALL OBJECTS ARE COMPOSED OF SUCH PARTICLES.
VREEEE!
OH, I LOVE ATHENS! GENIUS ON EVERY CORNER!
KA-KA-KROOOO
IT SEEMS ZEUS IS AWAKENING AGAIN...
POWERING UP ALREADY? WHERE'S ALL THE JUICE COMING FROM?
WE'D BETTER HURRY!

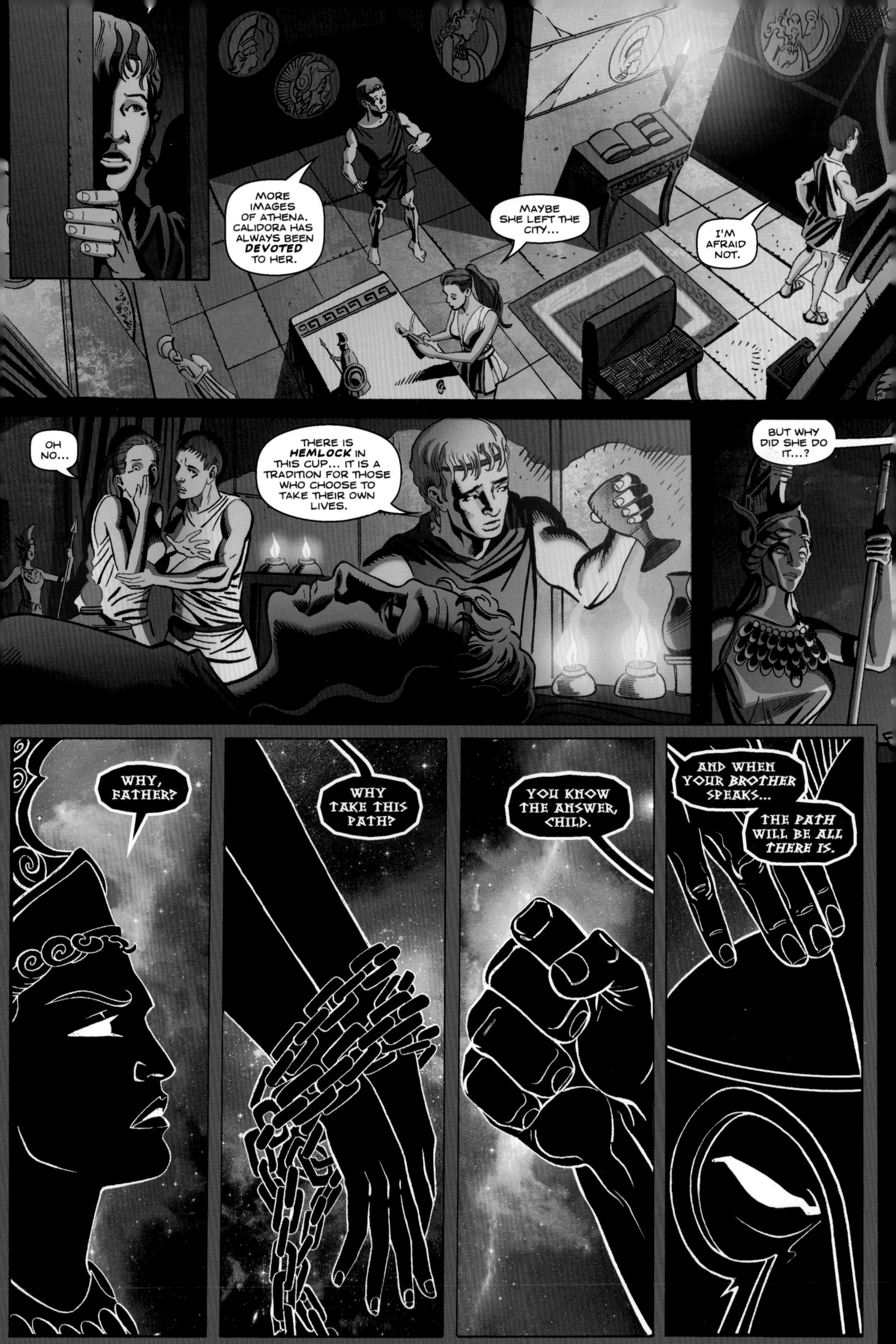
MORE IMAGES OF ATHENA. CALIDORA HAS ALWAYS BEEN DEVOTED TO HER.
MAYBE SHE LEFT THE CITY...
I'M AFRAID NOT.
OH NO...
THERE IS HEMLOCK IN THIS CUP... IT IS A TRADITION FOR THOSE WHO CHOOSE TO TAKE THEIR OWN LIVES.
BUT WHY DID SHE DO IT...?
WHY, FATHER?
WHY TAKE THIS PATH?
YOU KNOW THE ANSWER, CHILD.
AND WHEN YOUR BROTHER SPEAKS...
THE PATH WILL BE ALL THERE IS.

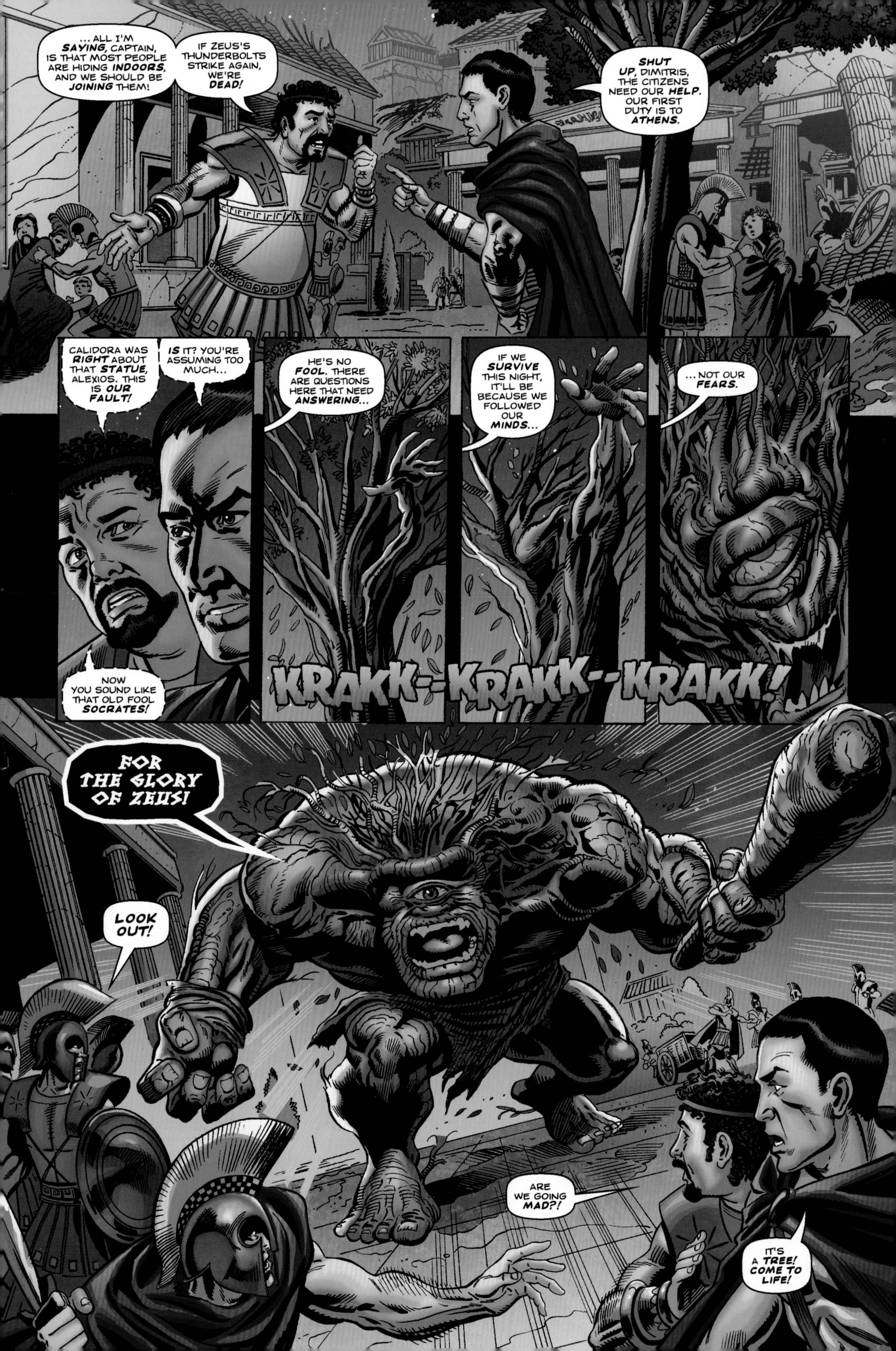
... ALL I'M SAYING, CAPTAIN, IS THAT MOST PEOPLE ARE HIDING INDOORS, AND WE SHOULD BE JOINING THEM!
IF ZEUS'S THUNDERBOLTS STRIKE AGAIN, WE'RE DEAD!
SHUT UP, DIMITRIS, THE CITIZENS NEED OUR HELP. OUR FIRST DUTY IS TO ATHENS.
CALIDORA WAS RIGHT ABOUT THAT STATUE, ALEXIOS. THIS IS OUR FAULT!
IS IT? YOU'RE ASSUMING TOO MUCH...
NOW YOU SOUND LIKE THAT OLD FOOL SOCRATES!
HE'S NO FOOL. THERE ARE QUESTIONS HERE THAT NEED ANSWERING...
IF WE SURVIVE THIS NIGHT, IT'LL BE BECAUSE WE FOLLOWED OUR MINDS...
... NOT OUR FEARS.
KRAKK-KRAKK-KRAKK!
FOR THE GLORY OF ZEUS!
LOOK OUT!
ARE WE GOING MAD?!
IT'S A TREE! COME TO LIFE!

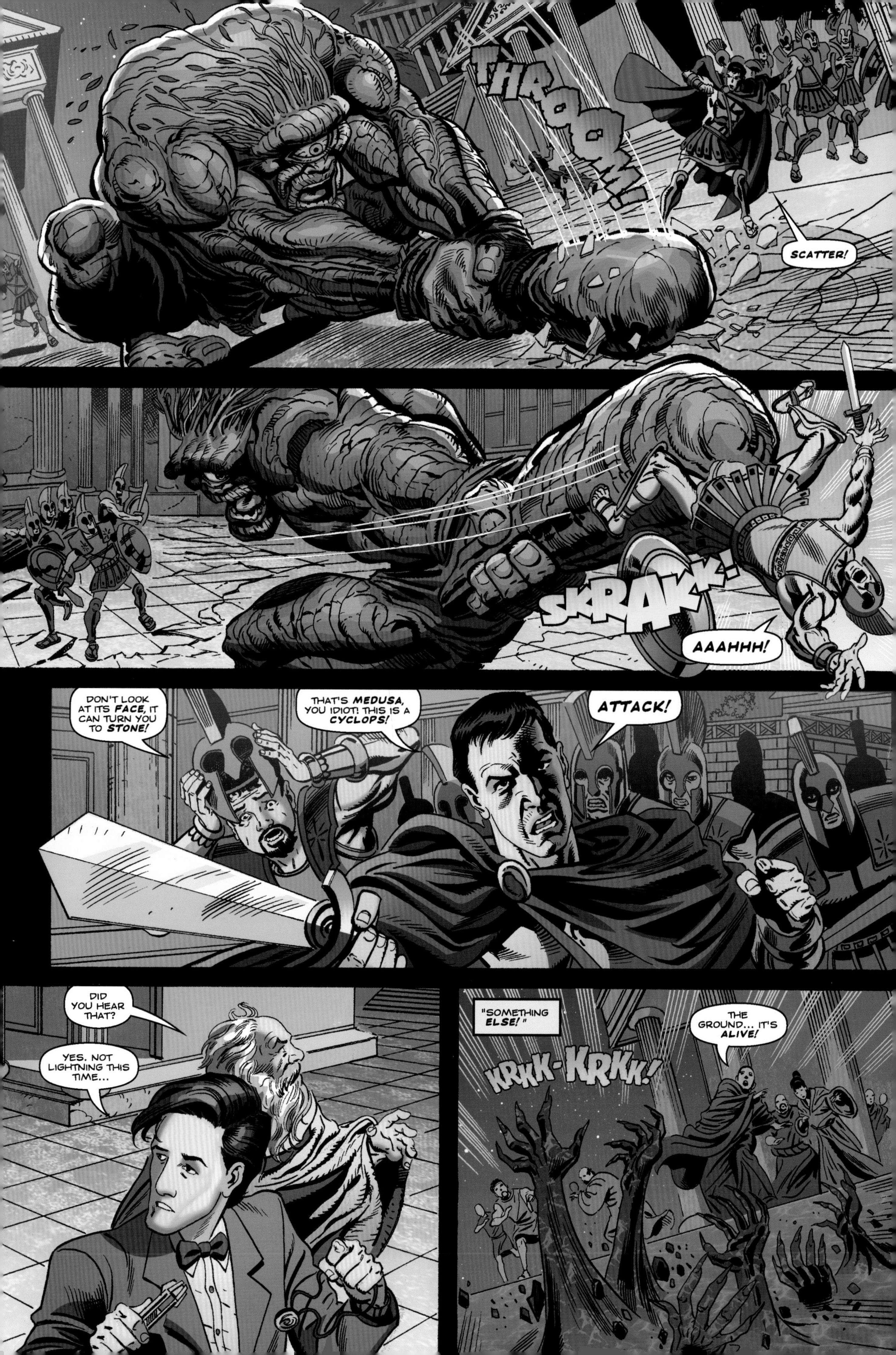
THRAOOM!
SCATTER!
SKRAKK!
AAAHHH!
DON'T LOOK AT ITS FACE, IT CAN TURN YOU TO STONE!
THAT'S MEDUSA, YOU IDIOT! THIS IS A CYCLOPS!
ATTACK!
DID YOU HEAR THAT?
YES. NOT LIGHTNING THIS TIME...
"SOMETHING ELSE!"
KRKK-KRKK!
THE GROUND... IT'S ALIVE!

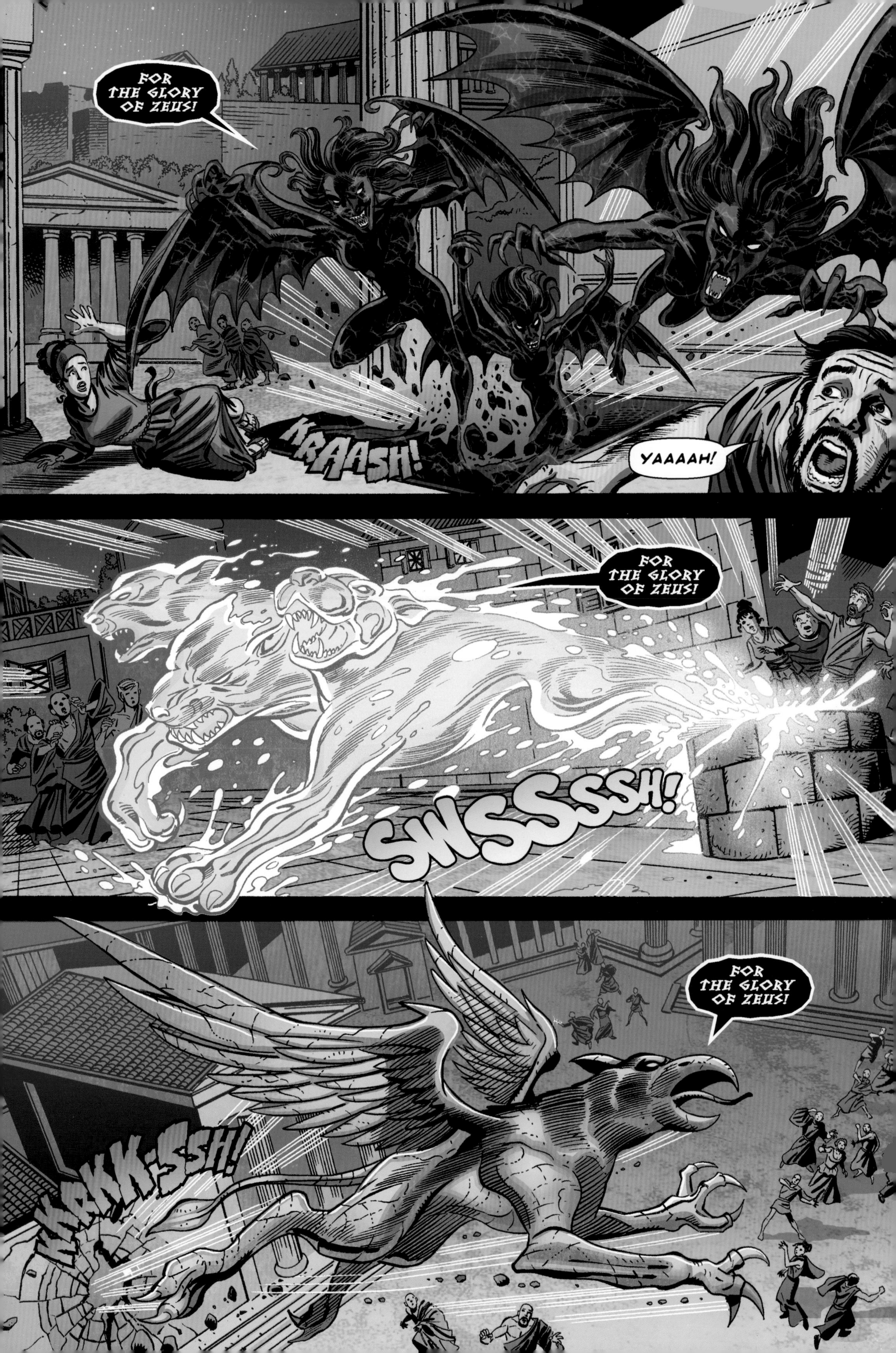
FOR THE GLORY OF ZEUS!
KRAASH!
YAAAAH!
FOR THE GLORY OF ZEUS!
SWSSSSSH!
FOR THE GLORY OF ZEUS!

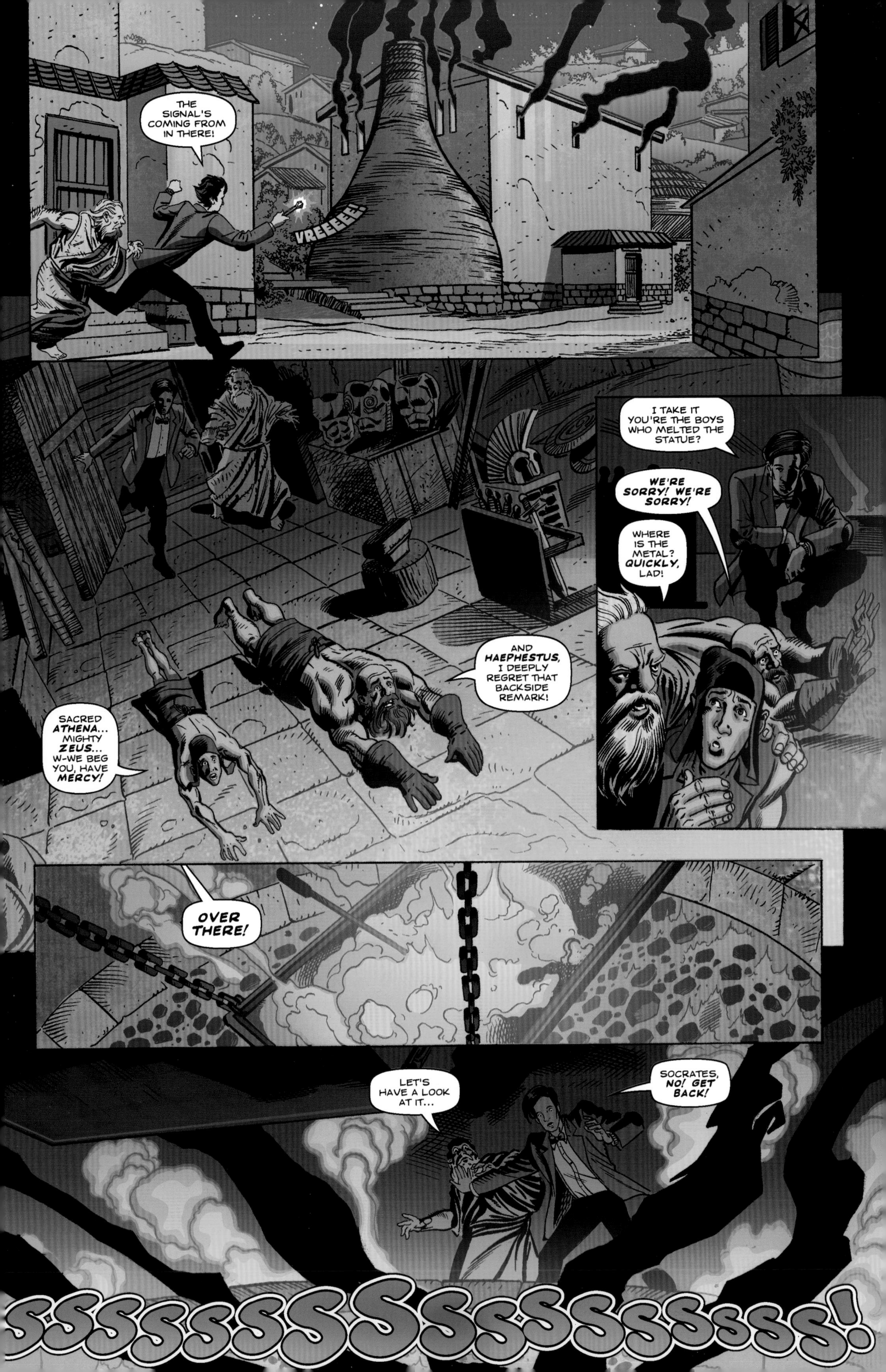

THE SIGNAL'S COMING FROM IN THERE!
VREEEEE!
SACRED ATHENA... MIGHTY ZEUS... W-WE BEG YOU, HAVE MERCY!
AND HAEPHESTUS, I DEEPLY REGRET THAT BACKSIDE REMARK!
I TAKE IT YOU'RE THE BOYS WHO MELTED THE STATUE?
WE'RE SORRY! WE'RE SORRY!
WHERE IS THE METAL? QUICKLY, LAD!
OVER THERE!
LET'S HAVE A LOOK AT IT...
SOCRATES, NO! GET BACK!
SSSSSSSSSSSSSSSS!

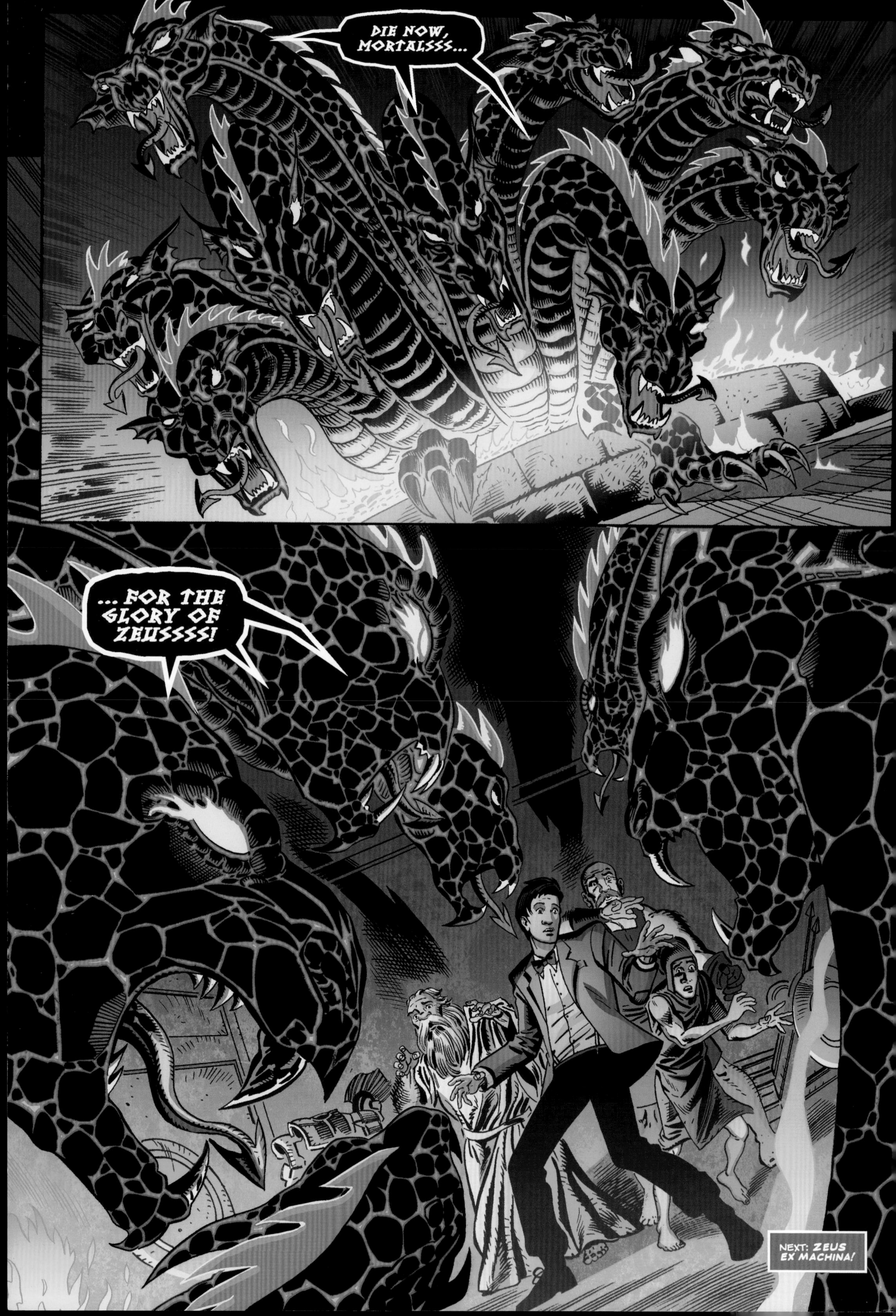
DIE NOW, MORTALSSS...
...FOR THE GLORY OF ZEUSSSSS!
NEXT: ZEUS EX MACHINA!

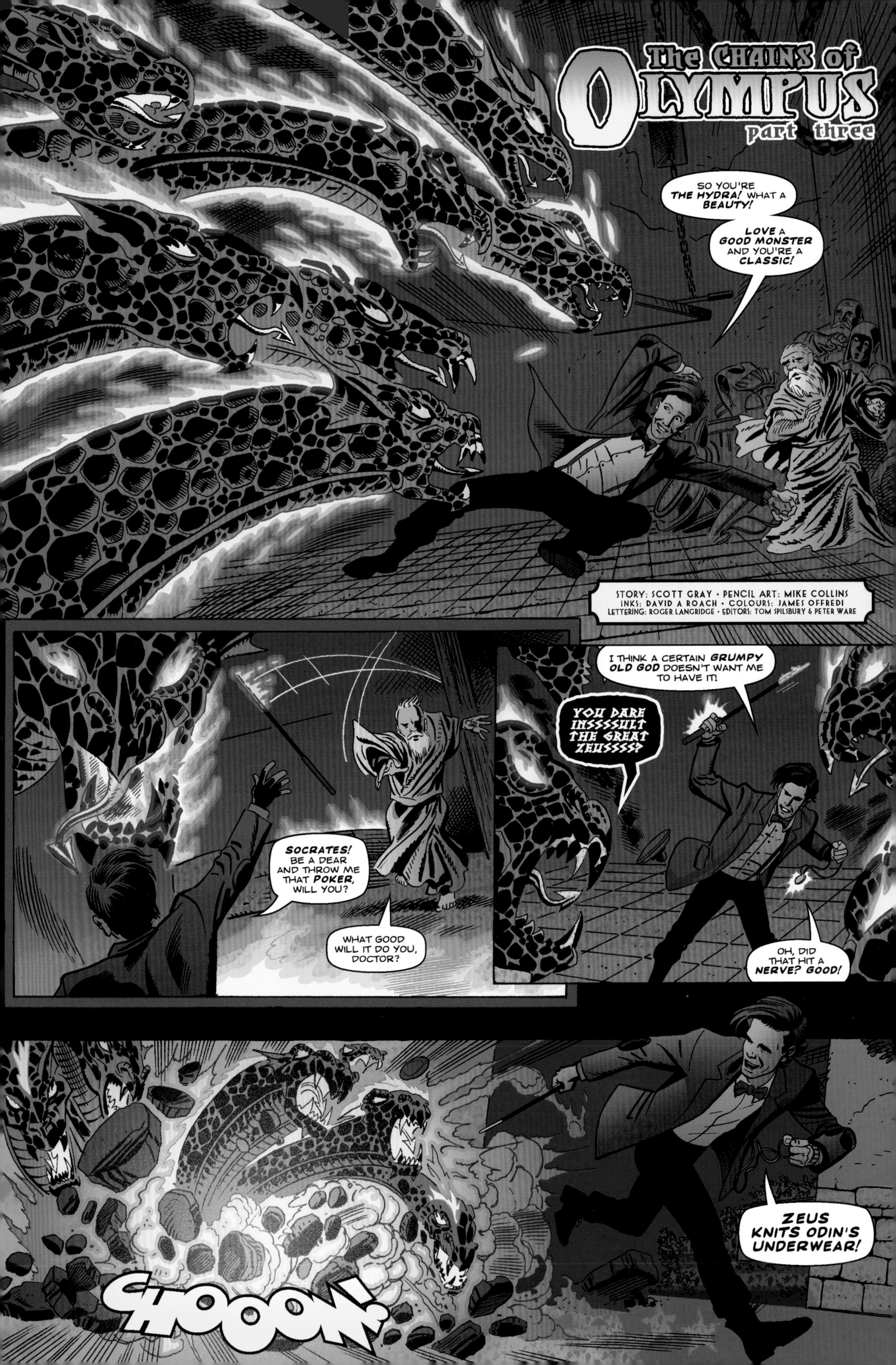
The CHAINS of OLYMPUS
part three
SO YOU'RE THE HYDRA! WHAT A BEAUTY!
LOVE A GOOD MONSTER AND YOU'RE A CLASSIC!
STORY: SCOTT GRAY • PENCIL ART: MIKE COLLINS
INKS: DAVID A ROACH • COLOURS: JAMES OFFREDI
LETTERING: ROGER LANGRIDGE • EDITORS: TOM SPILSBURY & PETER WARE
SOCRATES! BE A DEAR AND THROW ME THAT POKER, WILL YOU?
WHAT GOOD WILL IT DO YOU, DOCTOR?
I THINK A CERTAIN GRUMPY OLD GOD DOESN'T WANT ME TO HAVE IT!
YOU DARE INSSSSULT THE GREAT ZEUSSSSS?
OH, DID THAT HIT A NERVE? GOOD!
ZEUS KNITS ODIN'S UNDERWEAR!
CHOOOM!

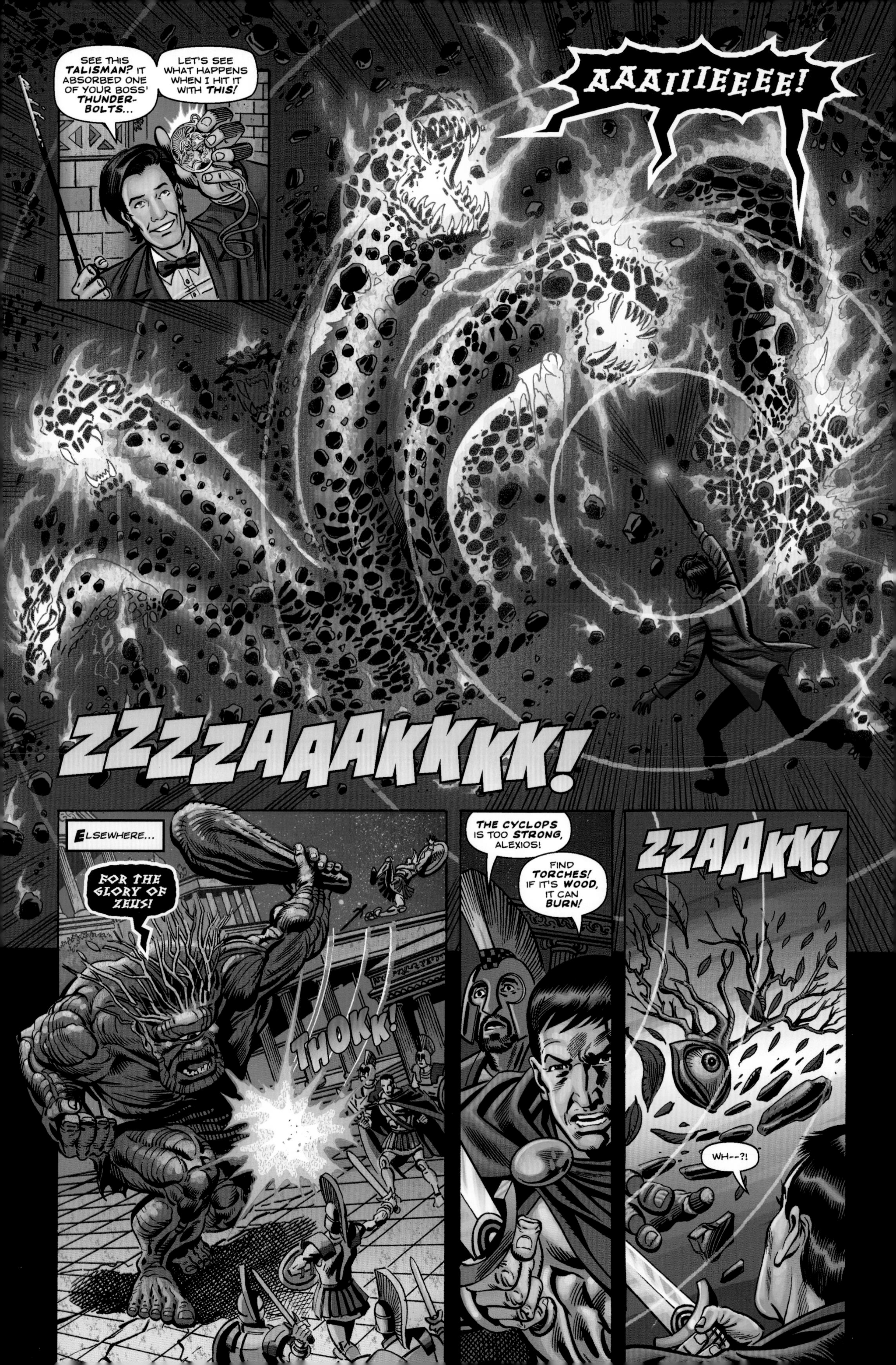
SEE THIS TALISMAN? IT ABSORBED ONE OF YOUR BOSS' THUNDER-BOLTS...
LET'S SEE WHAT HAPPENS WHEN I HIT IT WITH THIS!
AAAIIIEEEE!
ZZZZAAAKKKK!
ELSEWHERE...
FOR THE GLORY OF ZEUS!
THOKK!
THE CYCLOPS IS TOO STRONG, ALEXIOS!
FIND TORCHES! IF IT'S WOOD, IT CAN BURN!
ZZAAKK!
WH--?!

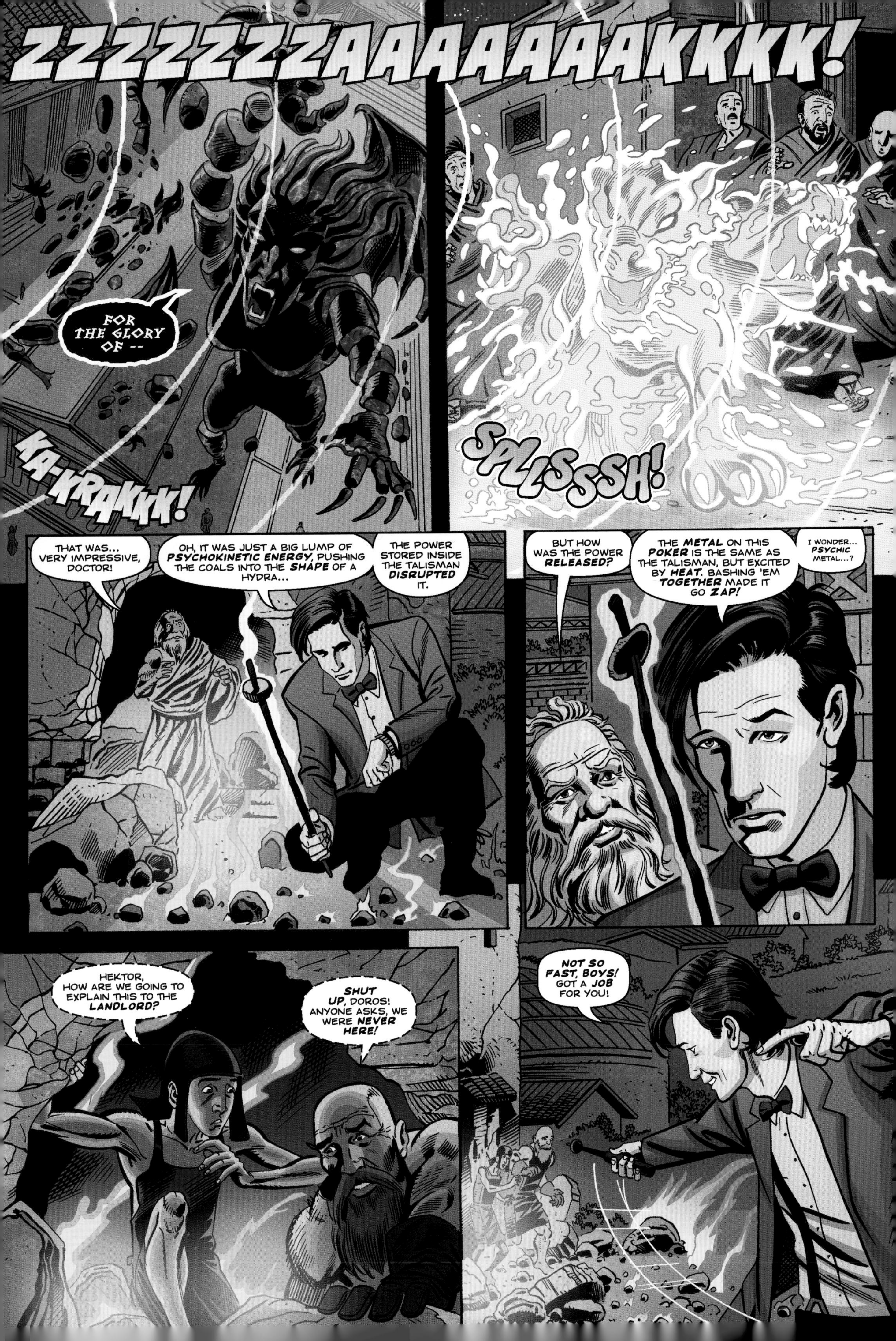
ZZZZZZZAAAAAAAAKKKK!
FOR THE GLORY OF --
KA-KRAKKK!
SPLISSSH!
THAT WAS... VERY IMPRESSIVE, DOCTOR!
OH, IT WAS JUST A BIG LUMP OF PSYCHOKINETIC ENERGY, PUSHING THE COALS INTO THE SHAPE OF A HYDRA...
THE POWER STORED INSIDE THE TALISMAN DISRUPTED IT.
BUT HOW WAS THE POWER RELEASED?
THE METAL ON THIS POKER IS THE SAME AS THE TALISMAN, BUT EXCITED BY HEAT. BASHING 'EM TOGETHER MADE IT GO ZAP!
I WONDER... PSYCHIC METAL...?
HEKTOR, HOW ARE WE GOING TO EXPLAIN THIS TO THE LANDLORD?
SHUT UP, DOROS! ANYONE ASKS, WE WERE NEVER HERE!
NOT SO FAST, BOYS! GOT A JOB FOR YOU!

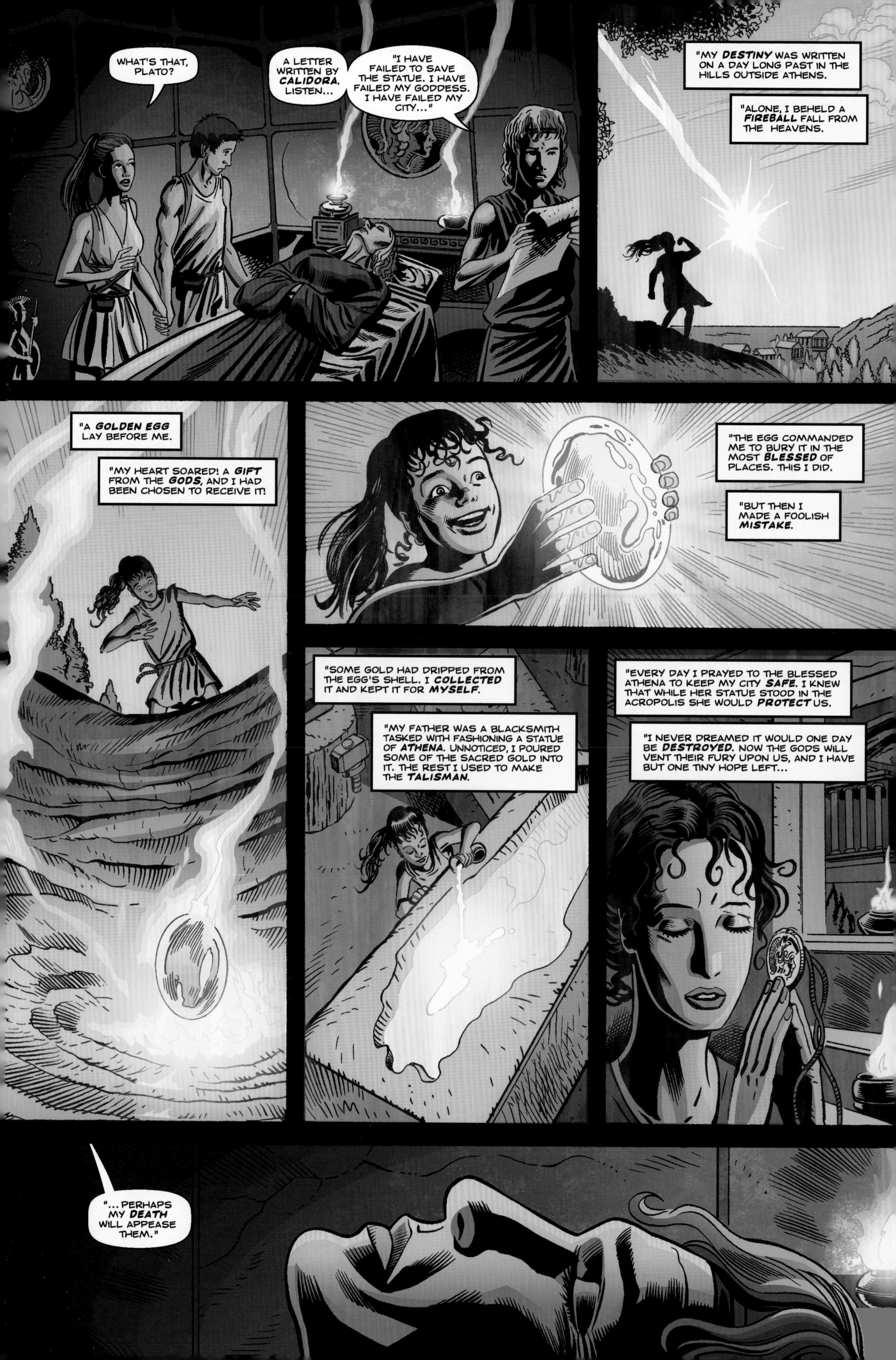
WHAT'S THAT, PLATO?
A LETTER WRITTEN BY CALIDORA. LISTEN...
"I HAVE FAILED TO SAVE THE STATUE. I HAVE FAILED MY GODDESS. I HAVE FAILED MY CITY..."
"MY DESTINY WAS WRITTEN ON A DAY LONG PAST IN THE HILLS OUTSIDE ATHENS.
"ALONE, I BEHELD A FIREBALL FALL FROM THE HEAVENS.
"A GOLDEN EGG LAY BEFORE ME.
"MY HEART SOARED! A GIFT FROM THE GODS, AND I HAD BEEN CHOSEN TO RECEIVE IT!
"THE EGG COMMANDED ME TO BURY IT IN THE MOST BLESSED OF PLACES. THIS I DID.
"BUT THEN I MADE A FOOLISH MISTAKE.
"SOME GOLD HAD DRIPPED FROM THE EGG'S SHELL. I COLLECTED IT AND KEPT IT FOR MYSELF.
"MY FATHER WAS A BLACKSMITH TASKED WITH FASHIONING A STATUE OF ATHENA. UNNOTICED, I POURED SOME OF THE SACRED GOLD INTO IT. THE REST I USED TO MAKE THE TALISMAN.
"EVERY DAY I PRAYED TO THE BLESSED ATHENA TO KEEP MY CITY SAFE. I KNEW THAT WHILE HER STATUE STOOD IN THE ACROPOLIS SHE WOULD PROTECT US.
"I NEVER DREAMED IT WOULD ONE DAY BE DESTROYED. NOW THE GODS WILL VENT THEIR FURY UPON US, AND I HAVE BUT ONE TINY HOPE LEFT...
"...PERHAPS MY DEATH WILL APPEASE THEM."

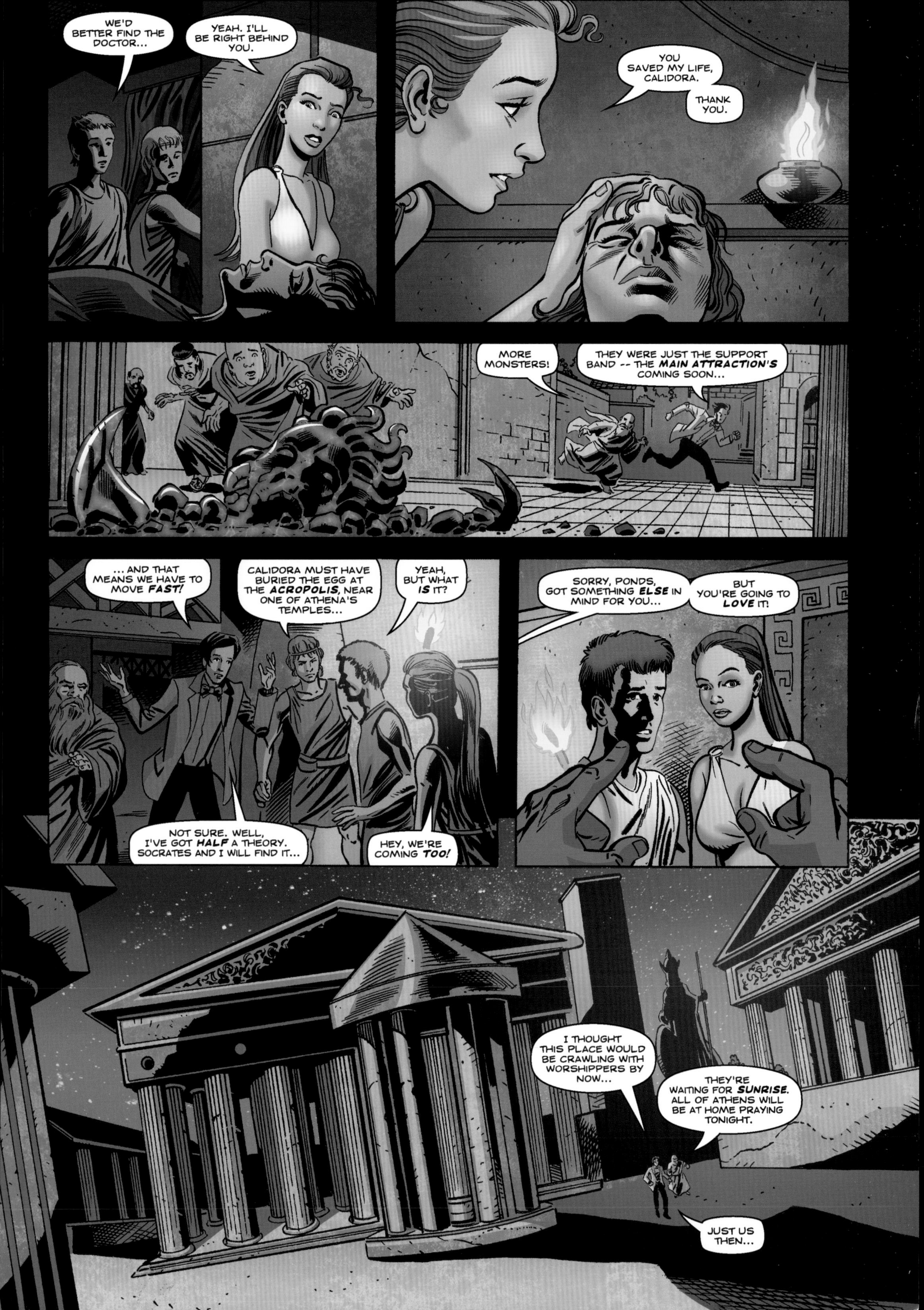
WE'D BETTER FIND THE DOCTOR...
YEAH. I'LL BE RIGHT BEHIND YOU.
YOU SAVED MY LIFE, CALIDORA.
THANK YOU.
MORE MONSTERS!
THEY WERE JUST THE SUPPORT BAND -- THE MAIN ATTRACTION'S COMING SOON...
... AND THAT MEANS WE HAVE TO MOVE FAST!
CALIDORA MUST HAVE BURIED THE EGG AT THE ACROPOLIS, NEAR ONE OF ATHENA'S TEMPLES...
YEAH, BUT WHAT IS IT?
NOT SURE. WELL, I'VE GOT HALF A THEORY. SOCRATES AND I WILL FIND IT...
HEY, WE'RE COMING TOO!
SORRY, PONDS, GOT SOMETHING ELSE IN MIND FOR YOU...
BUT YOU'RE GOING TO LOVE IT!
I THOUGHT THIS PLACE WOULD BE CRAWLING WITH WORSHIPPERS BY NOW...
THEY'RE WAITING FOR SUNRISE. ALL OF ATHENS WILL BE AT HOME PRAYING TONIGHT.
JUST US THEN...

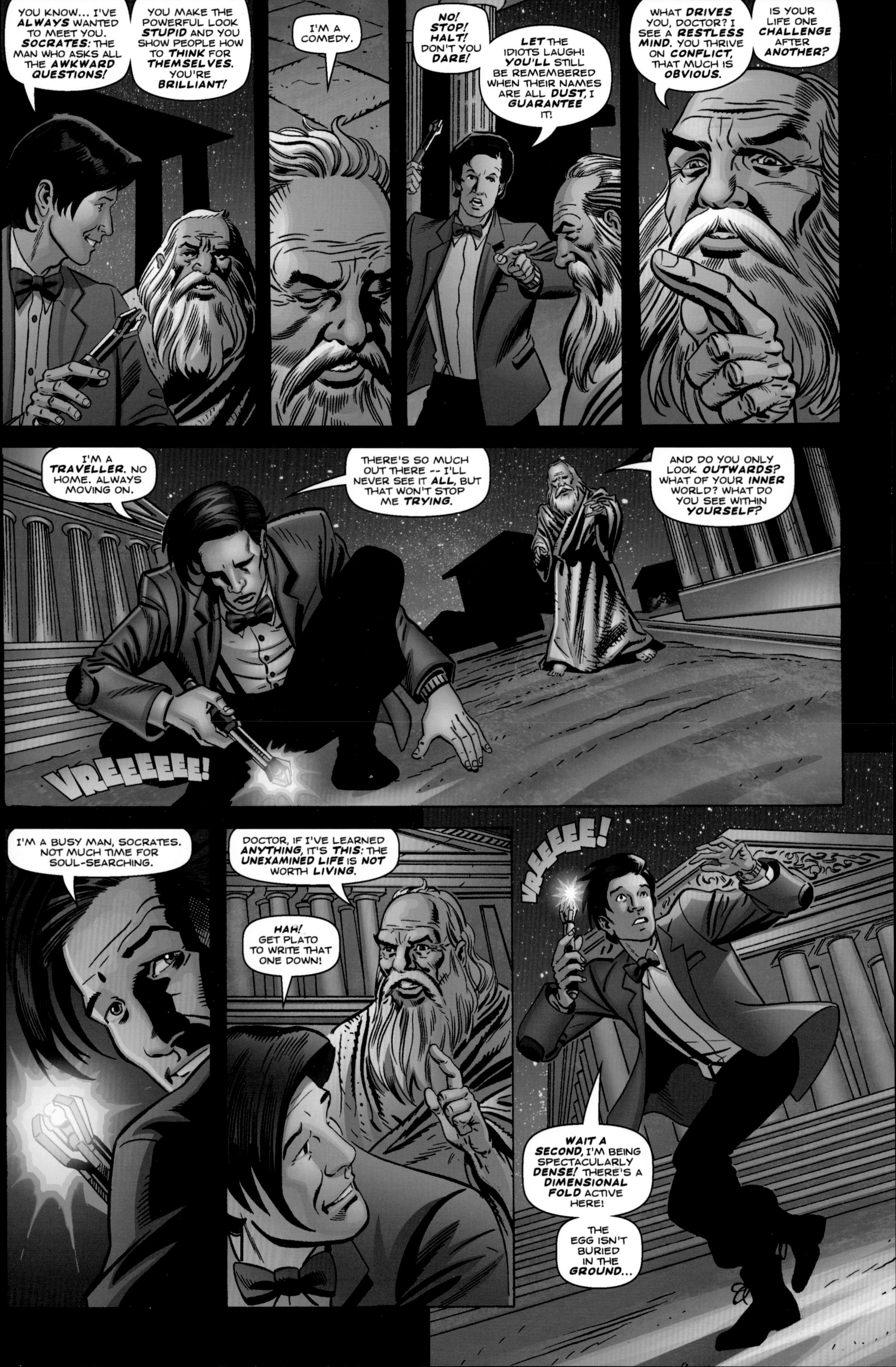
YOU KNOW... I'VE ALWAYS WANTED TO MEET YOU. SOCRATES: THE MAN WHO ASKS ALL THE AWKWARD QUESTIONS!
YOU MAKE THE POWERFUL LOOK STUPID AND YOU SHOW PEOPLE HOW TO THINK FOR THEMSELVES. YOU'RE BRILLIANT!
I'M A COMEDY.
NO! STOP! HALT! DON'T YOU DARE!
LET THE IDIOTS LAUGH! YOU'LL STILL BE REMEMBERED WHEN THEIR NAMES ARE ALL DUST, I GUARANTEE IT!
WHAT DRIVES YOU, DOCTOR? I SEE A RESTLESS MIND. YOU THRIVE ON CONFLICT, THAT MUCH IS OBVIOUS.
IS YOUR LIFE ONE CHALLENGE AFTER ANOTHER?
I'M A TRAVELLER. NO HOME. ALWAYS MOVING ON.
THERE'S SO MUCH OUT THERE -- I'LL NEVER SEE IT ALL, BUT THAT WON'T STOP ME TRYING.
AND DO YOU ONLY LOOK OUTWARDS? WHAT OF YOUR INNER WORLD? WHAT DO YOU SEE WITHIN YOURSELF?
VREEEEEE!
I'M A BUSY MAN, SOCRATES. NOT MUCH TIME FOR SOUL-SEARCHING.
DOCTOR, IF I'VE LEARNED ANYTHING, IT'S THIS: THE UNEXAMINED LIFE IS NOT WORTH LIVING.
HAH! GET PLATO TO WRITE THAT ONE DOWN!
VREEEEE!
WAIT A SECOND, I'M BEING SPECTACULARLY DENSE! THERE'S A DIMENSIONAL FOLD ACTIVE HERE!
THE EGG ISN'T BURIED IN THE GROUND...

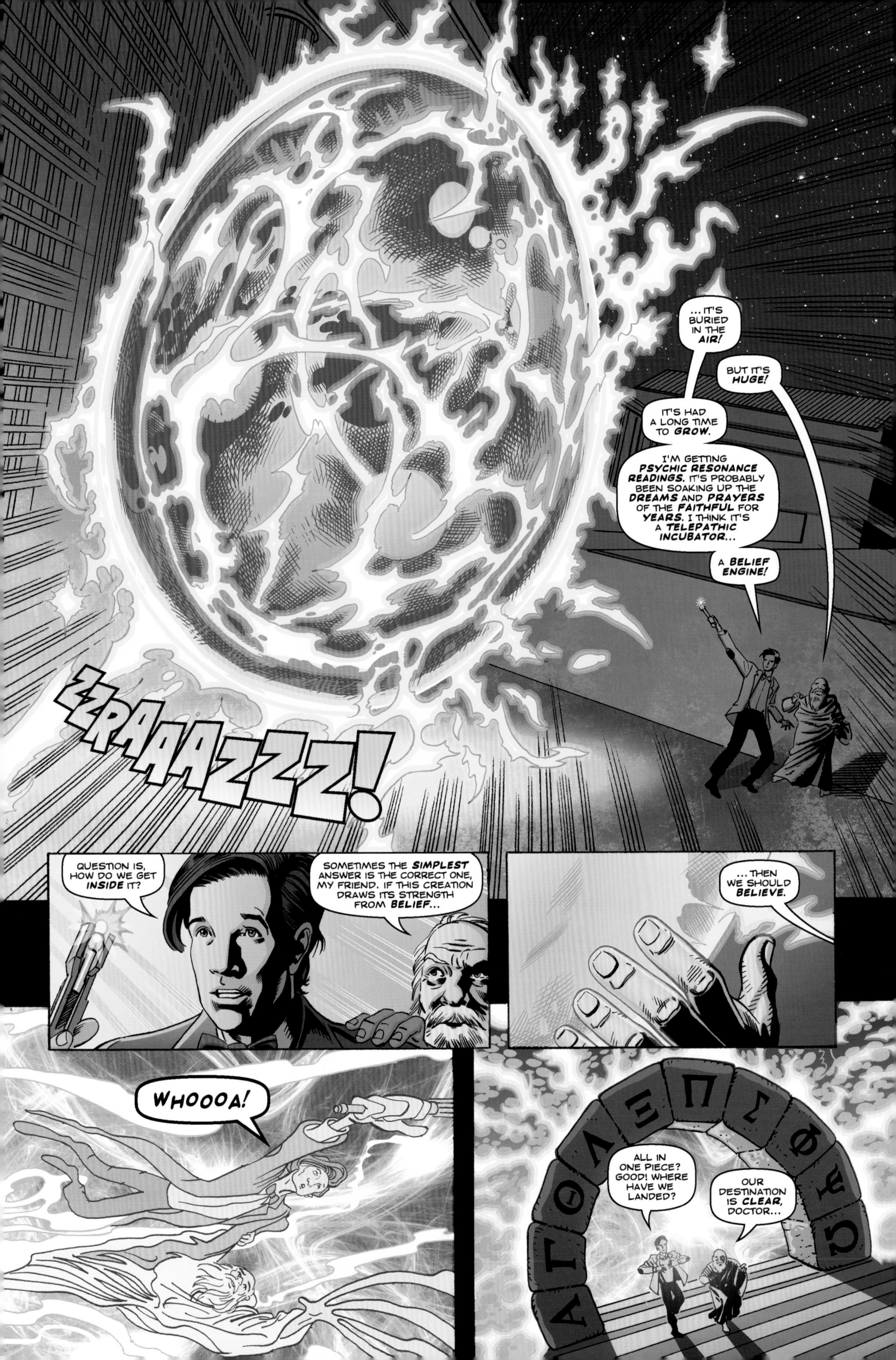

ZZRAAAZZZ!
...IT'S BURIED IN THE AIR!
BUT IT'S HUGE!
IT'S HAD A LONG TIME TO GROW.
I'M GETTING PSYCHIC RESONANCE READINGS. IT'S PROBABLY BEEN SOAKING UP THE DREAMS AND PRAYERS OF THE FAITHFUL FOR YEARS. I THINK IT'S A TELEPATHIC INCUBATOR...
A BELIEF ENGINE!
QUESTION IS, HOW DO WE GET INSIDE IT?
SOMETIMES THE SIMPLEST ANSWER IS THE CORRECT ONE, MY FRIEND. IF THIS CREATION DRAWS ITS STRENGTH FROM BELIEF...
...THEN WE SHOULD BELIEVE.
WHOOOA!
ALL IN ONE PIECE? GOOD! WHERE HAVE WE LANDED?
OUR DESTINATION IS CLEAR, DOCTOR...

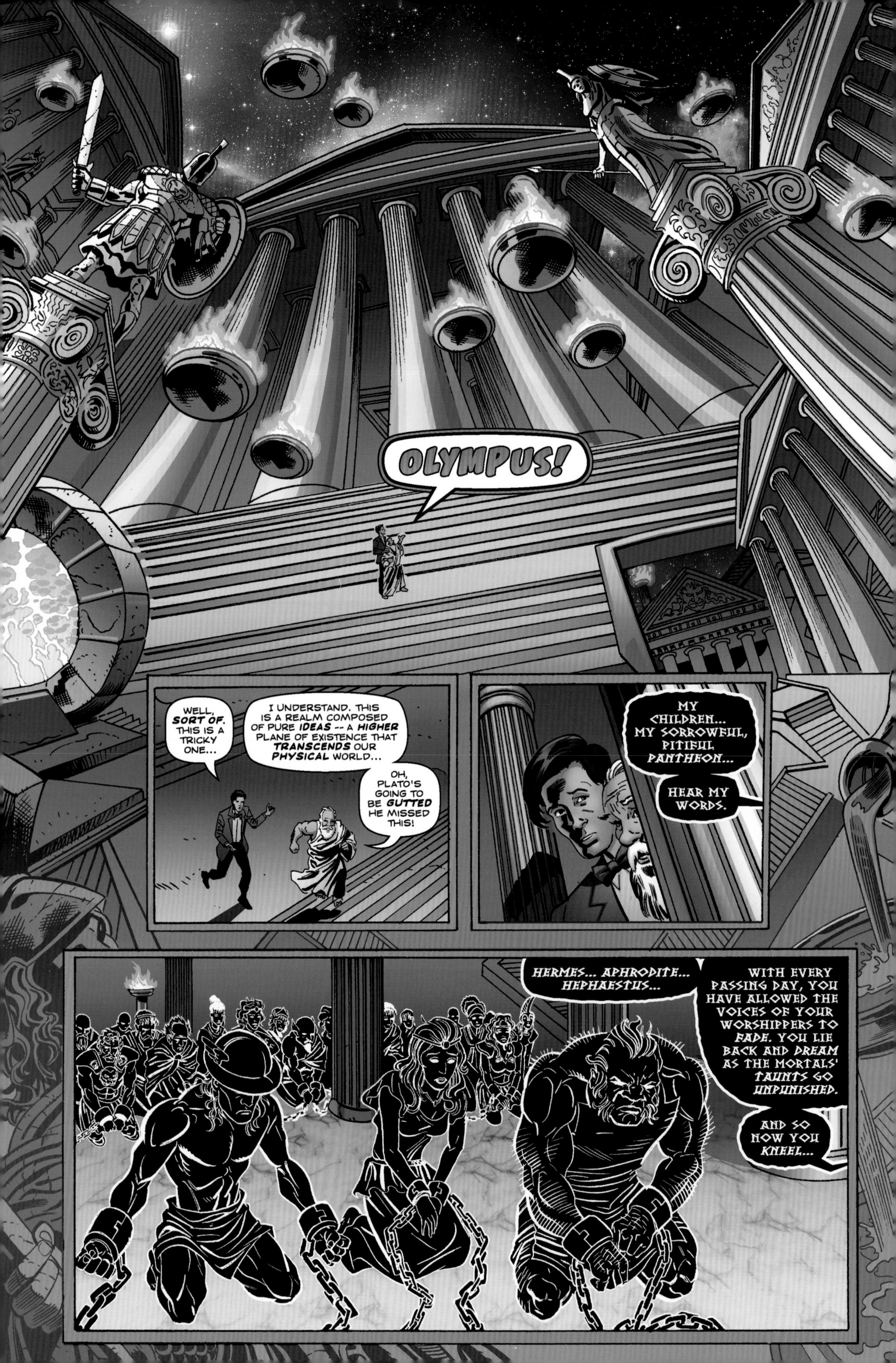
OLYMPUS!
I UNDERSTAND. THIS IS A REALM COMPOSED OF PURE IDEAS -- A HIGHER PLANE OF EXISTENCE THAT TRANSCENDS OUR PHYSICAL WORLD...
WELL, SORT OF. THIS IS A TRICKY ONE...
OH, PLATO'S GOING TO BE GUTTED HE MISSED THIS!
MY CHILDREN... MY SORROWFUL, PITIFUL PANTHEON...
HEAR MY WORDS.
HERMES... APHRODITE... HEPHAESTUS...
WITH EVERY PASSING DAY, YOU HAVE ALLOWED THE VOICES OF YOUR WORSHIPPERS TO FADE. YOU LIE BACK AND DREAM AS THE MORTALS' TAUNTS GO UNPUNISHED.
AND SO NOW YOU KNEEL...

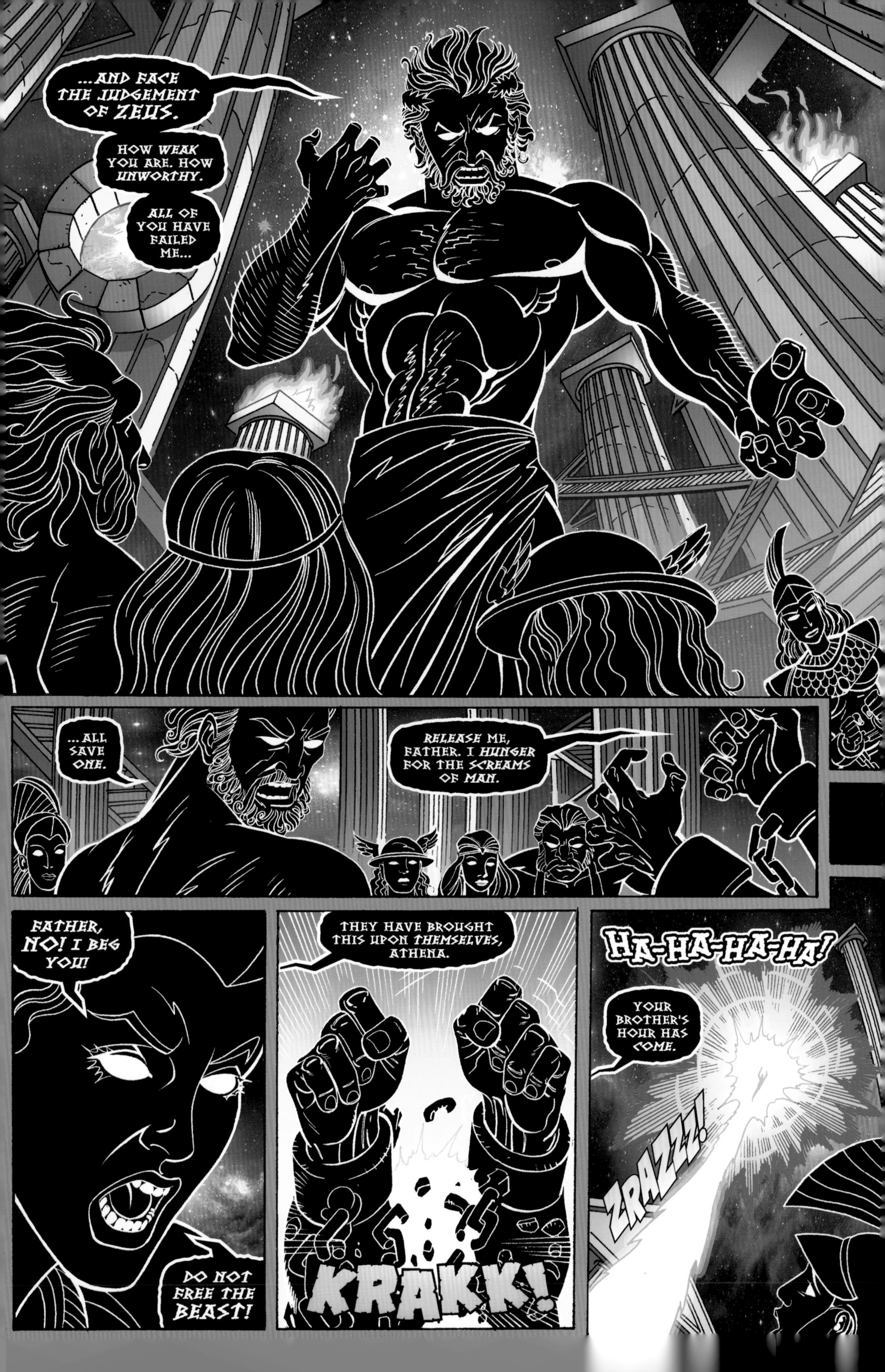
...AND FACE THE JUDGEMENT OF ZEUS.
HOW WEAK YOU ARE. HOW UNWORTHY.
ALL OF YOU HAVE FAILED ME...
...ALL SAVE ONE.
RELEASE ME, FATHER. I HUNGER FOR THE SCREAMS OF MAN.
FATHER, NO! I BEG YOU!
DO NOT FREE THE BEAST!
THEY HAVE BROUGHT THIS UPON THEMSELVES, ATHENA.
KRAKK!
HA-HA-HA-HA!
YOUR BROTHER'S HOUR HAS COME.
ZRAZZZZ!

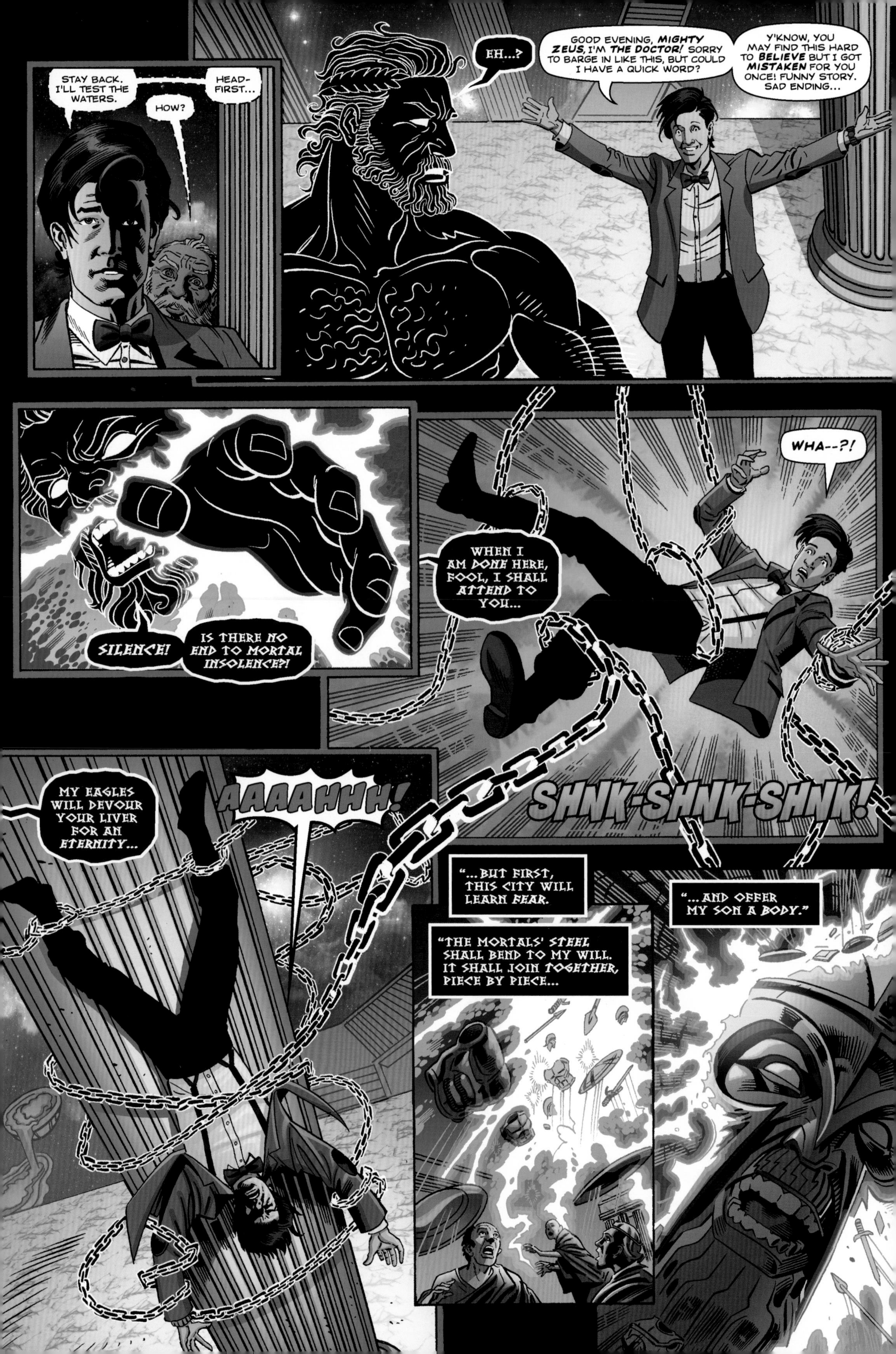
STAY BACK. I'LL TEST THE WATERS.
HOW?
HEAD-FIRST...
EH...?
GOOD EVENING, MIGHTY ZEUS, I'M THE DOCTOR! SORRY TO BARGE IN LIKE THIS, BUT COULD I HAVE A QUICK WORD?
Y'KNOW, YOU MAY FIND THIS HARD TO BELIEVE BUT I GOT MISTAKEN FOR YOU ONCE! FUNNY STORY. SAD ENDING...
SILENCE!
IS THERE NO END TO MORTAL INSOLENCE?!
WHEN I AM DONE HERE, FOOL, I SHALL ATTEND TO YOU...
WHA--?!
SHNK-SHNK-SHNK!
MY EAGLES WILL DEVOUR YOUR LIVER FOR AN ETERNITY...
AAAAHHH!
"...BUT FIRST, THIS CITY WILL LEARN FEAR.
"THE MORTALS' STEEL SHALL BEND TO MY WILL. IT SHALL JOIN TOGETHER, PIECE BY PIECE...
"...AND OFFER MY SON A BODY."

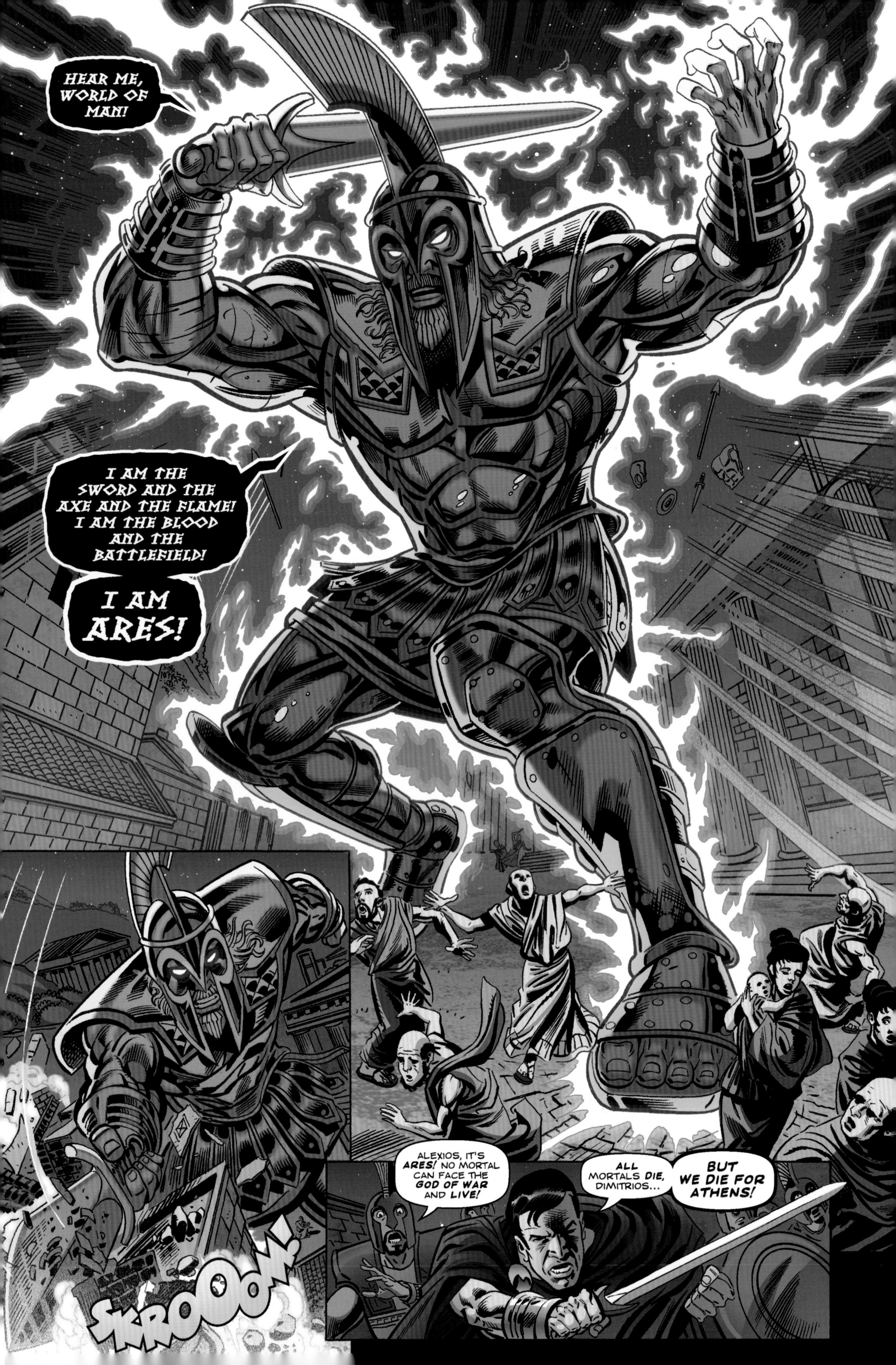
HEAR ME, WORLD OF MAN!
I AM THE SWORD AND THE AXE AND THE FLAME! I AM THE BLOOD AND THE BATTLEFIELD!
I AM ARES!
SKROOOOM!
ALEXIOS, IT'S ARES! NO MORTAL CAN FACE THE GOD OF WAR AND LIVE!
ALL MORTALS DIE, DIMITRIOS...
BUT WE DIE FOR ATHENS!

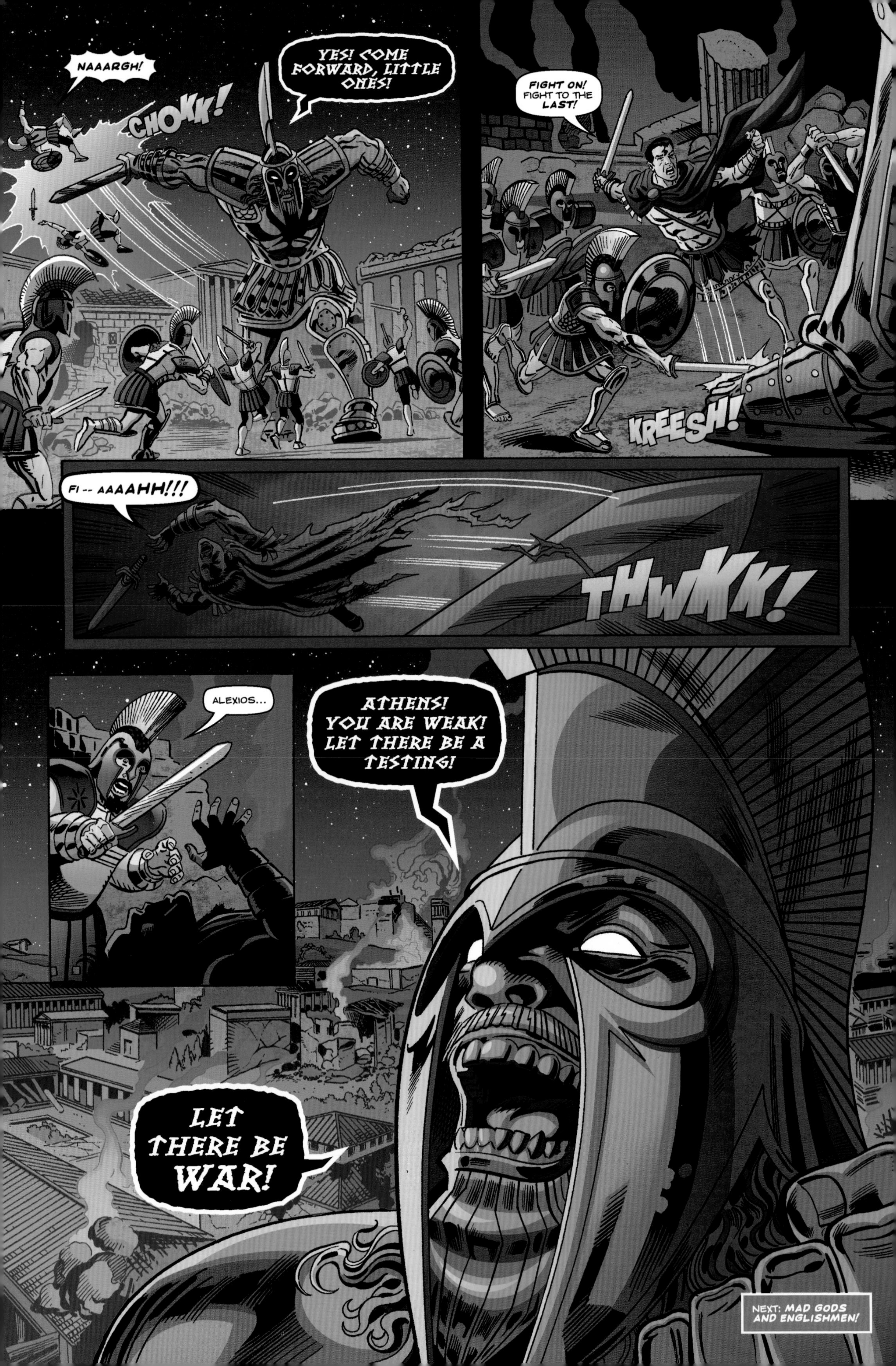
NAAARGH!
YES! COME FORWARD, LITTLE ONES!
CHOKK!
FIGHT ON! FIGHT TO THE LAST!
KREESH!
FI -- AAAAHH!!!
THWKK!
ALEXIOS...
ATHENS! YOU ARE WEAK! LET THERE BE A TESTING!
LET THERE BE WAR!
NEXT: MAD GODS AND ENGLISHMEN!

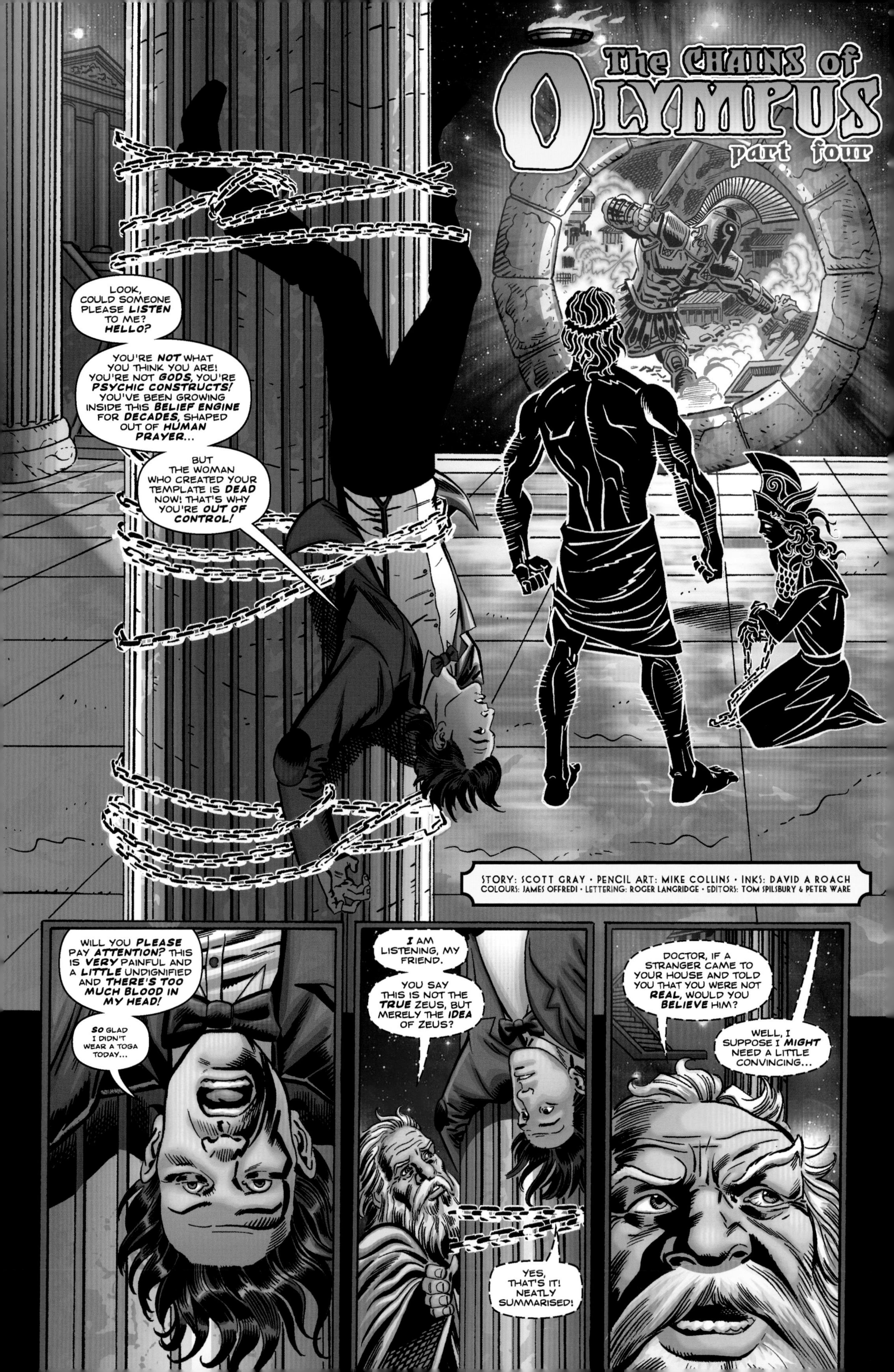
The CHAINS of OLYMPUS
part four
LOOK, COULD SOMEONE PLEASE LISTEN TO ME? HELLO?
YOU'RE NOT WHAT YOU THINK YOU ARE! YOU'RE NOT GODS, YOU'RE PSYCHIC CONSTRUCTS! YOU'VE BEEN GROWING INSIDE THIS BELIEF ENGINE FOR DECADES, SHAPED OUT OF HUMAN PRAYER...
BUT THE WOMAN WHO CREATED YOUR TEMPLATE IS DEAD NOW! THAT'S WHY YOU'RE OUT OF CONTROL!
STORY: SCOTT GRAY • PENCIL ART: MIKE COLLINS • INKS: DAVID A ROACH
COLOURS: JAMES OFFREDI • LETTERING: ROGER LANGRIDGE • EDITORS: TOM SPILSBURY & PETER WARE
WILL YOU PLEASE PAY ATTENTION? THIS IS VERY PAINFUL AND A LITTLE UNDIGNIFIED AND THERE'S TOO MUCH BLOOD IN MY HEAD!
SO GLAD I DIDN'T WEAR A TOGA TODAY...
I AM LISTENING, MY FRIEND.
YOU SAY THIS IS NOT THE TRUE ZEUS, BUT MERELY THE IDEA OF ZEUS?
YES, THAT'S IT! NEATLY SUMMARISED!
DOCTOR, IF A STRANGER CAME TO YOUR HOUSE AND TOLD YOU THAT YOU WERE NOT REAL, WOULD YOU BELIEVE HIM?
WELL, I SUPPOSE I MIGHT NEED A LITTLE CONVINCING...

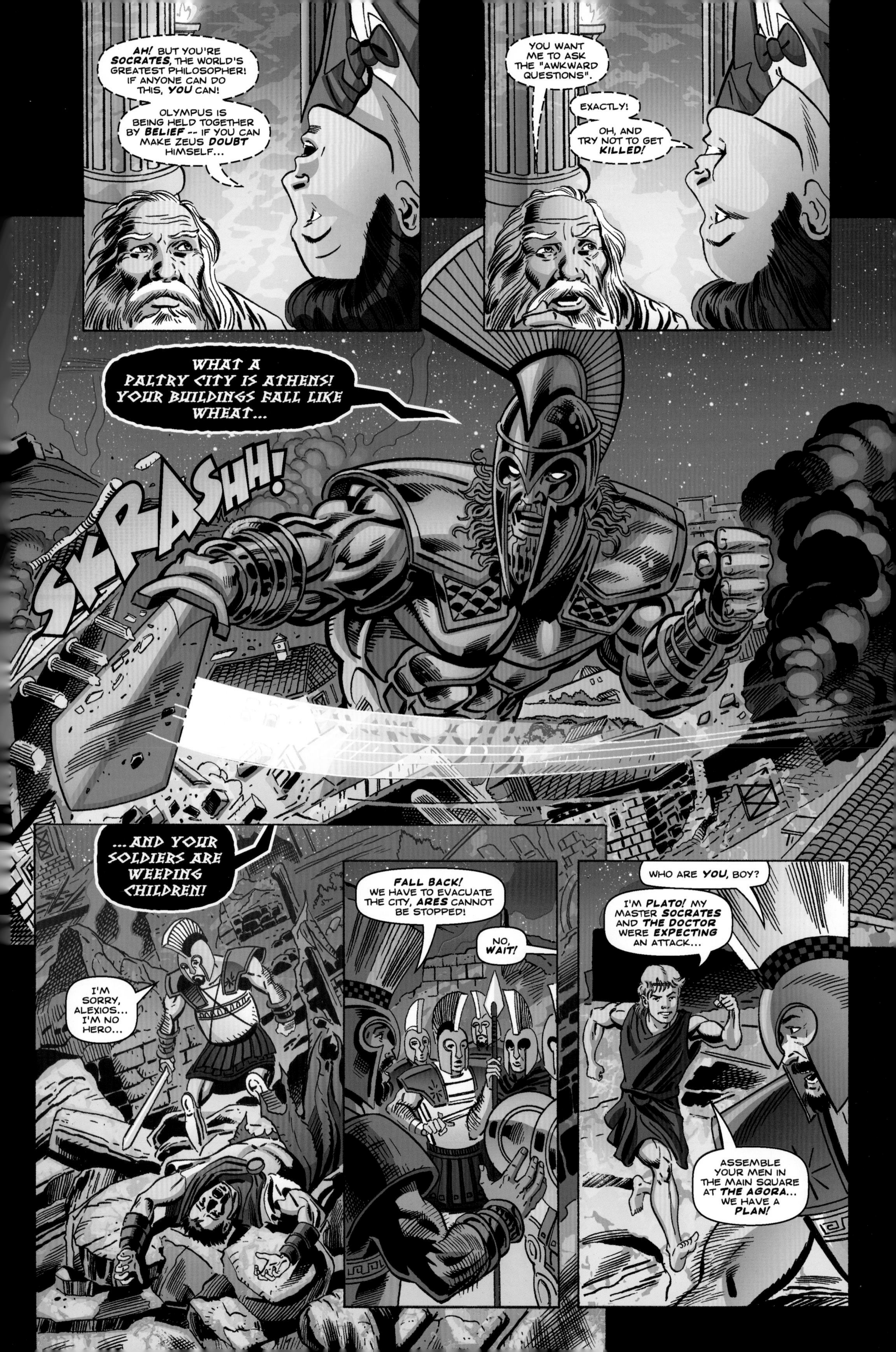
AH! BUT YOU'RE SOCRATES, THE WORLD'S GREATEST PHILOSOPHER! IF ANYONE CAN DO THIS, YOU CAN!
OLYMPUS IS BEING HELD TOGETHER BY BELIEF -- IF YOU CAN MAKE ZEUS DOUBT HIMSELF...
YOU WANT ME TO ASK THE "AWKWARD QUESTIONS".
EXACTLY!
OH, AND TRY NOT TO GET KILLED!
WHAT A PALTRY CITY IS ATHENS! YOUR BUILDINGS FALL LIKE WHEAT...
SKRASHH!
...AND YOUR SOLDIERS ARE WEEPING CHILDREN!
I'M SORRY, ALEXIOS... I'M NO HERO...
FALL BACK! WE HAVE TO EVACUATE THE CITY, ARES CANNOT BE STOPPED!
NO, WAIT!
WHO ARE YOU, BOY?
I'M PLATO! MY MASTER SOCRATES AND THE DOCTOR WERE EXPECTING AN ATTACK...
ASSEMBLE YOUR MEN IN THE MAIN SQUARE AT THE AGORA... WE HAVE A PLAN!

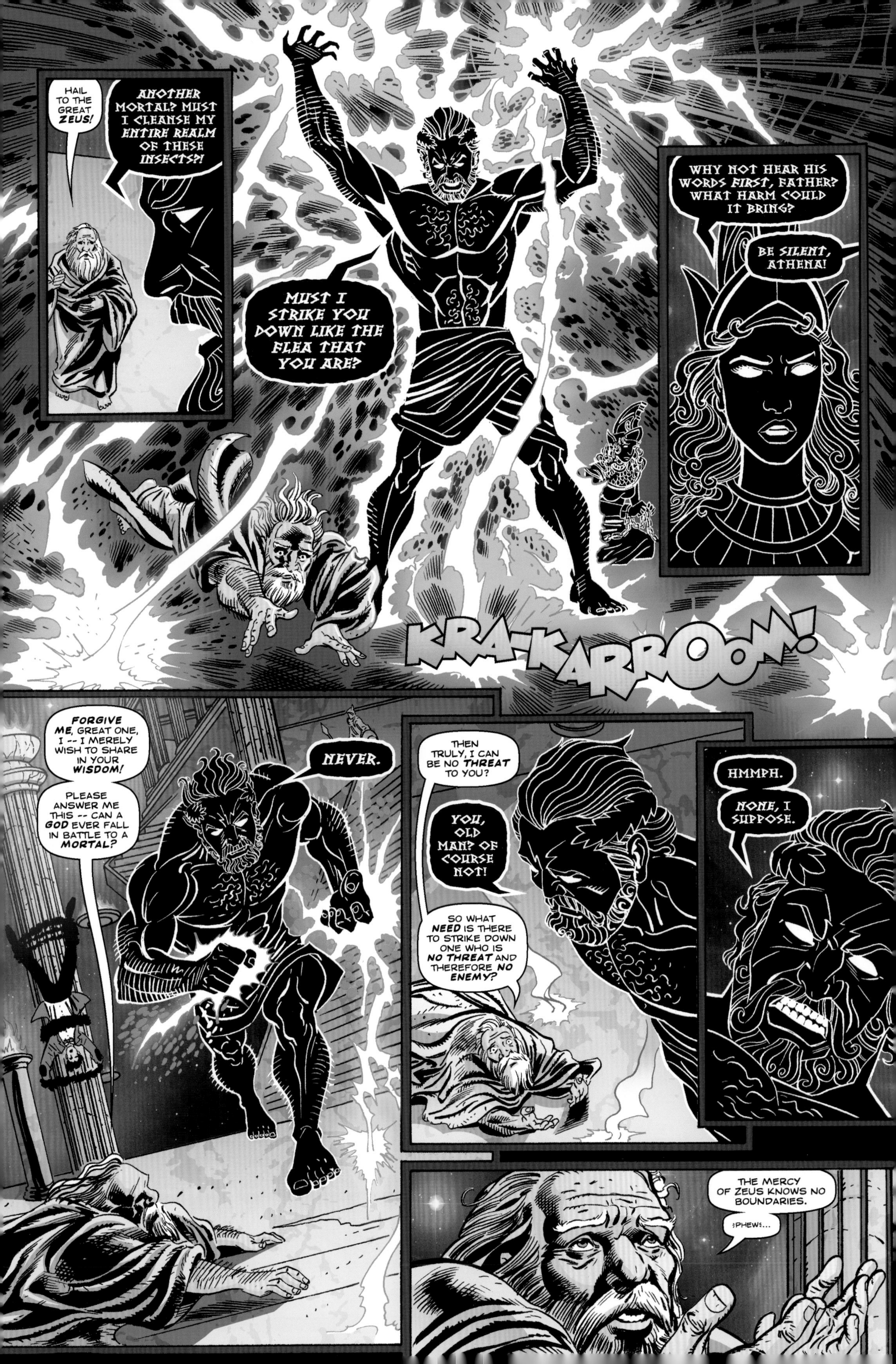
HAIL TO THE GREAT ZEUS!
ANOTHER MORTAL? MUST I CLEANSE MY ENTIRE REALM OF THESE INSECTS?!
MUST I STRIKE YOU DOWN LIKE THE FLEA THAT YOU ARE?
WHY NOT HEAR HIS WORDS FIRST, FATHER? WHAT HARM COULD IT BRING?
BE SILENT, ATHENA!
KRA-KARROOM!
FORGIVE ME, GREAT ONE, I -- I MERELY WISH TO SHARE IN YOUR WISDOM!
PLEASE ANSWER ME THIS -- CAN A GOD EVER FALL IN BATTLE TO A MORTAL?
NEVER.
THEN TRULY, I CAN BE NO THREAT TO YOU?
YOU, OLD MAN? OF COURSE NOT!
SO WHAT NEED IS THERE TO STRIKE DOWN ONE WHO IS NO THREAT AND THEREFORE NO ENEMY?
HMMPH.
NONE, I SUPPOSE.
THE MERCY OF ZEUS KNOWS NO BOUNDARIES.
PHEW...

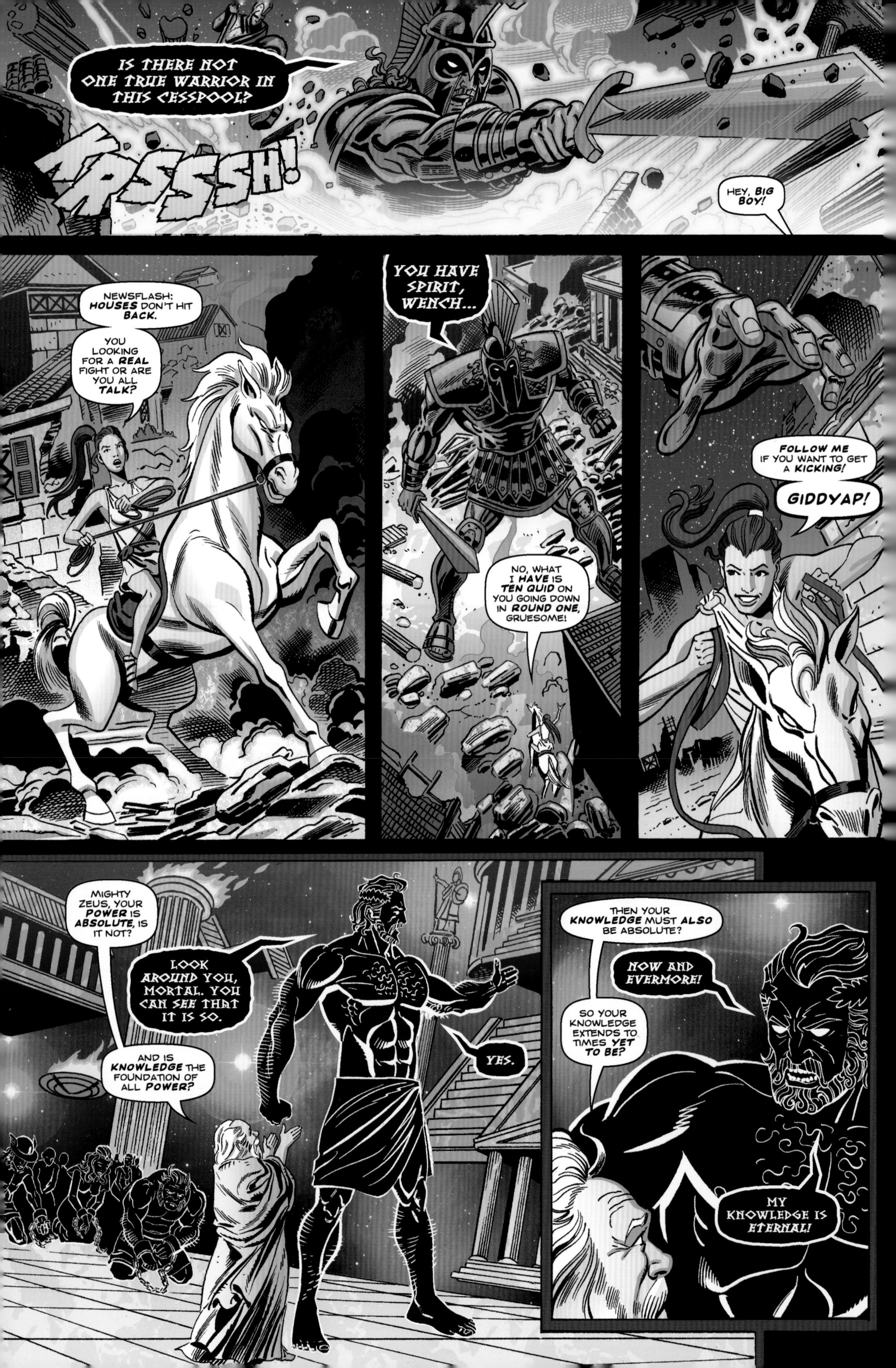
IS THERE NOT ONE TRUE WARRIOR IN THIS CESSPOOL?
KRSSSH!
HEY, BIG BOY!
NEWSFLASH: HOUSES DON'T HIT BACK.
YOU LOOKING FOR A REAL FIGHT OR ARE YOU ALL TALK?
YOU HAVE SPIRIT, WENCH...
NO, WHAT I HAVE IS TEN QUID ON YOU GOING DOWN IN ROUND ONE, GRUESOME!
FOLLOW ME IF YOU WANT TO GET A KICKING!
GIDDYAP!
MIGHTY ZEUS, YOUR POWER IS ABSOLUTE, IS IT NOT?
LOOK AROUND YOU, MORTAL. YOU CAN SEE THAT IT IS SO.
AND IS KNOWLEDGE THE FOUNDATION OF ALL POWER?
YES.
THEN YOUR KNOWLEDGE MUST ALSO BE ABSOLUTE?
NOW AND EVERMORE!
SO YOUR KNOWLEDGE EXTENDS TO TIMES YET TO BE?
MY KNOWLEDGE IS ETERNAL!

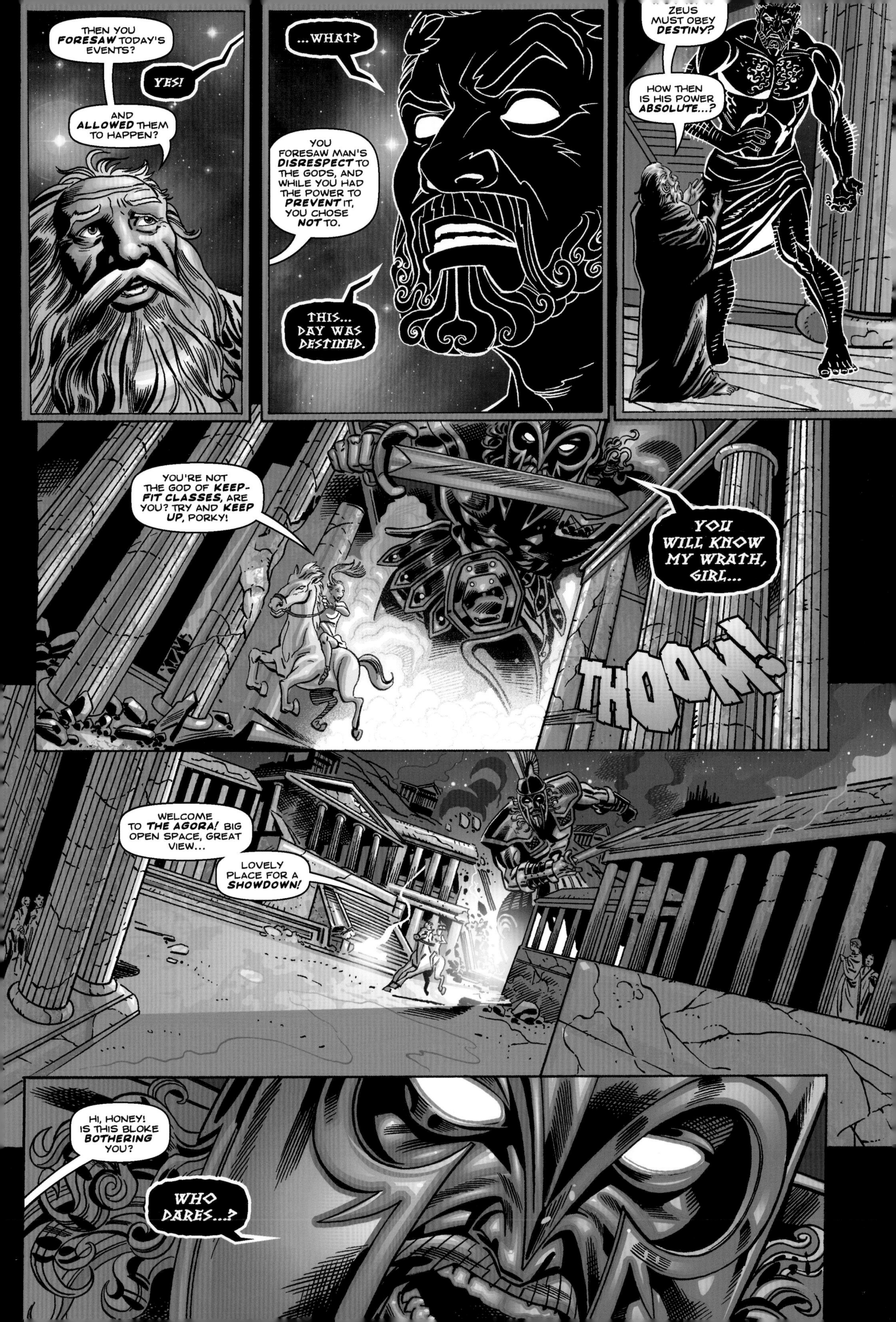
THEN YOU FORESAW TODAY'S EVENTS?
YES!
AND ALLOWED THEM TO HAPPEN?
...WHAT?
YOU FORESAW MAN'S DISRESPECT TO THE GODS, AND WHILE YOU HAD THE POWER TO PREVENT IT, YOU CHOSE NOT TO.
THIS... DAY WAS DESTINED.
ZEUS MUST OBEY DESTINY?
HOW THEN IS HIS POWER ABSOLUTE...?
YOU'RE NOT THE GOD OF KEEP-FIT CLASSES, ARE YOU? TRY AND KEEP UP, PORKY!
YOU WILL KNOW MY WRATH, GIRL...
THOOM!
WELCOME TO THE AGORA! BIG OPEN SPACE, GREAT VIEW...
LOVELY PLACE FOR A SHOWDOWN!
HI, HONEY! IS THIS BLOKE BOTHERING YOU?
WHO DARES...?

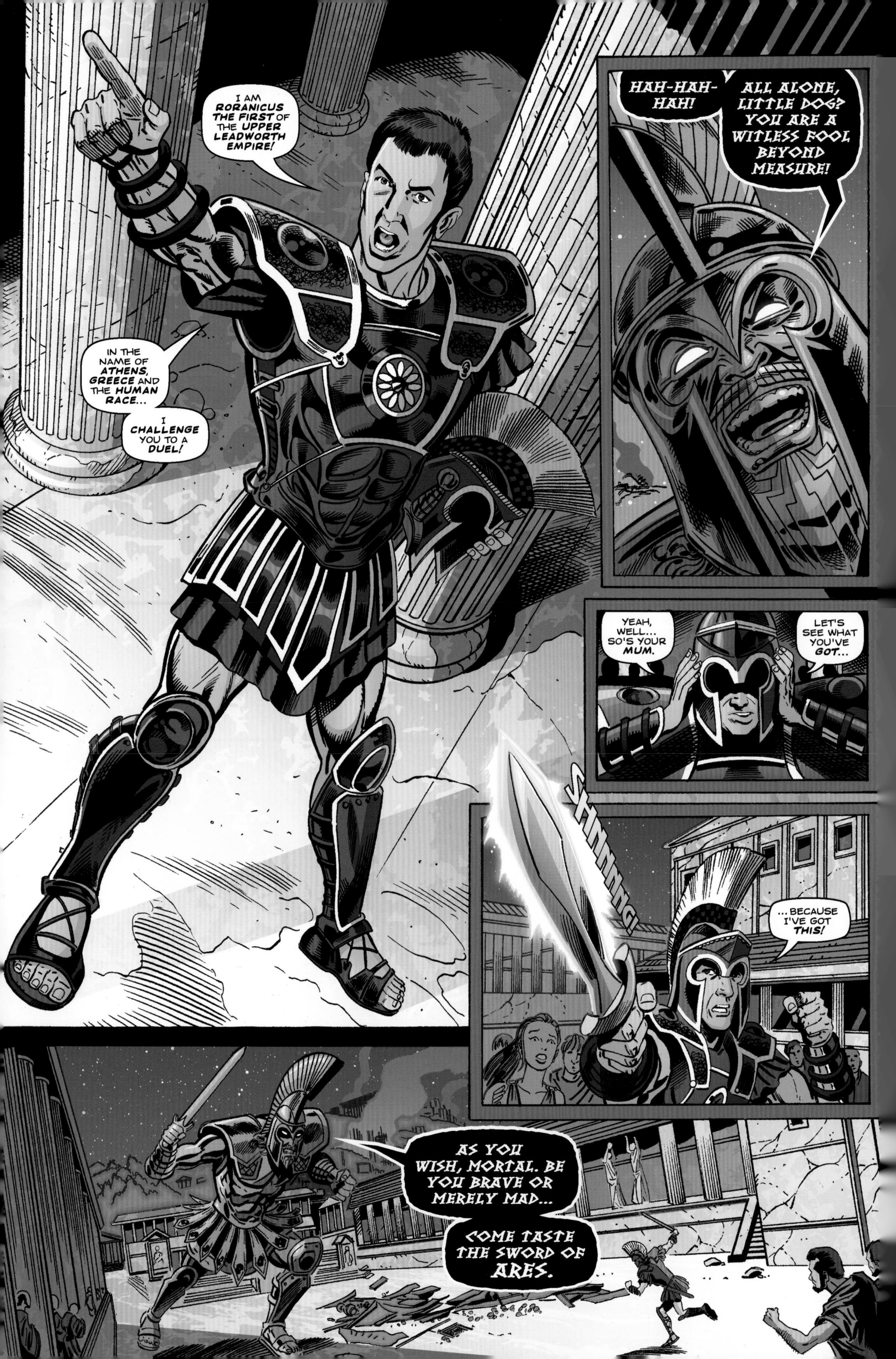

I AM RORANICUS THE FIRST OF THE UPPER LEADWORTH EMPIRE!
IN THE NAME OF ATHENS, GREECE AND THE HUMAN RACE...
I CHALLENGE YOU TO A DUEL!
HAH-HAH-HAH!
ALL ALONE, LITTLE DOG? YOU ARE A WITLESS FOOL BEYOND MEASURE!
YEAH, WELL... SO'S YOUR MUM.
LET'S SEE WHAT YOU'VE GOT...
SHHHHNG!
...BECAUSE I'VE GOT THIS!
AS YOU WISH, MORTAL. BE YOU BRAVE OR MERELY MAD...
COME TASTE THE SWORD OF ARES.

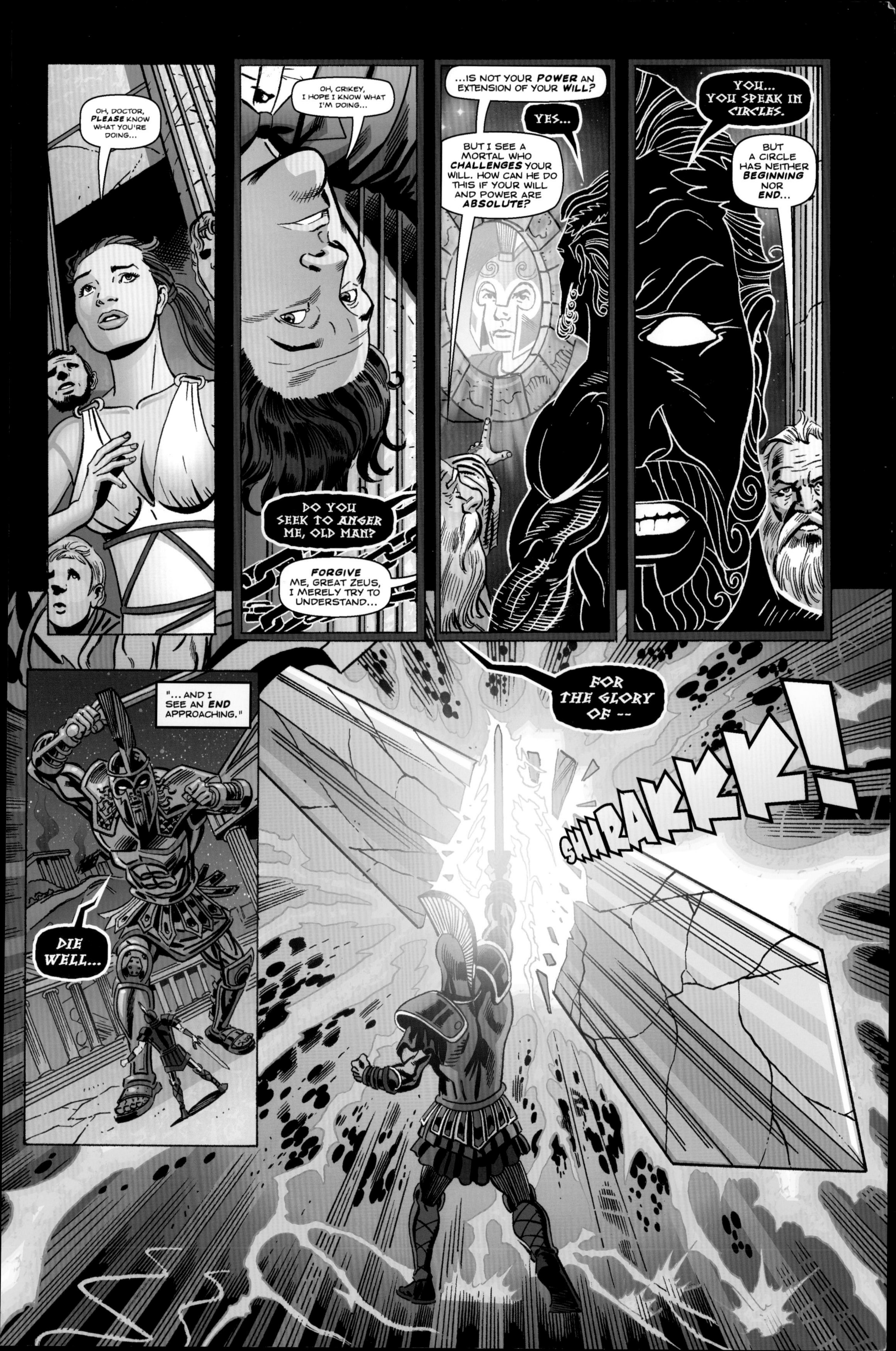

OH, DOCTOR, PLEASE KNOW WHAT YOU'RE DOING...
OH, CRIKEY, I HOPE I KNOW WHAT I'M DOING...
DO YOU SEEK TO ANGER ME, OLD MAN?
FORGIVE ME, GREAT ZEUS, I MERELY TRY TO UNDERSTAND...
...IS NOT YOUR POWER AN EXTENSION OF YOUR WILL?
YES...
BUT I SEE A MORTAL WHO CHALLENGES YOUR WILL. HOW CAN HE DO THIS IF YOUR WILL AND POWER ARE ABSOLUTE?
YOU... YOU SPEAK IN CIRCLES.
BUT A CIRCLE HAS NEITHER BEGINNING NOR END...
"...AND I SEE AN END APPROACHING."
DIE WELL...
FOR THE GLORY OF --
SHRAKKK!

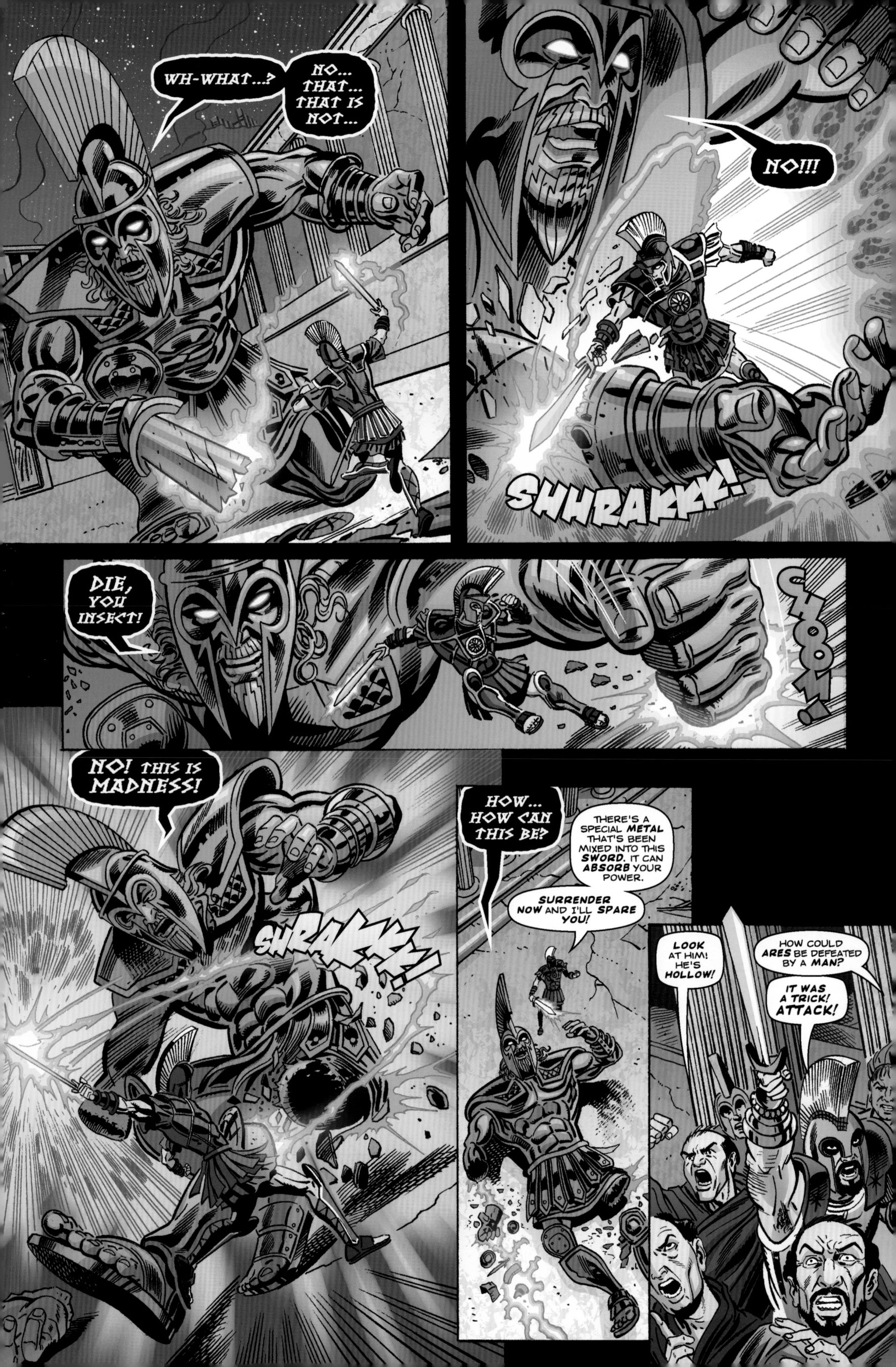
WH-WHAT...?
NO... THAT... THAT IS NOT...
NO!!!
SHHRAKKK!
DIE, YOU INSECT!
CHOOM!
NO! THIS IS MADNESS!
SHRAKKK!
HOW... HOW CAN THIS BE?
THERE'S A SPECIAL METAL THAT'S BEEN MIXED INTO THIS SWORD. IT CAN ABSORB YOUR POWER.
SURRENDER NOW AND I'LL SPARE YOU!
LOOK AT HIM! HE'S HOLLOW!
HOW COULD ARES BE DEFEATED BY A MAN?
IT WAS A TRICK! ATTACK!

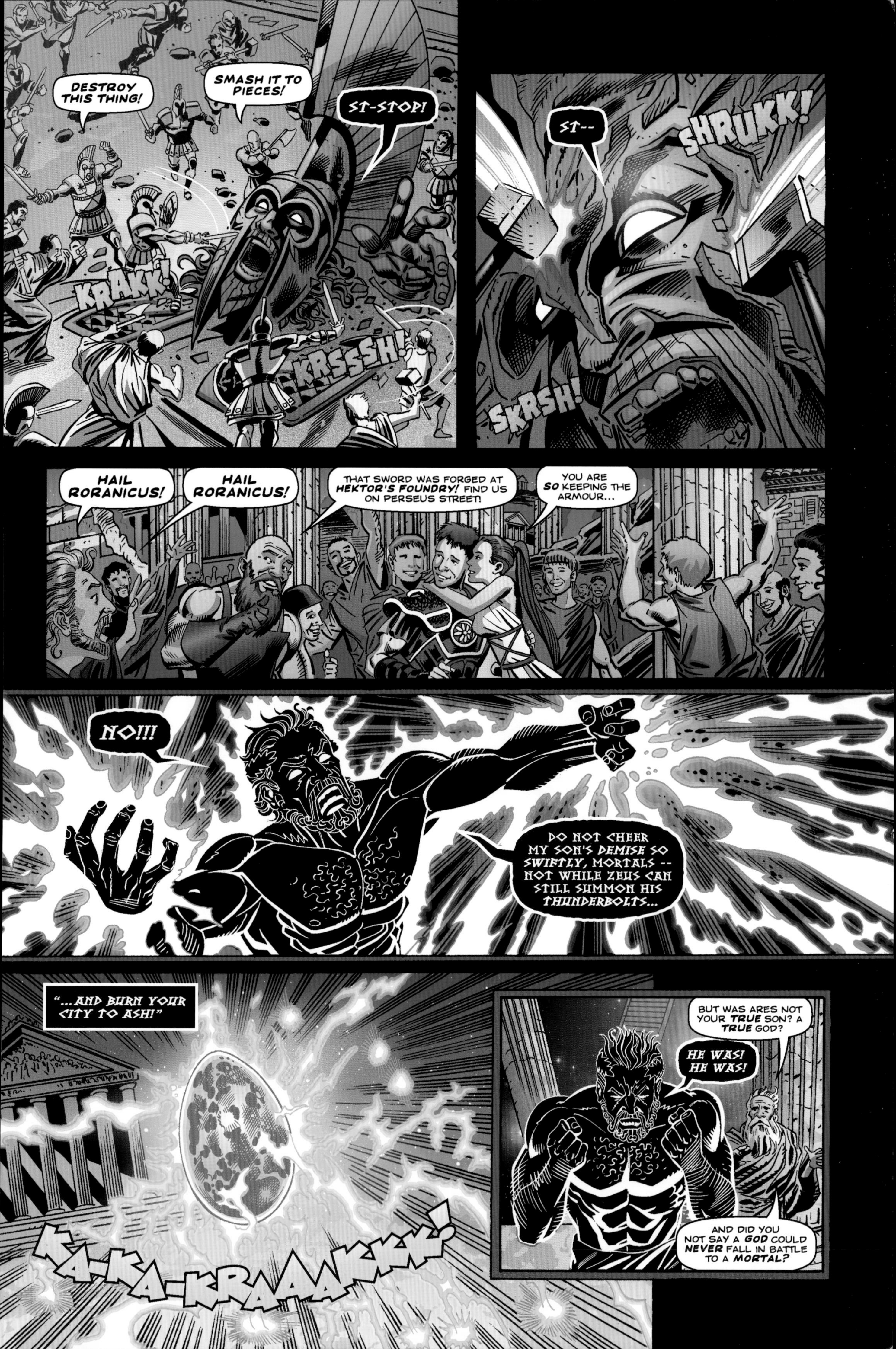
DESTROY THIS THING!
SMASH IT TO PIECES!
ST-STOP!
KRAKK!
KRSSSH!
ST--
SHRUKK!
SKRSH!
HAIL RORANICUS!
HAIL RORANICUS!
THAT SWORD WAS FORGED AT HEKTOR'S FOUNDRY! FIND US ON PERSEUS STREET!
YOU ARE SO KEEPING THE ARMOUR...
NO!!!
DO NOT CHEER MY SON'S DEMISE SO SWIFTLY, MORTALS -- NOT WHILE ZEUS CAN STILL SUMMON HIS THUNDERBOLTS...
"...AND BURN YOUR CITY TO ASH!"
KA-KA-KRAAAKK!
BUT WAS ARES NOT YOUR TRUE SON? A TRUE GOD?
HE WAS! HE WAS!
AND DID YOU NOT SAY A GOD COULD NEVER FALL IN BATTLE TO A MORTAL?

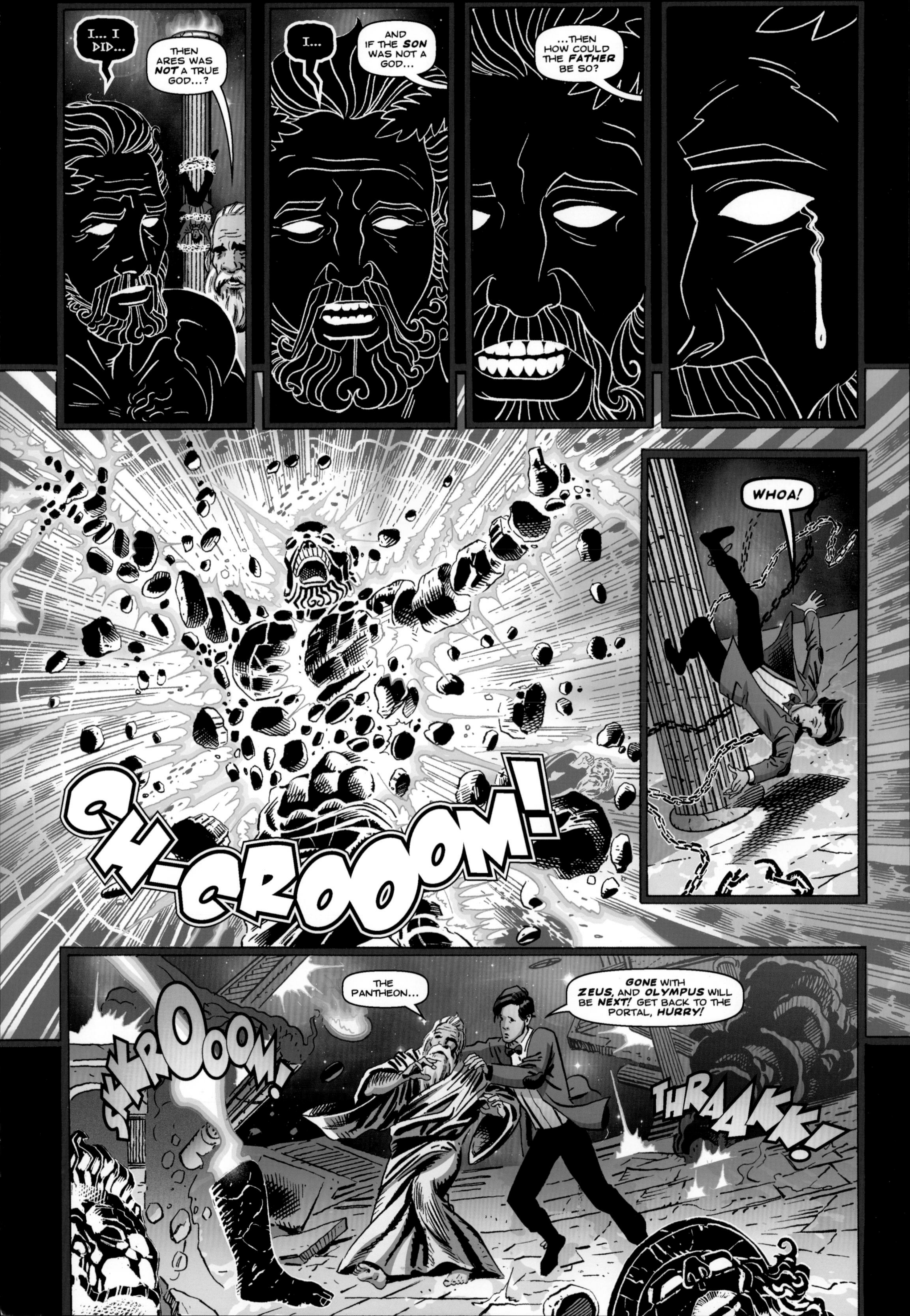
I... I DID...
THEN ARES WAS NOT A TRUE GOD...?
I...
AND IF THE SON WAS NOT A GOD...
...THEN HOW COULD THE FATHER BE SO?
CH-CROOOOM!
WHOA!
THE PANTHEON...
GONE WITH ZEUS, AND OLYMPUS WILL BE NEXT! GET BACK TO THE PORTAL, HURRY!
SHROOOOM!
THRAAKK!

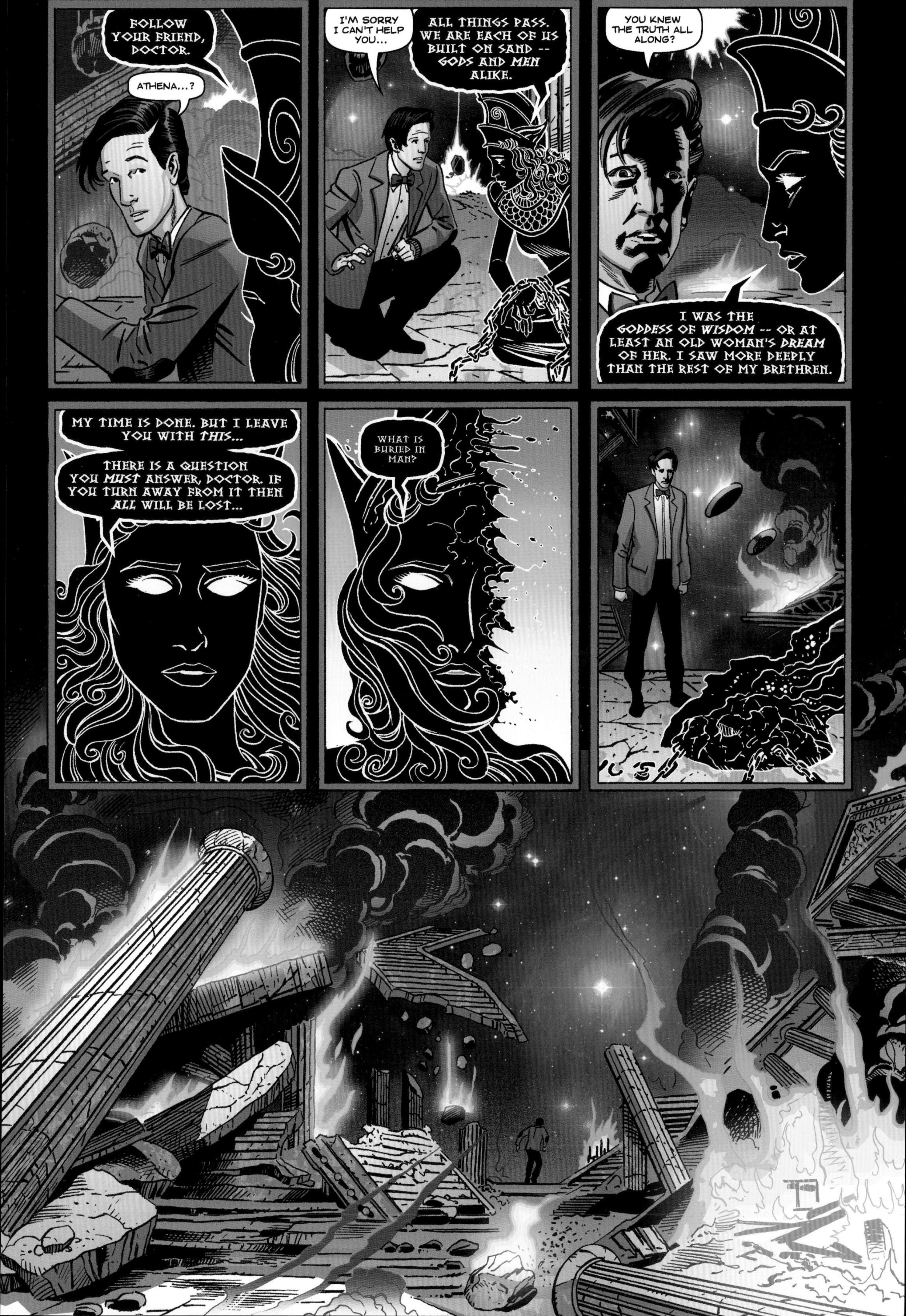
FOLLOW YOUR FRIEND, DOCTOR.
ATHENA...?
I'M SORRY I CAN'T HELP YOU...
ALL THINGS PASS. WE ARE EACH OF US BUILT ON SAND -- GODS AND MEN ALIKE.
YOU KNEW THE TRUTH ALL ALONG?
I WAS THE GODDESS OF WISDOM -- OR AT LEAST AN OLD WOMAN'S DREAM OF HER. I SAW MORE DEEPLY THAN THE REST OF MY BRETHREN.
MY TIME IS DONE. BUT I LEAVE YOU WITH THIS...
THERE IS A QUESTION YOU MUST ANSWER, DOCTOR. IF YOU TURN AWAY FROM IT THEN ALL WILL BE LOST...
WHAT IS BURIED IN MAN?

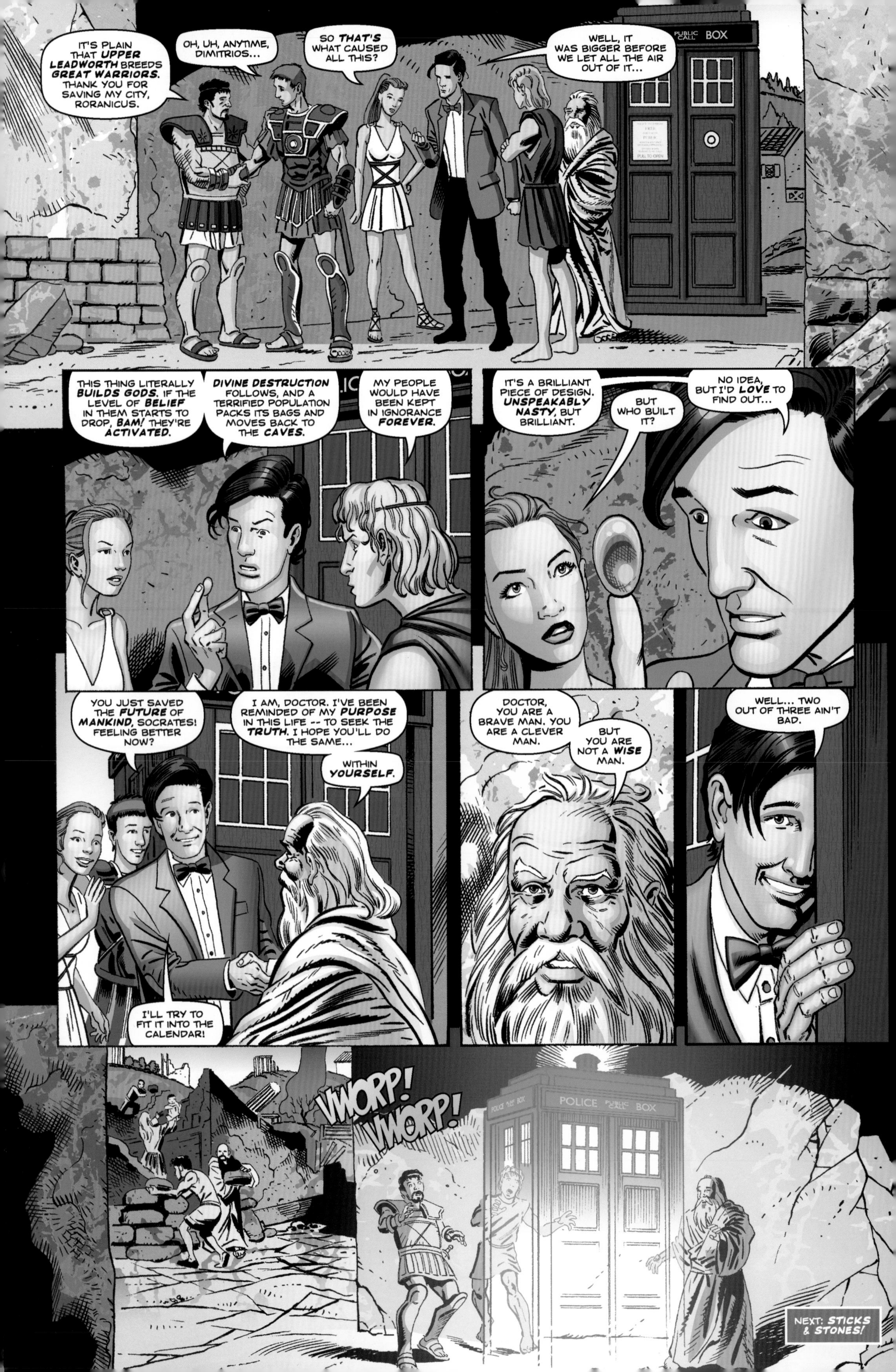
IT'S PLAIN THAT UPPER LEADWORTH BREEDS GREAT WARRIORS. THANK YOU FOR SAVING MY CITY, RORANICUS.
OH, UH, ANYTIME, DIMITRIOS...
SO THAT'S WHAT CAUSED ALL THIS?
WELL, IT WAS BIGGER BEFORE WE LET ALL THE AIR OUT OF IT...
POLICE PUBLIC CALL BOX
THIS THING LITERALLY BUILDS GODS. IF THE LEVEL OF BELIEF IN THEM STARTS TO DROP, BAM! THEY'RE ACTIVATED.
DIVINE DESTRUCTION FOLLOWS, AND A TERRIFIED POPULATION PACKS ITS BAGS AND MOVES BACK TO THE CAVES.
MY PEOPLE WOULD HAVE BEEN KEPT IN IGNORANCE FOREVER.
IT'S A BRILLIANT PIECE OF DESIGN. UNSPEAKABLY NASTY, BUT BRILLIANT.
BUT WHO BUILT IT?
NO IDEA, BUT I'D LOVE TO FIND OUT...
YOU JUST SAVED THE FUTURE OF MANKIND, SOCRATES! FEELING BETTER NOW?
I AM, DOCTOR. I'VE BEEN REMINDED OF MY PURPOSE IN THIS LIFE -- TO SEEK THE TRUTH. I HOPE YOU'LL DO THE SAME...
WITHIN YOURSELF.
I'LL TRY TO FIT IT INTO THE CALENDAR!
DOCTOR, YOU ARE A BRAVE MAN. YOU ARE A CLEVER MAN.
BUT YOU ARE NOT A WISE MAN.
WELL... TWO OUT OF THREE AIN'T BAD.
VWORP! VWORP!
POLICE PUBLIC CALL BOX
NEXT: STICKS & STONES!

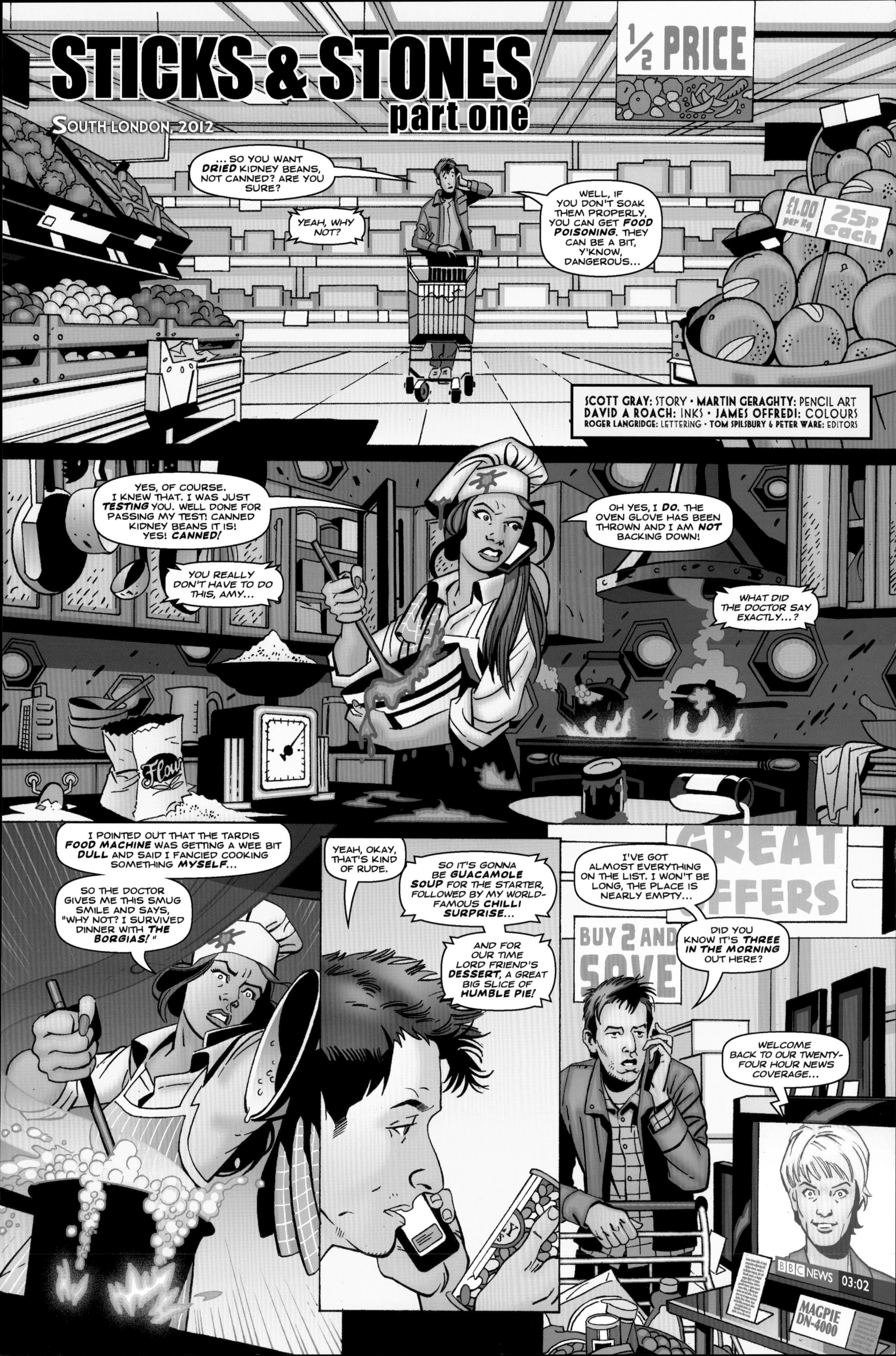
STICKS & STONES
part one
½ PRICE
SOUTH LONDON, 2012
...SO YOU WANT DRIED KIDNEY BEANS, NOT CANNED? ARE YOU SURE?
YEAH, WHY NOT?
WELL, IF YOU DON'T SOAK THEM PROPERLY, YOU CAN GET FOOD POISONING. THEY CAN BE A BIT, Y'KNOW, DANGEROUS...
£1.00 per Kg
25p each
SCOTT GRAY: STORY • MARTIN GERAGHTY: PENCIL ART
DAVID A ROACH: INKS • JAMES OFFREDI: COLOURS
ROGER LANGRIDGE: LETTERING • TOM SPILSBURY & PETER WARE: EDITORS
YES, OF COURSE. I KNEW THAT. I WAS JUST TESTING YOU. WELL DONE FOR PASSING MY TEST! CANNED KIDNEY BEANS IT IS! YES! CANNED!
YOU REALLY DON'T HAVE TO DO THIS, AMY...
OH YES, I DO. THE OVEN GLOVE HAS BEEN THROWN AND I AM NOT BACKING DOWN!
WHAT DID THE DOCTOR SAY EXACTLY...?
Flour
I POINTED OUT THAT THE TARDIS FOOD MACHINE WAS GETTING A WEE BIT DULL AND SAID I FANCIED COOKING SOMETHING MYSELF...
SO THE DOCTOR GIVES ME THIS SMUG SMILE AND SAYS, "WHY NOT? I SURVIVED DINNER WITH THE BORGIAS!"
YEAH, OKAY, THAT'S KIND OF RUDE.
SO IT'S GONNA BE GUACAMOLE SOUP FOR THE STARTER, FOLLOWED BY MY WORLD-FAMOUS CHILLI SURPRISE...
AND FOR OUR TIME LORD FRIEND'S DESSERT, A GREAT BIG SLICE OF HUMBLE PIE!
GREAT OFFERS
BUY 2 AND SAVE
I'VE GOT ALMOST EVERYTHING ON THE LIST. I WON'T BE LONG, THE PLACE IS NEARLY EMPTY...
DID YOU KNOW IT'S THREE IN THE MORNING OUT HERE?
WELCOME BACK TO OUR TWENTY-FOUR HOUR NEWS COVERAGE...
BBC NEWS 03:02
MAGPIE DN-4000

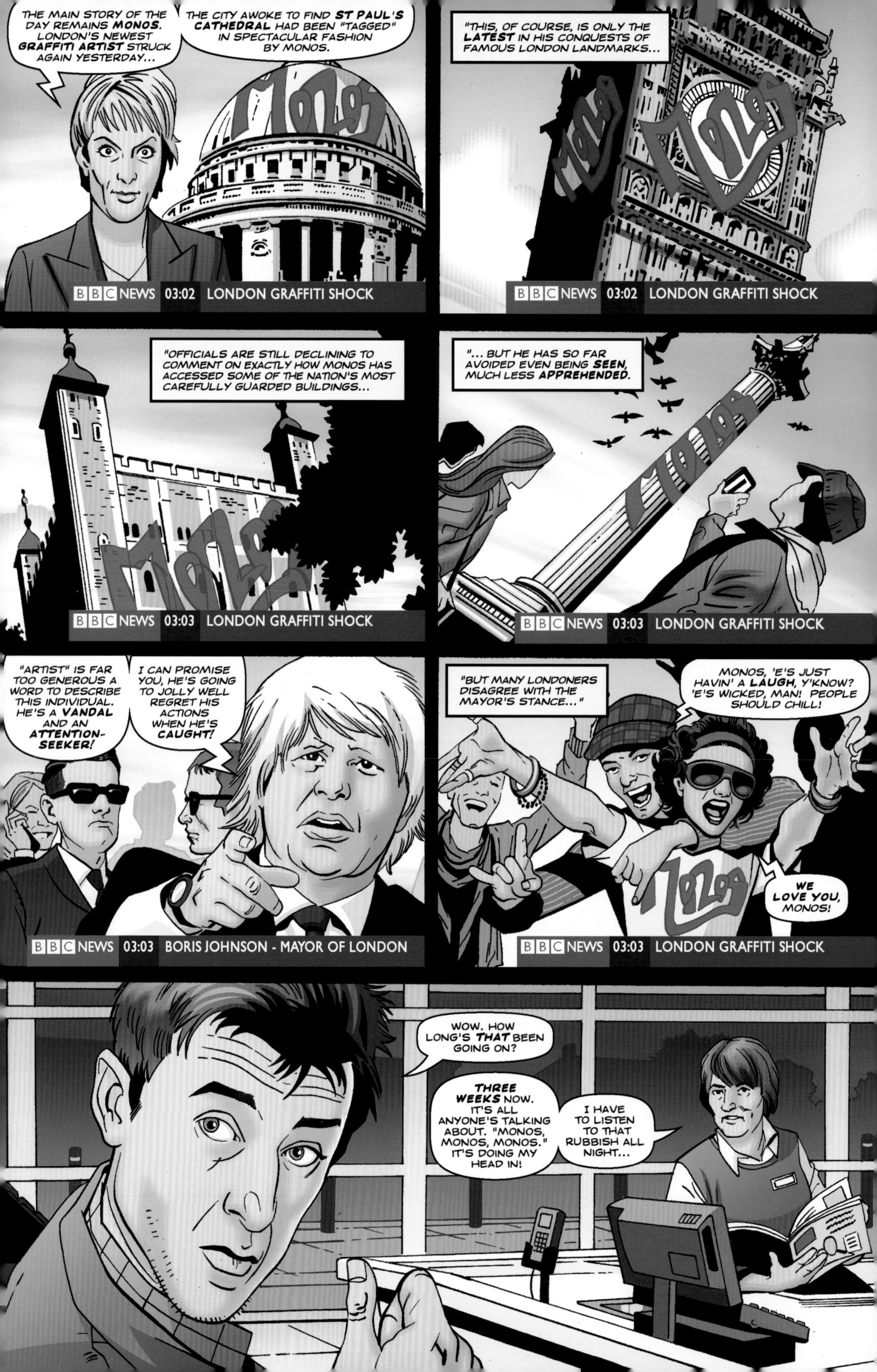
THE MAIN STORY OF THE DAY REMAINS MONOS. LONDON'S NEWEST GRAFFITI ARTIST STRUCK AGAIN YESTERDAY...
THE CITY AWOKE TO FIND ST PAUL'S CATHEDRAL HAD BEEN "TAGGED" IN SPECTACULAR FASHION BY MONOS.
BBC NEWS 03:02 LONDON GRAFFITI SHOCK
"THIS, OF COURSE, IS ONLY THE LATEST IN HIS CONQUESTS OF FAMOUS LONDON LANDMARKS...
BBC NEWS 03:02 LONDON GRAFFITI SHOCK
"OFFICIALS ARE STILL DECLINING TO COMMENT ON EXACTLY HOW MONOS HAS ACCESSED SOME OF THE NATION'S MOST CAREFULLY GUARDED BUILDINGS...
BBC NEWS 03:03 LONDON GRAFFITI SHOCK
"... BUT HE HAS SO FAR AVOIDED EVEN BEING SEEN, MUCH LESS APPREHENDED.
BBC NEWS 03:03 LONDON GRAFFITI SHOCK
"ARTIST" IS FAR TOO GENEROUS A WORD TO DESCRIBE THIS INDIVIDUAL. HE'S A VANDAL AND AN ATTENTION-SEEKER!
I CAN PROMISE YOU, HE'S GOING TO JOLLY WELL REGRET HIS ACTIONS WHEN HE'S CAUGHT!
BBC NEWS 03:03 BORIS JOHNSON - MAYOR OF LONDON
"BUT MANY LONDONERS DISAGREE WITH THE MAYOR'S STANCE..."
MONOS, 'E'S JUST HAVIN' A LAUGH, Y'KNOW? 'E'S WICKED, MAN! PEOPLE SHOULD CHILL!
WE LOVE YOU, MONOS!
BBC NEWS 03:03 LONDON GRAFFITI SHOCK
WOW. HOW LONG'S THAT BEEN GOING ON?
THREE WEEKS NOW. IT'S ALL ANYONE'S TALKING ABOUT. "MONOS, MONOS, MONOS." IT'S DOING MY HEAD IN!
I HAVE TO LISTEN TO THAT RUBBISH ALL NIGHT...

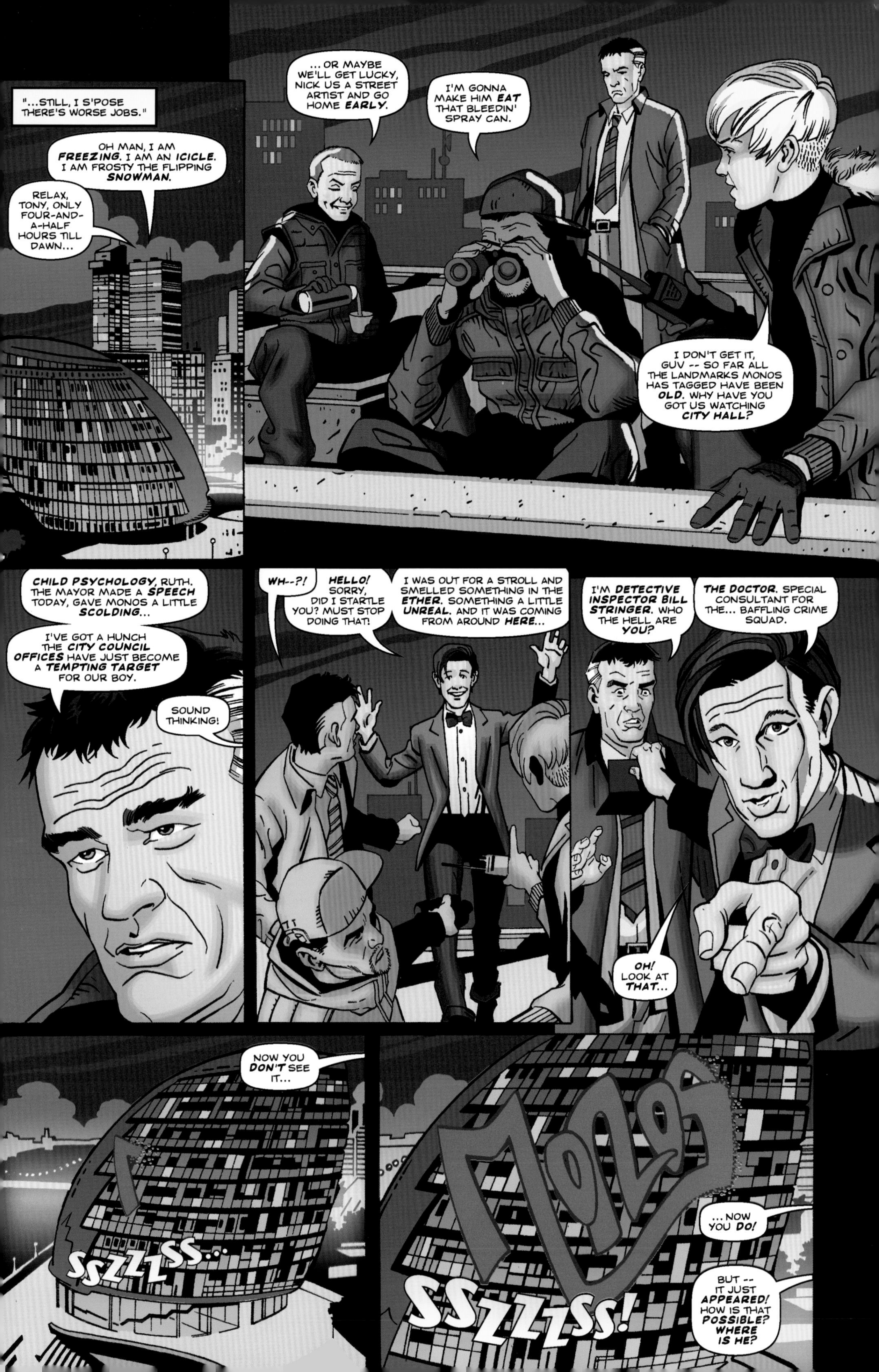
"...STILL, I S'POSE THERE'S WORSE JOBS."
OH MAN, I AM FREEZING. I AM AN ICICLE. I AM FROSTY THE FLIPPING SNOWMAN.
RELAX, TONY, ONLY FOUR-AND-A-HALF HOURS TILL DAWN...
...OR MAYBE WE'LL GET LUCKY, NICK US A STREET ARTIST AND GO HOME EARLY.
I'M GONNA MAKE HIM EAT THAT BLEEDIN' SPRAY CAN.
I DON'T GET IT, GUV -- SO FAR ALL THE LANDMARKS MONOS HAS TAGGED HAVE BEEN OLD. WHY HAVE YOU GOT US WATCHING CITY HALL?
CHILD PSYCHOLOGY, RUTH. THE MAYOR MADE A SPEECH TODAY, GAVE MONOS A LITTLE SCOLDING...
I'VE GOT A HUNCH THE CITY COUNCIL OFFICES HAVE JUST BECOME A TEMPTING TARGET FOR OUR BOY.
SOUND THINKING!
WH--?!
HELLO! SORRY, DID I STARTLE YOU? MUST STOP DOING THAT!
I WAS OUT FOR A STROLL AND SMELLED SOMETHING IN THE ETHER. SOMETHING A LITTLE UNREAL. AND IT WAS COMING FROM AROUND HERE...
I'M DETECTIVE INSPECTOR BILL STRINGER. WHO THE HELL ARE YOU?
THE DOCTOR. SPECIAL CONSULTANT FOR THE... BAFFLING CRIME SQUAD.
OH! LOOK AT THAT...
NOW YOU DON'T SEE IT...
SSZZZSS...
...NOW YOU DO!
MONOS
SSZZZSS!
BUT -- IT JUST APPEARED! HOW IS THAT POSSIBLE? WHERE IS HE?

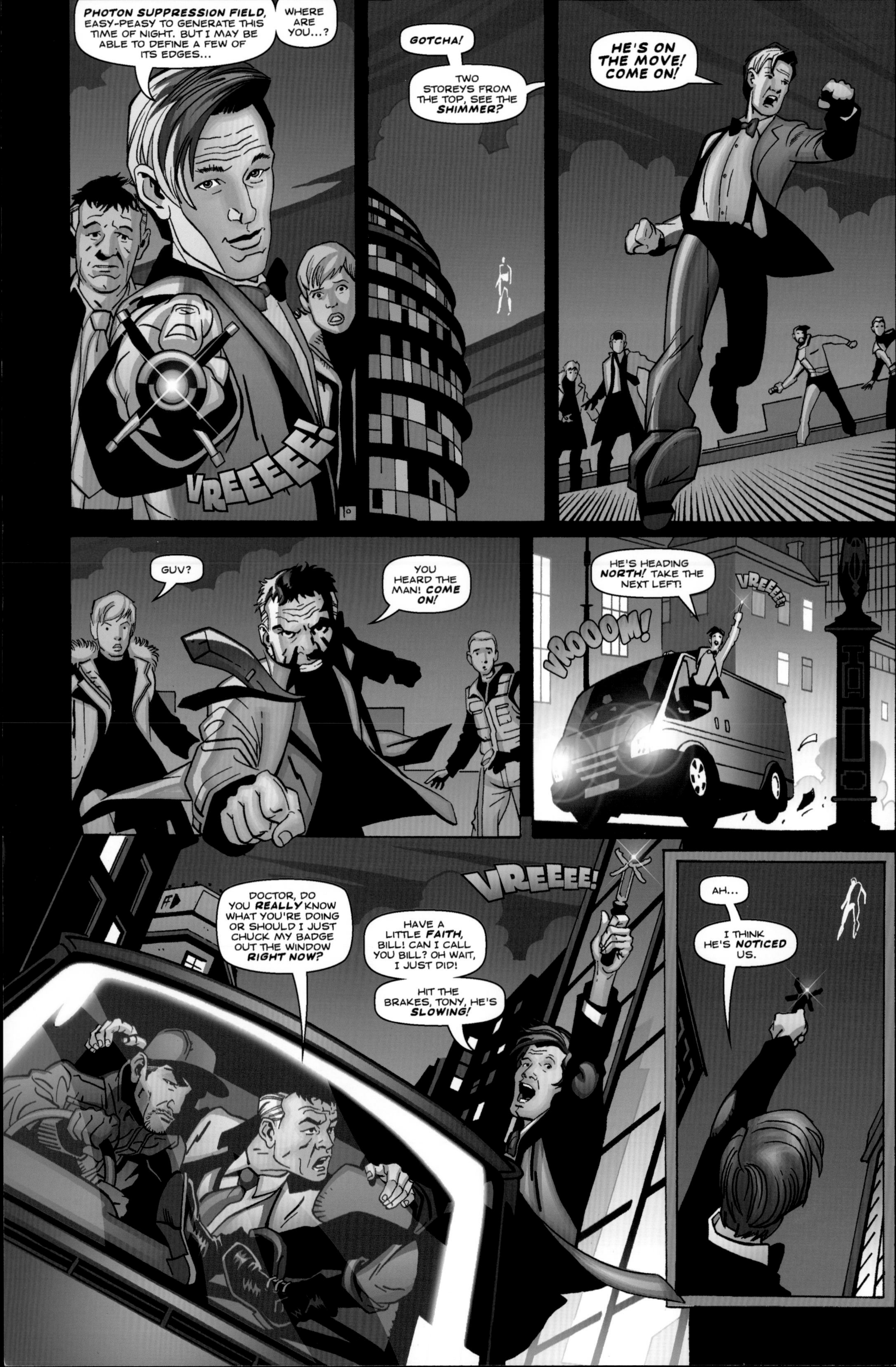
PHOTON SUPPRESSION FIELD, EASY-PEASY TO GENERATE THIS TIME OF NIGHT. BUT I MAY BE ABLE TO DEFINE A FEW OF ITS EDGES...
WHERE ARE YOU...?
VREEEEE!
GOTCHA!
TWO STOREYS FROM THE TOP, SEE THE SHIMMER?
HE'S ON THE MOVE! COME ON!
GUV?
YOU HEARD THE MAN! COME ON!
HE'S HEADING NORTH! TAKE THE NEXT LEFT!
VREEEE!
VROOOM!
DOCTOR, DO YOU REALLY KNOW WHAT YOU'RE DOING OR SHOULD I JUST CHUCK MY BADGE OUT THE WINDOW RIGHT NOW?
VREEEE!
HAVE A LITTLE FAITH, BILL! CAN I CALL YOU BILL? OH WAIT, I JUST DID!
HIT THE BRAKES, TONY, HE'S SLOWING!
AH...
I THINK HE'S NOTICED US.

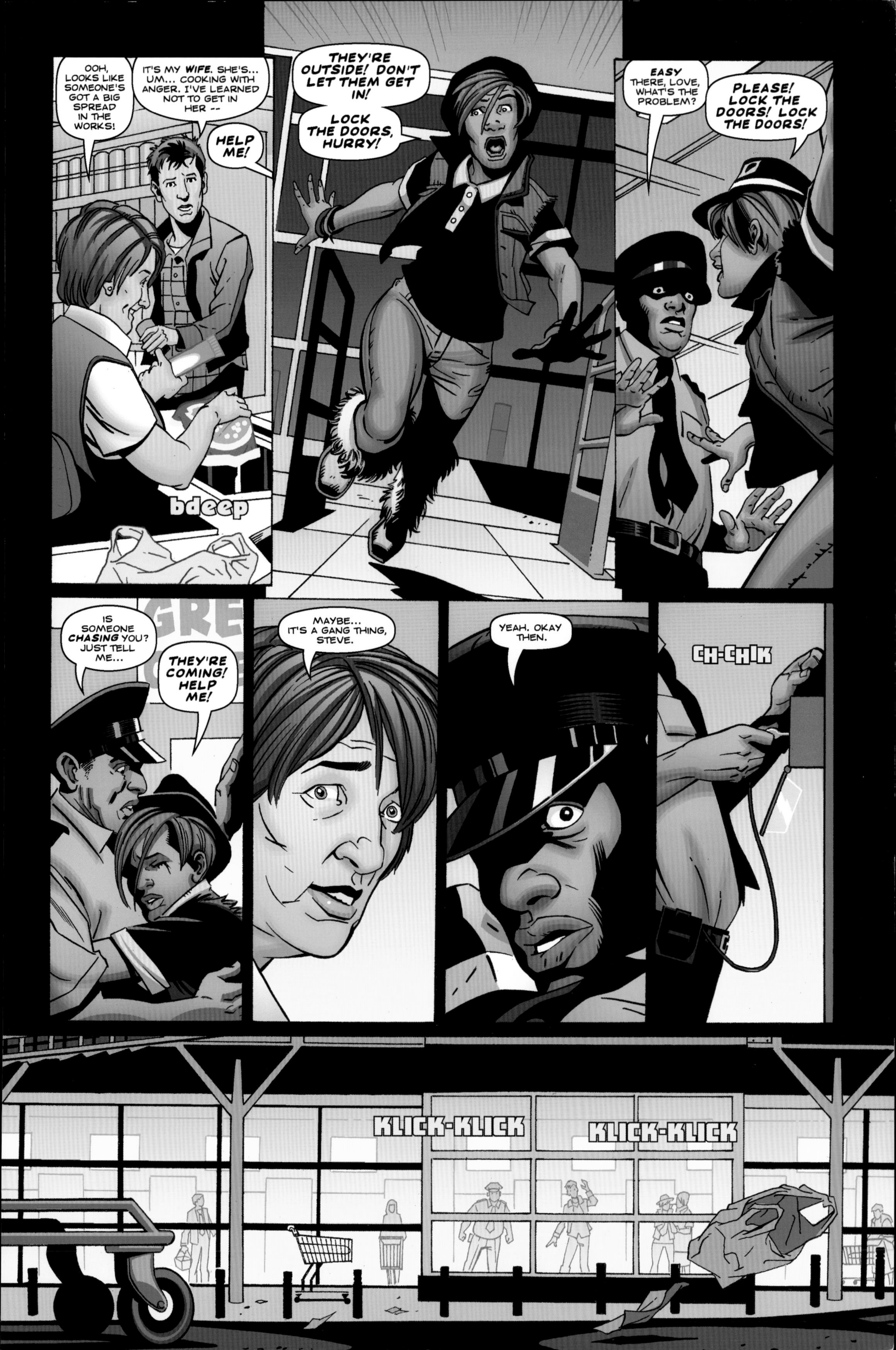
OOH, LOOKS LIKE SOMEONE'S GOT A BIG SPREAD IN THE WORKS!
IT'S MY WIFE. SHE'S... UM... COOKING WITH ANGER. I'VE LEARNED NOT TO GET IN HER --
HELP ME!
bdeep
THEY'RE OUTSIDE! DON'T LET THEM GET IN!
LOCK THE DOORS, HURRY!
EASY THERE, LOVE, WHAT'S THE PROBLEM?
PLEASE! LOCK THE DOORS! LOCK THE DOORS!
IS SOMEONE CHASING YOU? JUST TELL ME...
THEY'RE COMING! HELP ME!
MAYBE... IT'S A GANG THING, STEVE.
YEAH. OKAY THEN.
CH-CHIK
KLICK-KLICK
KLICK-KLICK

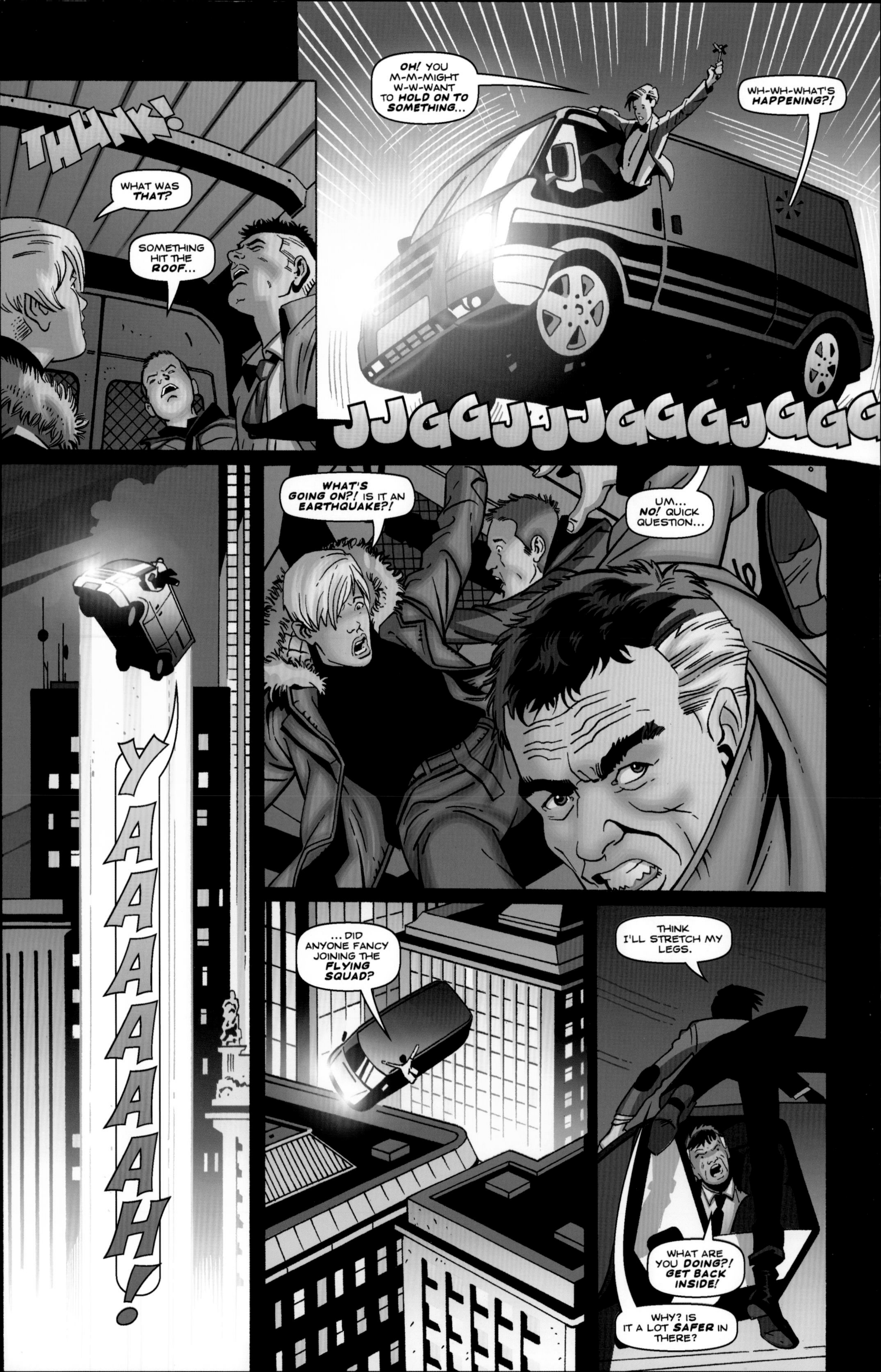

THUNK!
WHAT WAS THAT?
SOMETHING HIT THE ROOF...
OH! YOU M-M-MIGHT W-W-WANT TO HOLD ON TO SOMETHING...
WH-WH-WHAT'S HAPPENING?!
JJGGJJJJGGGGJGGG
YAAAAAAAAAH!
WHAT'S GOING ON?! IS IT AN EARTHQUAKE?!
UM... NO! QUICK QUESTION...
... DID ANYONE FANCY JOINING THE FLYING SQUAD?
THINK I'LL STRETCH MY LEGS.
WHAT ARE YOU DOING?! GET BACK INSIDE!
WHY? IS IT A LOT SAFER IN THERE?

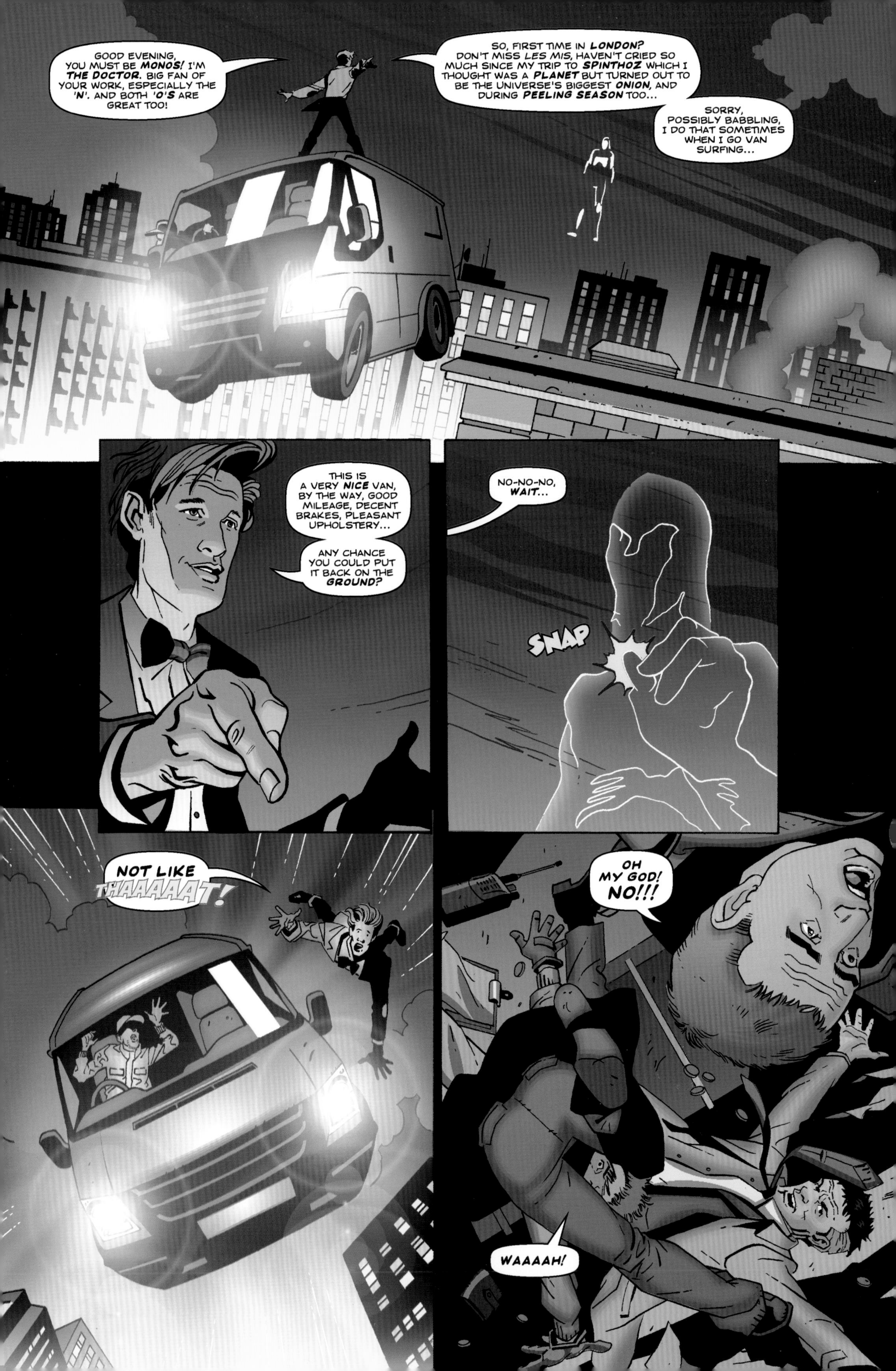
GOOD EVENING, YOU MUST BE MONOS! I'M THE DOCTOR. BIG FAN OF YOUR WORK, ESPECIALLY THE 'N'. AND BOTH 'O'S ARE GREAT TOO!
SO, FIRST TIME IN LONDON? DON'T MISS LES MIS, HAVEN'T CRIED SO MUCH SINCE MY TRIP TO SPINTHOZ WHICH I THOUGHT WAS A PLANET BUT TURNED OUT TO BE THE UNIVERSE'S BIGGEST ONION, AND DURING PEELING SEASON TOO...
SORRY, POSSIBLY BABBLING, I DO THAT SOMETIMES WHEN I GO VAN SURFING...
THIS IS A VERY NICE VAN, BY THE WAY, GOOD MILEAGE, DECENT BRAKES, PLEASANT UPHOLSTERY...
ANY CHANCE YOU COULD PUT IT BACK ON THE GROUND?
NO-NO-NO, WAIT...
SNAP
NOT LIKE THAAAAAT!
OH MY GOD! NO!!!
WAAAAH!

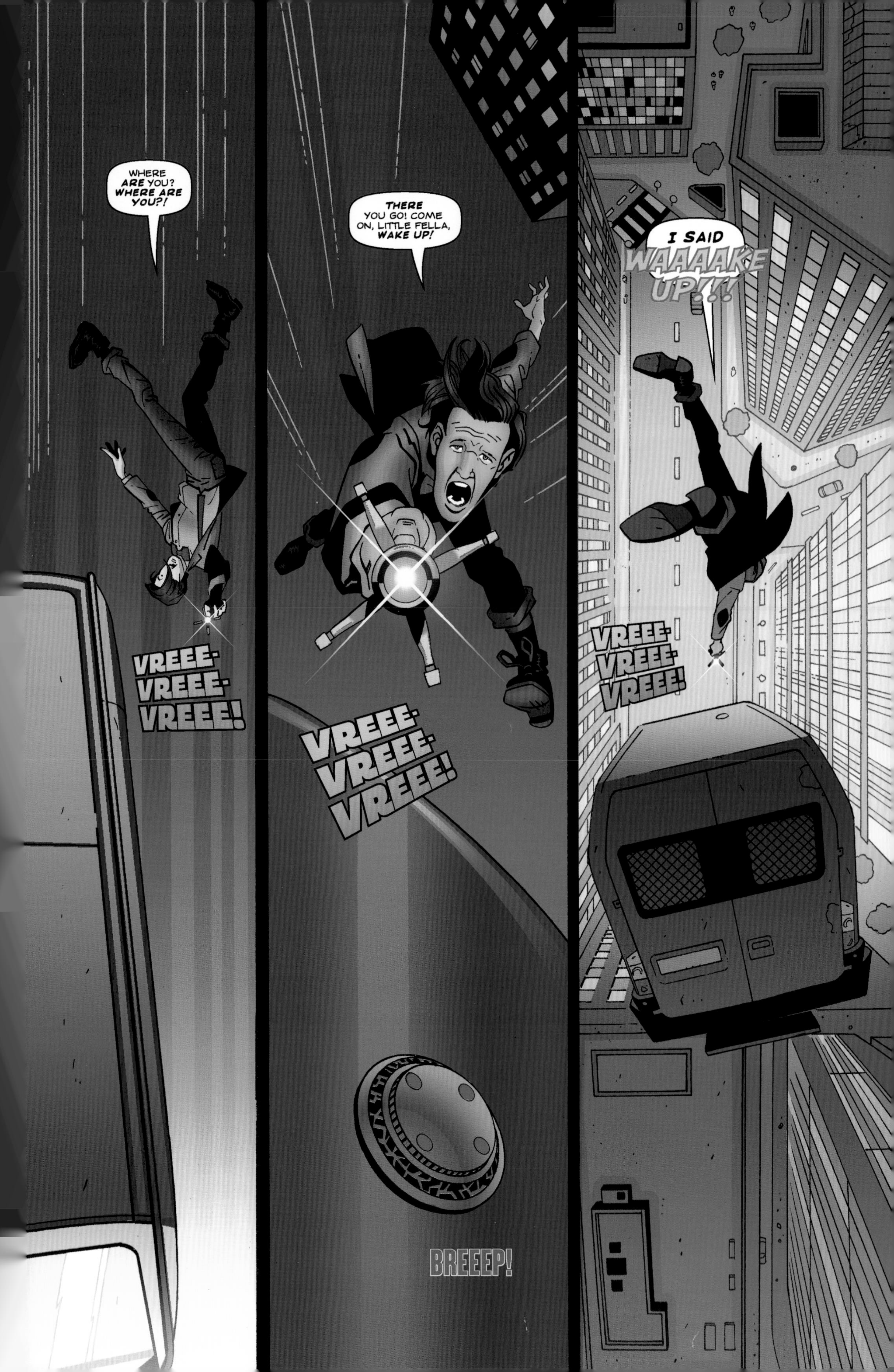
WHERE ARE YOU? WHERE ARE YOU?!
VREEE-VREEE-VREEE!
THERE YOU GO! COME ON, LITTLE FELLA, WAKE UP!
VREEE-VREEE-VREEE!
BREEEP!
I SAID WAAAAKE UP!!!
VREEE-VREEE-VREEE!

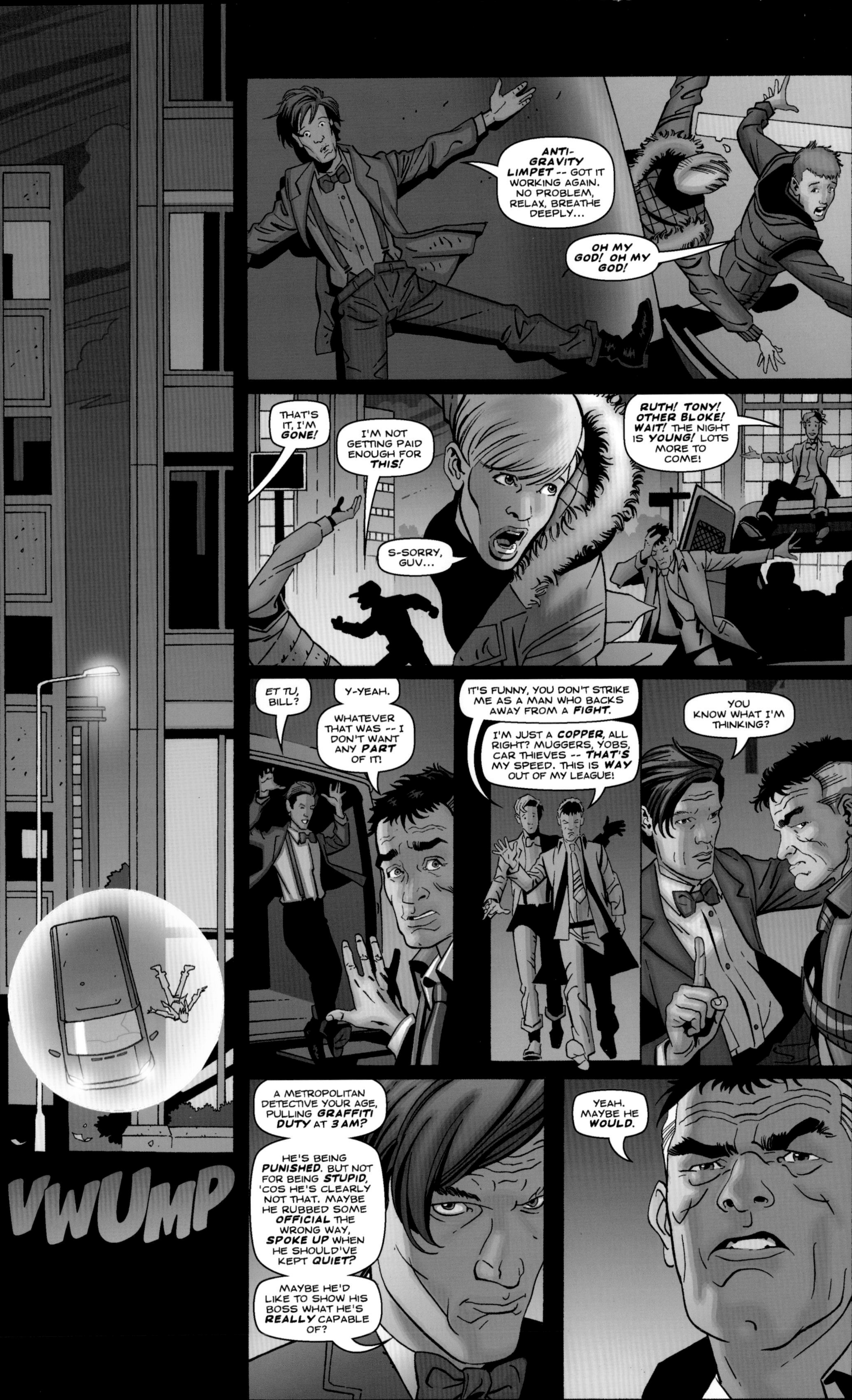
VWUMP
ANTI-GRAVITY LIMPET -- GOT IT WORKING AGAIN. NO PROBLEM, RELAX, BREATHE DEEPLY...
OH MY GOD! OH MY GOD!
THAT'S IT, I'M GONE!
I'M NOT GETTING PAID ENOUGH FOR THIS!
S-SORRY, GUV...
RUTH! TONY! OTHER BLOKE! WAIT! THE NIGHT IS YOUNG! LOTS MORE TO COME!
ET TU, BILL?
Y-YEAH.
WHATEVER THAT WAS -- I DON'T WANT ANY PART OF IT!
IT'S FUNNY, YOU DON'T STRIKE ME AS A MAN WHO BACKS AWAY FROM A FIGHT.
I'M JUST A COPPER, ALL RIGHT? MUGGERS, YOBS, CAR THIEVES -- THAT'S MY SPEED. THIS IS WAY OUT OF MY LEAGUE!
YOU KNOW WHAT I'M THINKING?
A METROPOLITAN DETECTIVE YOUR AGE, PULLING GRAFFITI DUTY AT 3 AM?
HE'S BEING PUNISHED. BUT NOT FOR BEING STUPID, 'COS HE'S CLEARLY NOT THAT. MAYBE HE RUBBED SOME OFFICIAL THE WRONG WAY, SPOKE UP WHEN HE SHOULD'VE KEPT QUIET?
MAYBE HE'D LIKE TO SHOW HIS BOSS WHAT HE'S REALLY CAPABLE OF?
YEAH. MAYBE HE WOULD.

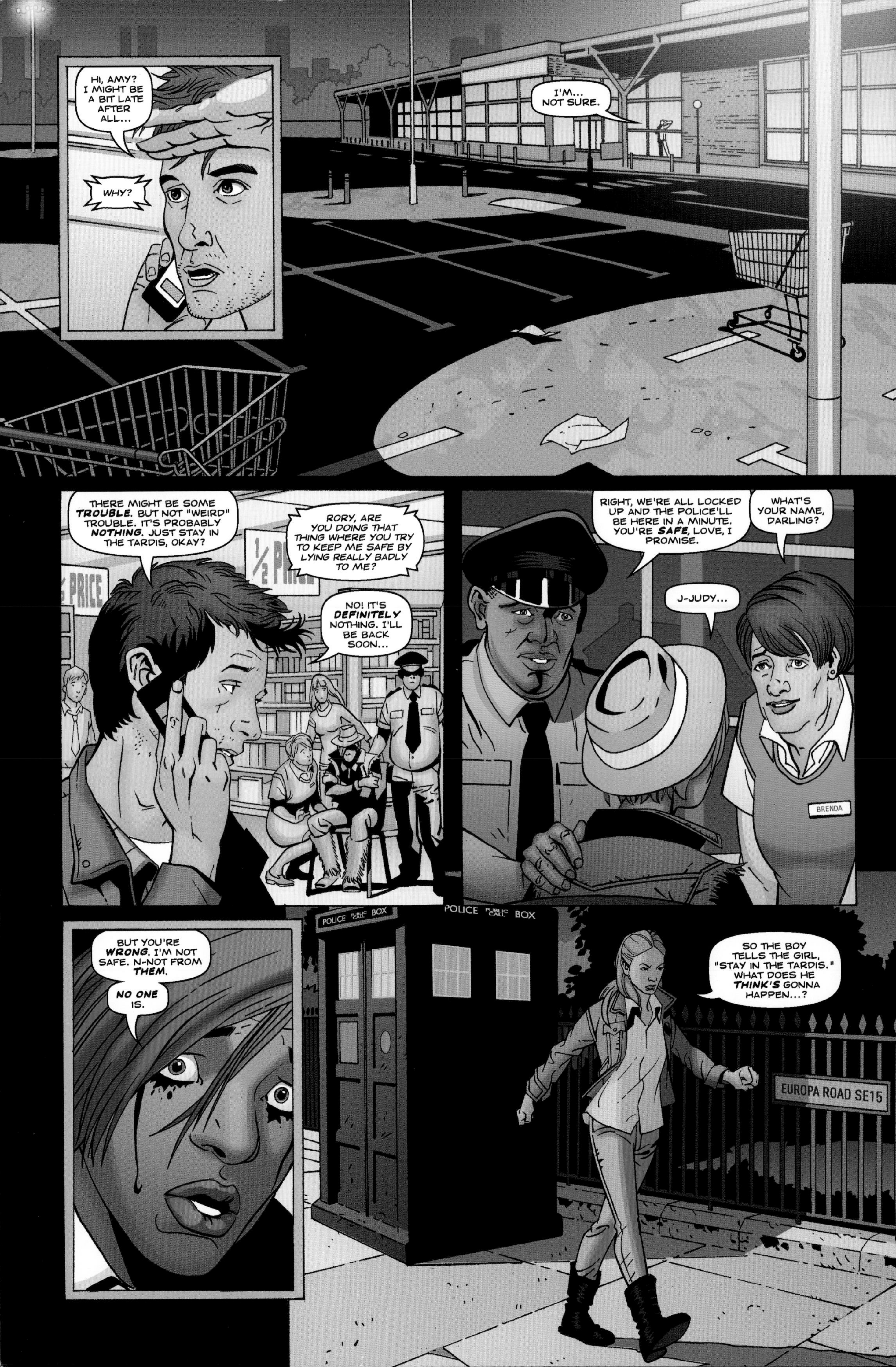

HI, AMY? I MIGHT BE A BIT LATE AFTER ALL...
WHY?
I'M... NOT SURE.
THERE MIGHT BE SOME TROUBLE. BUT NOT "WEIRD" TROUBLE. IT'S PROBABLY NOTHING. JUST STAY IN THE TARDIS, OKAY?
RORY, ARE YOU DOING THAT THING WHERE YOU TRY TO KEEP ME SAFE BY LYING REALLY BADLY TO ME?
NO! IT'S DEFINITELY NOTHING. I'LL BE BACK SOON...
1/2 PRICE
PRICE
RIGHT, WE'RE ALL LOCKED UP AND THE POLICE'LL BE HERE IN A MINUTE. YOU'RE SAFE, LOVE, I PROMISE.
WHAT'S YOUR NAME, DARLING?
J-JUDY...
BRENDA
BUT YOU'RE WRONG. I'M NOT SAFE. N-NOT FROM THEM.
NO ONE IS.
POLICE PUBLIC CALL BOX
POLICE PUBLIC CALL BOX
SO THE BOY TELLS THE GIRL, "STAY IN THE TARDIS." WHAT DOES HE THINK'S GONNA HAPPEN...?
EUROPA ROAD SE15

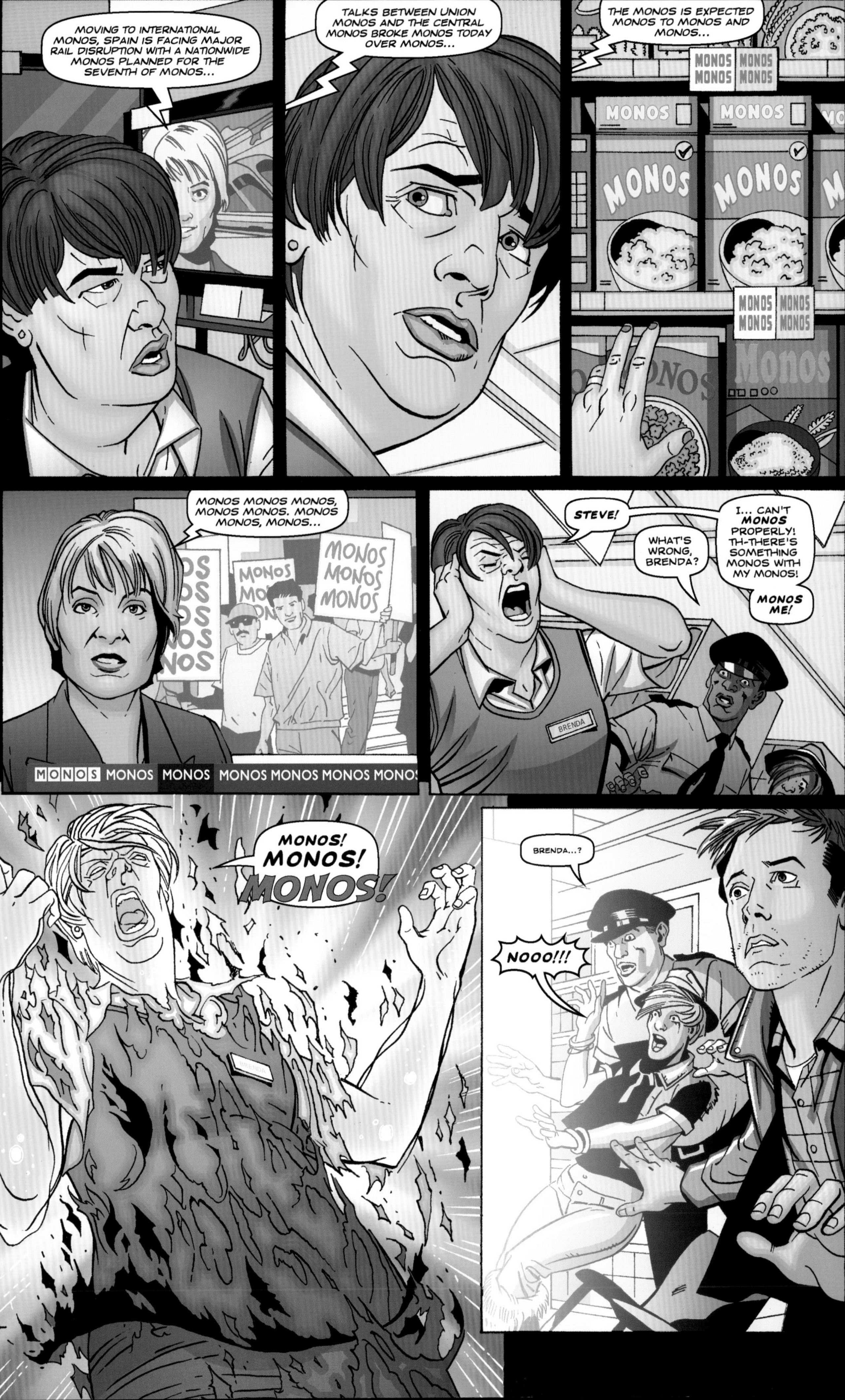
MOVING TO INTERNATIONAL MONOS, SPAIN IS FACING MAJOR RAIL DISRUPTION WITH A NATIONWIDE MONOS PLANNED FOR THE SEVENTH OF MONOS...
TALKS BETWEEN UNION MONOS AND THE CENTRAL MONOS BROKE MONOS TODAY OVER MONOS...
THE MONOS IS EXPECTED MONOS TO MONOS AND MONOS...
MONOS MONOS MONOS MONOS
MONOS
MONOS
MONOS MONOS MONOS MONOS
Monos
MONOS MONOS MONOS, MONOS MONOS. MONOS MONOS, MONOS...
MONOS MONOS MONOS
MONOS MONOS MONOS MONOS MONOS MONOS MONOS
STEVE!
WHAT'S WRONG, BRENDA?
I... CAN'T MONOS PROPERLY! TH-THERE'S SOMETHING MONOS WITH MY MONOS!
MONOS ME!
BRENDA
MONOS! MONOS! MONOS!
BRENDA...?
NOOO!!!

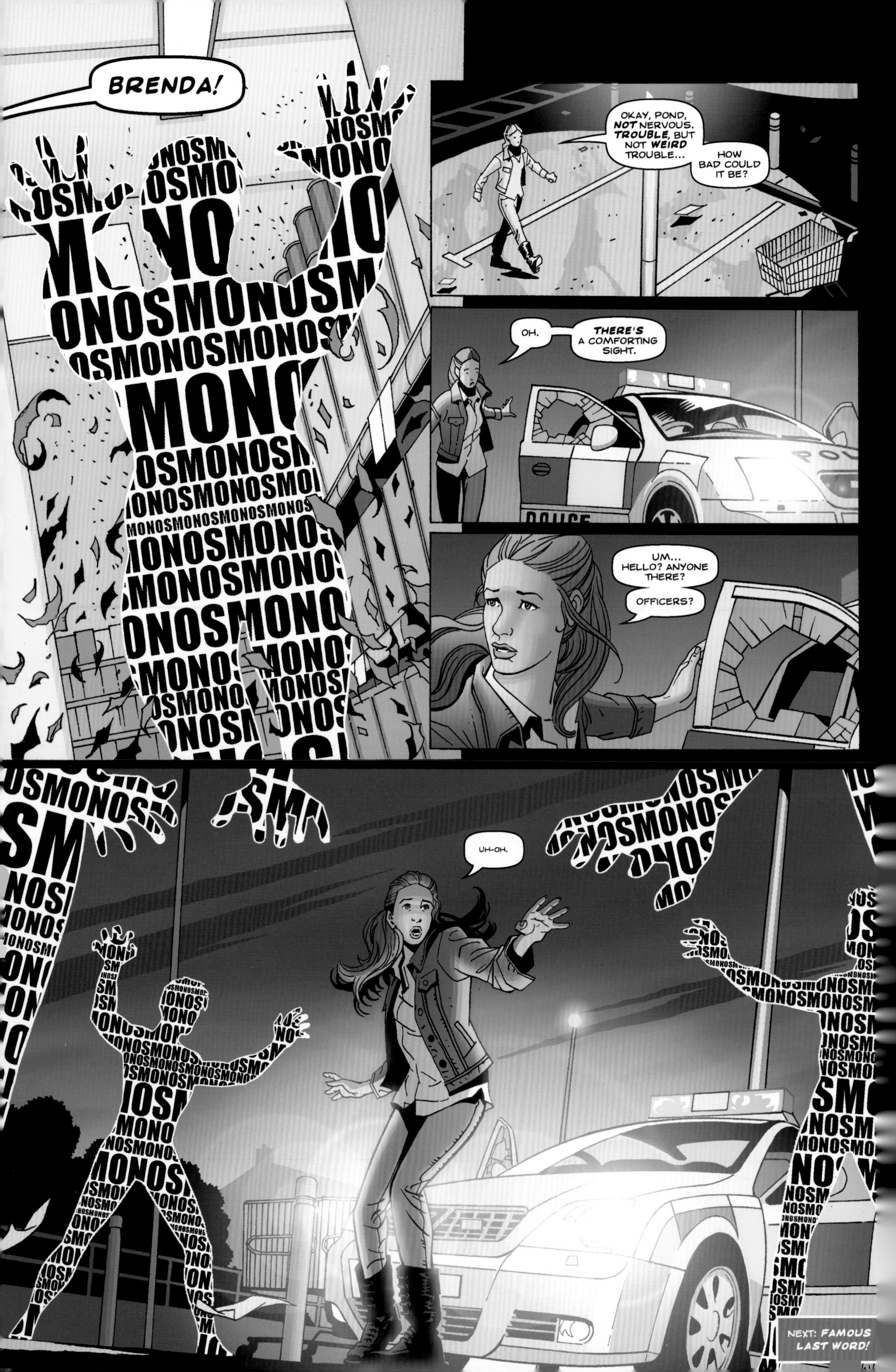
BRENDA!
OKAY, POND, NOT NERVOUS. TROUBLE, BUT NOT WEIRD TROUBLE...
HOW BAD COULD IT BE?
OH.
THERE'S A COMFORTING SIGHT.
UM... HELLO? ANYONE THERE?
OFFICERS?
UH-OH.
NEXT: FAMOUS LAST WORD!

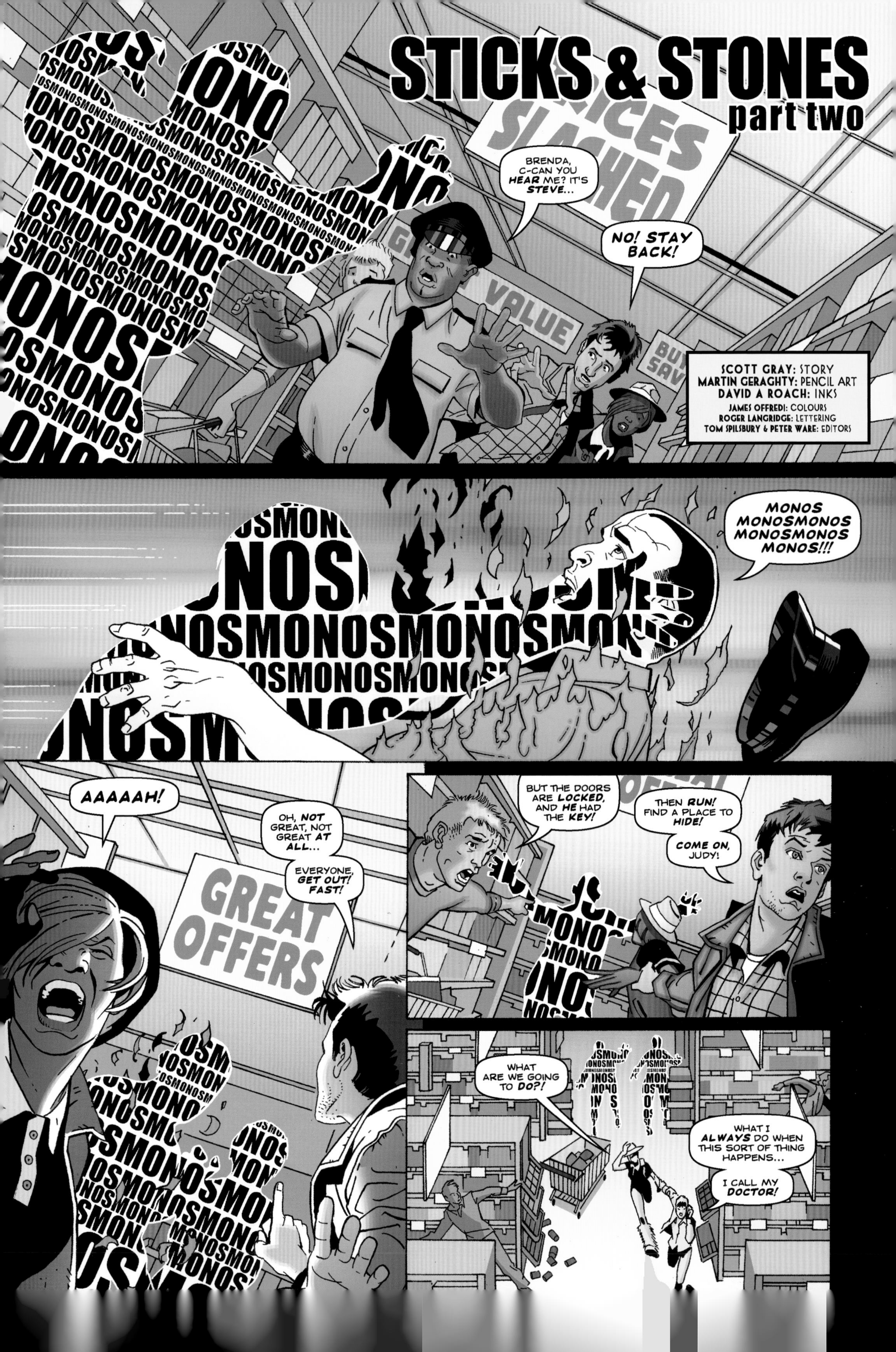
STICKS & STONES
part two
SCOTT GRAY: STORY
MARTIN GERAGHTY: PENCIL ART
DAVID A ROACH: INKS
JAMES OFFREDI: COLOURS
ROGER LANGRIDGE: LETTERING
TOM SPILSBURY & PETER WARE: EDITORS
BRENDA, C-CAN YOU HEAR ME? IT'S STEVE...
NO! STAY BACK!
MONOS MONOSMONOS MONOSMONOS MONOS!!!
AAAAAH!
OH, NOT GREAT, NOT GREAT AT ALL...
EVERYONE, GET OUT! FAST!
GREAT OFFERS
BUT THE DOORS ARE LOCKED, AND HE HAD THE KEY!
THEN RUN! FIND A PLACE TO HIDE!
COME ON, JUDY!
WHAT ARE WE GOING TO DO?!
WHAT I ALWAYS DO WHEN THIS SORT OF THING HAPPENS...
I CALL MY DOCTOR!

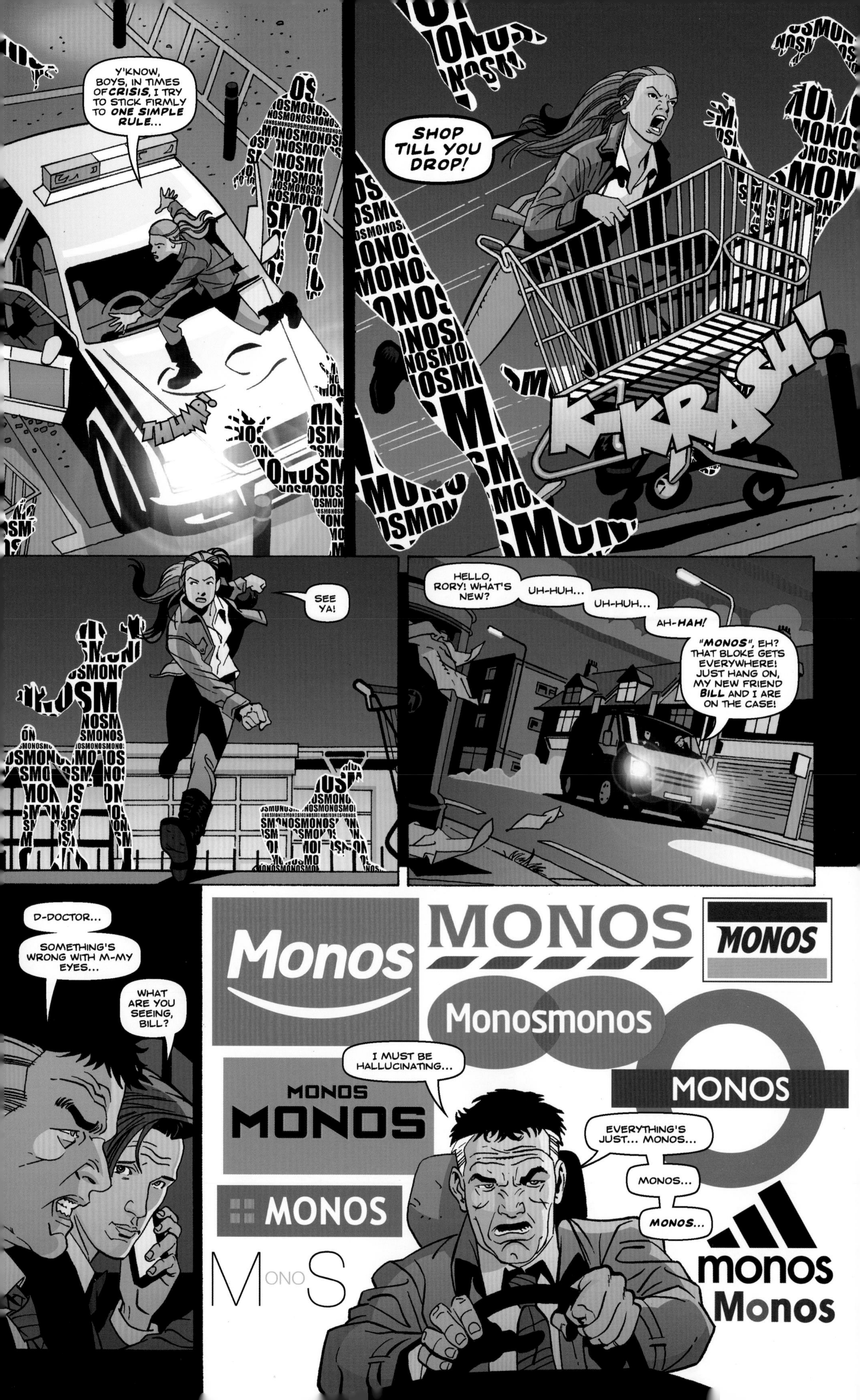
Y'KNOW, BOYS, IN TIMES OF CRISIS, I TRY TO STICK FIRMLY TO ONE SIMPLE RULE...
THUMP!
SHOP TILL YOU DROP!
K-KRASH!
SEE YA!
HELLO, RORY! WHAT'S NEW?
UH-HUH...
UH-HUH...
AH-HAH!
"MONOS", EH? THAT BLOKE GETS EVERYWHERE! JUST HANG ON, MY NEW FRIEND BILL AND I ARE ON THE CASE!
D-DOCTOR...
SOMETHING'S WRONG WITH M-MY EYES...
WHAT ARE YOU SEEING, BILL?
Monos
MONOS
MONOS
Monosmonos
I MUST BE HALLUCINATING...
MONOS MONOS
MONOS
EVERYTHING'S JUST... MONOS...
MONOS...
MONOS...
MONOS
MonoS
monos
Monos

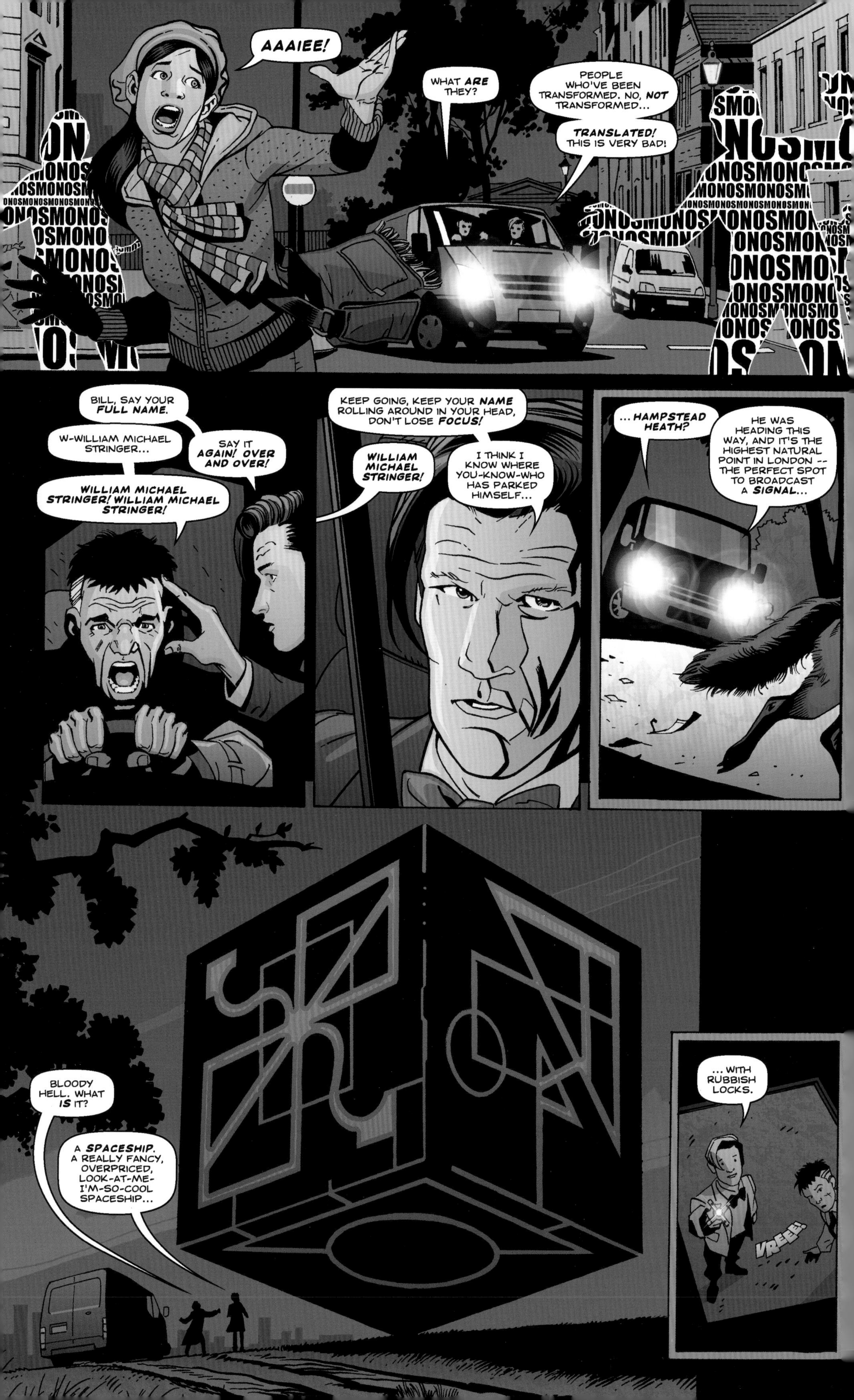
AAAIEE!
WHAT ARE THEY?
PEOPLE WHO'VE BEEN TRANSFORMED. NO, NOT TRANSFORMED...
TRANSLATED! THIS IS VERY BAD!
BILL, SAY YOUR FULL NAME.
W-WILLIAM MICHAEL STRINGER...
SAY IT AGAIN! OVER AND OVER!
WILLIAM MICHAEL STRINGER! WILLIAM MICHAEL STRINGER!
KEEP GOING, KEEP YOUR NAME ROLLING AROUND IN YOUR HEAD, DON'T LOSE FOCUS!
WILLIAM MICHAEL STRINGER!
I THINK I KNOW WHERE YOU-KNOW-WHO HAS PARKED HIMSELF...
...HAMPSTEAD HEATH?
HE WAS HEADING THIS WAY, AND IT'S THE HIGHEST NATURAL POINT IN LONDON -- THE PERFECT SPOT TO BROADCAST A SIGNAL...
BLOODY HELL. WHAT IS IT?
A SPACESHIP. A REALLY FANCY, OVERPRICED, LOOK-AT-ME-I'M-SO-COOL SPACESHIP...
...WITH RUBBISH LOCKS.
VREEE!

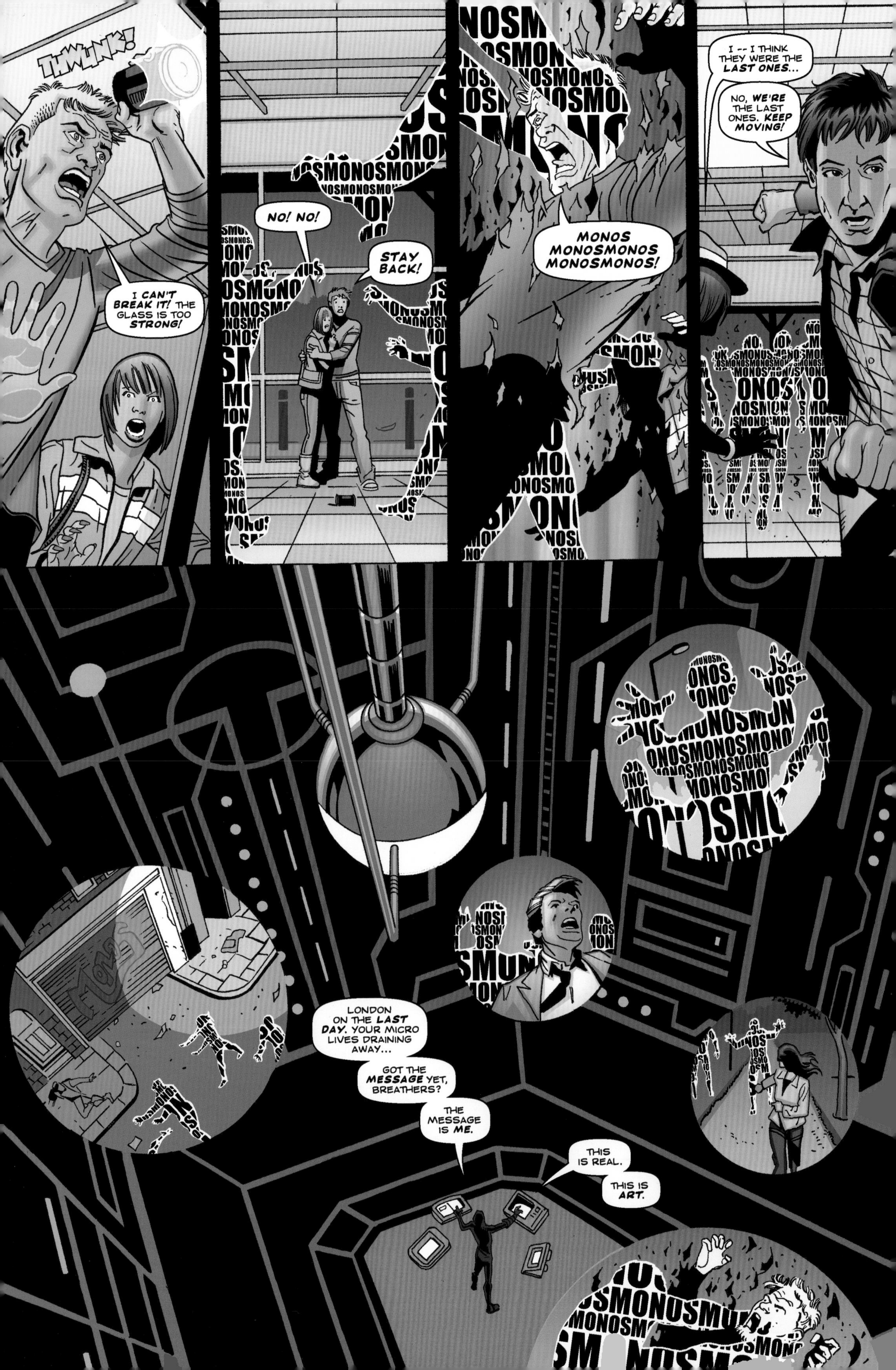
THWUNK!
I CAN'T BREAK IT! THE GLASS IS TOO STRONG!
NO! NO!
STAY BACK!
MONOS MONOSMONOS MONOSMONOS!
I -- I THINK THEY WERE THE LAST ONES...
NO, WE'RE THE LAST ONES. KEEP MOVING!
LONDON ON THE LAST DAY. YOUR MICRO LIVES DRAINING AWAY...
GOT THE MESSAGE YET, BREATHERS?
THE MESSAGE IS ME.
THIS IS REAL.
THIS IS ART.

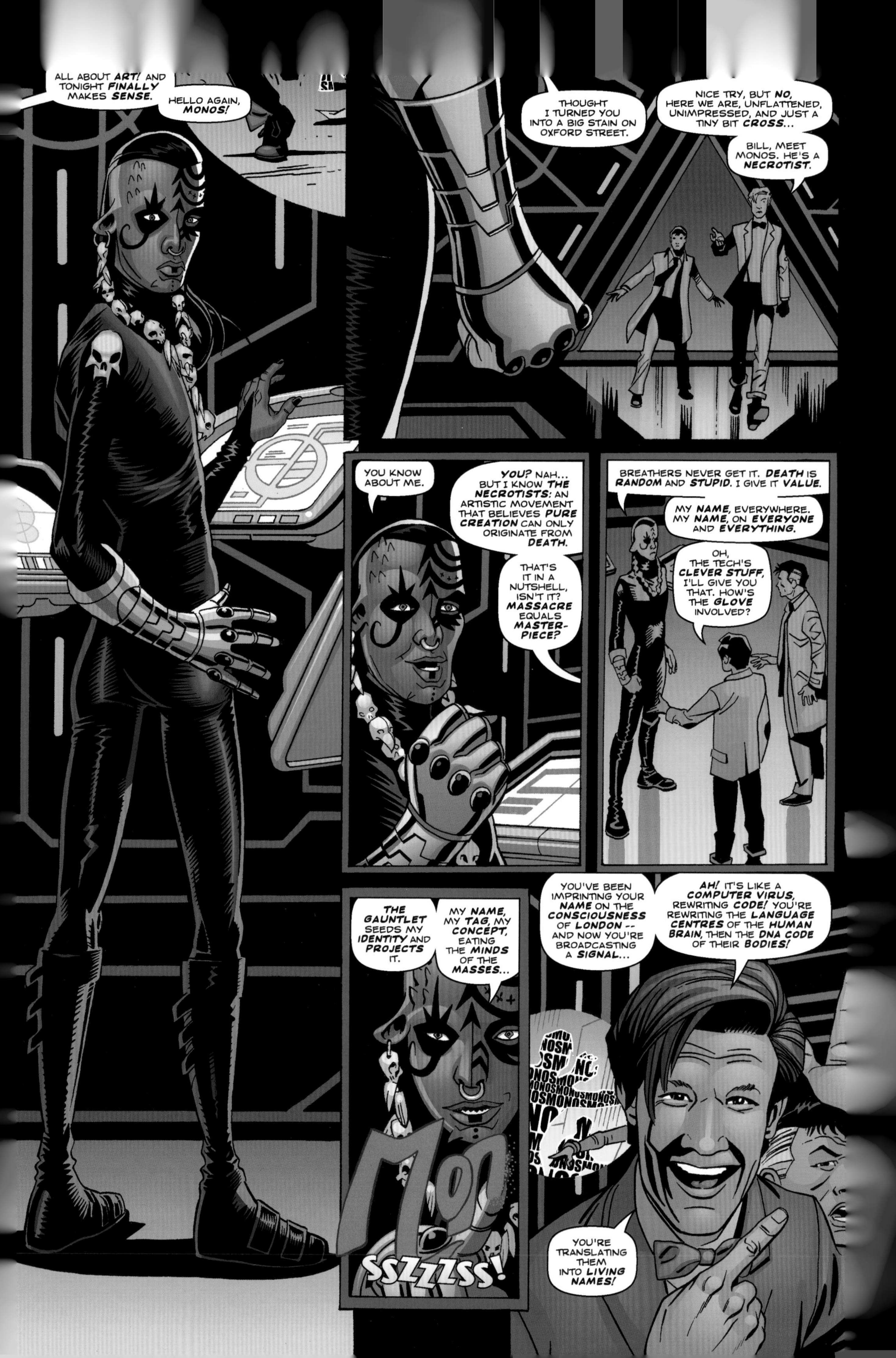
ALL ABOUT ART! AND TONIGHT FINALLY MAKES SENSE.
HELLO AGAIN, MONOS!
THOUGHT I TURNED YOU INTO A BIG STAIN ON OXFORD STREET.
NICE TRY, BUT NO, HERE WE ARE, UNFLATTENED, UNIMPRESSED, AND JUST A TINY BIT CROSS...
BILL, MEET MONOS. HE'S A NECROTIST.
YOU KNOW ABOUT ME.
YOU? NAH... BUT I KNOW THE NECROTISTS: AN ARTISTIC MOVEMENT THAT BELIEVES PURE CREATION CAN ONLY ORIGINATE FROM DEATH.
THAT'S IT IN A NUTSHELL, ISN'T IT? MASSACRE EQUALS MASTER-PIECE?
BREATHERS NEVER GET IT. DEATH IS RANDOM AND STUPID. I GIVE IT VALUE.
MY NAME, EVERYWHERE. MY NAME, ON EVERYONE AND EVERYTHING.
OH, THE TECH'S CLEVER STUFF, I'LL GIVE YOU THAT. HOW'S THE GLOVE INVOLVED?
THE GAUNTLET SEEDS MY IDENTITY AND PROJECTS IT.
MY NAME, MY TAG, MY CONCEPT, EATING THE MINDS OF THE MASSES...
SSZZZSS!
YOU'VE BEEN IMPRINTING YOUR NAME ON THE CONSCIOUSNESS OF LONDON -- AND NOW YOU'RE BROADCASTING A SIGNAL...
AH! IT'S LIKE A COMPUTER VIRUS, REWRITING CODE! YOU'RE REWRITING THE LANGUAGE CENTRES OF THE HUMAN BRAIN, THEN THE DNA CODE OF THEIR BODIES!
YOU'RE TRANSLATING THEM INTO LIVING NAMES!

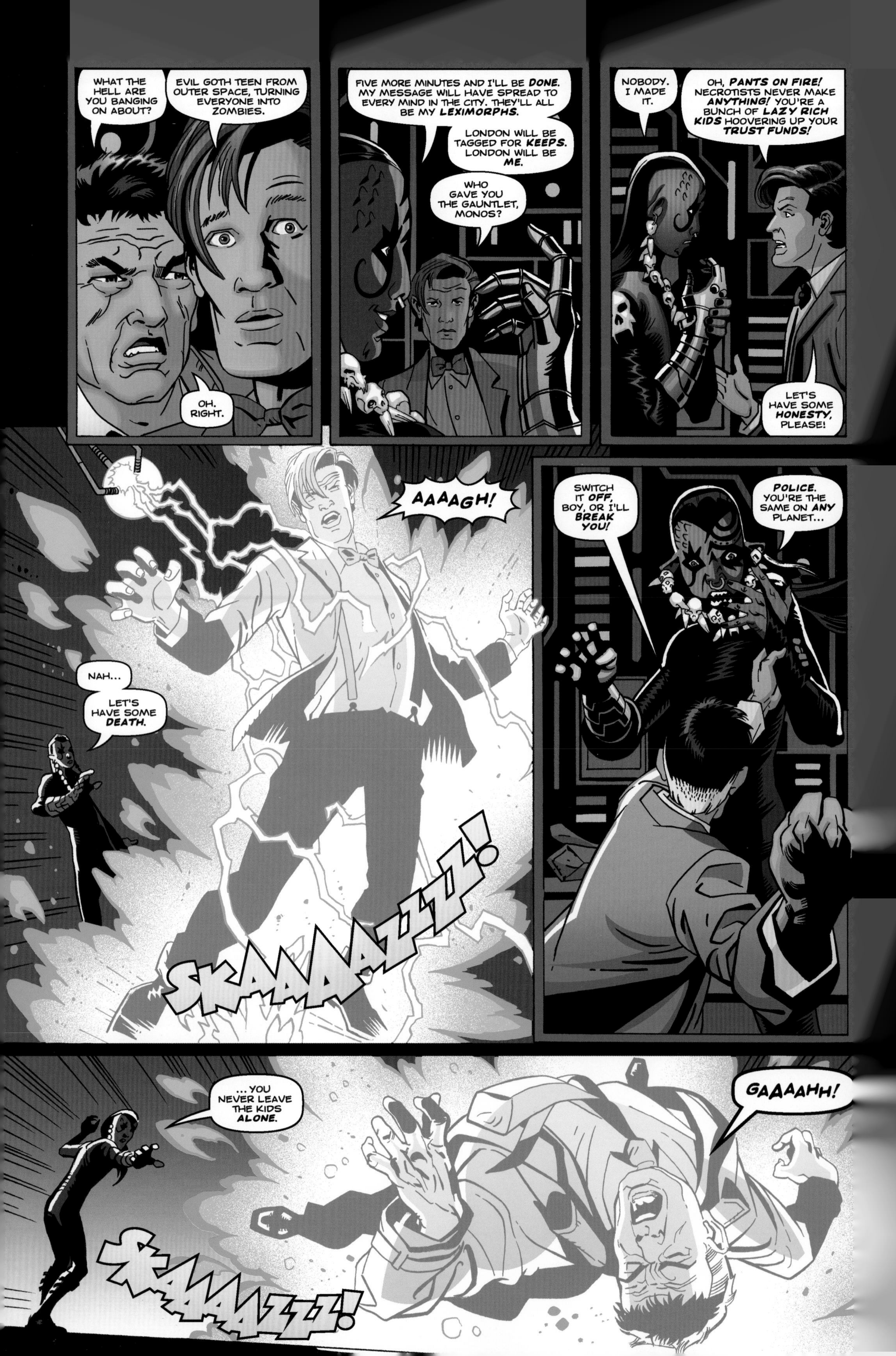
WHAT THE HELL ARE YOU BANGING ON ABOUT?
EVIL GOTH TEEN FROM OUTER SPACE, TURNING EVERYONE INTO ZOMBIES.
OH. RIGHT.
FIVE MORE MINUTES AND I'LL BE DONE. MY MESSAGE WILL HAVE SPREAD TO EVERY MIND IN THE CITY. THEY'LL ALL BE MY LEXIMORPHS.
LONDON WILL BE TAGGED FOR KEEPS. LONDON WILL BE ME.
WHO GAVE YOU THE GAUNTLET, MONOS?
NOBODY. I MADE IT.
OH, PANTS ON FIRE! NECROTISTS NEVER MAKE ANYTHING! YOU'RE A BUNCH OF LAZY RICH KIDS HOOVERING UP YOUR TRUST FUNDS!
LET'S HAVE SOME HONESTY, PLEASE!
AAAAGH!
NAH...
LET'S HAVE SOME DEATH.
SKAAAAZZZZ!
SWITCH IT OFF, BOY, OR I'LL BREAK YOU!
POLICE. YOU'RE THE SAME ON ANY PLANET...
...YOU NEVER LEAVE THE KIDS ALONE.
GAAAAHH!
SKAAAAZZZZ!

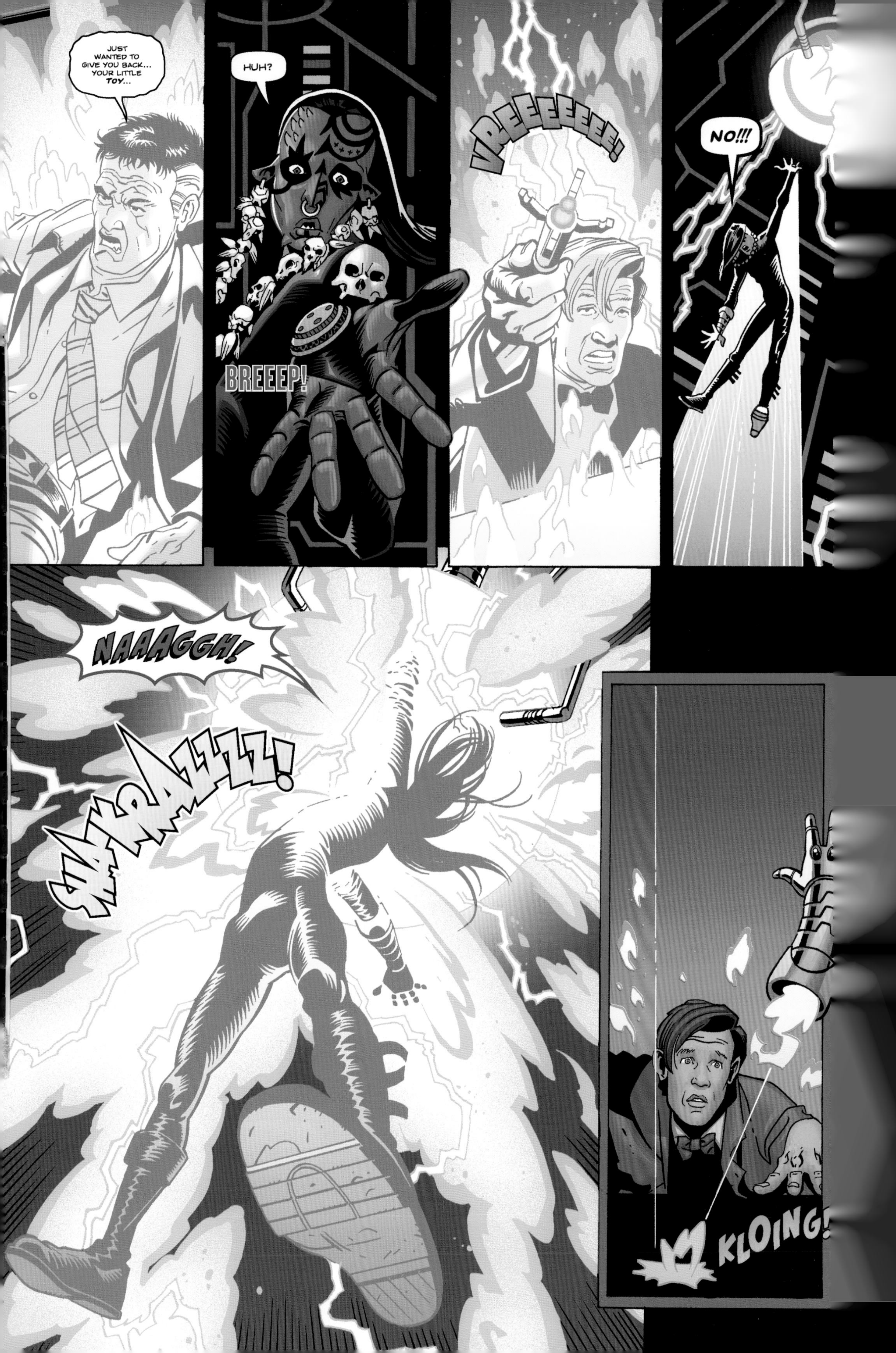

JUST WANTED TO GIVE YOU BACK... YOUR LITTLE TOY...
HUH?
BREEEP!
VREEEEEEE!
NO!!!
NAAAGGH!
SHAKRAZZZZ!
KLOING!

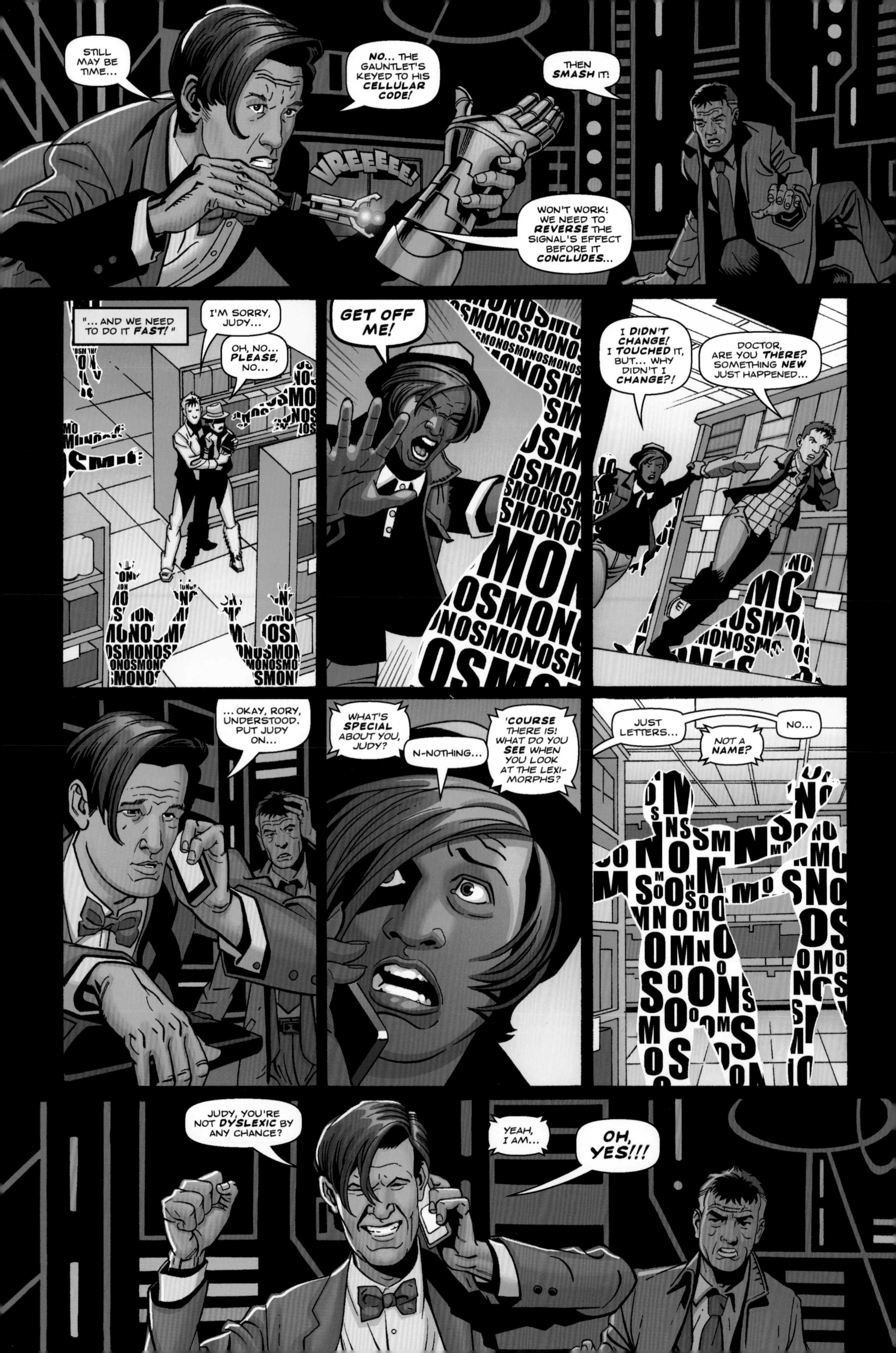

STILL MAY BE TIME...
NO... THE GAUNTLET'S KEYED TO HIS CELLULAR CODE!
THEN SMASH IT!
VREEEEE!
WON'T WORK! WE NEED TO REVERSE THE SIGNAL'S EFFECT BEFORE IT CONCLUDES...
"... AND WE NEED TO DO IT FAST!"
I'M SORRY, JUDY...
OH, NO... PLEASE, NO...
GET OFF ME!
I DIDN'T CHANGE! I TOUCHED IT, BUT... WHY DIDN'T I CHANGE?!
DOCTOR, ARE YOU THERE? SOMETHING NEW JUST HAPPENED...
... OKAY, RORY, UNDERSTOOD. PUT JUDY ON...
WHAT'S SPECIAL ABOUT YOU, JUDY?
N-NOTHING...
'COURSE THERE IS! WHAT DO YOU SEE WHEN YOU LOOK AT THE LEXI-MORPHS?
JUST LETTERS...
NOT A NAME?
NO...
JUDY, YOU'RE NOT DYSLEXIC BY ANY CHANCE?
YEAH, I AM...
OH, YES!!!

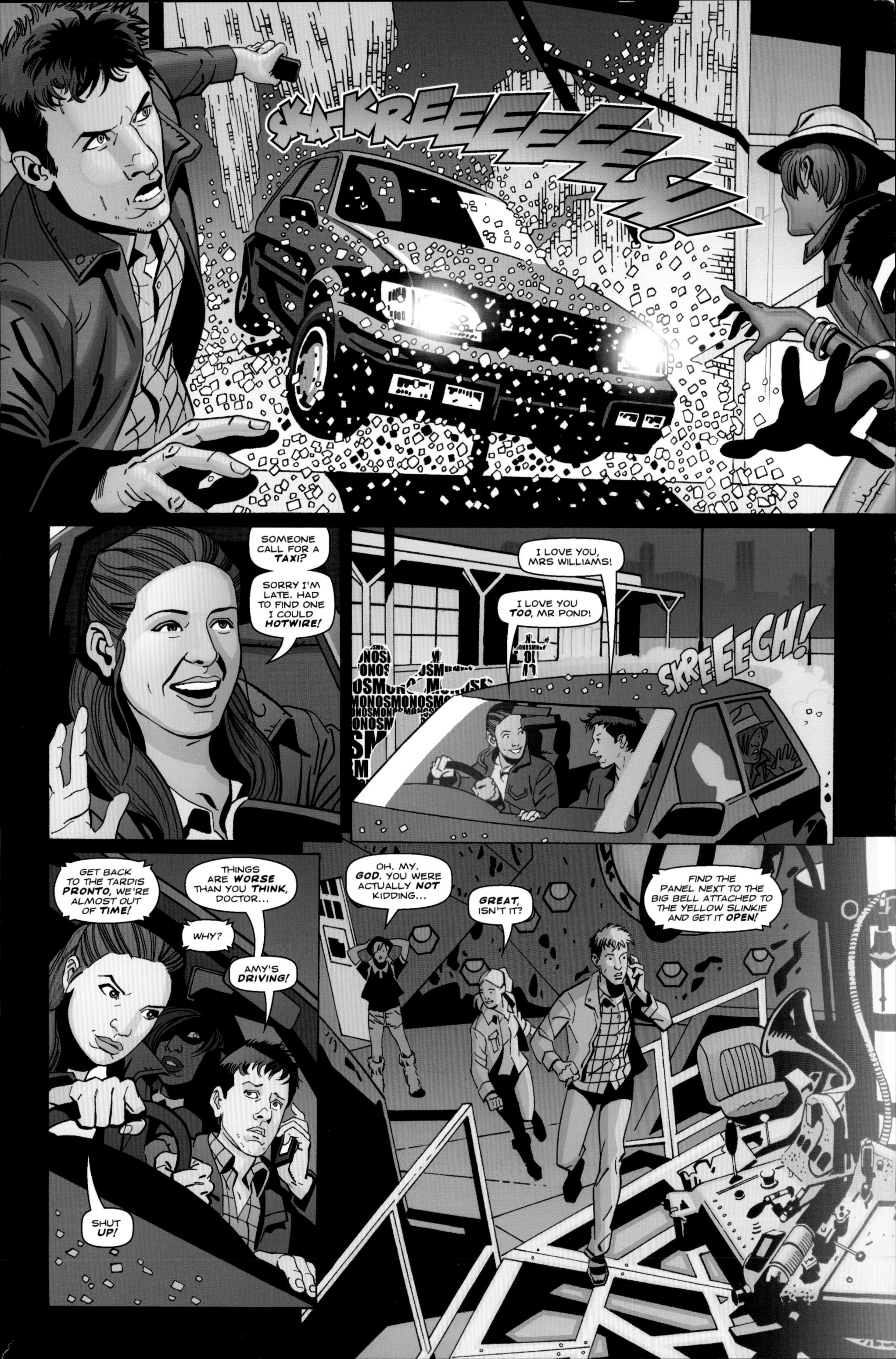
SKA-KREEEEEEE!!
SOMEONE CALL FOR A TAXI?
SORRY I'M LATE. HAD TO FIND ONE I COULD HOTWIRE!
I LOVE YOU, MRS WILLIAMS!
I LOVE YOU TOO, MR POND!
SKREEECH!
GET BACK TO THE TARDIS PRONTO, WE'RE ALMOST OUT OF TIME!
THINGS ARE WORSE THAN YOU THINK, DOCTOR...
WHY?
AMY'S DRIVING!
SHUT UP!
OH. MY. GOD. YOU WERE ACTUALLY NOT KIDDING...
GREAT, ISN'T IT?
FIND THE PANEL NEXT TO THE BIG BELL ATTACHED TO THE YELLOW SLINKIE AND GET IT OPEN!

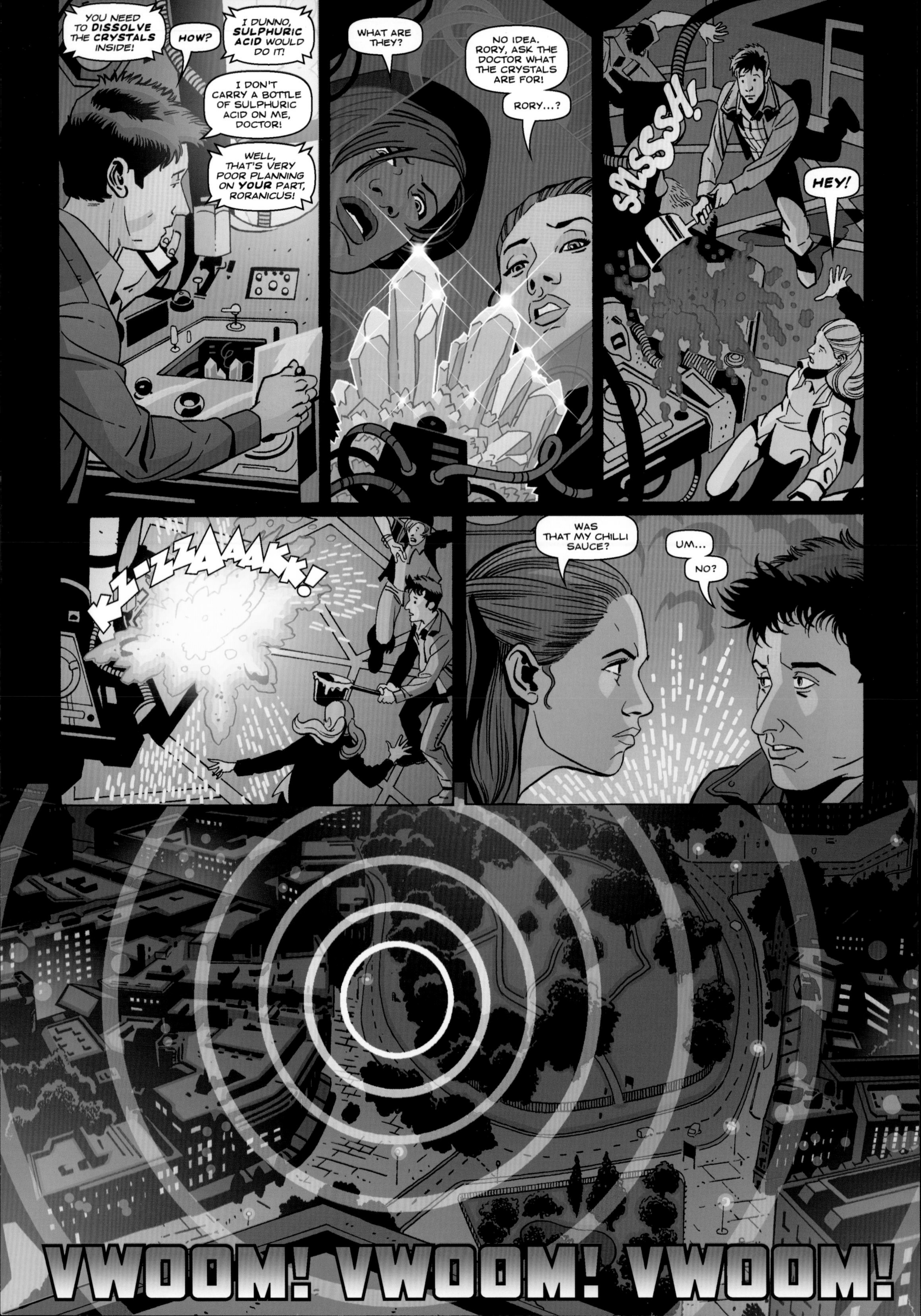
YOU NEED TO DISSOLVE THE CRYSTALS INSIDE!
HOW?
I DUNNO, SULPHURIC ACID WOULD DO IT!
I DON'T CARRY A BOTTLE OF SULPHURIC ACID ON ME, DOCTOR!
WELL, THAT'S VERY POOR PLANNING ON YOUR PART, RORANICUS!
WHAT ARE THEY?
NO IDEA. RORY, ASK THE DOCTOR WHAT THE CRYSTALS ARE FOR!
RORY...?
SSSSSH!
HEY!
KZ-ZZAAAKK!
WAS THAT MY CHILLI SAUCE?
UM...
NO?
VWOOM! VWOOM! VWOOM!

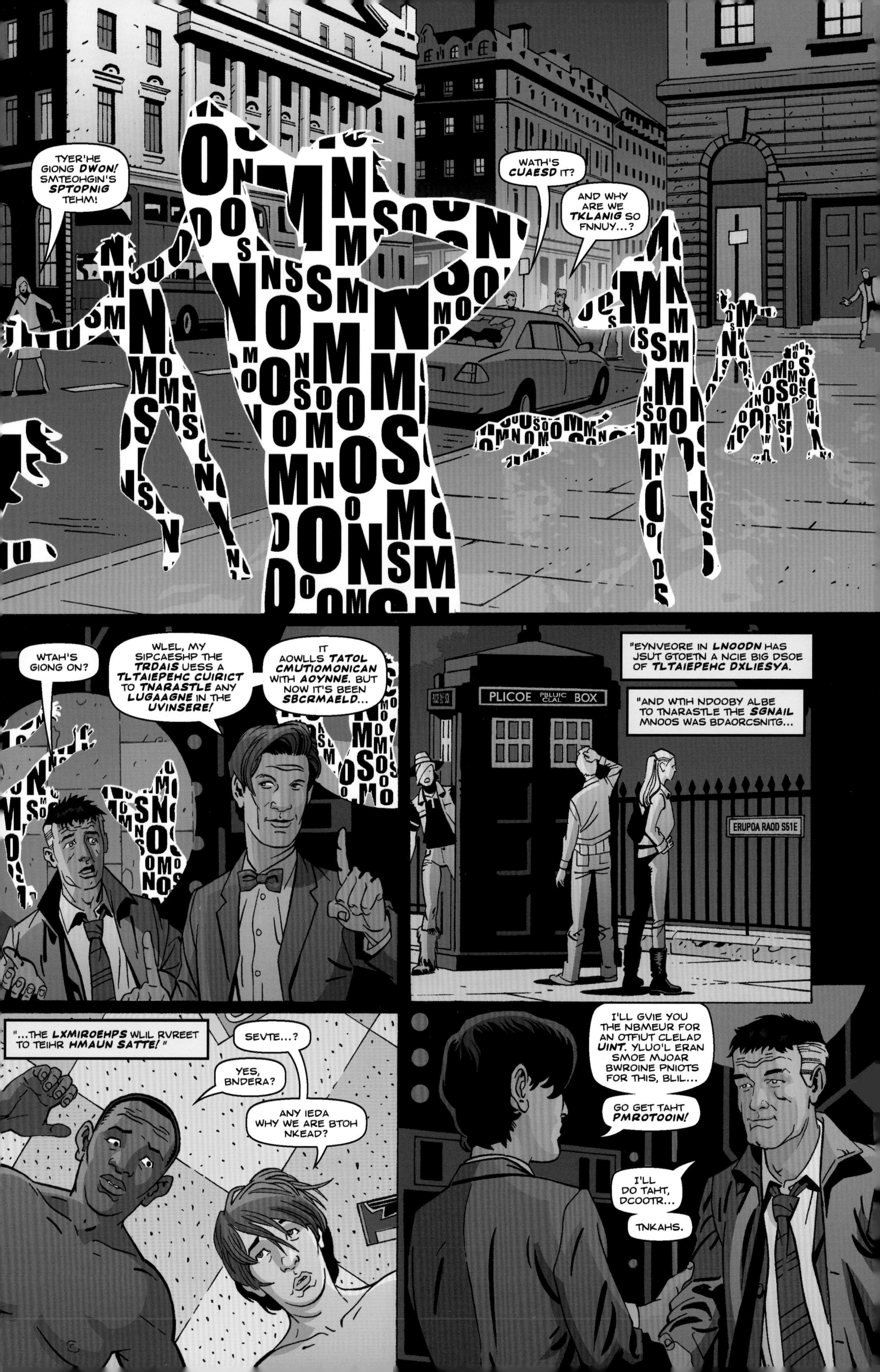

TYER'HE GIONG DWON! SMTEOHGIN'S SPTOPNIG TEHM!
WATH'S CUAESD IT?
AND WHY ARE WE TKLANIG SO FNNUY...?
WTAH'S GIONG ON?
WLEL, MY SIPCAESHP THE TRDAIS UESS A TLTAIEPEHC CUIRICT TO TNARASTLE ANY LUGAAGNE IN THE UVINSERE!
IT AOWLLS TATOL CMUTIOMONICAN WITH AOYNNE. BUT NOW IT'S BEEN SBCRMAELD...
"EYNVEORE IN LNOODN HAS JSUT GTOETN A NCIE BIG DSOE OF TLTAIEPEHC DXLIESYA.
"AND WTIH NDOOBY ALBE TO TNARASTLE THE SGNAIL MNOOS WAS BDAORCSNITG...
PLICOE PBLUIC CLAL BOX
ERUPOA RAOD S51E
"...THE LXMIROEHPS WLIL RVREET TO TEIHR HMAUN SATTE!"
SEVTE...?
YES, BNDERA?
ANY IEDA WHY WE ARE BTOH NKEAD?
I'LL GVIE YOU THE NBMEUR FOR AN OTFIUT CLELAD UINT. YLUO'L ERAN SMOE MJOAR BWROINE PNIOTS FOR THIS, BLIL...
GO GET TAHT PMROTOOIN!
I'LL DO TAHT, DCOOTR...
TNKAHS.

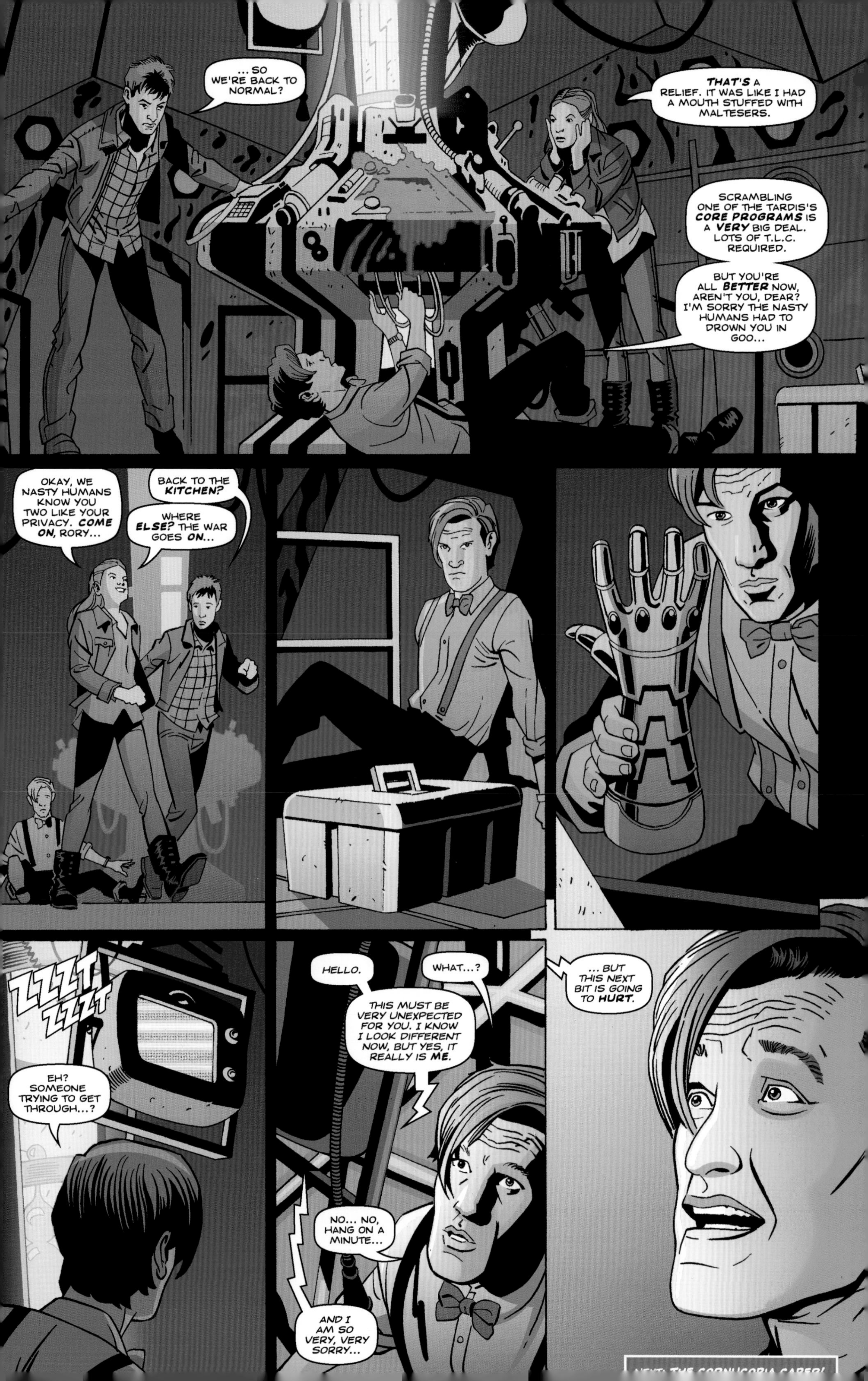
... SO WE'RE BACK TO NORMAL?
THAT'S A RELIEF. IT WAS LIKE I HAD A MOUTH STUFFED WITH MALTESERS.
SCRAMBLING ONE OF THE TARDIS'S CORE PROGRAMS IS A VERY BIG DEAL. LOTS OF T.L.C. REQUIRED.
BUT YOU'RE ALL BETTER NOW, AREN'T YOU, DEAR? I'M SORRY THE NASTY HUMANS HAD TO DROWN YOU IN GOO...
OKAY, WE NASTY HUMANS KNOW YOU TWO LIKE YOUR PRIVACY. COME ON, RORY...
BACK TO THE KITCHEN?
WHERE ELSE? THE WAR GOES ON...
ZZZT ZZZT
EH? SOMEONE TRYING TO GET THROUGH...?
HELLO.
WHAT...?
THIS MUST BE VERY UNEXPECTED FOR YOU. I KNOW I LOOK DIFFERENT NOW, BUT YES, IT REALLY IS ME.
NO... NO, HANG ON A MINUTE...
AND I AM SO VERY, VERY SORRY...
... BUT THIS NEXT BIT IS GOING TO HURT.
NEXT: THE CORNUCOPIA CAPER!

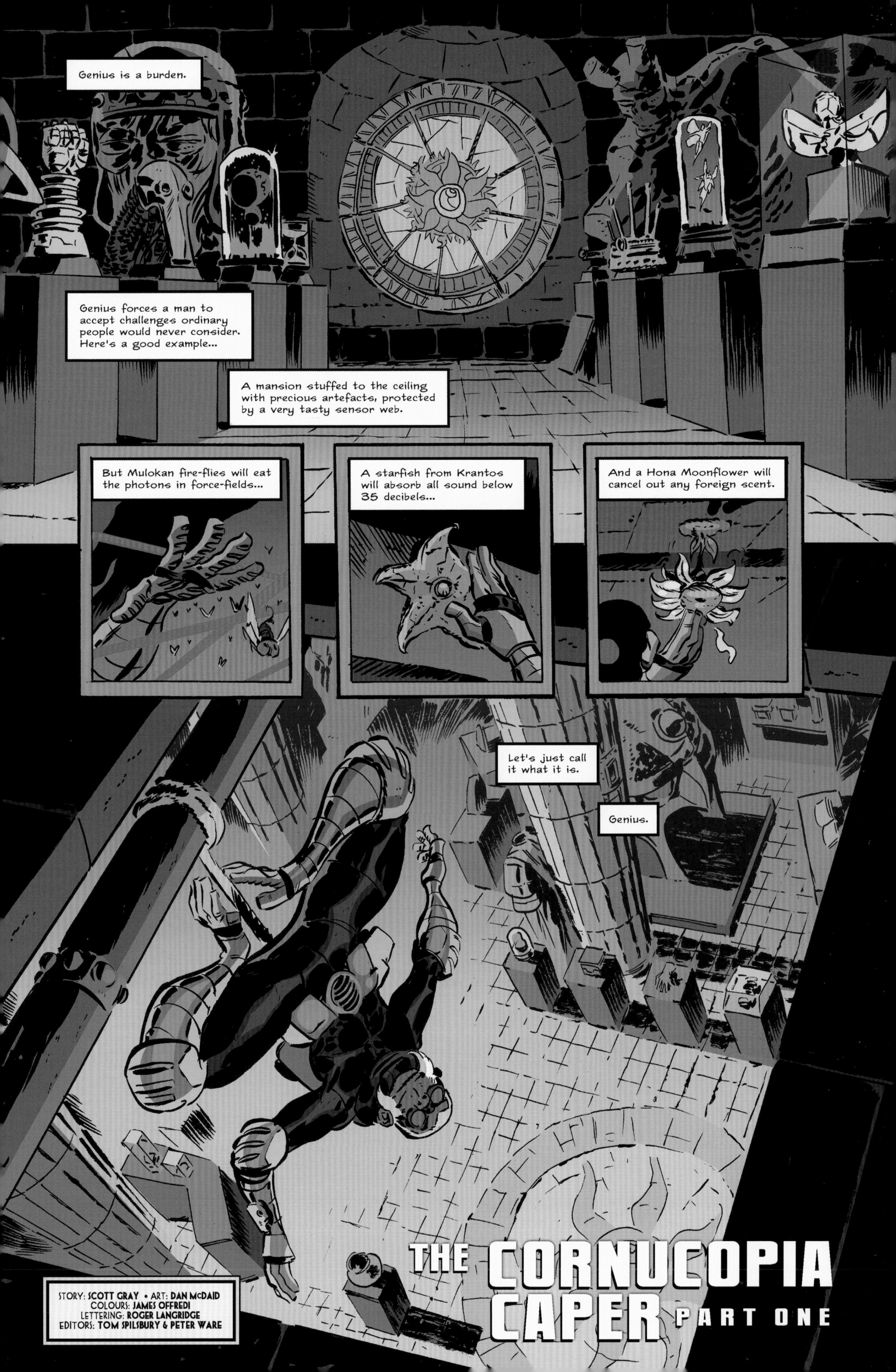

Genius is a burden.
Genius forces a man to accept challenges ordinary people would never consider. Here's a good example...
A mansion stuffed to the ceiling with precious artefacts, protected by a very tasty sensor web.
But Mulokan fire-flies will eat the photons in force-fields...
A starfish from Krantos will absorb all sound below 35 decibels...
And a Hona Moonflower will cancel out any foreign scent.
Let's just call it what it is.
Genius.
THE CORNUCOPIA CAPER PART ONE
STORY: SCOTT GRAY • ART: DAN McDAID
COLOURS: JAMES OFFREDI
LETTERING: ROGER LANGRIDGE
EDITORS: TOM SPILSBURY & PETER WARE

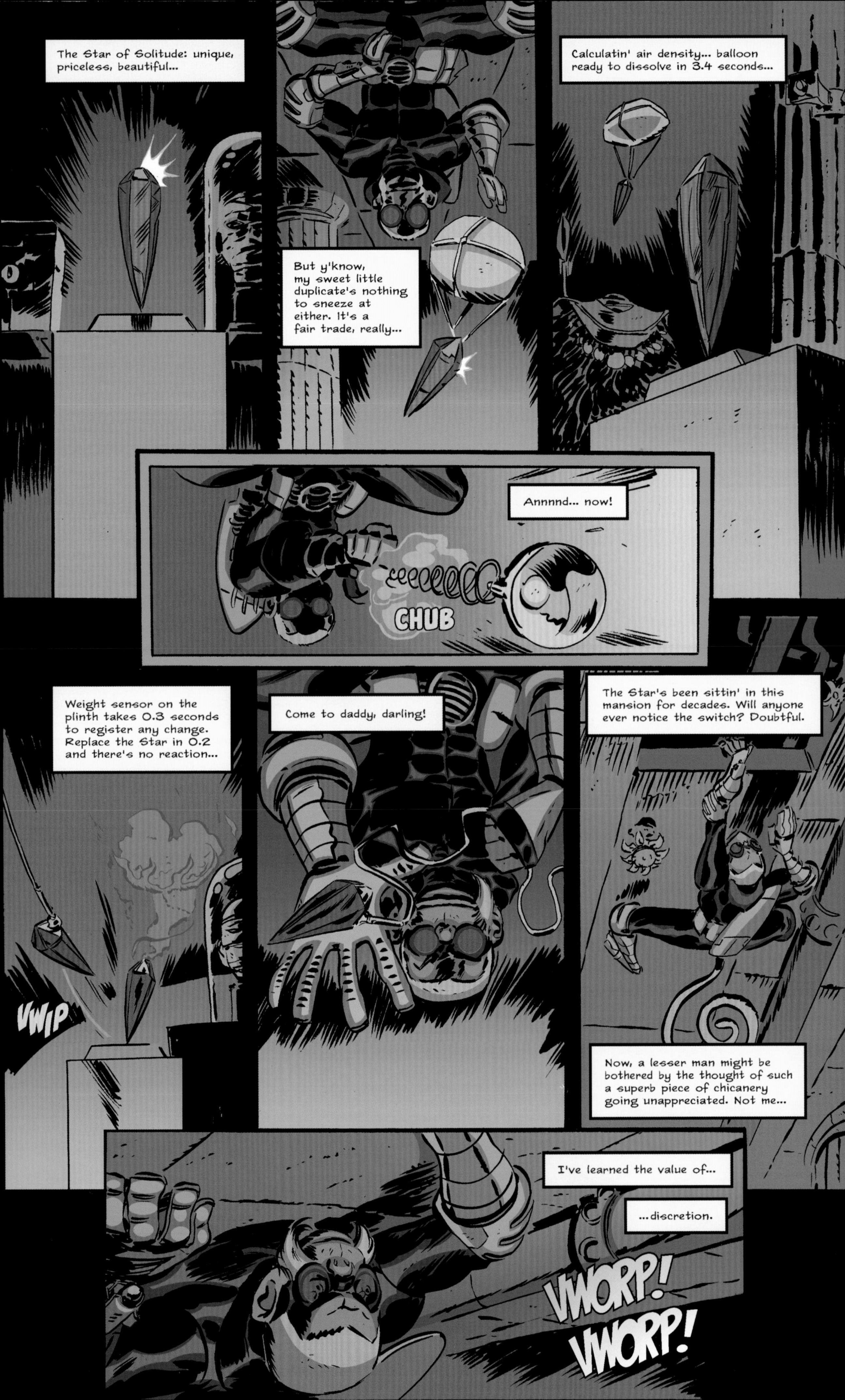
The Star of Solitude: unique, priceless, beautiful...
But y'know, my sweet little duplicate's nothing to sneeze at either. It's a fair trade, really...
Calculatin' air density... balloon ready to dissolve in 3.4 seconds...
Annnnd... now!
CHUB
Weight sensor on the plinth takes 0.3 seconds to register any change. Replace the Star in 0.2 and there's no reaction...
VWIP
Come to daddy, darling!
The Star's been sittin' in this mansion for decades. Will anyone ever notice the switch? Doubtful.
Now, a lesser man might be bothered by the thought of such a superb piece of chicanery going unappreciated. Not me...
I've learned the value of...
...discretion.
VWORP!
VWORP!

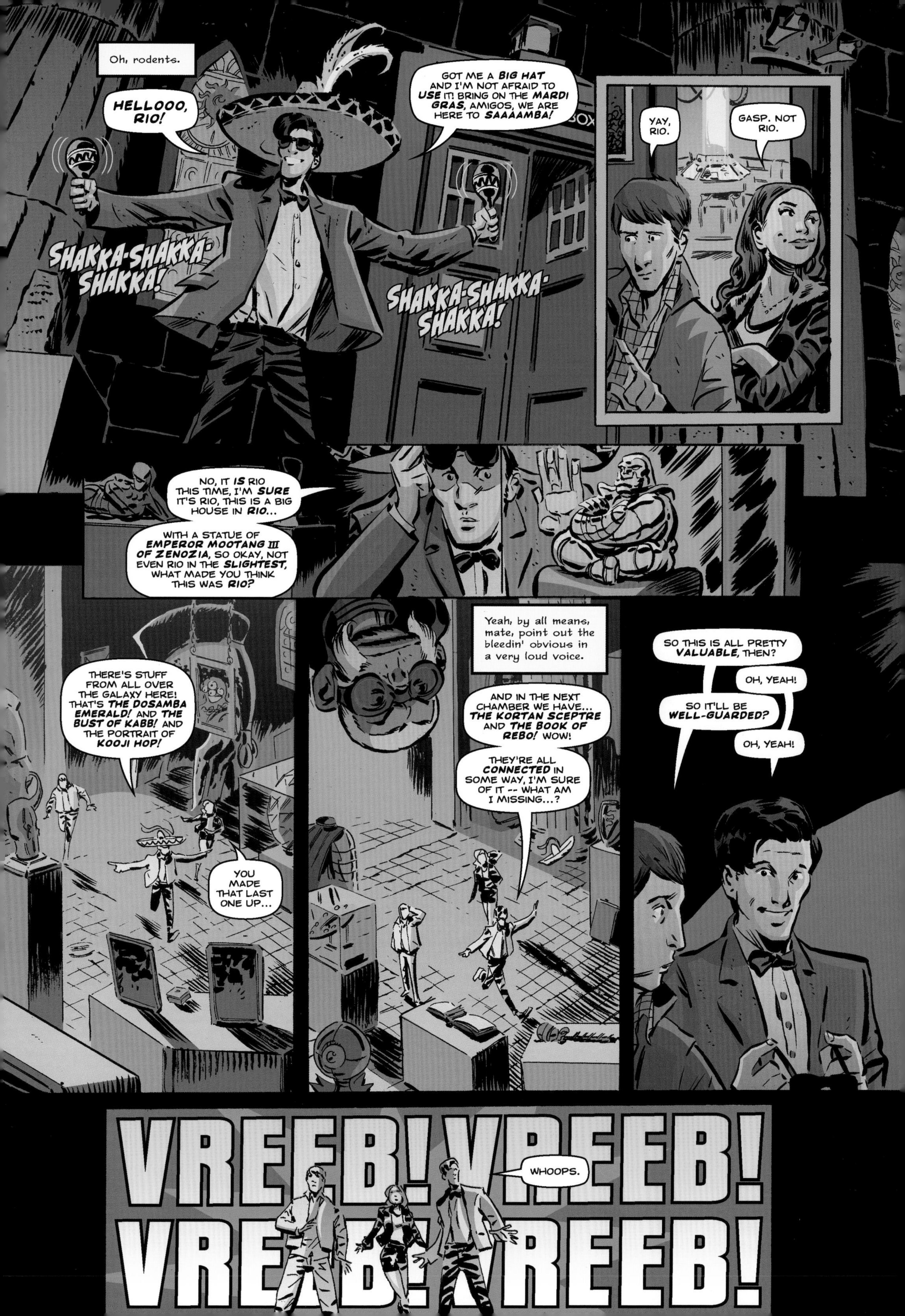

Oh, rodents.
HELLOOO, RIO!
GOT ME A BIG HAT AND I'M NOT AFRAID TO USE IT! BRING ON THE MARDI GRAS, AMIGOS, WE ARE HERE TO SAAAAMBA!
SHAKKA-SHAKKA-SHAKKA!
SHAKKA-SHAKKA-SHAKKA!
YAY, RIO.
GASP. NOT RIO.
NO, IT IS RIO THIS TIME, I'M SURE IT'S RIO, THIS IS A BIG HOUSE IN RIO...
WITH A STATUE OF EMPEROR MOOTANG III OF ZENOZIA, SO OKAY, NOT EVEN RIO IN THE SLIGHTEST, WHAT MADE YOU THINK THIS WAS RIO?
THERE'S STUFF FROM ALL OVER THE GALAXY HERE! THAT'S THE DOSAMBA EMERALD! AND THE BUST OF KABB! AND THE PORTRAIT OF KOOJI HOP!
YOU MADE THAT LAST ONE UP...
Yeah, by all means, mate, point out the bleedin' obvious in a very loud voice.
AND IN THE NEXT CHAMBER WE HAVE... THE KORTAN SCEPTRE AND THE BOOK OF REBO! WOW!
THEY'RE ALL CONNECTED IN SOME WAY, I'M SURE OF IT -- WHAT AM I MISSING...?
SO THIS IS ALL PRETTY VALUABLE, THEN?
OH, YEAH!
SO IT'LL BE WELL-GUARDED?
OH, YEAH!
VREEB! VREEB! VREEB! VREEB!
WHOOPS.

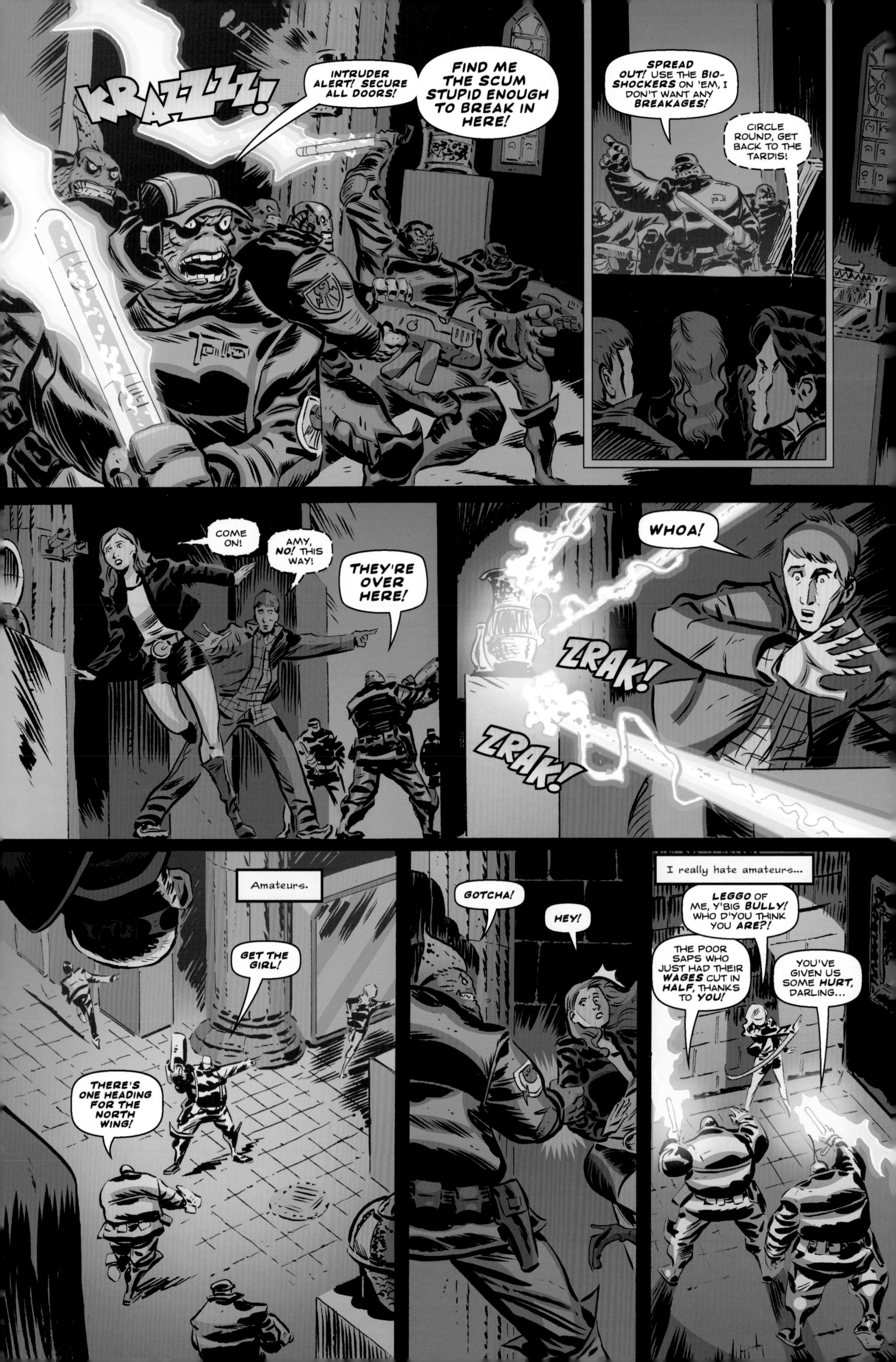
KRAZZZZ!
INTRUDER ALERT! SECURE ALL DOORS!
FIND ME THE SCUM STUPID ENOUGH TO BREAK IN HERE!
SPREAD OUT! USE THE BIO-SHOCKERS ON 'EM, I DON'T WANT ANY BREAKAGES!
CIRCLE ROUND, GET BACK TO THE TARDIS!
COME ON!
AMY, NO! THIS WAY!
THEY'RE OVER HERE!
WHOA!
ZRAK!
ZRAK!
Amateurs.
GET THE GIRL!
THERE'S ONE HEADING FOR THE NORTH WING!
GOTCHA!
HEY!
I really hate amateurs...
LEGGO OF ME, Y'BIG BULLY! WHO D'YOU THINK YOU ARE?!
THE POOR SAPS WHO JUST HAD THEIR WAGES CUT IN HALF, THANKS TO YOU!
YOU'VE GIVEN US SOME HURT, DARLING...

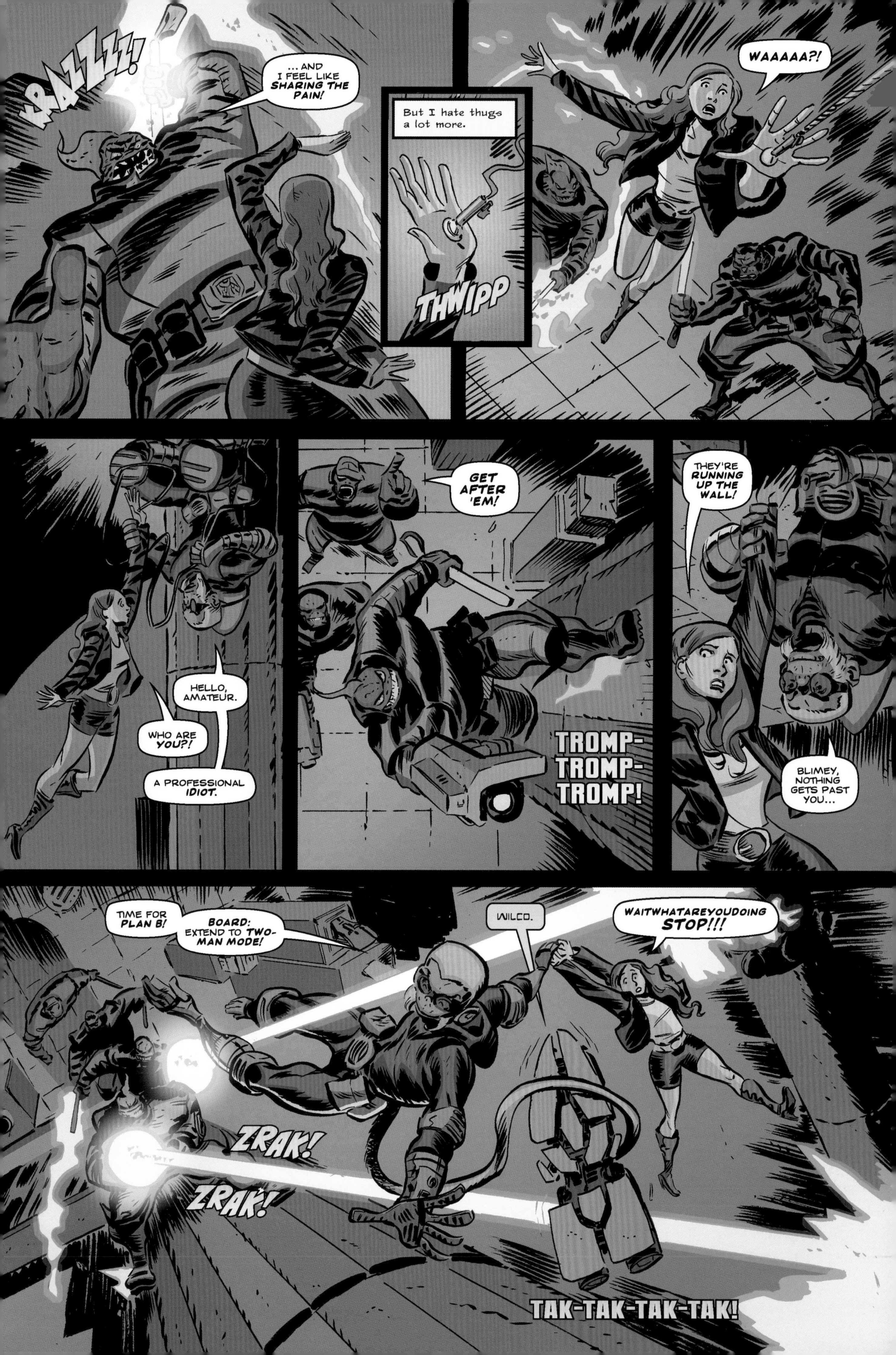
KRAZZZZ!
... AND I FEEL LIKE SHARING THE PAIN!
But I hate thugs a lot more.
THWIPP
WAAAAA?!
HELLO, AMATEUR.
WHO ARE YOU?!
A PROFESSIONAL IDIOT.
GET AFTER 'EM!
TROMP-TROMP-TROMP!
THEY'RE RUNNING UP THE WALL!
BLIMEY, NOTHING GETS PAST YOU...
TIME FOR PLAN B!
BOARD: EXTEND TO TWO-MAN MODE!
WILCO.
WAITWHATAREYOUDOING STOP!!!
ZRAK!
ZRAK!
TAK-TAK-TAK-TAK!

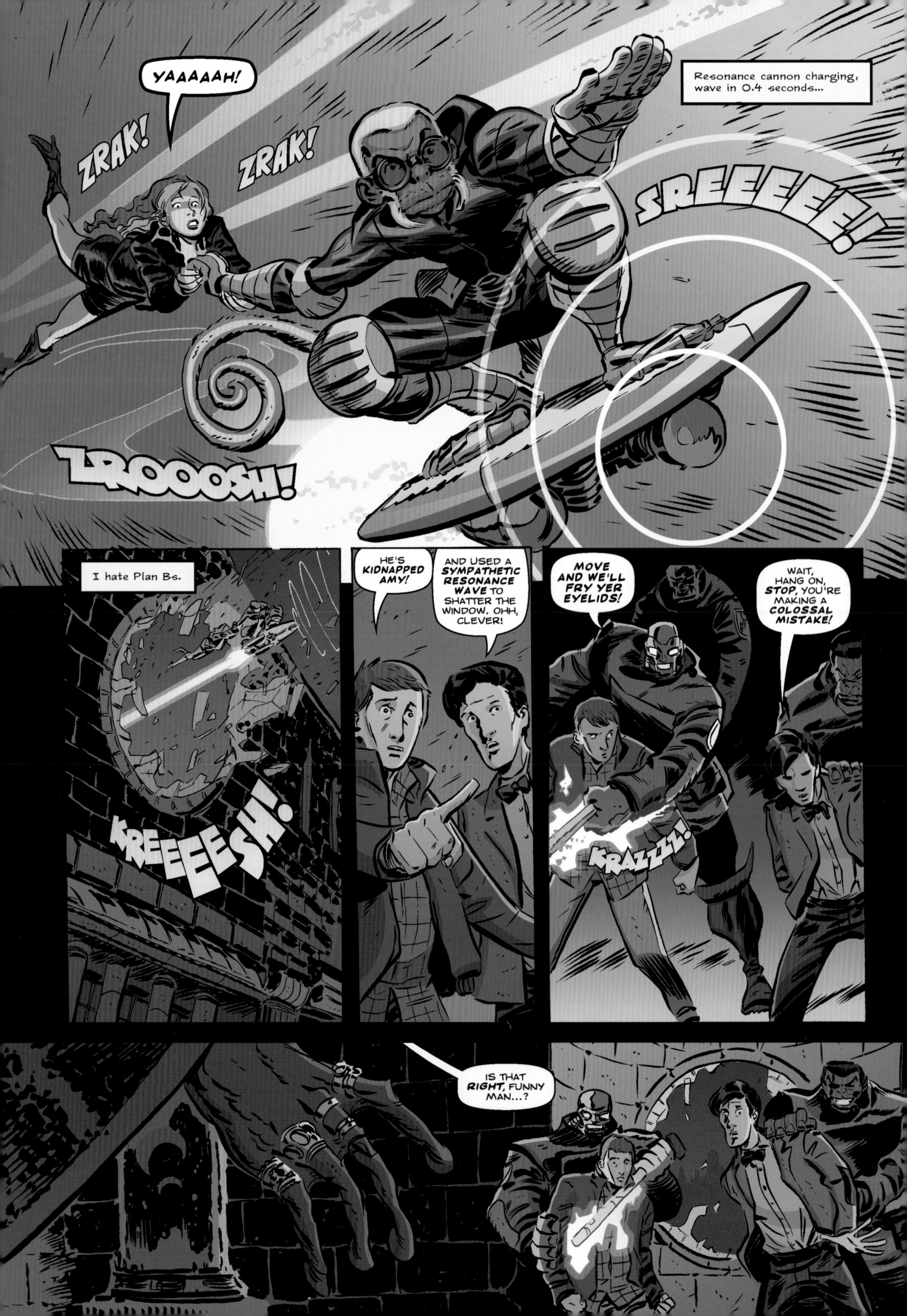
YAAAAAH!
ZRAK!
ZRAK!
Resonance cannon charging, wave in 0.4 seconds...
SREEEEE!
ZROOOSH!
I hate Plan Bs.
KREEEESH!
HE'S KIDNAPPED AMY!
AND USED A SYMPATHETIC RESONANCE WAVE TO SHATTER THE WINDOW. OHH, CLEVER!
MOVE AND WE'LL FRY YER EYELIDS!
WAIT, HANG ON, STOP, YOU'RE MAKING A COLOSSAL MISTAKE!
KRAZZZZ!
IS THAT RIGHT, FUNNY MAN...?

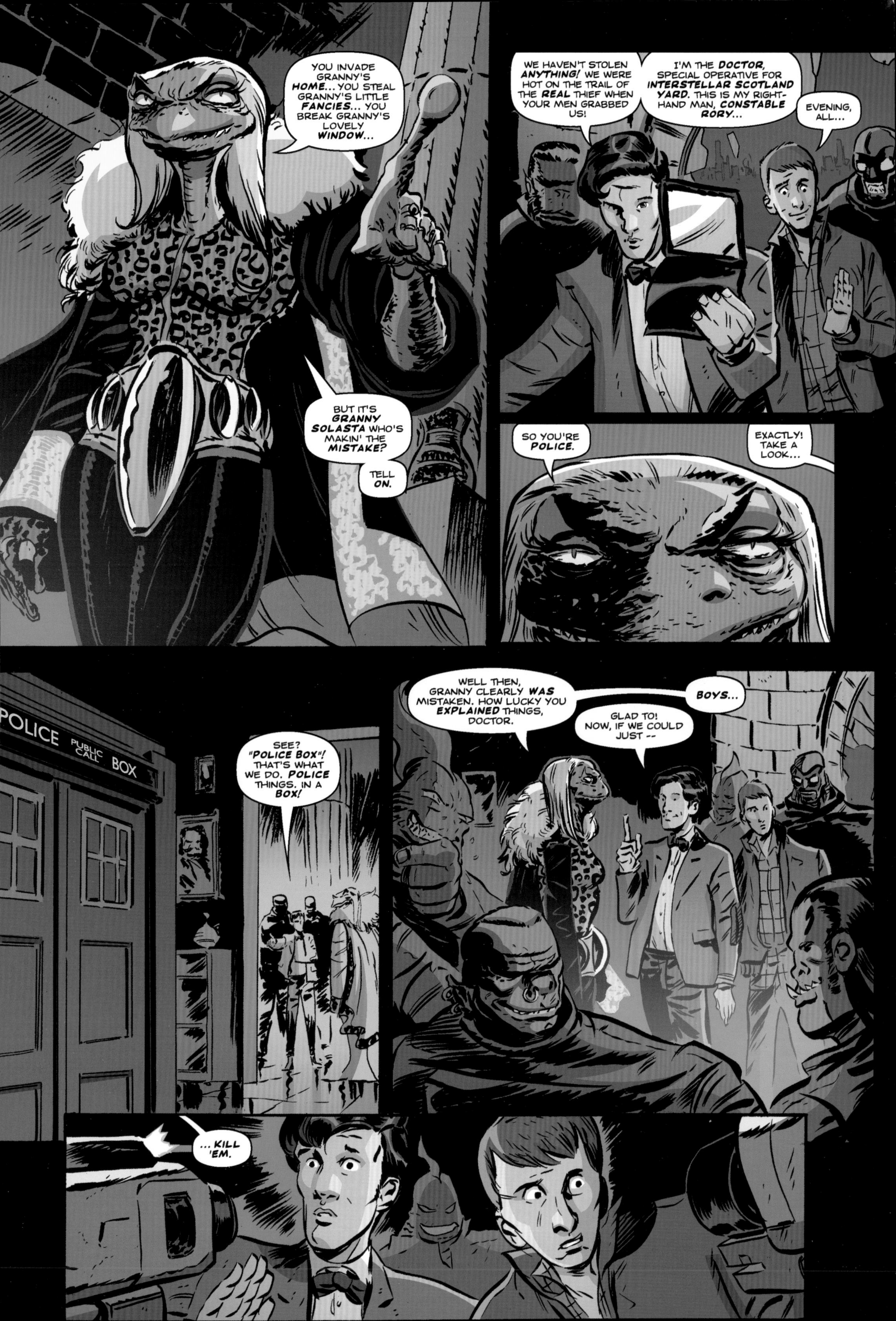
YOU INVADE GRANNY'S HOME... YOU STEAL GRANNY'S LITTLE FANCIES... YOU BREAK GRANNY'S LOVELY WINDOW...
BUT IT'S GRANNY SOLASTA WHO'S MAKIN' THE MISTAKE?
TELL ON.
WE HAVEN'T STOLEN ANYTHING! WE WERE HOT ON THE TRAIL OF THE REAL THIEF WHEN YOUR MEN GRABBED US!
I'M THE DOCTOR, SPECIAL OPERATIVE FOR INTERSTELLAR SCOTLAND YARD. THIS IS MY RIGHT-HAND MAN, CONSTABLE RORY...
EVENING, ALL...
SO YOU'RE POLICE.
EXACTLY! TAKE A LOOK...
POLICE PUBLIC CALL BOX
SEE? "POLICE BOX"! THAT'S WHAT WE DO. POLICE THINGS. IN A BOX!
WELL THEN, GRANNY CLEARLY WAS MISTAKEN. HOW LUCKY YOU EXPLAINED THINGS, DOCTOR.
BOYS...
GLAD TO! NOW, IF WE COULD JUST --
...KILL 'EM.

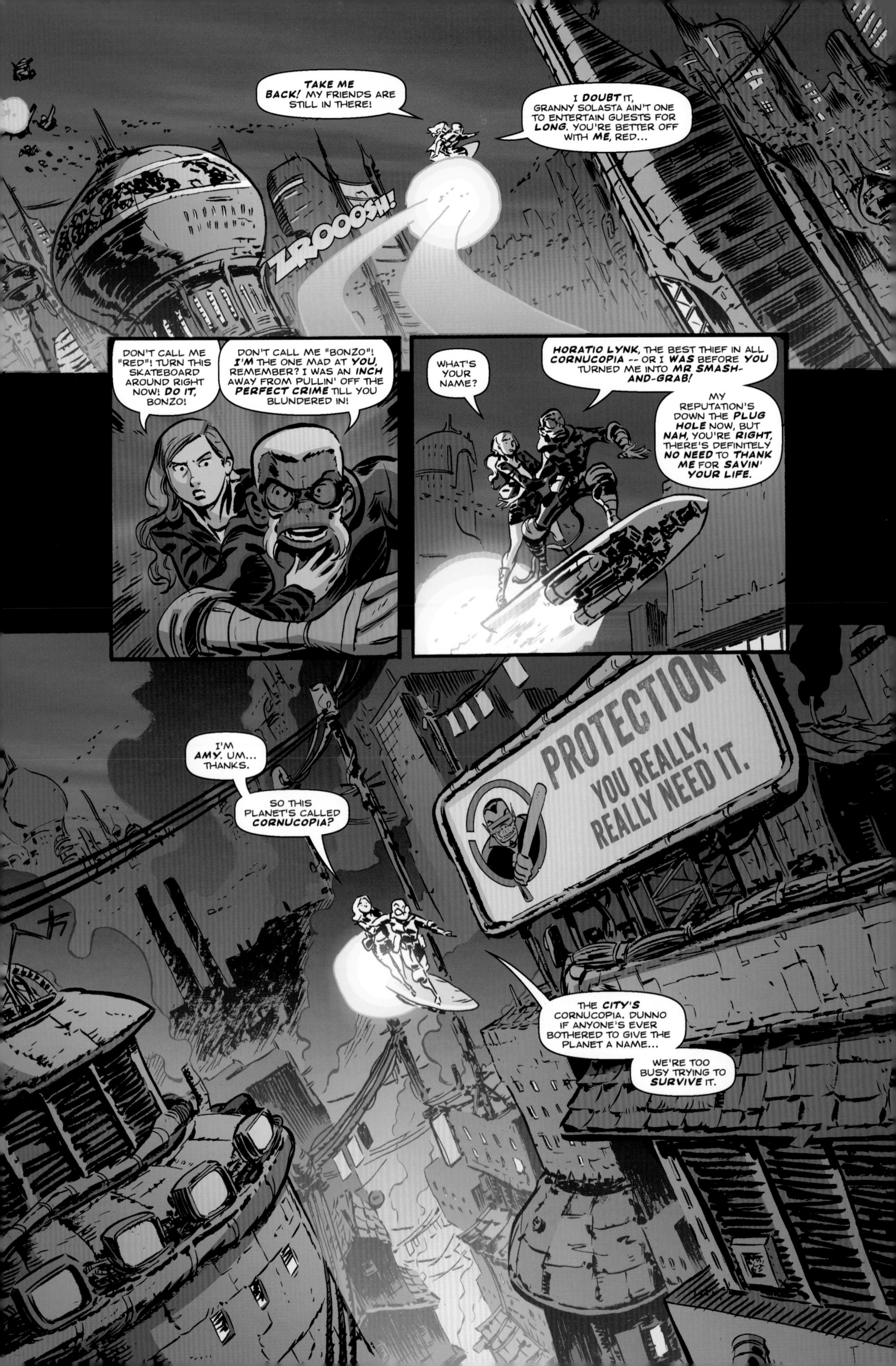
TAKE ME BACK! MY FRIENDS ARE STILL IN THERE!
I DOUBT IT, GRANNY SOLASTA AIN'T ONE TO ENTERTAIN GUESTS FOR LONG. YOU'RE BETTER OFF WITH ME, RED...
ZROOOSH!
DON'T CALL ME "RED"! TURN THIS SKATEBOARD AROUND RIGHT NOW! DO IT, BONZO!
DON'T CALL ME "BONZO"! I'M THE ONE MAD AT YOU, REMEMBER? I WAS AN INCH AWAY FROM PULLIN' OFF THE PERFECT CRIME TILL YOU BLUNDERED IN!
WHAT'S YOUR NAME?
HORATIO LYNK, THE BEST THIEF IN ALL CORNUCOPIA -- OR I WAS BEFORE YOU TURNED ME INTO MR SMASH-AND-GRAB!
MY REPUTATION'S DOWN THE PLUG HOLE NOW, BUT NAH, YOU'RE RIGHT, THERE'S DEFINITELY NO NEED TO THANK ME FOR SAVIN' YOUR LIFE.
PROTECTION
YOU REALLY, REALLY NEED IT.
I'M AMY. UM... THANKS.
SO THIS PLANET'S CALLED CORNUCOPIA?
THE CITY'S CORNUCOPIA. DUNNO IF ANYONE'S EVER BOTHERED TO GIVE THE PLANET A NAME...
WE'RE TOO BUSY TRYING TO SURVIVE IT.

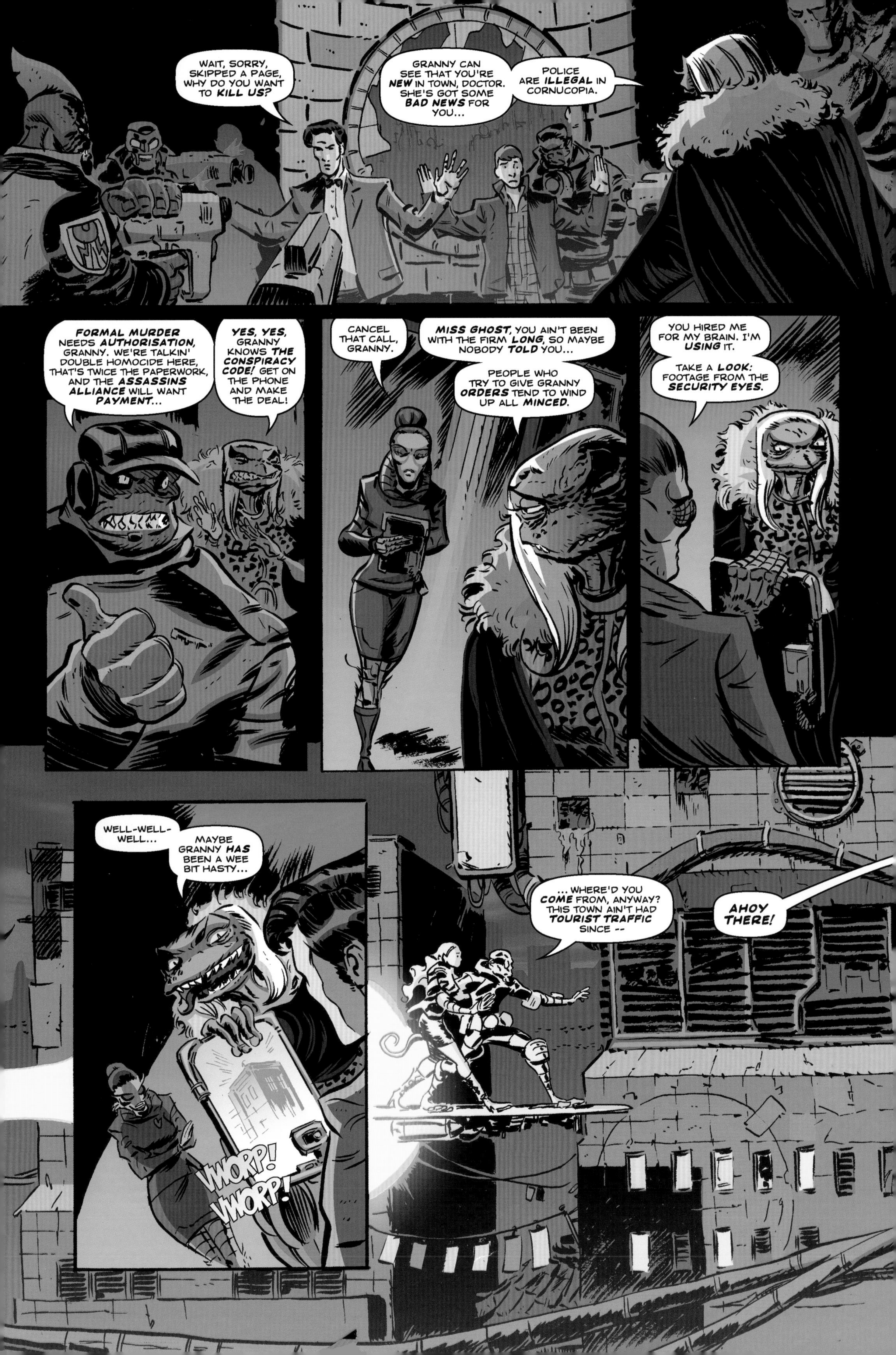
WAIT, SORRY, SKIPPED A PAGE, WHY DO YOU WANT TO KILL US?
GRANNY CAN SEE THAT YOU'RE NEW IN TOWN, DOCTOR. SHE'S GOT SOME BAD NEWS FOR YOU...
POLICE ARE ILLEGAL IN CORNUCOPIA.
FORMAL MURDER NEEDS AUTHORISATION, GRANNY. WE'RE TALKIN' DOUBLE HOMOCIDE HERE, THAT'S TWICE THE PAPERWORK, AND THE ASSASSINS ALLIANCE WILL WANT PAYMENT...
YES, YES, GRANNY KNOWS THE CONSPIRACY CODE! GET ON THE PHONE AND MAKE THE DEAL!
CANCEL THAT CALL, GRANNY.
MISS GHOST, YOU AIN'T BEEN WITH THE FIRM LONG, SO MAYBE NOBODY TOLD YOU...
PEOPLE WHO TRY TO GIVE GRANNY ORDERS TEND TO WIND UP ALL MINCED.
YOU HIRED ME FOR MY BRAIN. I'M USING IT.
TAKE A LOOK: FOOTAGE FROM THE SECURITY EYES.
WELL-WELL-WELL...
MAYBE GRANNY HAS BEEN A WEE BIT HASTY...
VWORP! VWORP!
... WHERE'D YOU COME FROM, ANYWAY? THIS TOWN AIN'T HAD TOURIST TRAFFIC SINCE --
AHOY THERE!

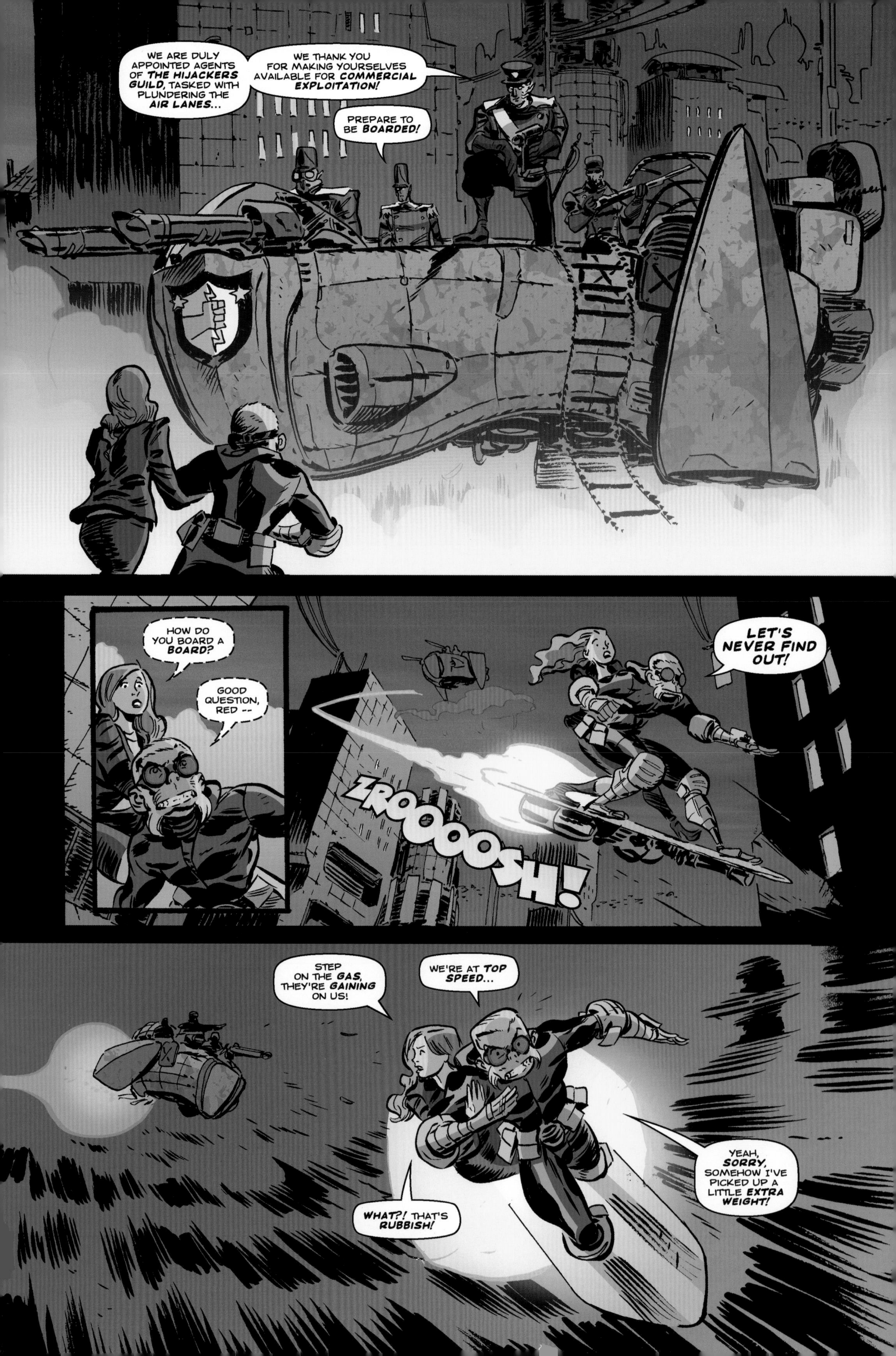
WE ARE DULY APPOINTED AGENTS OF THE HIJACKERS GUILD, TASKED WITH PLUNDERING THE AIR LANES...
WE THANK YOU FOR MAKING YOURSELVES AVAILABLE FOR COMMERCIAL EXPLOITATION!
PREPARE TO BE BOARDED!
HOW DO YOU BOARD A BOARD?
GOOD QUESTION, RED --
LET'S NEVER FIND OUT!
ZROOOOOSH!
STEP ON THE GAS, THEY'RE GAINING ON US!
WE'RE AT TOP SPEED...
YEAH, SORRY, SOMEHOW I'VE PICKED UP A LITTLE EXTRA WEIGHT!
WHAT?! THAT'S RUBBISH!

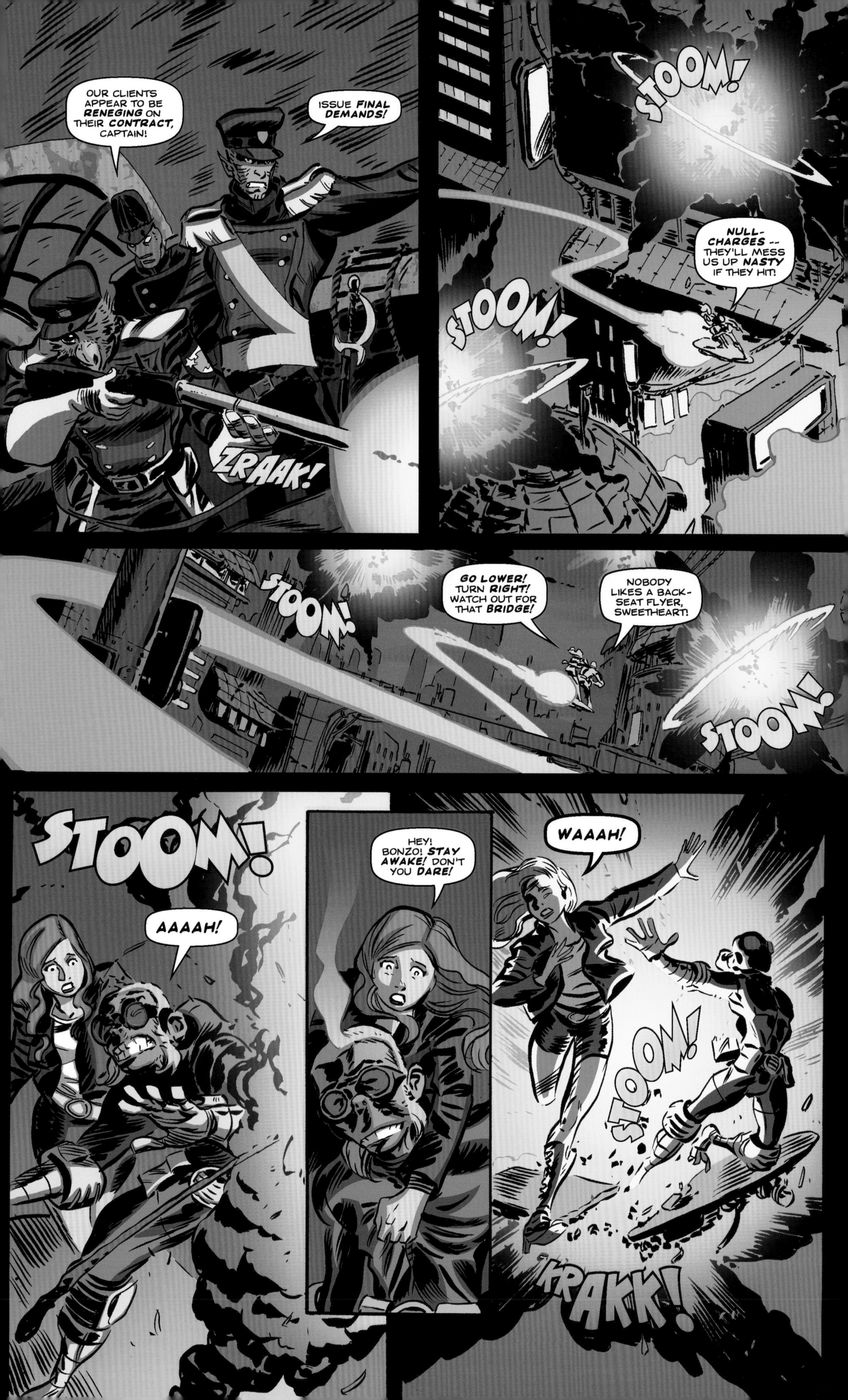
OUR CLIENTS APPEAR TO BE RENEGING ON THEIR CONTRACT, CAPTAIN!
ISSUE FINAL DEMANDS!
ZRAAK!
STOOM!
NULL-CHARGES -- THEY'LL MESS US UP NASTY IF THEY HIT!
STOOM!
STOOM!
GO LOWER! TURN RIGHT! WATCH OUT FOR THAT BRIDGE!
NOBODY LIKES A BACK-SEAT FLYER, SWEETHEART!
STOOM!
STOOM!
AAAAH!
HEY! BONZO! STAY AWAKE! DON'T YOU DARE!
WAAAH!
STOOM!
KRAKK!

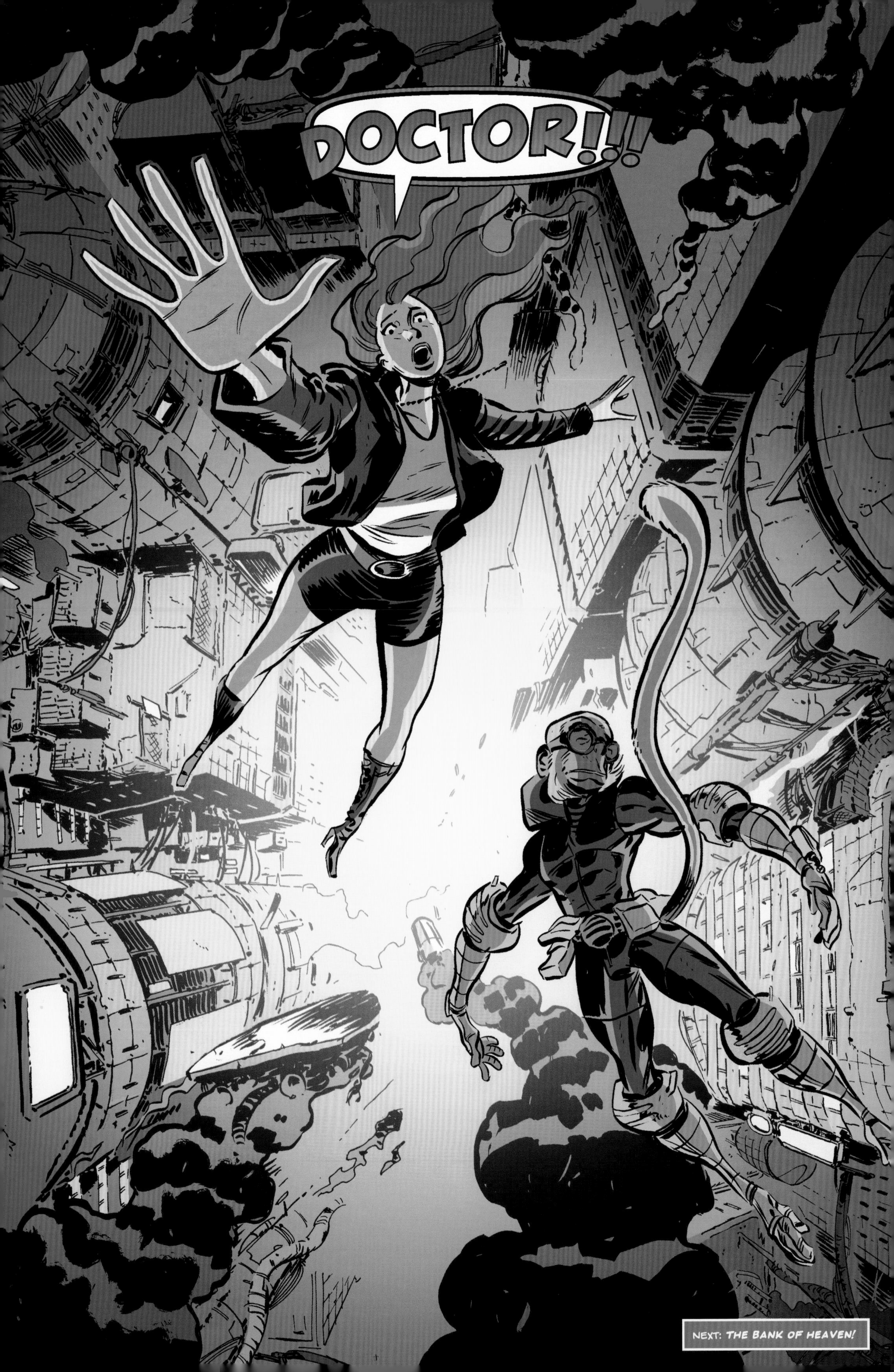
DOCTOR!!!
NEXT: THE BANK OF HEAVEN!

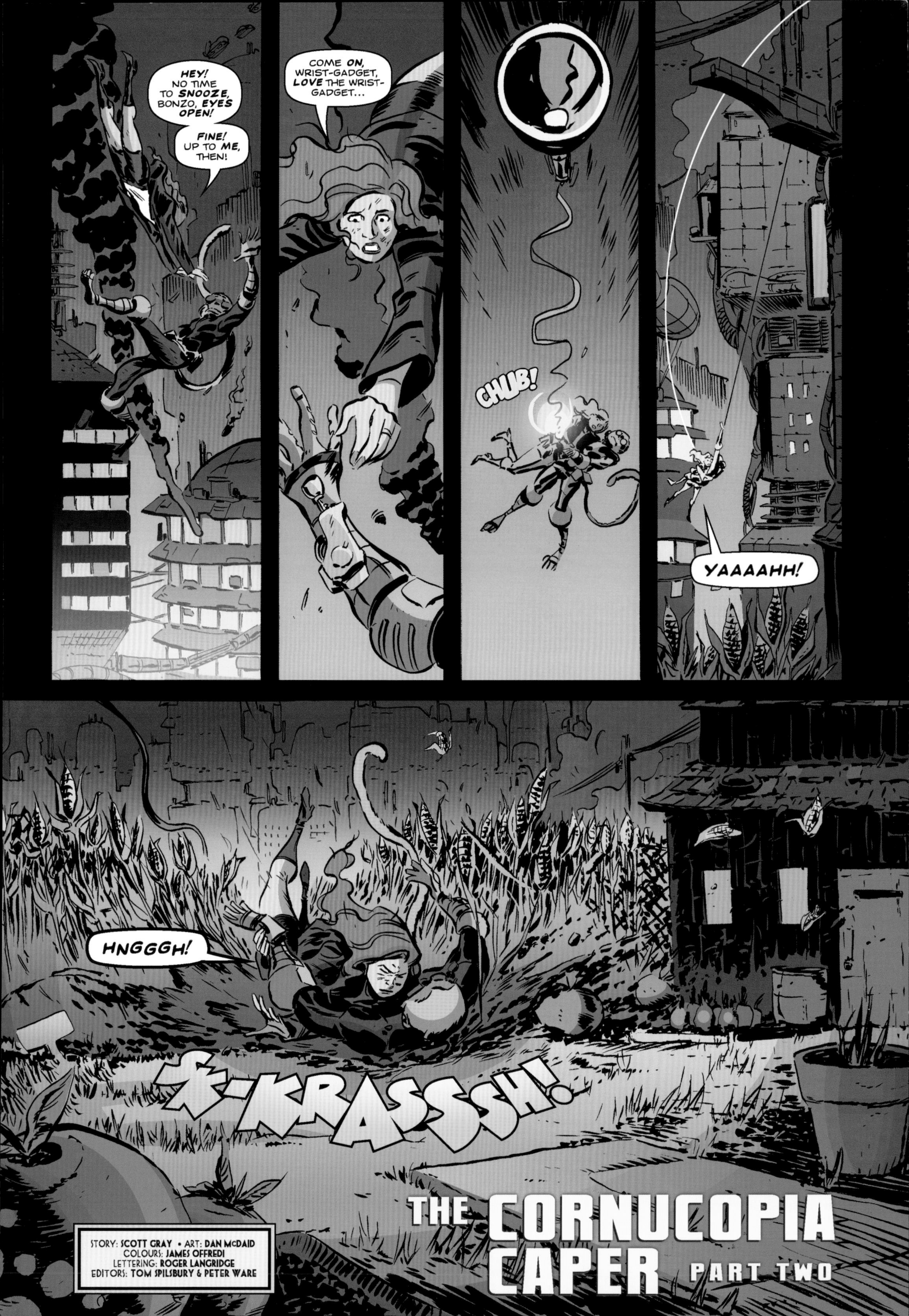
HEY! NO TIME TO SNOOZE, BONZO, EYES OPEN!
FINE! UP TO ME, THEN!
COME ON, WRIST-GADGET, LOVE THE WRIST-GADGET...
CHUB!
YAAAAHH!
HNGGGH!
K-KRASSSH!
THE CORNUCOPIA CAPER PART TWO
STORY: SCOTT GRAY • ART: DAN McDAID
COLOURS: JAMES OFFREDI
LETTERING: ROGER LANGRIDGE
EDITORS: TOM SPILSBURY & PETER WARE

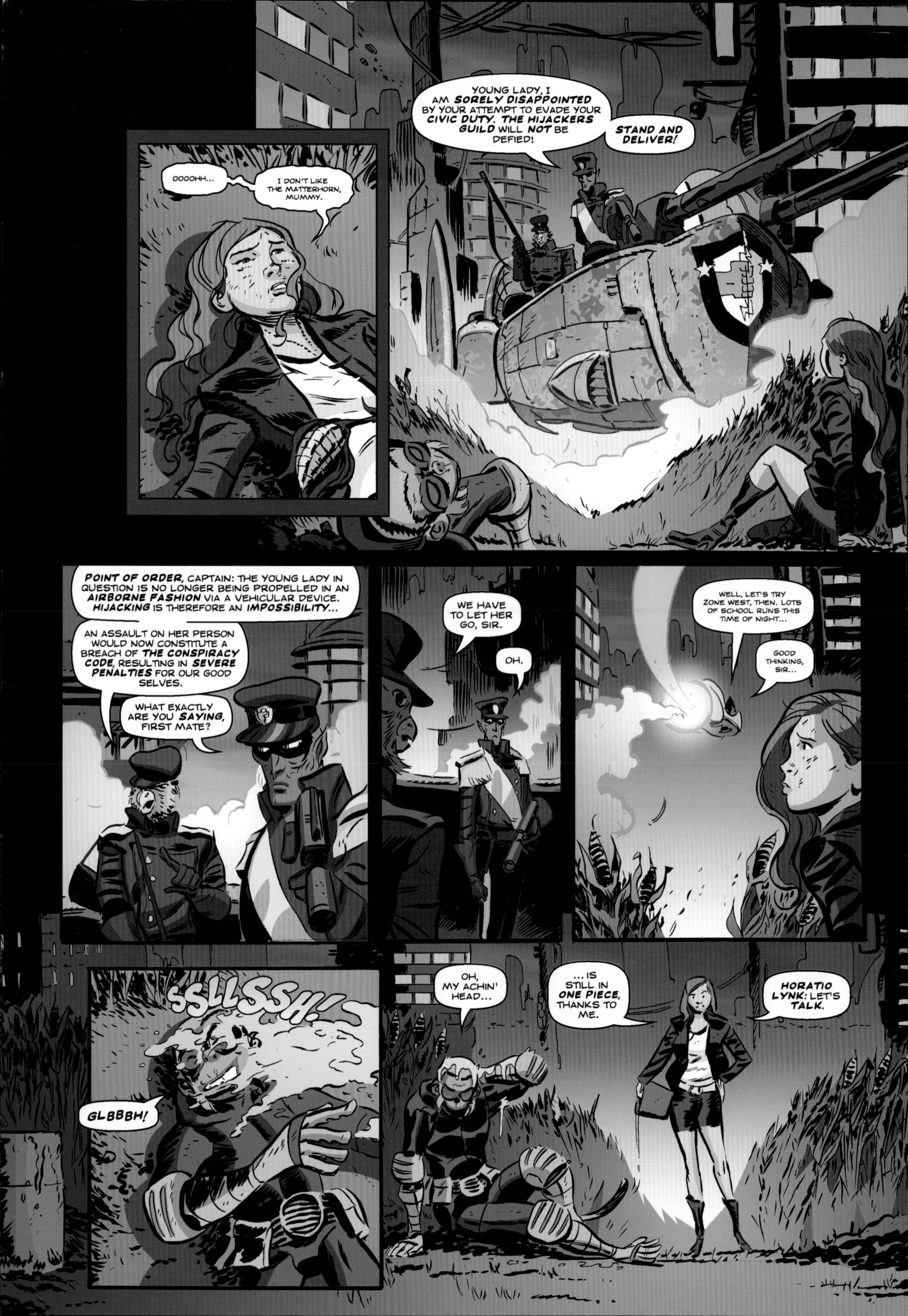
OOOOHH...
I DON'T LIKE THE MATTERHORN, MUMMY.
YOUNG LADY, I AM SORELY DISAPPOINTED BY YOUR ATTEMPT TO EVADE YOUR CIVIC DUTY. THE HIJACKERS GUILD WILL NOT BE DEFIED!
STAND AND DELIVER!
POINT OF ORDER, CAPTAIN: THE YOUNG LADY IN QUESTION IS NO LONGER BEING PROPELLED IN AN AIRBORNE FASHION VIA A VEHICULAR DEVICE. HIJACKING IS THEREFORE AN IMPOSSIBILITY...
AN ASSAULT ON HER PERSON WOULD NOW CONSTITUTE A BREACH OF THE CONSPIRACY CODE, RESULTING IN SEVERE PENALTIES FOR OUR GOOD SELVES.
WHAT EXACTLY ARE YOU SAYING, FIRST MATE?
WE HAVE TO LET HER GO, SIR.
OH.
WELL, LET'S TRY ZONE WEST, THEN. LOTS OF SCHOOL RUNS THIS TIME OF NIGHT...
GOOD THINKING, SIR...
SSLLSSH!
GLBBBH!
OH, MY ACHIN' HEAD...
... IS STILL IN ONE PIECE, THANKS TO ME.
HORATIO LYNK: LET'S TALK.

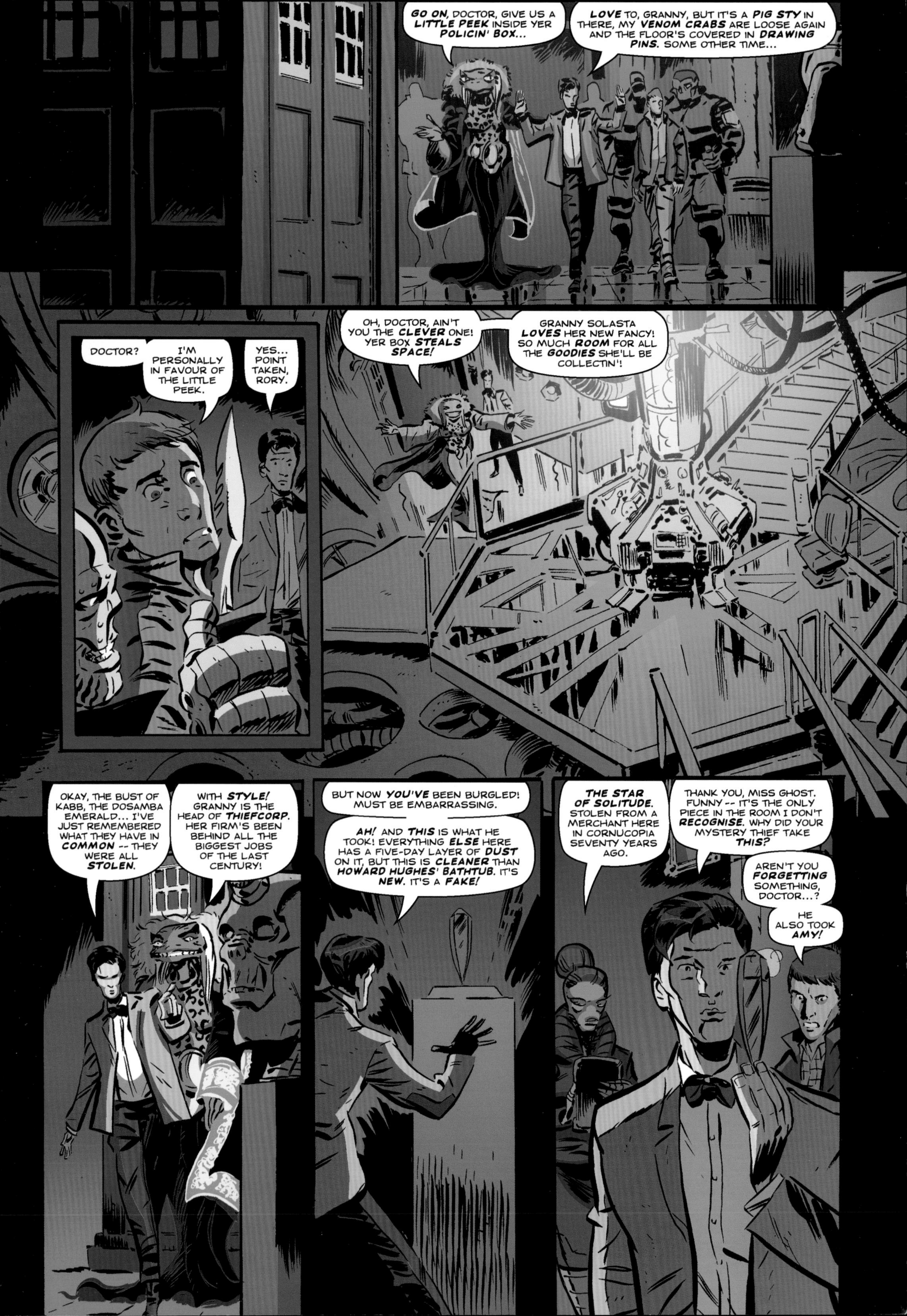
GO ON, DOCTOR, GIVE US A LITTLE PEEK INSIDE YER POLICIN' BOX...
LOVE TO, GRANNY, BUT IT'S A PIG STY IN THERE, MY VENOM CRABS ARE LOOSE AGAIN AND THE FLOOR'S COVERED IN DRAWING PINS. SOME OTHER TIME...
DOCTOR?
I'M PERSONALLY IN FAVOUR OF THE LITTLE PEEK.
YES... POINT TAKEN, RORY.
OH, DOCTOR, AIN'T YOU THE CLEVER ONE! YER BOX STEALS SPACE!
GRANNY SOLASTA LOVES HER NEW FANCY! SO MUCH ROOM FOR ALL THE GOODIES SHE'LL BE COLLECTIN'!
OKAY, THE BUST OF KABB, THE DOSAMBA EMERALD... I'VE JUST REMEMBERED WHAT THEY HAVE IN COMMON -- THEY WERE ALL STOLEN.
WITH STYLE! GRANNY IS THE HEAD OF THIEFCORP. HER FIRM'S BEEN BEHIND ALL THE BIGGEST JOBS OF THE LAST CENTURY!
BUT NOW YOU'VE BEEN BURGLED! MUST BE EMBARRASSING.
AH! AND THIS IS WHAT HE TOOK! EVERYTHING ELSE HERE HAS A FIVE-DAY LAYER OF DUST ON IT, BUT THIS IS CLEANER THAN HOWARD HUGHES' BATHTUB. IT'S NEW. IT'S A FAKE!
THE STAR OF SOLITUDE. STOLEN FROM A MERCHANT HERE IN CORNUCOPIA SEVENTY YEARS AGO.
THANK YOU, MISS GHOST. FUNNY -- IT'S THE ONLY PIECE IN THE ROOM I DON'T RECOGNISE. WHY DID YOUR MYSTERY THIEF TAKE THIS?
AREN'T YOU FORGETTING SOMETHING, DOCTOR...?
HE ALSO TOOK AMY!

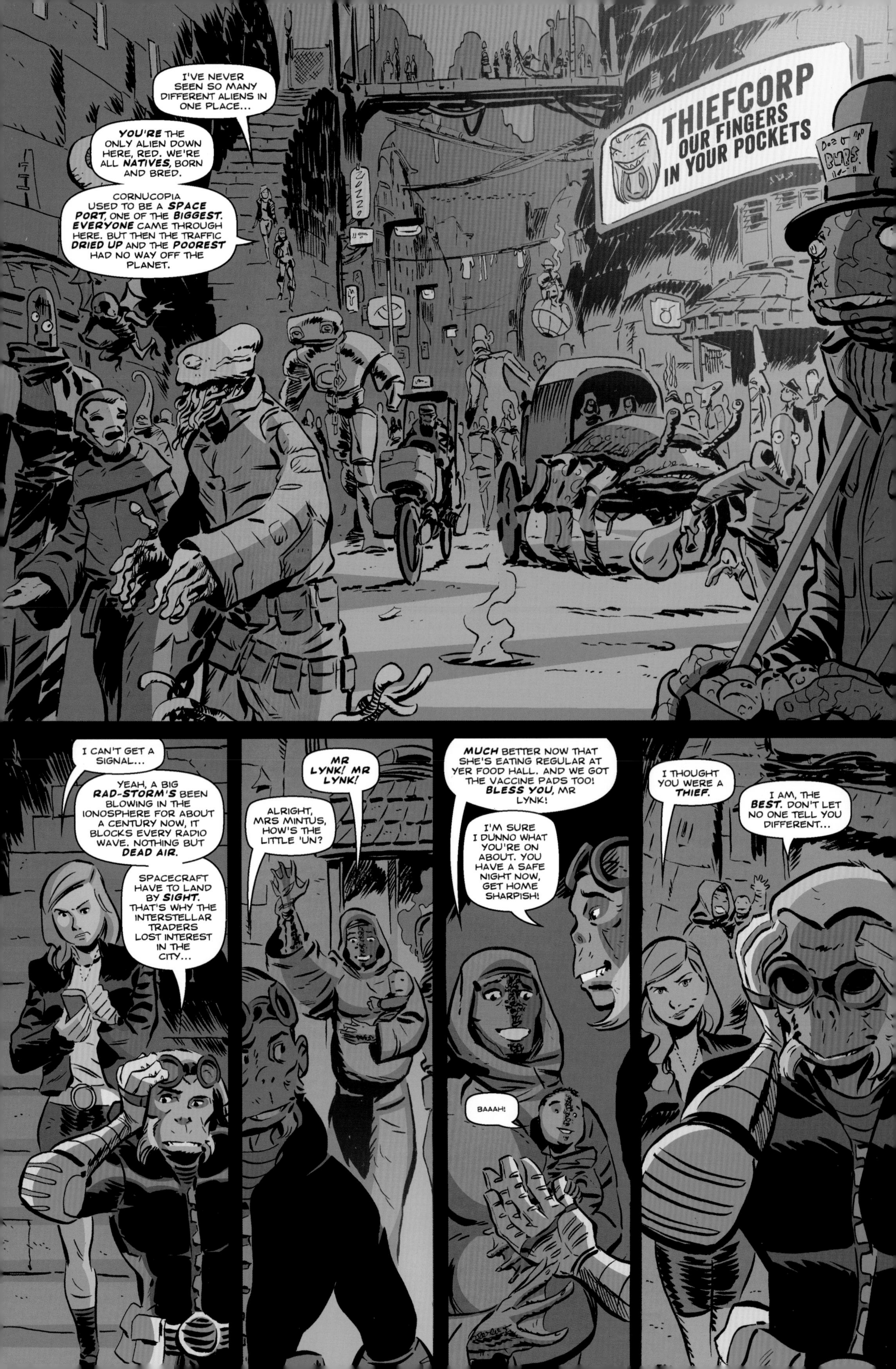
I'VE NEVER SEEN SO MANY DIFFERENT ALIENS IN ONE PLACE...
YOU'RE THE ONLY ALIEN DOWN HERE, RED. WE'RE ALL NATIVES, BORN AND BRED.
CORNUCOPIA USED TO BE A SPACE PORT, ONE OF THE BIGGEST. EVERYONE CAME THROUGH HERE. BUT THEN THE TRAFFIC DRIED UP AND THE POOREST HAD NO WAY OFF THE PLANET.
THIEFCORP
OUR FINGERS IN YOUR POCKETS
I CAN'T GET A SIGNAL...
YEAH, A BIG RAD-STORM'S BEEN BLOWING IN THE IONOSPHERE FOR ABOUT A CENTURY NOW, IT BLOCKS EVERY RADIO WAVE. NOTHING BUT DEAD AIR.
SPACECRAFT HAVE TO LAND BY SIGHT. THAT'S WHY THE INTERSTELLAR TRADERS LOST INTEREST IN THE CITY...
MR LYNK! MR LYNK!
ALRIGHT, MRS MINTUS, HOW'S THE LITTLE 'UN?
MUCH BETTER NOW THAT SHE'S EATING REGULAR AT YER FOOD HALL. AND WE GOT THE VACCINE PADS TOO! BLESS YOU, MR LYNK!
I'M SURE I DUNNO WHAT YOU'RE ON ABOUT. YOU HAVE A SAFE NIGHT NOW, GET HOME SHARPISH!
BAAAH!
I THOUGHT YOU WERE A THIEF.
I AM, THE BEST. DON'T LET NO ONE TELL YOU DIFFERENT...

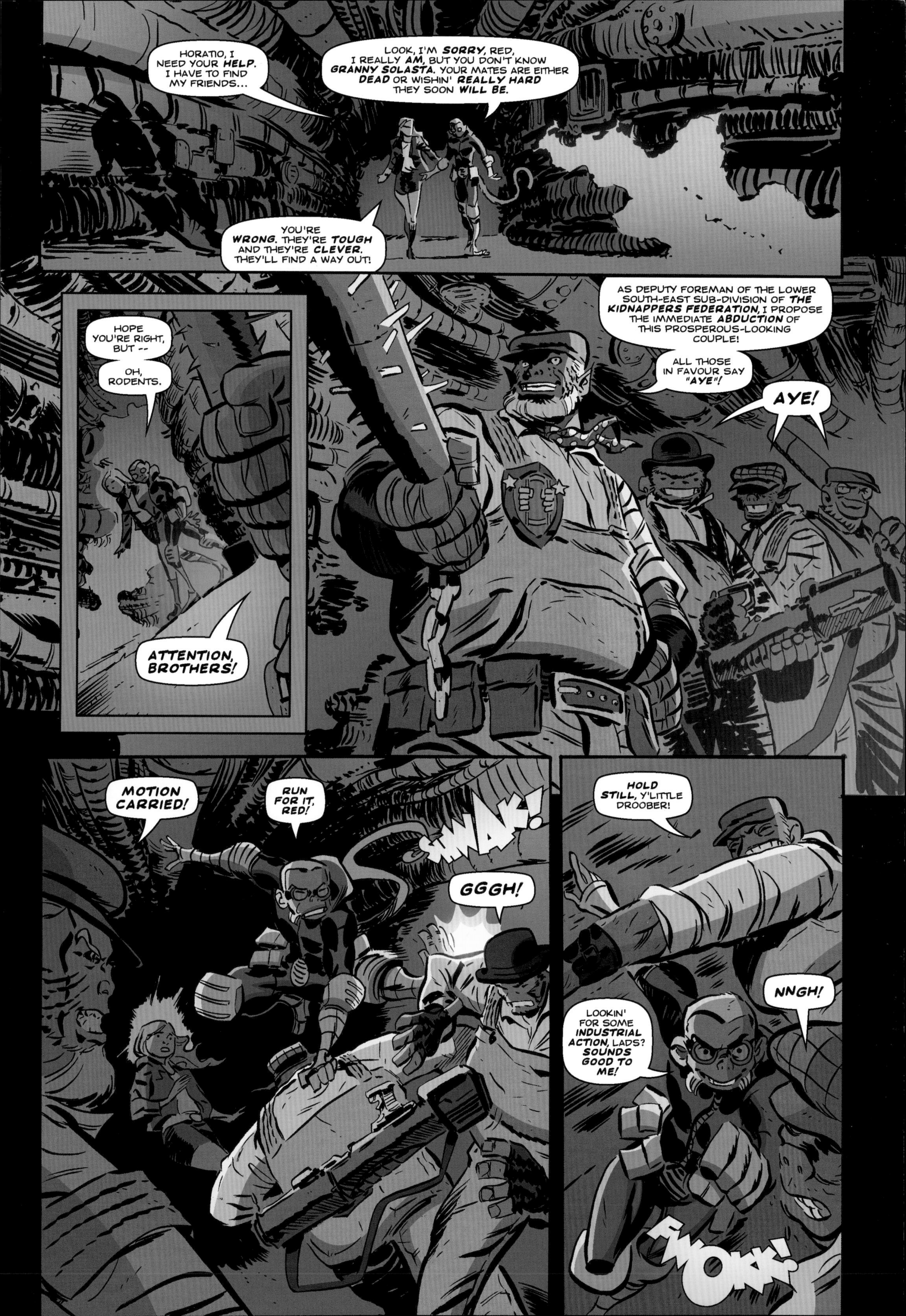
HORATIO, I NEED YOUR HELP. I HAVE TO FIND MY FRIENDS...
LOOK, I'M SORRY, RED, I REALLY AM, BUT YOU DON'T KNOW GRANNY SOLASTA. YOUR MATES ARE EITHER DEAD OR WISHIN' REALLY HARD THEY SOON WILL BE.
YOU'RE WRONG. THEY'RE TOUGH AND THEY'RE CLEVER. THEY'LL FIND A WAY OUT!
HOPE YOU'RE RIGHT, BUT --
OH, RODENTS.
ATTENTION, BROTHERS!
AS DEPUTY FOREMAN OF THE LOWER SOUTH-EAST SUB-DIVISION OF THE KIDNAPPERS FEDERATION, I PROPOSE THE IMMEDIATE ABDUCTION OF THIS PROSPEROUS-LOOKING COUPLE!
ALL THOSE IN FAVOUR SAY "AYE"!
AYE!
MOTION CARRIED!
RUN FOR IT, RED!
SWAK!
GGGH!
HOLD STILL, Y'LITTLE DROOBER!
LOOKIN' FOR SOME INDUSTRIAL ACTION, LADS? SOUNDS GOOD TO ME!
NNGH!
FWOK!

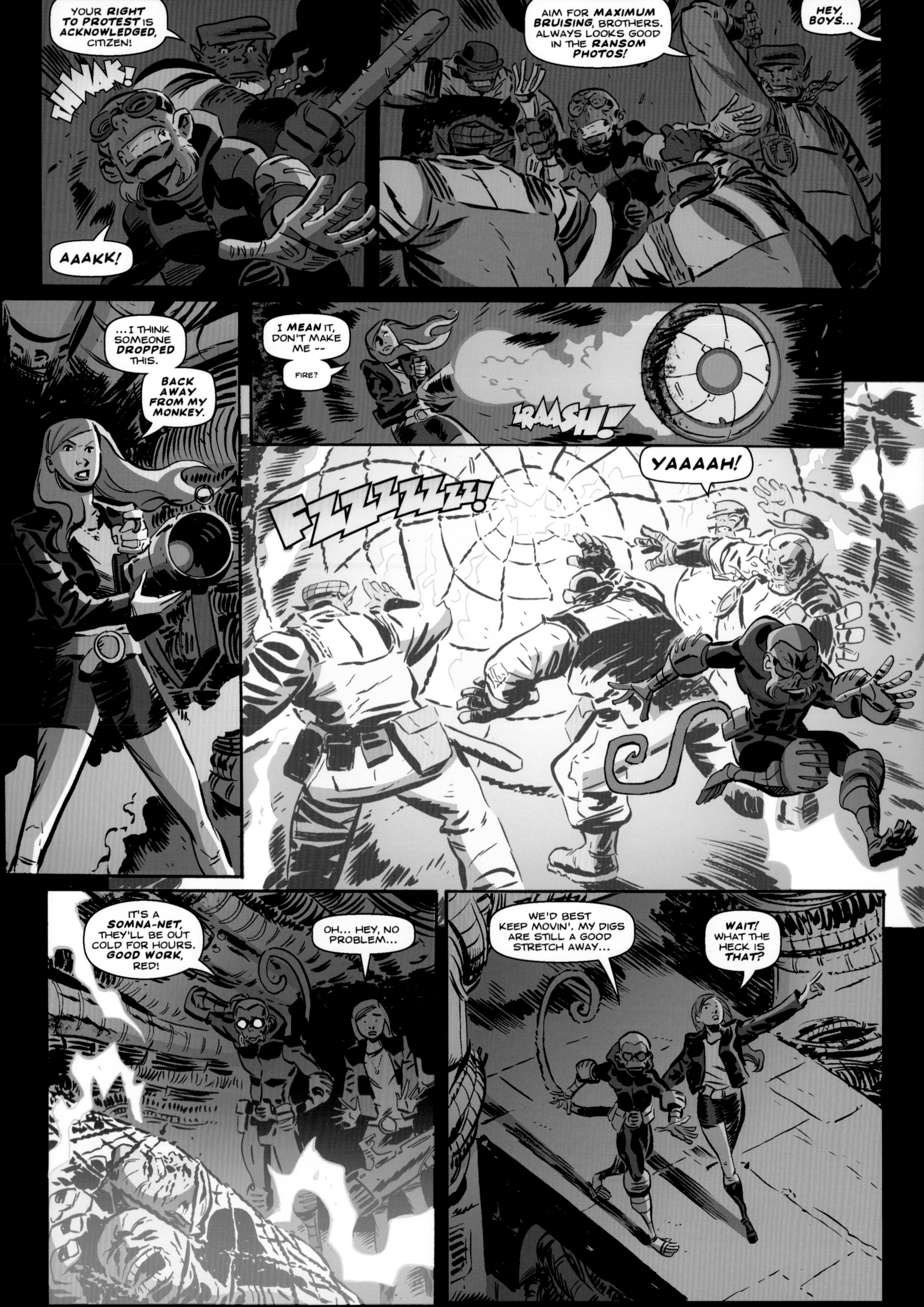
YOUR RIGHT TO PROTEST IS ACKNOWLEDGED, CITIZEN!
THWAK!
AAAKK!
AIM FOR MAXIMUM BRUISING, BROTHERS. ALWAYS LOOKS GOOD IN THE RANSOM PHOTOS!
HEY, BOYS...
...I THINK SOMEONE DROPPED THIS.
BACK AWAY FROM MY MONKEY.
I MEAN IT, DON'T MAKE ME --
FIRE?
KRAASH!
YAAAAH!
FZZZZZZZZ!
IT'S A SOMNA-NET, THEY'LL BE OUT COLD FOR HOURS. GOOD WORK, RED!
OH... HEY, NO PROBLEM...
WE'D BEST KEEP MOVIN'. MY DIGS ARE STILL A GOOD STRETCH AWAY...
WAIT! WHAT THE HECK IS THAT?

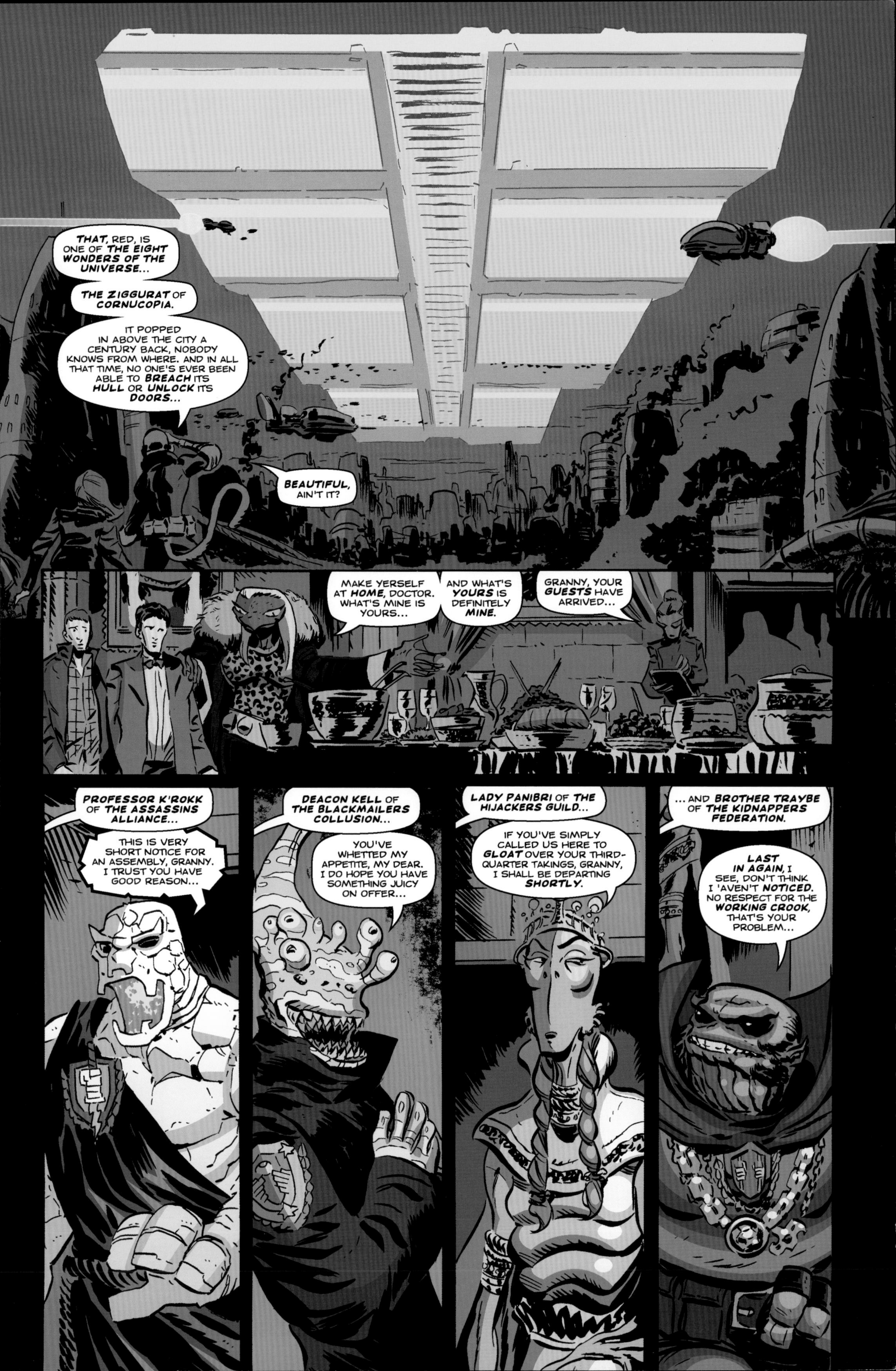
THAT, RED, IS ONE OF THE EIGHT WONDERS OF THE UNIVERSE...
THE ZIGGURAT OF CORNUCOPIA.
IT POPPED IN ABOVE THE CITY A CENTURY BACK, NOBODY KNOWS FROM WHERE. AND IN ALL THAT TIME, NO ONE'S EVER BEEN ABLE TO BREACH ITS HULL OR UNLOCK ITS DOORS...
BEAUTIFUL, AIN'T IT?
MAKE YERSELF AT HOME, DOCTOR. WHAT'S MINE IS YOURS...
AND WHAT'S YOURS IS DEFINITELY MINE.
GRANNY, YOUR GUESTS HAVE ARRIVED...
PROFESSOR K'ROKK OF THE ASSASSINS ALLIANCE...
THIS IS VERY SHORT NOTICE FOR AN ASSEMBLY, GRANNY. I TRUST YOU HAVE GOOD REASON...
DEACON KELL OF THE BLACKMAILERS COLLUSION...
YOU'VE WHETTED MY APPETITE, MY DEAR. I DO HOPE YOU HAVE SOMETHING JUICY ON OFFER...
LADY PANIBRI OF THE HIJACKERS GUILD...
IF YOU'VE SIMPLY CALLED US HERE TO GLOAT OVER YOUR THIRD-QUARTER TAKINGS, GRANNY, I SHALL BE DEPARTING SHORTLY.
...AND BROTHER TRAYBE OF THE KIDNAPPERS FEDERATION.
LAST IN AGAIN, I SEE, DON'T THINK I 'AVEN'T NOTICED. NO RESPECT FOR THE WORKING CROOK, THAT'S YOUR PROBLEM...

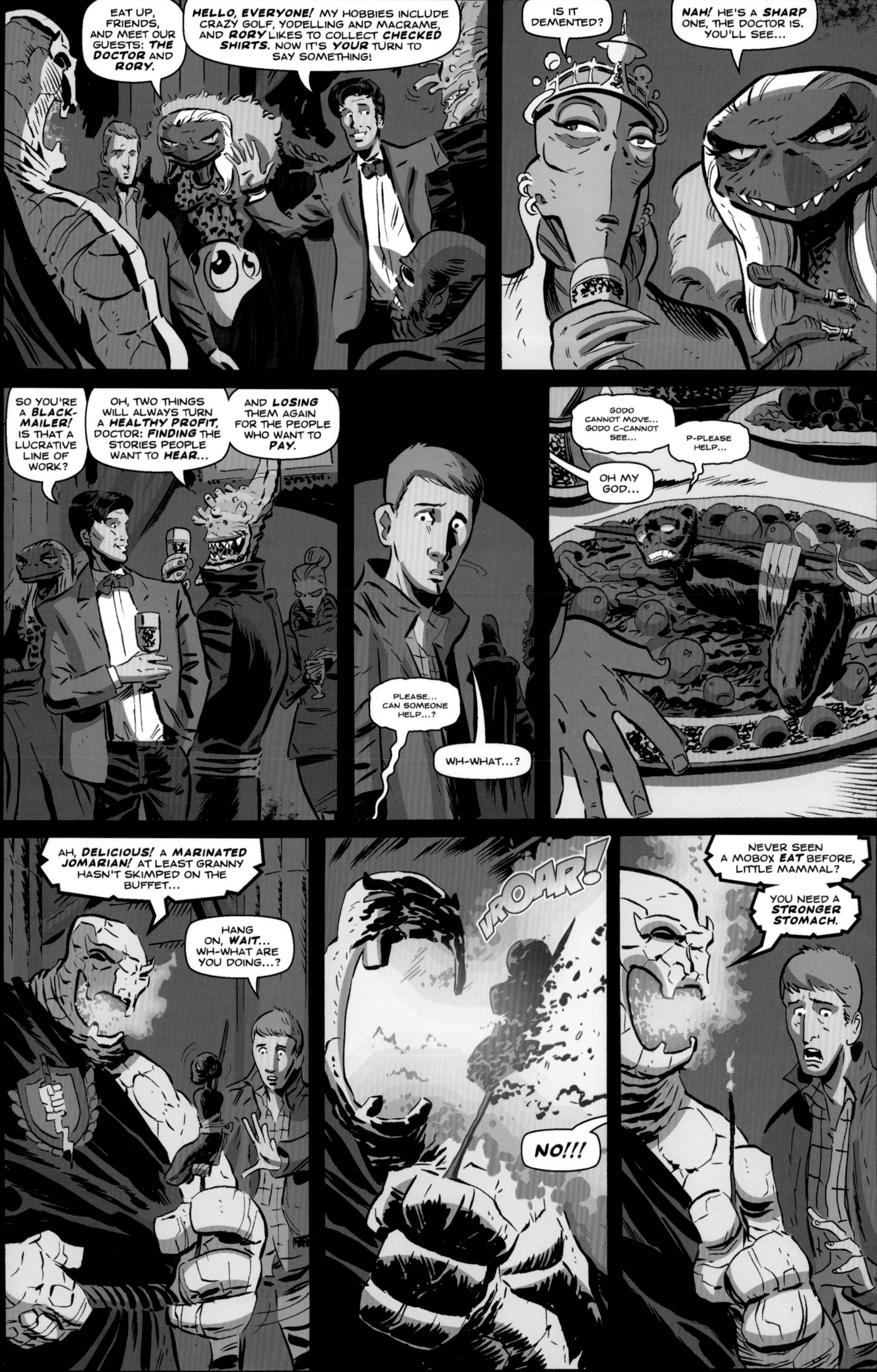
EAT UP, FRIENDS, AND MEET OUR GUESTS: THE DOCTOR AND RORY.
HELLO, EVERYONE! MY HOBBIES INCLUDE CRAZY GOLF, YODELLING AND MACRAME, AND RORY LIKES TO COLLECT CHECKED SHIRTS. NOW IT'S YOUR TURN TO SAY SOMETHING!
IS IT DEMENTED?
NAH! HE'S A SHARP ONE, THE DOCTOR IS. YOU'LL SEE...
SO YOU'RE A BLACK-MAILER! IS THAT A LUCRATIVE LINE OF WORK?
OH, TWO THINGS WILL ALWAYS TURN A HEALTHY PROFIT, DOCTOR: FINDING THE STORIES PEOPLE WANT TO HEAR...
AND LOSING THEM AGAIN FOR THE PEOPLE WHO WANT TO PAY.
PLEASE... CAN SOMEONE HELP...?
WH-WHAT...?
GODO CANNOT MOVE... GODO C-CANNOT SEE...
P-PLEASE HELP...
OH MY GOD...
AH, DELICIOUS! A MARINATED JOMARIAN! AT LEAST GRANNY HASN'T SKIMPED ON THE BUFFET...
HANG ON, WAIT... WH-WHAT ARE YOU DOING...?
UROAR!
NO!!!
NEVER SEEN A MOBOX EAT BEFORE, LITTLE MAMMAL?
YOU NEED A STRONGER STOMACH.

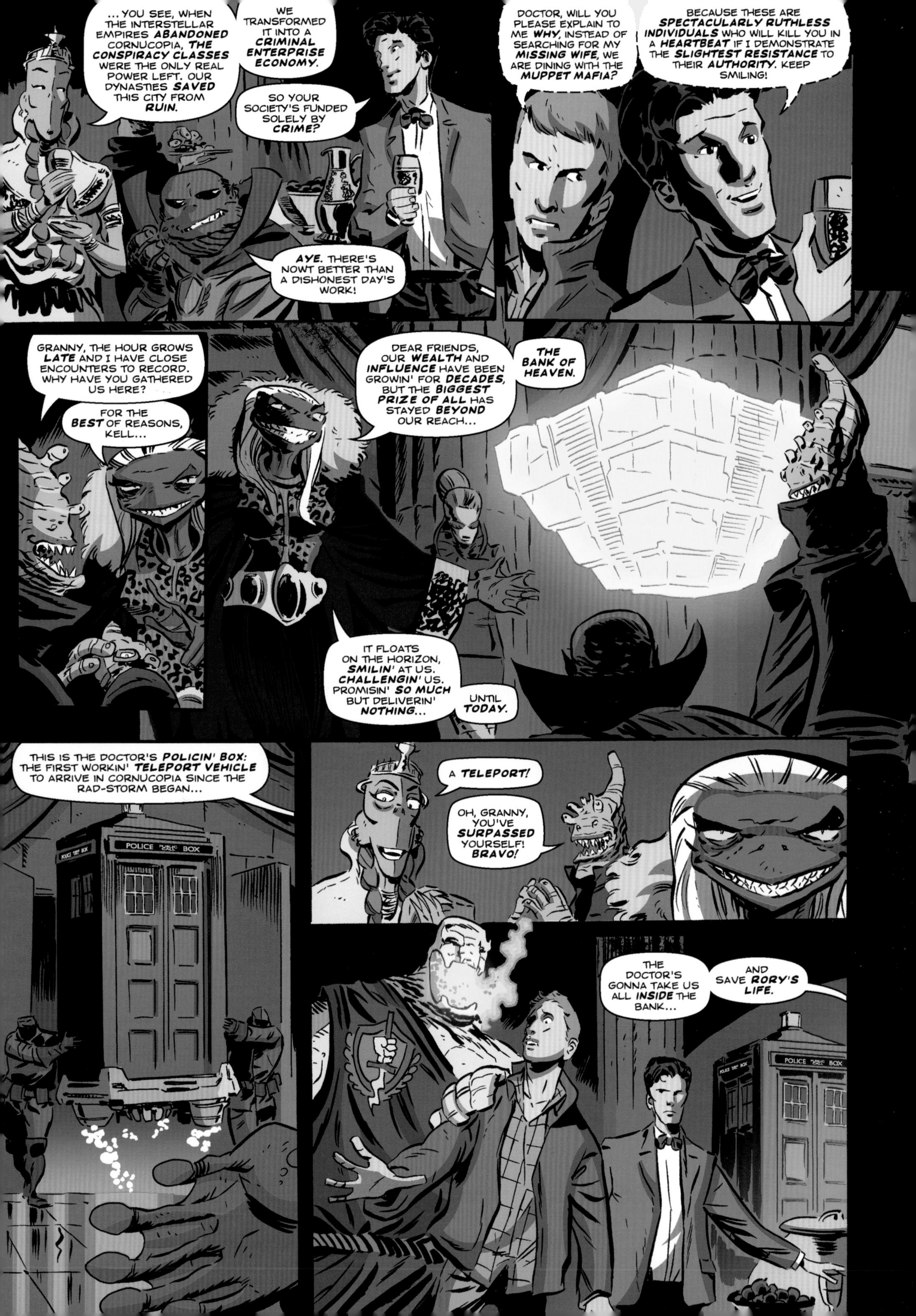
...YOU SEE, WHEN THE INTERSTELLAR EMPIRES ABANDONED CORNUCOPIA, THE CONSPIRACY CLASSES WERE THE ONLY REAL POWER LEFT. OUR DYNASTIES SAVED THIS CITY FROM RUIN.
WE TRANSFORMED IT INTO A CRIMINAL ENTERPRISE ECONOMY.
SO YOUR SOCIETY'S FUNDED SOLELY BY CRIME?
AYE. THERE'S NOWT BETTER THAN A DISHONEST DAY'S WORK!
DOCTOR, WILL YOU PLEASE EXPLAIN TO ME WHY, INSTEAD OF SEARCHING FOR MY MISSING WIFE, WE ARE DINING WITH THE MUPPET MAFIA?
BECAUSE THESE ARE SPECTACULARLY RUTHLESS INDIVIDUALS WHO WILL KILL YOU IN A HEARTBEAT IF I DEMONSTRATE THE SLIGHTEST RESISTANCE TO THEIR AUTHORITY. KEEP SMILING!
GRANNY, THE HOUR GROWS LATE AND I HAVE CLOSE ENCOUNTERS TO RECORD. WHY HAVE YOU GATHERED US HERE?
FOR THE BEST OF REASONS, KELL...
DEAR FRIENDS, OUR WEALTH AND INFLUENCE HAVE BEEN GROWIN' FOR DECADES, BUT THE BIGGEST PRIZE OF ALL HAS STAYED BEYOND OUR REACH...
THE BANK OF HEAVEN.
IT FLOATS ON THE HORIZON, SMILIN' AT US. CHALLENGIN' US. PROMISIN' SO MUCH BUT DELIVERIN' NOTHING...
UNTIL TODAY.
THIS IS THE DOCTOR'S POLICIN' BOX: THE FIRST WORKIN' TELEPORT VEHICLE TO ARRIVE IN CORNUCOPIA SINCE THE RAD-STORM BEGAN...
POLICE PUBLIC CALL BOX
A TELEPORT!
OH, GRANNY, YOU'VE SURPASSED YOURSELF! BRAVO!
THE DOCTOR'S GONNA TAKE US ALL INSIDE THE BANK...
AND SAVE RORY'S LIFE.
POLICE PUBLIC CALL BOX

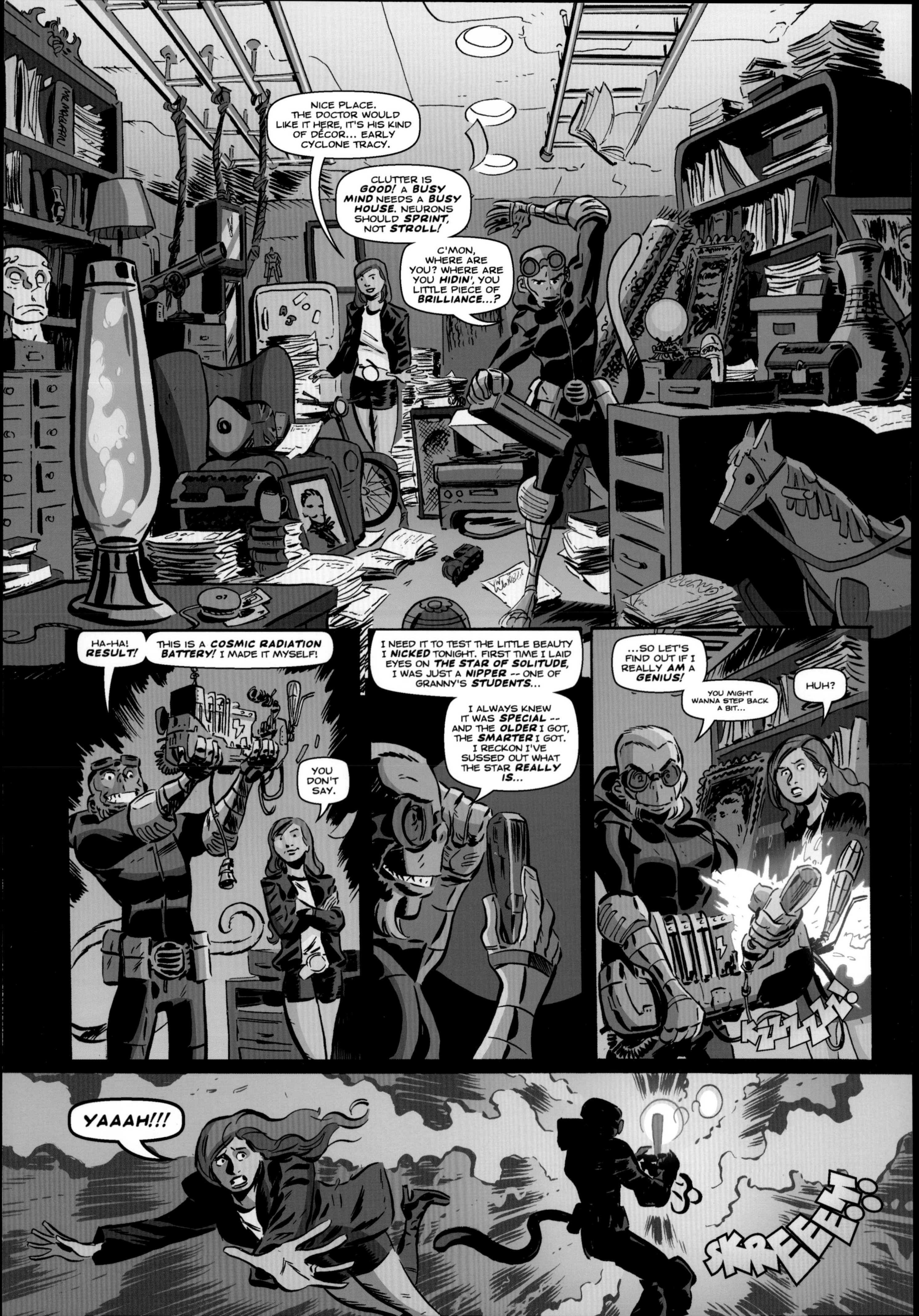
NICE PLACE. THE DOCTOR WOULD LIKE IT HERE, IT'S HIS KIND OF DÉCOR... EARLY CYCLONE TRACY.
CLUTTER IS GOOD! A BUSY MIND NEEDS A BUSY HOUSE. NEURONS SHOULD SPRINT, NOT STROLL!
C'MON, WHERE ARE YOU? WHERE ARE YOU HIDIN', YOU LITTLE PIECE OF BRILLIANCE...?
HA-HA! RESULT!
THIS IS A COSMIC RADIATION BATTERY! I MADE IT MYSELF!
YOU DON'T SAY.
I NEED IT TO TEST THE LITTLE BEAUTY I NICKED TONIGHT. FIRST TIME I LAID EYES ON THE STAR OF SOLITUDE, I WAS JUST A NIPPER -- ONE OF GRANNY'S STUDENTS...
I ALWAYS KNEW IT WAS SPECIAL -- AND THE OLDER I GOT, THE SMARTER I GOT. I RECKON I'VE SUSSED OUT WHAT THE STAR REALLY IS...
...SO LET'S FIND OUT IF I REALLY AM A GENIUS!
YOU MIGHT WANNA STEP BACK A BIT...
HUH?
KZZZZT!
YAAAH!!!
SKREEEEM...

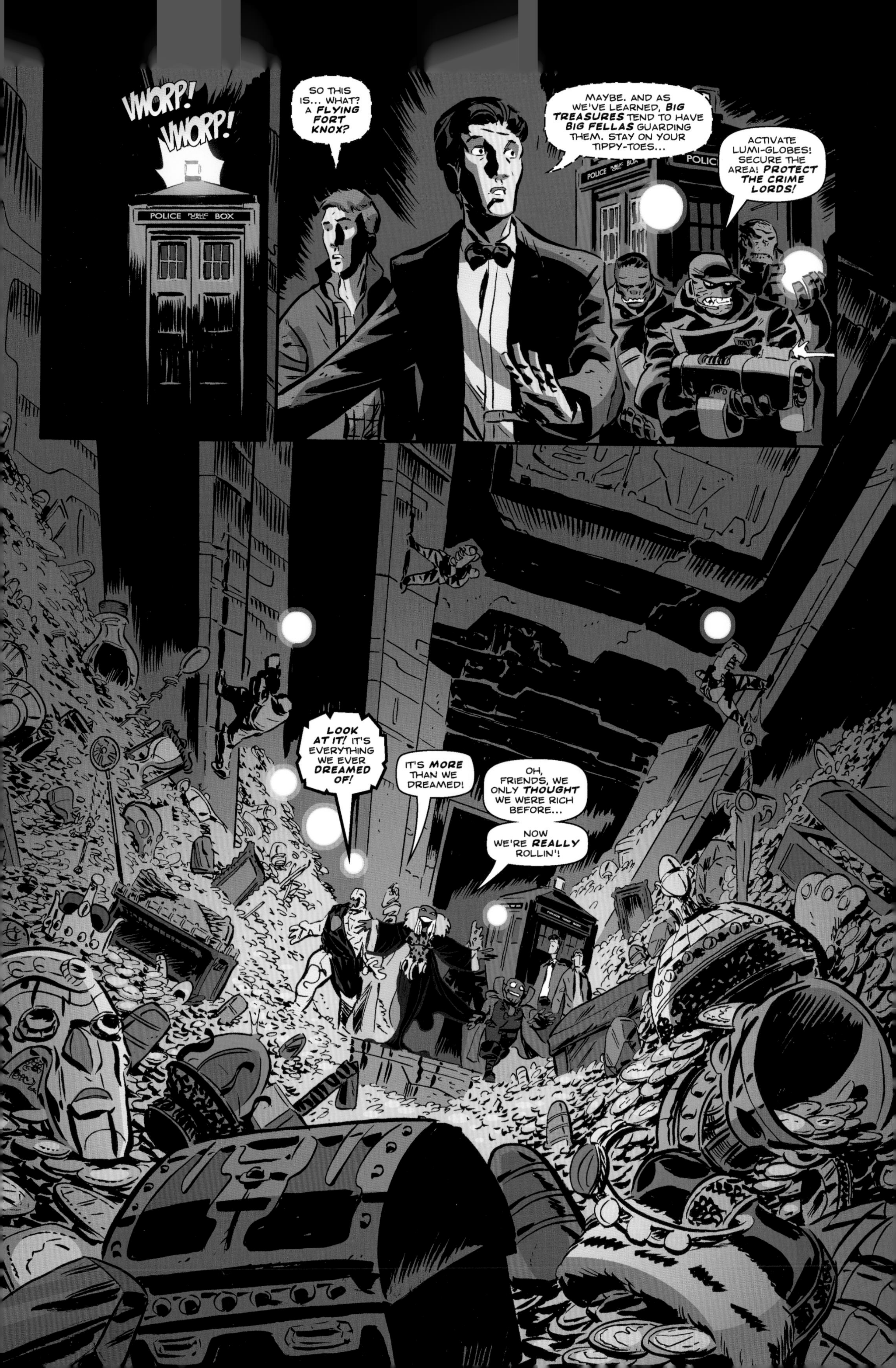
VWORP! VWORP!
POLICE PUBLIC CALL BOX
SO THIS IS... WHAT? A FLYING FORT KNOX?
MAYBE. AND AS WE'VE LEARNED, BIG TREASURES TEND TO HAVE BIG FELLAS GUARDING THEM. STAY ON YOUR TIPPY-TOES...
ACTIVATE LUMI-GLOBES! SECURE THE AREA! PROTECT THE CRIME LORDS!
LOOK AT IT! IT'S EVERYTHING WE EVER DREAMED OF!
IT'S MORE THAN WE DREAMED!
OH, FRIENDS, WE ONLY THOUGHT WE WERE RICH BEFORE...
NOW WE'RE REALLY ROLLIN'!

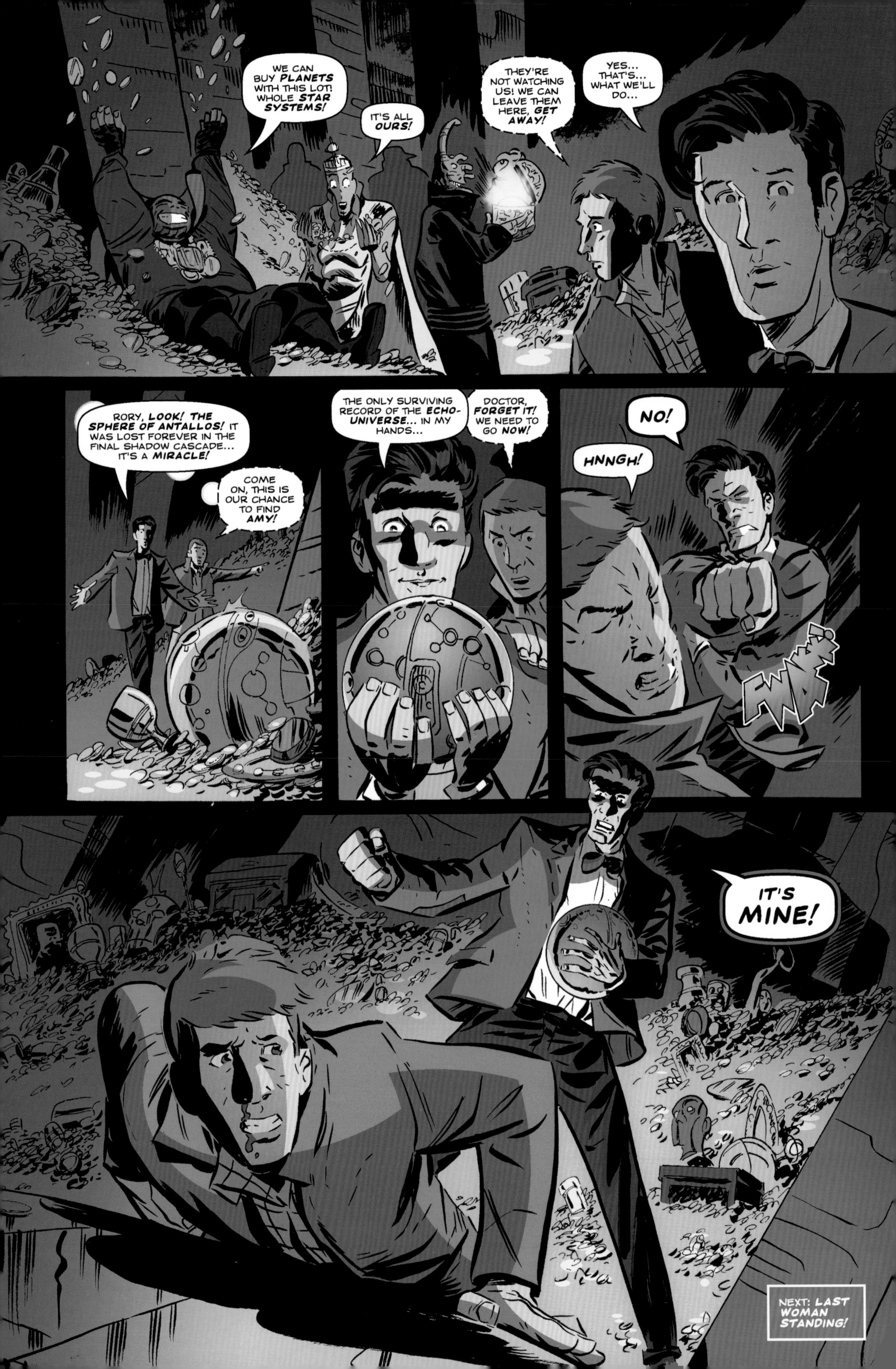
WE CAN BUY **PLANETS** WITH THIS LOT! WHOLE **STAR SYSTEMS!**
IT'S ALL **OURS!**
THEY'RE NOT WATCHING US! WE CAN LEAVE THEM HERE, **GET AWAY!**
YES... THAT'S... WHAT WE'LL DO...
RORY, **LOOK! THE SPHERE OF ANTALLOS!** IT WAS LOST FOREVER IN THE FINAL SHADOW CASCADE... IT'S A **MIRACLE!**
COME ON, THIS IS OUR CHANCE TO FIND **AMY!**
THE ONLY SURVIVING RECORD OF THE **ECHO-UNIVERSE...** IN MY HANDS...
DOCTOR, **FORGET IT!** WE NEED TO GO **NOW!**
NO!
HNNGH!
FWAM!
IT'S MINE!
NEXT: **LAST WOMAN STANDING!**

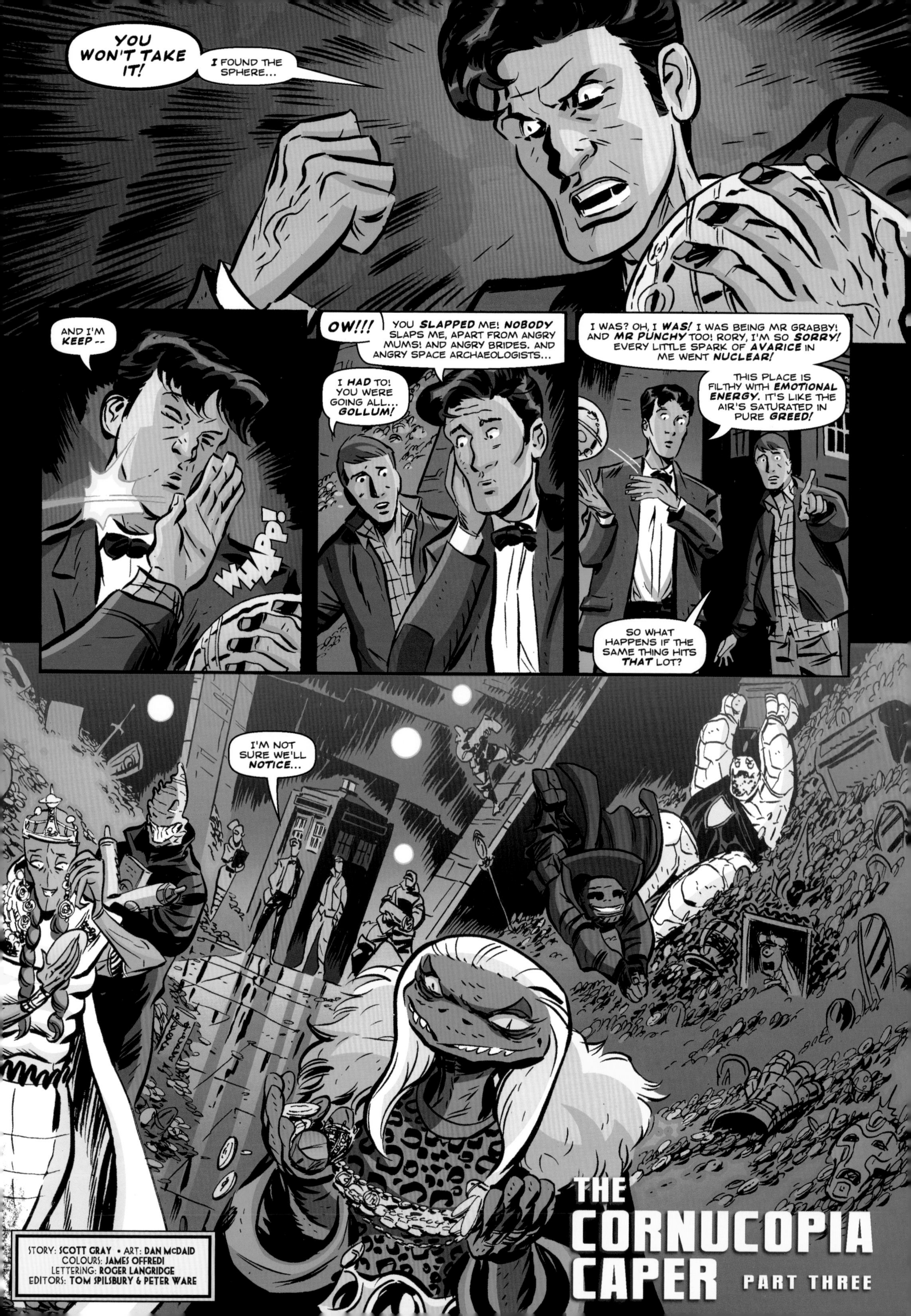
YOU WON'T TAKE IT!
I FOUND THE SPHERE...
AND I'M KEEP --
WHAPP!
OW!!!
YOU SLAPPED ME! NOBODY SLAPS ME, APART FROM ANGRY MUMS! AND ANGRY BRIDES. AND ANGRY SPACE ARCHAEOLOGISTS...
I HAD TO! YOU WERE GOING ALL... GOLLUM!
I WAS? OH, I WAS! I WAS BEING MR GRABBY! AND MR PUNCHY TOO! RORY, I'M SO SORRY! EVERY LITTLE SPARK OF AVARICE IN ME WENT NUCLEAR!
THIS PLACE IS FILTHY WITH EMOTIONAL ENERGY. IT'S LIKE THE AIR'S SATURATED IN PURE GREED!
SO WHAT HAPPENS IF THE SAME THING HITS THAT LOT?
I'M NOT SURE WE'LL NOTICE...
STORY: SCOTT GRAY • ART: DAN McDAID
COLOURS: JAMES OFFREDI
LETTERING: ROGER LANGRIDGE
EDITORS: TOM SPILSBURY & PETER WARE
THE CORNUCOPIA CAPER PART THREE

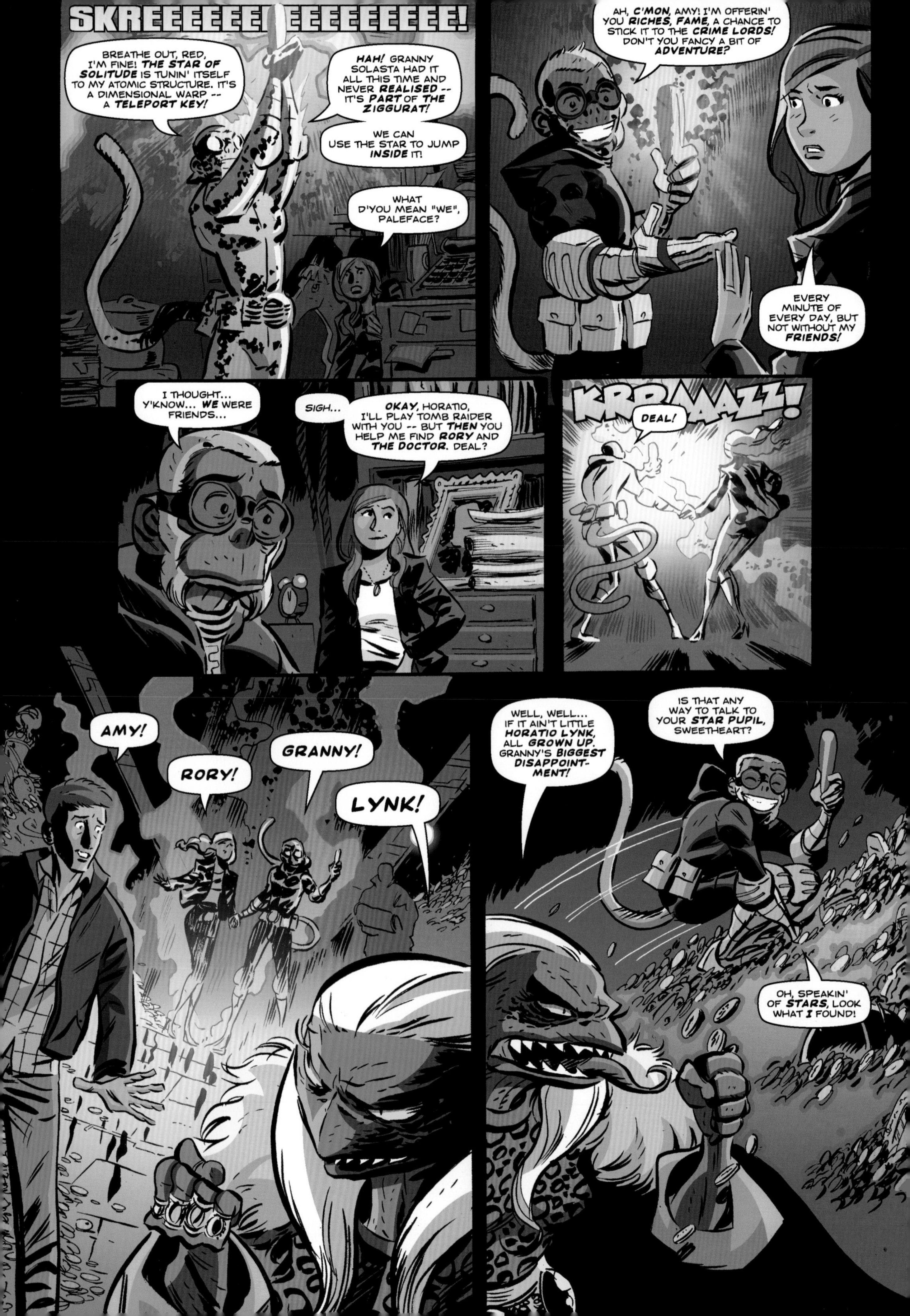
SKREEEEEEEEEEEEEEEEEE!
BREATHE OUT, RED, I'M FINE! **THE STAR OF SOLITUDE** IS TUNIN' ITSELF TO MY ATOMIC STRUCTURE. IT'S A DIMENSIONAL WARP -- A **TELEPORT KEY!**
HAH! GRANNY SOLASTA HAD IT ALL THIS TIME AND NEVER **REALISED** -- IT'S **PART** OF **THE ZIGGURAT!**
WE CAN USE THE STAR TO JUMP **INSIDE** IT!
WHAT D'YOU MEAN "WE", PALEFACE?
AH, **C'MON**, AMY! I'M OFFERIN' YOU **RICHES, FAME**, A CHANCE TO STICK IT TO THE **CRIME LORDS!** DON'T YOU FANCY A BIT OF **ADVENTURE?**
EVERY MINUTE OF EVERY DAY, BUT NOT WITHOUT MY **FRIENDS!**
I THOUGHT... Y'KNOW... **WE** WERE FRIENDS...
SIGH...
OKAY, HORATIO, I'LL PLAY TOMB RAIDER WITH YOU -- BUT **THEN** YOU HELP ME FIND **RORY** AND **THE DOCTOR**. DEAL?
KRRAAAZZ!
DEAL!
AMY!
RORY!
GRANNY!
LYNK!
WELL, WELL... IF IT AIN'T LITTLE **HORATIO LYNK**, ALL **GROWN UP**. GRANNY'S **BIGGEST DISAPPOINT-MENT!**
IS THAT ANY WAY TO TALK TO YOUR **STAR PUPIL**, SWEETHEART?
OH, SPEAKIN' OF **STARS**, LOOK WHAT **I** FOUND!

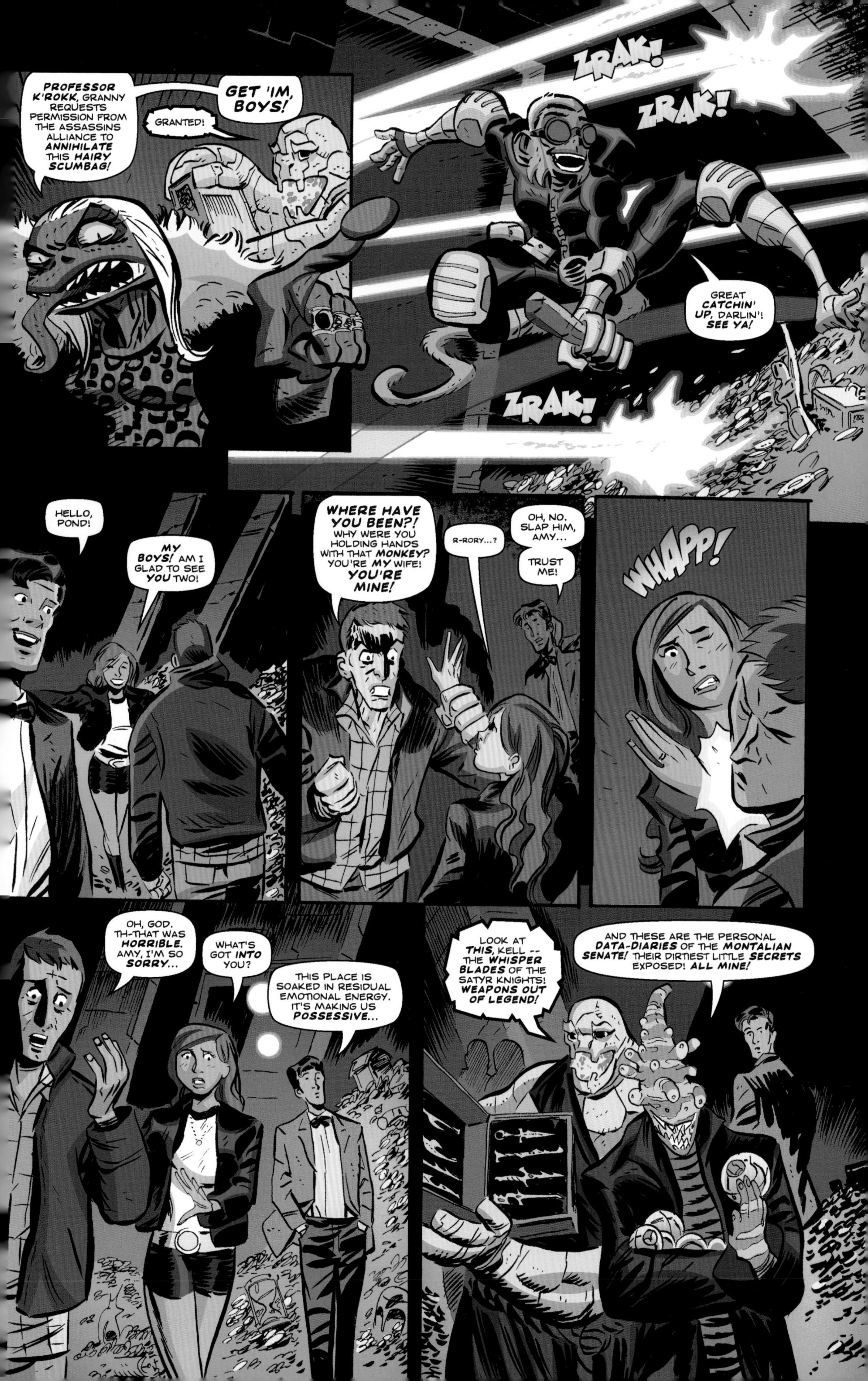

PROFESSOR K'ROKK, GRANNY REQUESTS PERMISSION FROM THE ASSASSINS ALLIANCE TO ANNIHILATE THIS HAIRY SCUMBAG!
GET 'IM, BOYS!
GRANTED!
ZRAK!
ZRAK!
GREAT CATCHIN' UP, DARLIN'! SEE YA!
ZRAK!
HELLO, POND!
MY BOYS! AM I GLAD TO SEE YOU TWO!
WHERE HAVE YOU BEEN?! WHY WERE YOU HOLDING HANDS WITH THAT MONKEY? YOU'RE MY WIFE! YOU'RE MINE!
R-RORY...?
OH, NO. SLAP HIM, AMY...
TRUST ME!
WHAPP!
OH, GOD. TH-THAT WAS HORRIBLE. AMY, I'M SO SORRY...
WHAT'S GOT INTO YOU?
THIS PLACE IS SOAKED IN RESIDUAL EMOTIONAL ENERGY. IT'S MAKING US POSSESSIVE...
LOOK AT THIS, KELL -- THE WHISPER BLADES OF THE SATYR KNIGHTS! WEAPONS OUT OF LEGEND!
AND THESE ARE THE PERSONAL DATA-DIARIES OF THE MONTALIAN SENATE! THEIR DIRTIEST LITTLE SECRETS EXPOSED! ALL MINE!

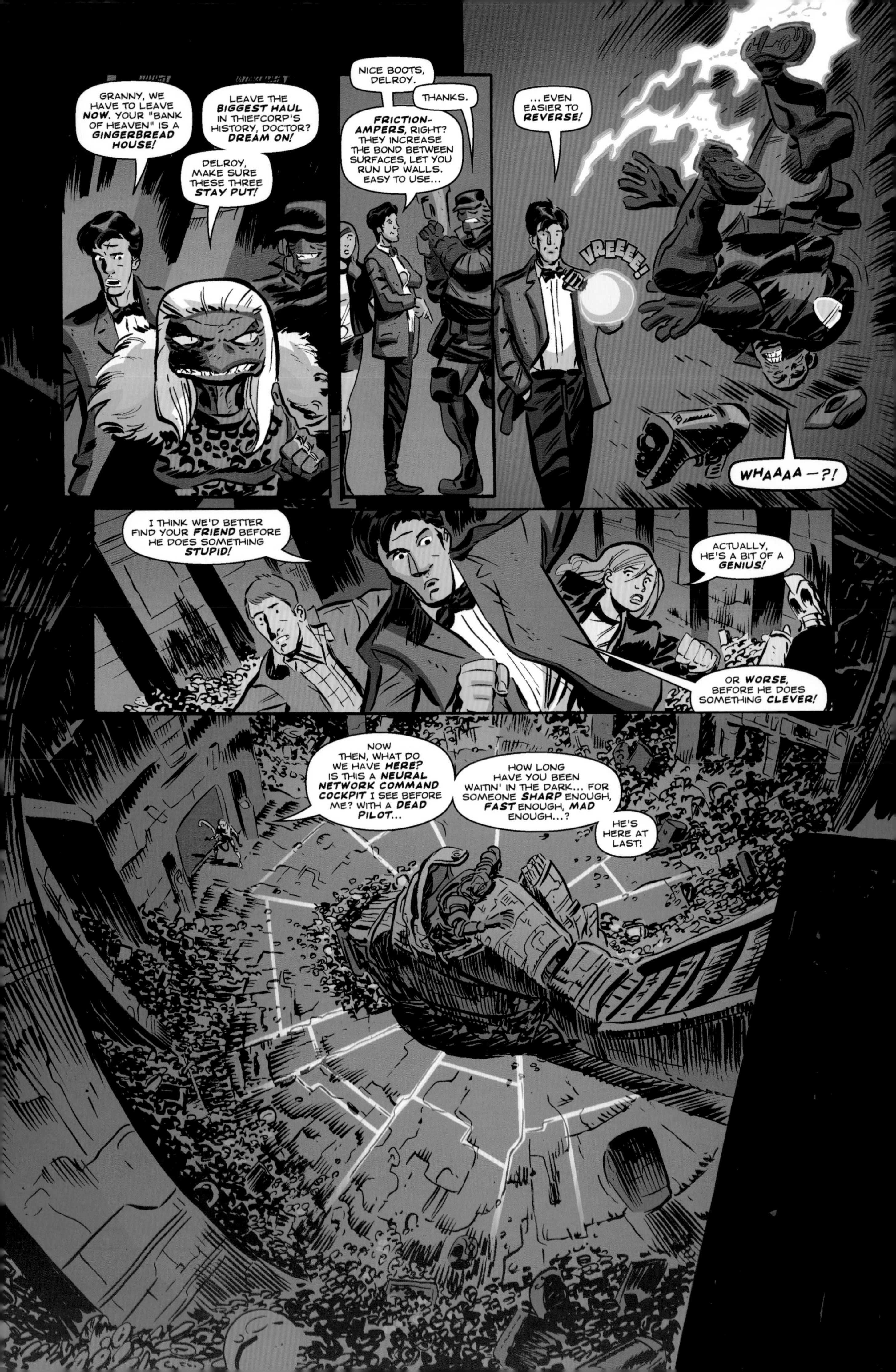
GRANNY, WE HAVE TO LEAVE NOW. YOUR "BANK OF HEAVEN" IS A GINGERBREAD HOUSE!
LEAVE THE BIGGEST HAUL IN THIEFCORP'S HISTORY, DOCTOR? DREAM ON!
DELROY, MAKE SURE THESE THREE STAY PUT!
NICE BOOTS, DELROY.
THANKS.
FRICTION-AMPERS, RIGHT? THEY INCREASE THE BOND BETWEEN SURFACES, LET YOU RUN UP WALLS. EASY TO USE...
... EVEN EASIER TO REVERSE!
VREEEE!
WHAAAA—?!
I THINK WE'D BETTER FIND YOUR FRIEND BEFORE HE DOES SOMETHING STUPID!
ACTUALLY, HE'S A BIT OF A GENIUS!
OR WORSE, BEFORE HE DOES SOMETHING CLEVER!
NOW THEN, WHAT DO WE HAVE HERE? IS THIS A NEURAL NETWORK COMMAND COCKPIT I SEE BEFORE ME? WITH A DEAD PILOT...
HOW LONG HAVE YOU BEEN WAITIN' IN THE DARK... FOR SOMEONE SHARP ENOUGH, FAST ENOUGH, MAD ENOUGH...?
HE'S HERE AT LAST!

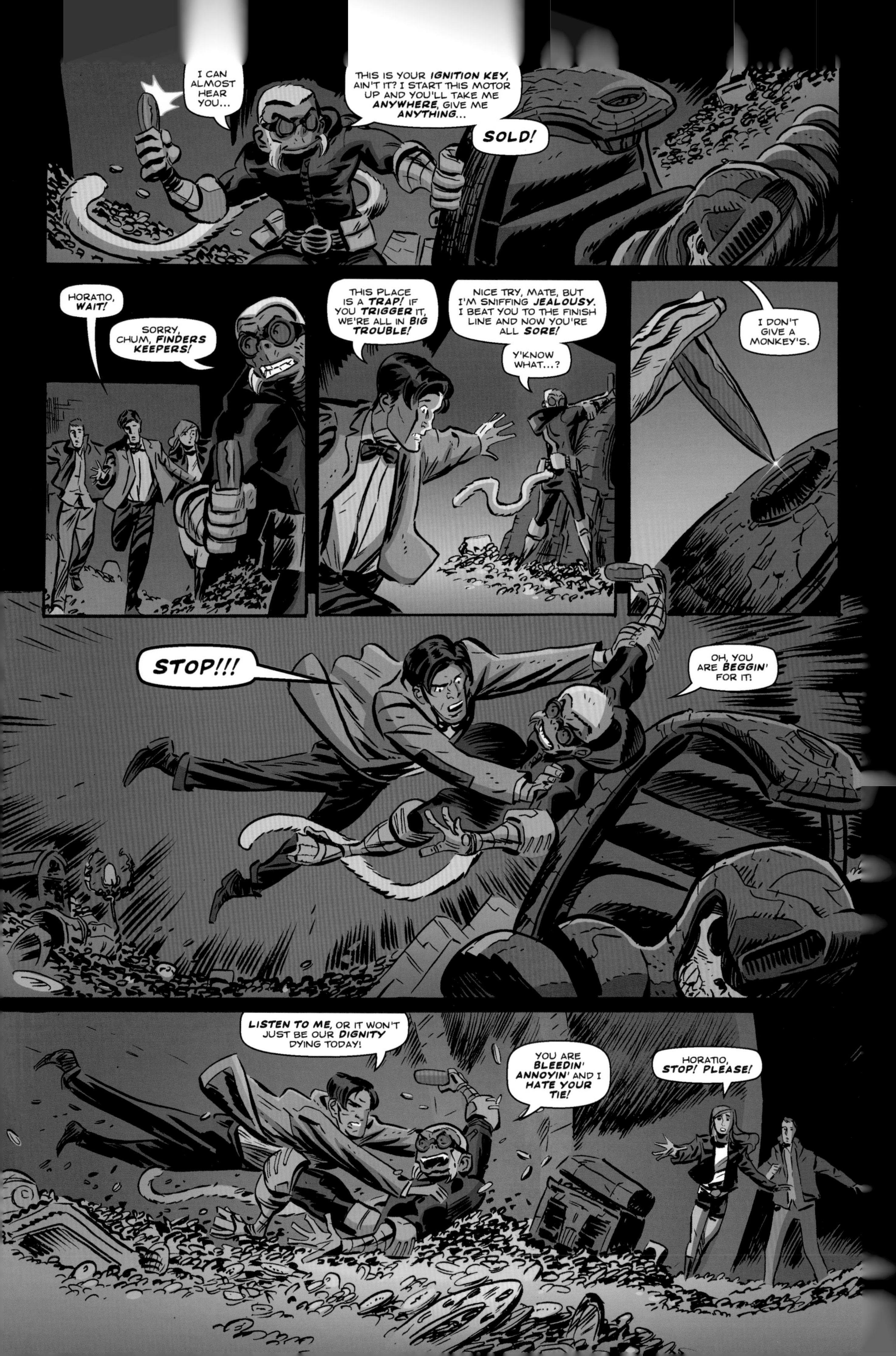
I CAN ALMOST HEAR YOU...
THIS IS YOUR IGNITION KEY, AIN'T IT? I START THIS MOTOR UP AND YOU'LL TAKE ME ANYWHERE, GIVE ME ANYTHING...
SOLD!
HORATIO, WAIT!
SORRY, CHUM, FINDERS KEEPERS!
THIS PLACE IS A TRAP! IF YOU TRIGGER IT, WE'RE ALL IN BIG TROUBLE!
NICE TRY, MATE, BUT I'M SNIFFING JEALOUSY. I BEAT YOU TO THE FINISH LINE AND NOW YOU'RE ALL SORE!
Y'KNOW WHAT...?
I DON'T GIVE A MONKEY'S.
STOP!!!
OH, YOU ARE BEGGIN' FOR IT!
LISTEN TO ME, OR IT WON'T JUST BE OUR DIGNITY DYING TODAY!
YOU ARE BLEEDIN' ANNOYIN' AND I HATE YOUR TIE!
HORATIO, STOP! PLEASE!

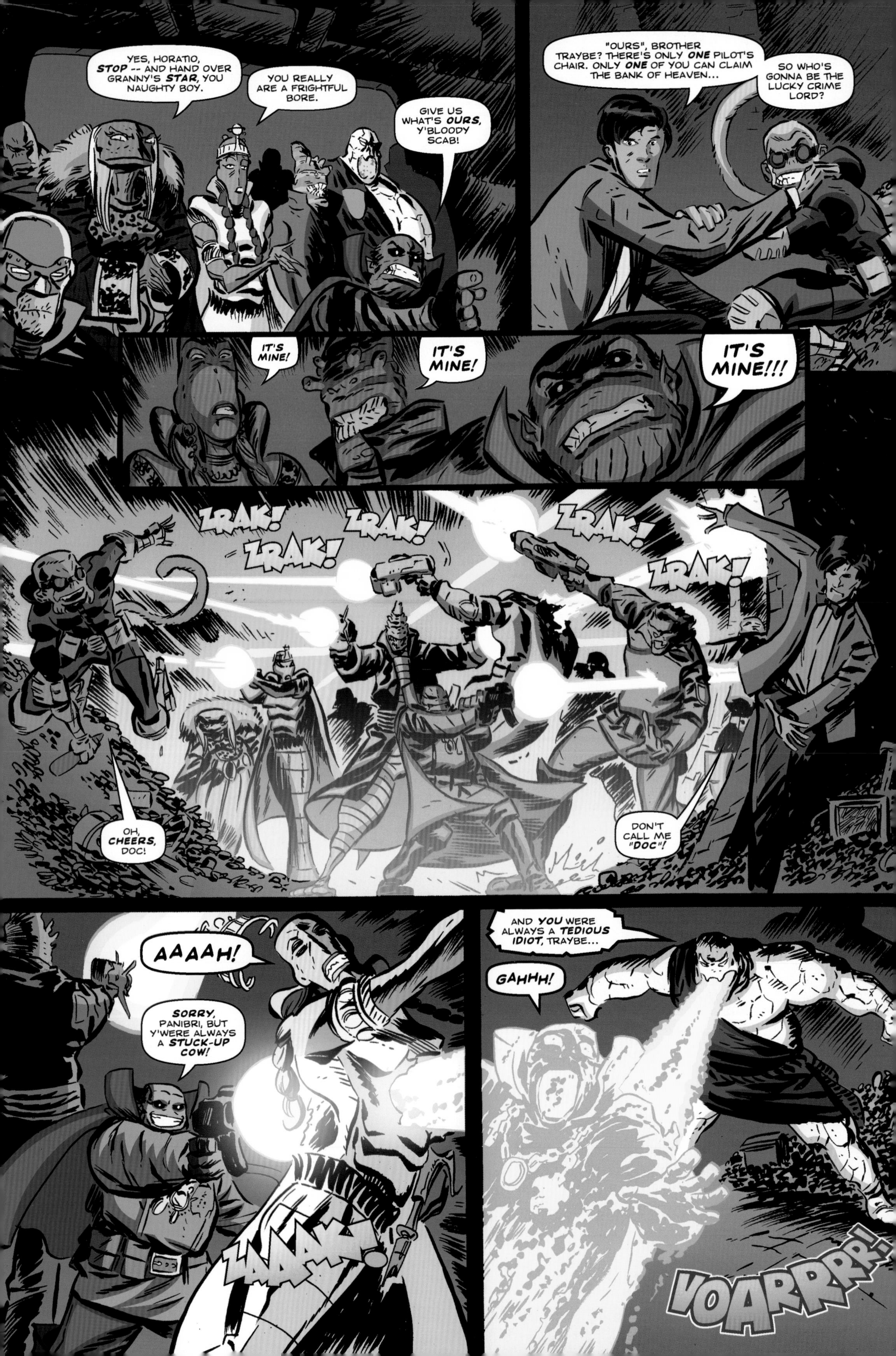
YES, HORATIO, STOP -- AND HAND OVER GRANNY'S STAR, YOU NAUGHTY BOY.
YOU REALLY ARE A FRIGHTFUL BORE.
GIVE US WHAT'S OURS, Y'BLOODY SCAB!
"OURS", BROTHER TRAYBE? THERE'S ONLY ONE PILOT'S CHAIR. ONLY ONE OF YOU CAN CLAIM THE BANK OF HEAVEN...
SO WHO'S GONNA BE THE LUCKY CRIME LORD?
IT'S MINE!
IT'S MINE!
IT'S MINE!!!
ZRAK!
ZRAK!
ZRAK!
ZRAK!
ZRAK!
OH, CHEERS, DOC!
DON'T CALL ME "DOC"!
AAAAH!
SORRY, PANIBRI, BUT Y'WERE ALWAYS A STUCK-UP COW!
AND YOU WERE ALWAYS A TEDIOUS IDIOT, TRAYBE...
GAHHH!
VOARRRR!

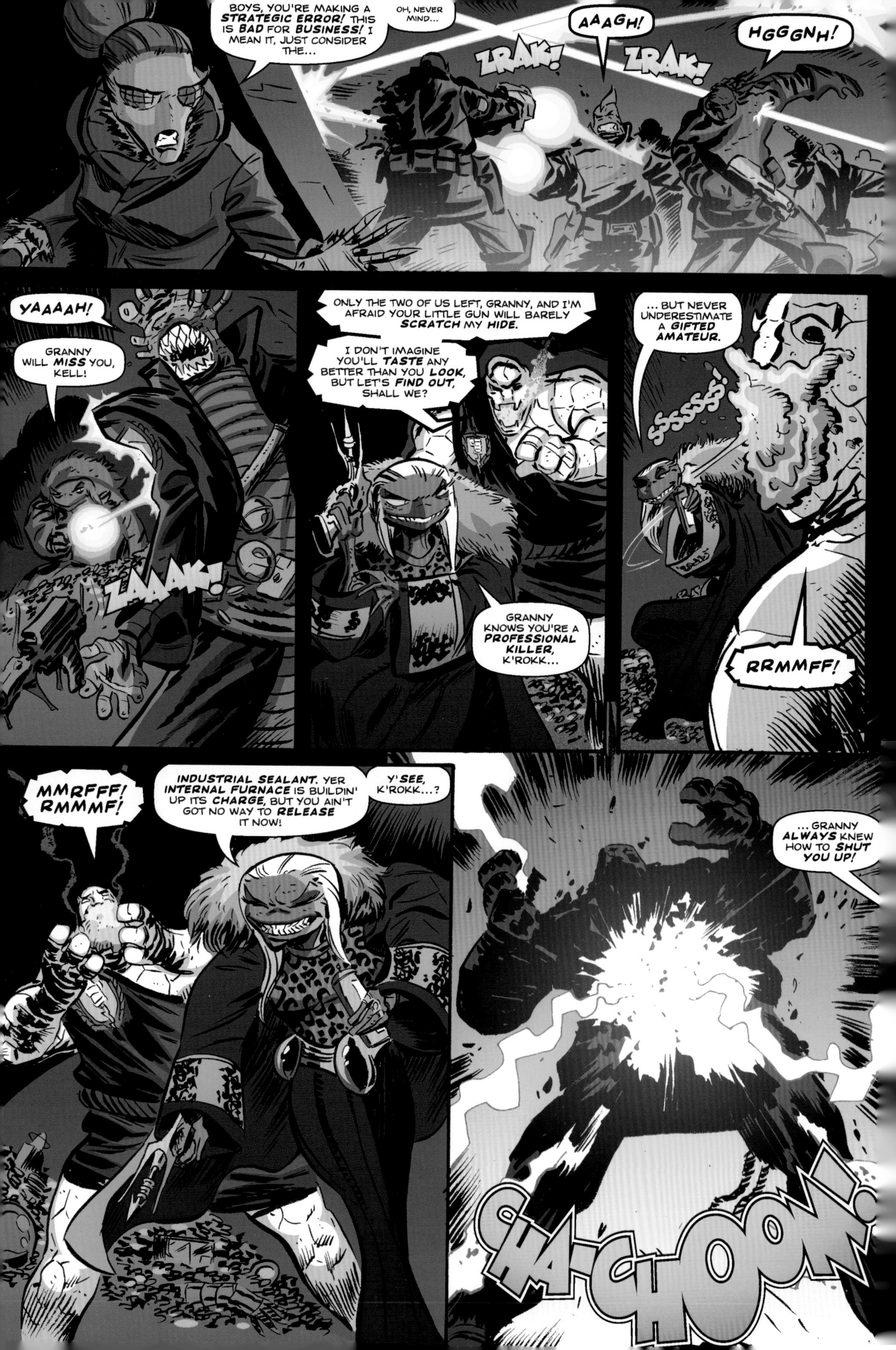
BOYS, YOU'RE MAKING A STRATEGIC ERROR! THIS IS BAD FOR BUSINESS! I MEAN IT, JUST CONSIDER THE...
OH, NEVER MIND...
ZRAK!
AAAGH!
ZRAK!
HGGGNH!
YAAAAH!
GRANNY WILL MISS YOU, KELL!
ZAAAK!
ONLY THE TWO OF US LEFT, GRANNY, AND I'M AFRAID YOUR LITTLE GUN WILL BARELY SCRATCH MY HIDE.
I DON'T IMAGINE YOU'LL TASTE ANY BETTER THAN YOU LOOK, BUT LET'S FIND OUT, SHALL WE?
GRANNY KNOWS YOU'RE A PROFESSIONAL KILLER, K'ROKK...
...BUT NEVER UNDERESTIMATE A GIFTED AMATEUR.
SSSSSS!
RRMMFF!
MMRFFF! RMMMF!
INDUSTRIAL SEALANT. YER INTERNAL FURNACE IS BUILDIN' UP ITS CHARGE, BUT YOU AIN'T GOT NO WAY TO RELEASE IT NOW!
Y'SEE, K'ROKK...?
...GRANNY ALWAYS KNEW HOW TO SHUT YOU UP!
SHA-CHOOM!

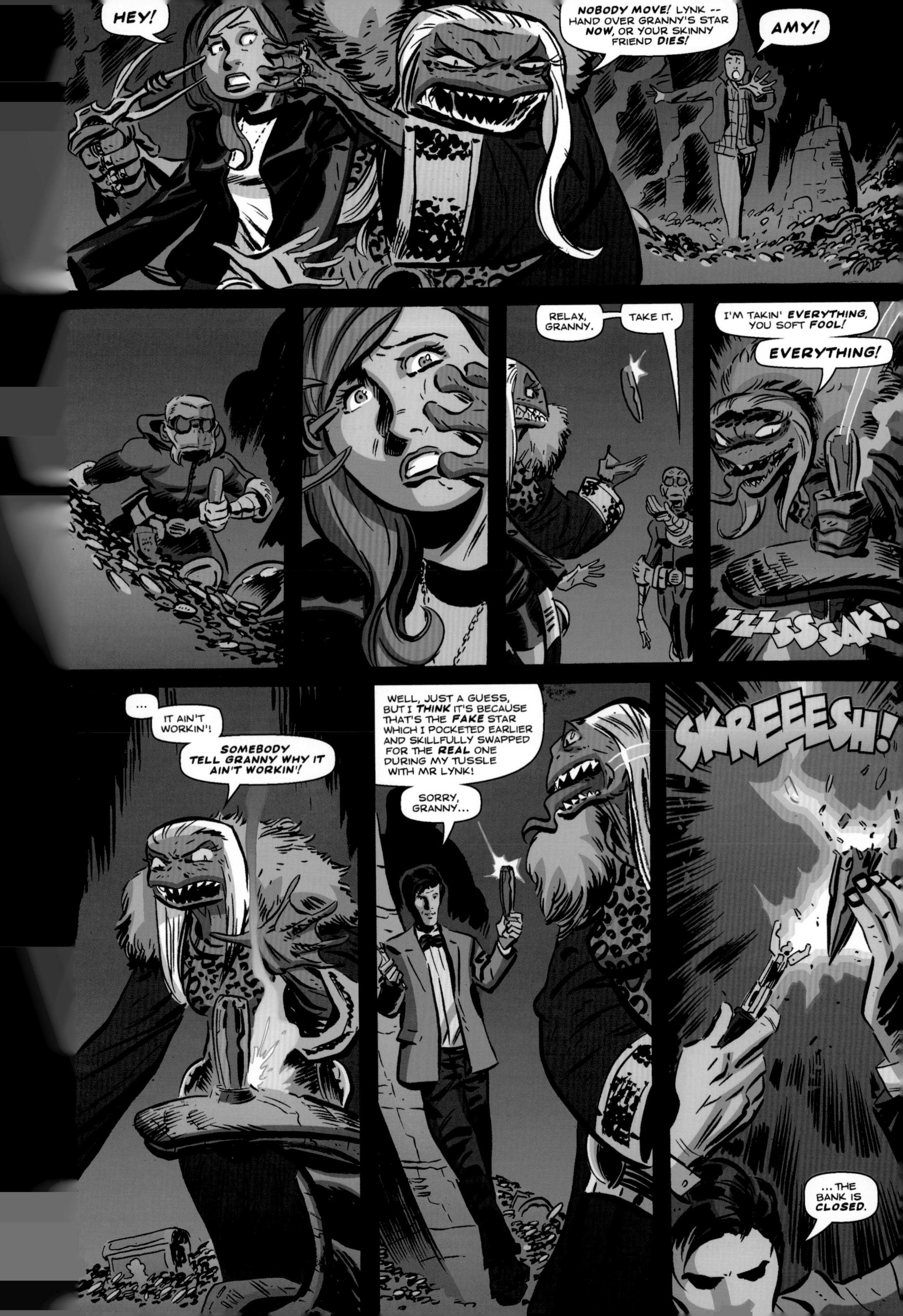
HEY!
NOBODY MOVE! LYNK -- HAND OVER GRANNY'S STAR NOW, OR YOUR SKINNY FRIEND DIES!
AMY!
RELAX, GRANNY.
TAKE IT.
I'M TAKIN' EVERYTHING, YOU SOFT FOOL!
EVERYTHING!
ZZZSSSAK!
...
IT AIN'T WORKIN'!
SOMEBODY TELL GRANNY WHY IT AIN'T WORKIN'!
WELL, JUST A GUESS, BUT I THINK IT'S BECAUSE THAT'S THE FAKE STAR WHICH I POCKETED EARLIER AND SKILLFULLY SWAPPED FOR THE REAL ONE DURING MY TUSSLE WITH MR LYNK!
SORRY, GRANNY...
SKREEEESH!
... THE BANK IS CLOSED.

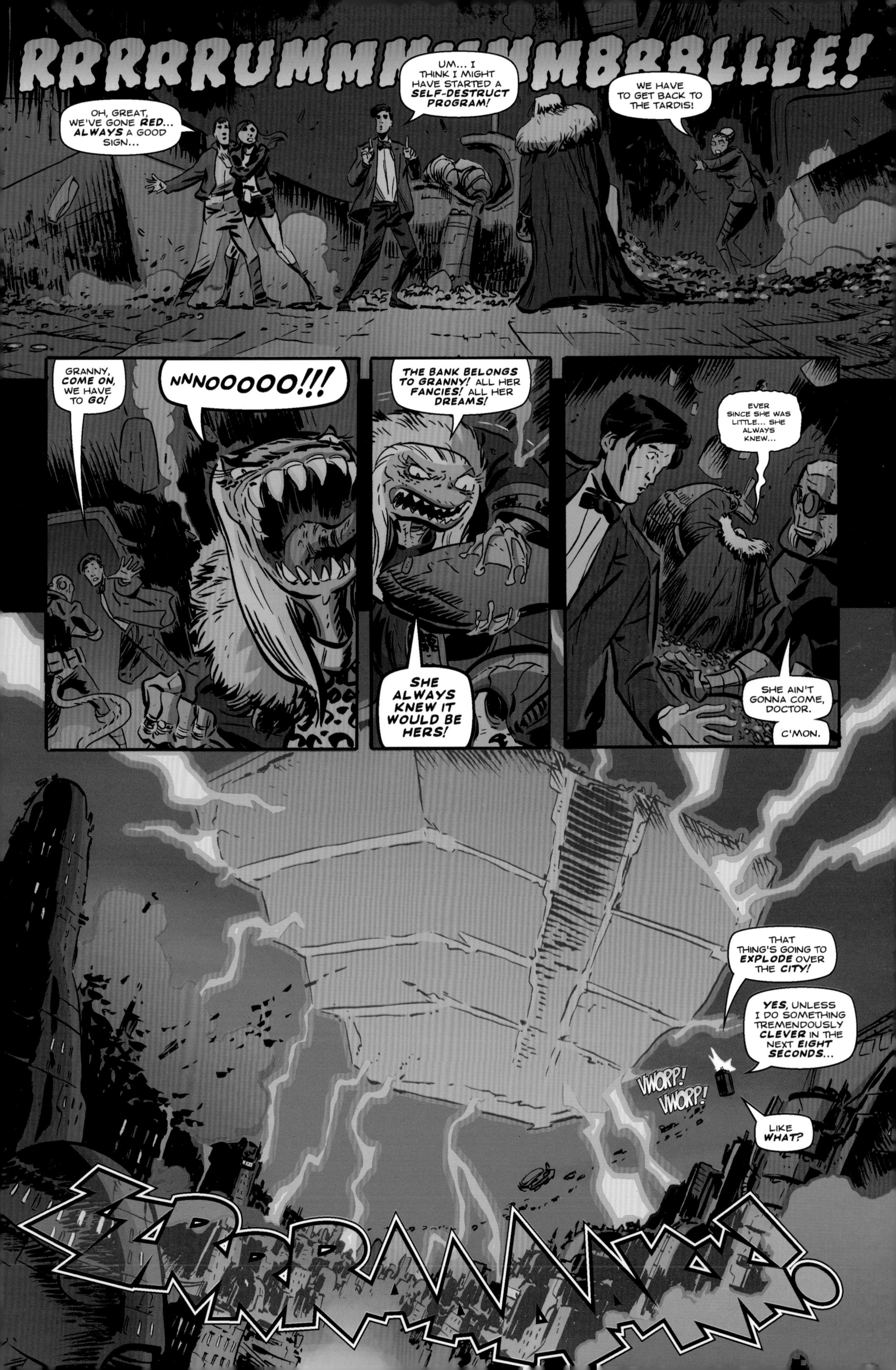
RRRRRUMMMMMMMBRRLLLE!
OH, GREAT, WE'VE GONE RED... ALWAYS A GOOD SIGN...
UM... I THINK I MIGHT HAVE STARTED A SELF-DESTRUCT PROGRAM!
WE HAVE TO GET BACK TO THE TARDIS!
GRANNY, COME ON, WE HAVE TO GO!
NNNOOOOO!!!
THE BANK BELONGS TO GRANNY! ALL HER FANCIES! ALL HER DREAMS!
SHE ALWAYS KNEW IT WOULD BE HERS!
EVER SINCE SHE WAS LITTLE... SHE ALWAYS KNEW...
SHE AIN'T GONNA COME, DOCTOR.
C'MON.
THAT THING'S GOING TO EXPLODE OVER THE CITY!
YES, UNLESS I DO SOMETHING TREMENDOUSLY CLEVER IN THE NEXT EIGHT SECONDS...
VWORP! VWORP!
LIKE WHAT?

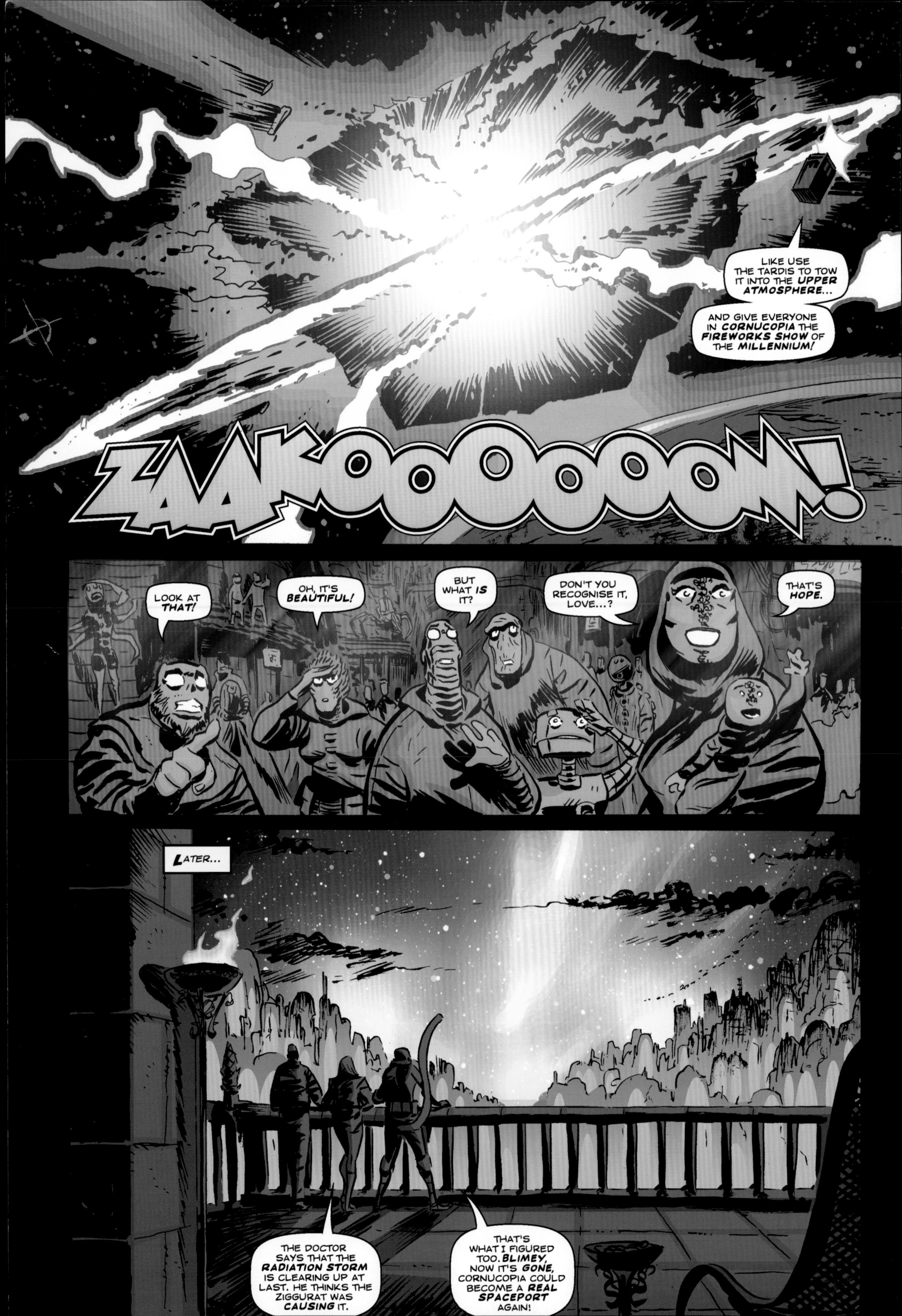
LIKE USE THE TARDIS TO TOW IT INTO THE UPPER ATMOSPHERE...
AND GIVE EVERYONE IN CORNUCOPIA THE FIREWORKS SHOW OF THE MILLENNIUM!
ZAAKOOOOOOOM!
LOOK AT THAT!
OH, IT'S BEAUTIFUL!
BUT WHAT IS IT?
DON'T YOU RECOGNISE IT, LOVE...?
THAT'S HOPE.
LATER...
THE DOCTOR SAYS THAT THE RADIATION STORM IS CLEARING UP AT LAST. HE THINKS THE ZIGGURAT WAS CAUSING IT.
THAT'S WHAT I FIGURED TOO. BLIMEY, NOW IT'S GONE, CORNUCOPIA COULD BECOME A REAL SPACEPORT AGAIN!

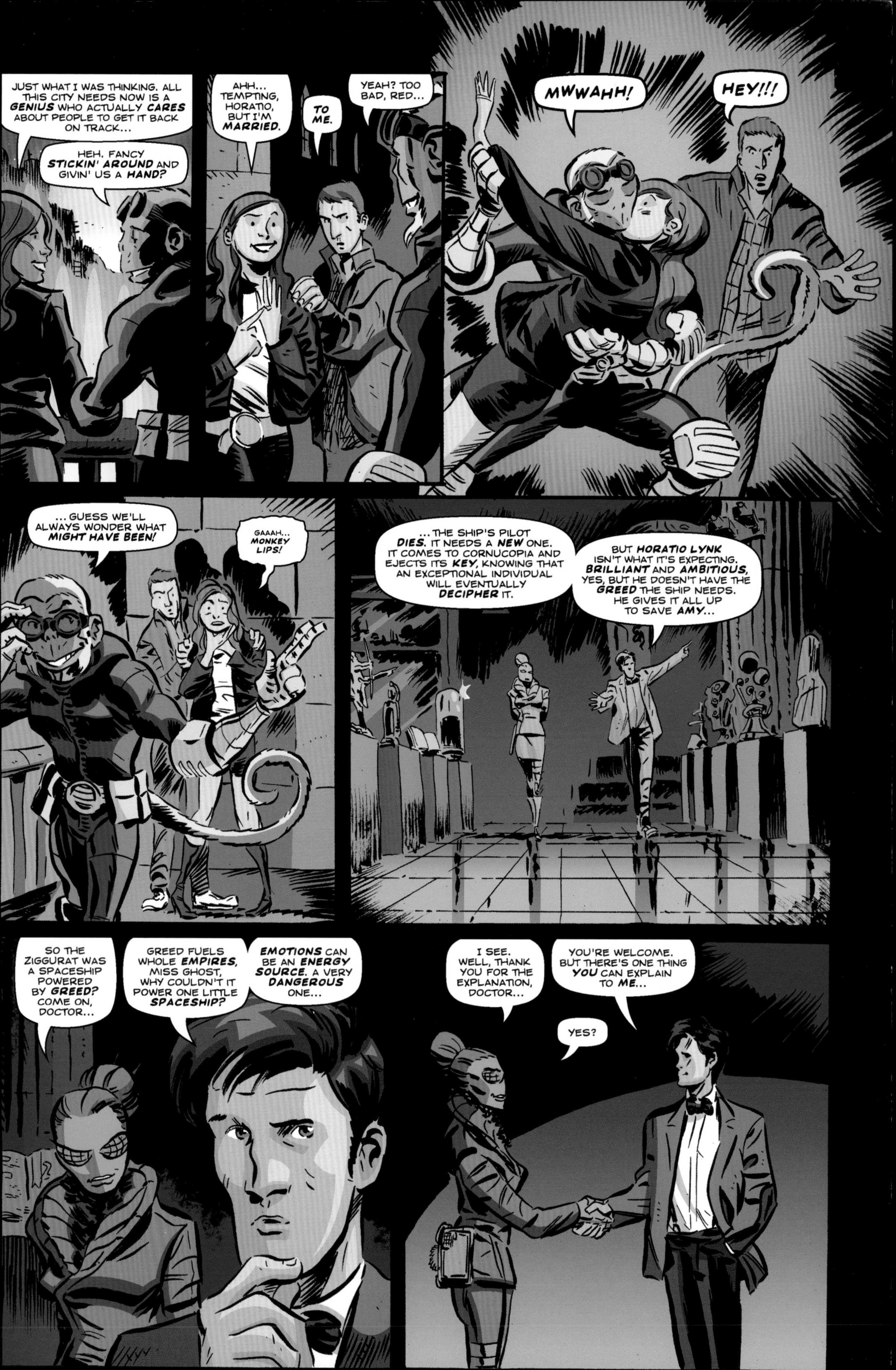
JUST WHAT I WAS THINKING. ALL THIS CITY NEEDS NOW IS A GENIUS WHO ACTUALLY CARES ABOUT PEOPLE TO GET IT BACK ON TRACK...
HEH. FANCY STICKIN' AROUND AND GIVIN' US A HAND?
AHH... TEMPTING, HORATIO, BUT I'M MARRIED.
TO ME.
YEAH? TOO BAD, RED...
MWWAHH!
HEY!!!
... GUESS WE'LL ALWAYS WONDER WHAT MIGHT HAVE BEEN!
GAAAH... MONKEY LIPS!
... THE SHIP'S PILOT DIES. IT NEEDS A NEW ONE. IT COMES TO CORNUCOPIA AND EJECTS ITS KEY, KNOWING THAT AN EXCEPTIONAL INDIVIDUAL WILL EVENTUALLY DECIPHER IT.
BUT HORATIO LYNK ISN'T WHAT IT'S EXPECTING. BRILLIANT AND AMBITIOUS, YES, BUT HE DOESN'T HAVE THE GREED THE SHIP NEEDS. HE GIVES IT ALL UP TO SAVE AMY...
SO THE ZIGGURAT WAS A SPACESHIP POWERED BY GREED? COME ON, DOCTOR...
GREED FUELS WHOLE EMPIRES, MISS GHOST, WHY COULDN'T IT POWER ONE LITTLE SPACESHIP?
EMOTIONS CAN BE AN ENERGY SOURCE. A VERY DANGEROUS ONE...
I SEE. WELL, THANK YOU FOR THE EXPLANATION, DOCTOR...
YOU'RE WELCOME. BUT THERE'S ONE THING YOU CAN EXPLAIN TO ME...
YES?

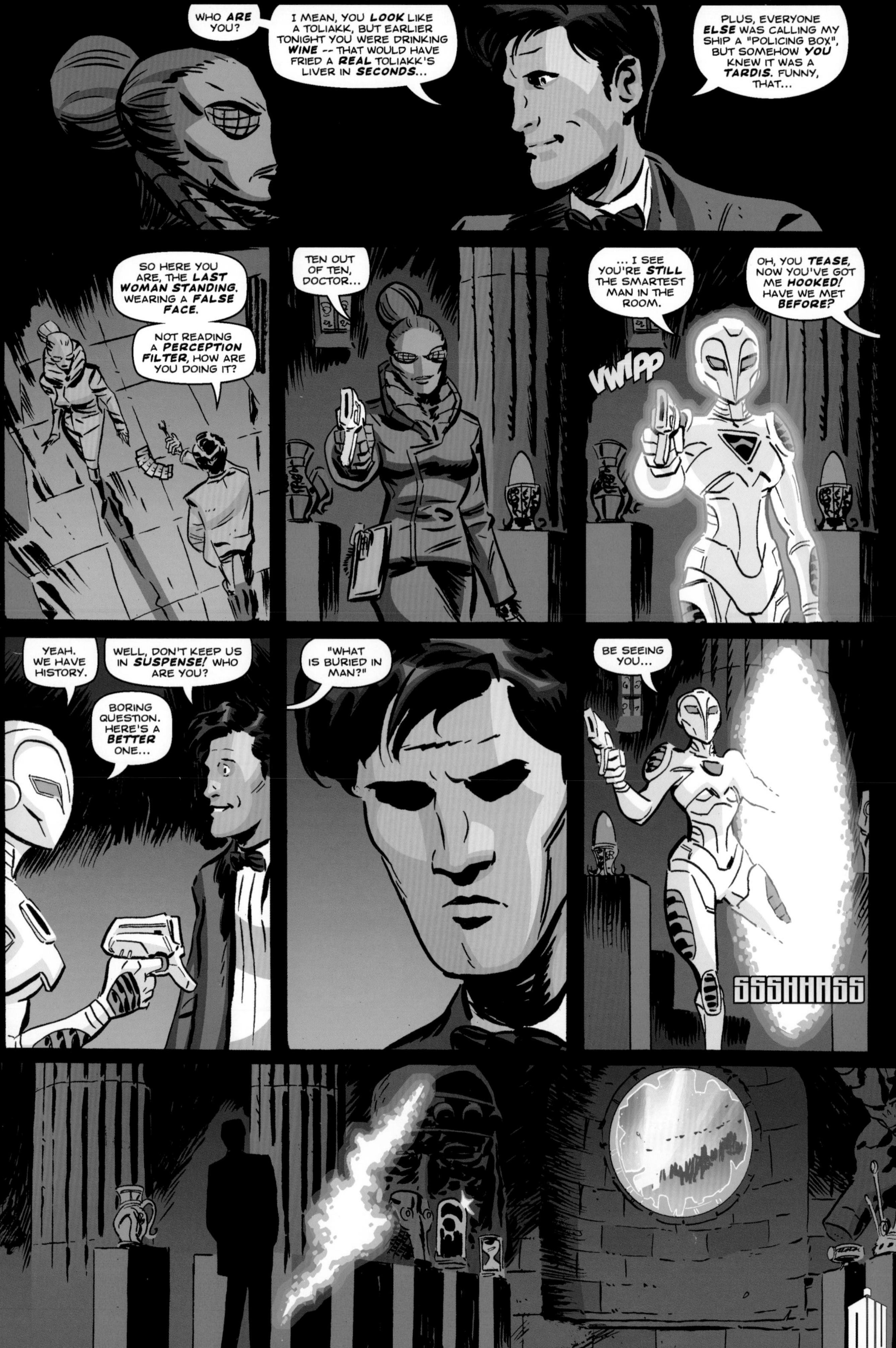
WHO ARE YOU?
I MEAN, YOU LOOK LIKE A TOLIAKK, BUT EARLIER TONIGHT YOU WERE DRINKING WINE -- THAT WOULD HAVE FRIED A REAL TOLIAKK'S LIVER IN SECONDS...
PLUS, EVERYONE ELSE WAS CALLING MY SHIP A "POLICING BOX", BUT SOMEHOW YOU KNEW IT WAS A TARDIS. FUNNY, THAT...
SO HERE YOU ARE, THE LAST WOMAN STANDING, WEARING A FALSE FACE.
NOT READING A PERCEPTION FILTER, HOW ARE YOU DOING IT?
TEN OUT OF TEN, DOCTOR...
... I SEE YOU'RE STILL THE SMARTEST MAN IN THE ROOM.
VWIPP
OH, YOU TEASE, NOW YOU'VE GOT ME HOOKED! HAVE WE MET BEFORE?
YEAH. WE HAVE HISTORY.
WELL, DON'T KEEP US IN SUSPENSE! WHO ARE YOU?
BORING QUESTION. HERE'S A BETTER ONE...
"WHAT IS BURIED IN MAN?"
BE SEEING YOU...
SSSHHHSS

Commentary

Introduction

Scott Gray

I'm of two minds about these kinds of behind-the-scenes pieces. Part of me thinks that we should all just keep schtum about the inner mechanics of stories. All types of storytellers – in comics, television, movies, novels, Punch & Judy shows, whatever – are united in a singular mission: we're here to convince you that what you're looking at is real. We want you to love these characters, fear for their lives, laugh at their jokes and hiss at their nastiness. You've spent both your money and your time with us; the least we can offer you is a genuine *experience*.

And then what do we do? We show up at the end and point out that what you've just seen *isn't* real – that everything you heard those interesting people say was scripted, that all those amazing visuals you've been enjoying were just lines of ink printed on paper. Aren't we killing the illusion here? Seriously, who really wants to see the magician explain how he made the elephant disappear?

But then another part of me – a larger part, to be sure – remembers that I *love* behind-the-scenes stuff. I'm fascinated by the whole creative process; of how stories take shape. I love the glimpses of what might have been: the ideas that get discarded, the designs unused. I love learning how a chance, random element can be added into the mix to produce something totally unexpected. I've been like this ever since I got my copy of *The Making of Doctor Who*, a book by Terrance Dicks and Malcolm Hulke, back in 1970-something. I read it to *death*.

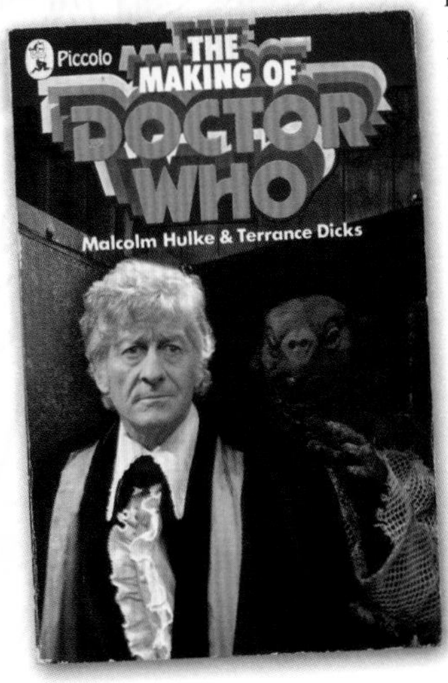
Piccolo
THE MAKING OF DOCTOR WHO
Malcolm Hulke & Terrance Dicks

There has never been any TV series as well-documented as *Doctor Who*. Nothing else even comes close. There have been hundreds of magazines, books and DVD features analysing the production of the show in nanoscopic detail, and you know what? It hasn't harmed the Doctor one little bit. He's as real in my head today as he was when I first met him as a five-year-old. The truth is that the characters and places in these stories will always feel real – usually far more so to the people behind the curtain than the ones in front of it. We live with these characters for weeks, months, sometimes years. We day-dream conversations with them. We laugh with them, get annoyed at them, and miss them when they leave us. They can't be killed by a few pages of documentation.

I think it's important to show young readers that stories are *achievable* – that through hard work, research, cooperation and, occasionally, a tiny bit of inspiration, they can be brought to life. That's what I learned from *The Making of Doctor Who*, and I wasn't the only one. A lot of people read that book and decided they wanted to go behind the scenes too. If you're reading this book now and wondering if you should do the same, then I say: what the heck are you waiting for? Get to work!

Stories are built. They are *designed*. The one thing they never, ever do is pop out, fully-formed, the way Athena did from daddy Zeus' forehead.

Speaking of which...

The Chains of Olympus

Scott Gray Writer

This story owes its life to Lord Melvyn Bragg. One fine day in the space year 2009 I was driving to work, listening to Melvyn's long-running Radio 4 programme *In Our Time*. The topic of discussion between Melvyn and his team of experts that morning was Socrates, the heavyweight champion of western philosophy. I knew very little about him. Thinking back, the sum total of my knowledge of the man amounted to this:

1) He lived in Greece.
2) He had a beard.
3) He's mentioned in Monty Python's *Philosophers Song*.
4) He assists Bill and Ted with their crucial history presentation.

It wasn't what you'd call a comprehensive library of information. So as I weaved my way through the Tunbridge Wells potholes, I listened to Melvyn's leisurely tones describe Socrates. He sounded *great*. (Socrates, I mean.) Here was a man who, while living in a culture that prided itself on intellectual discourse, still stood head-and-shoulders above the pack.

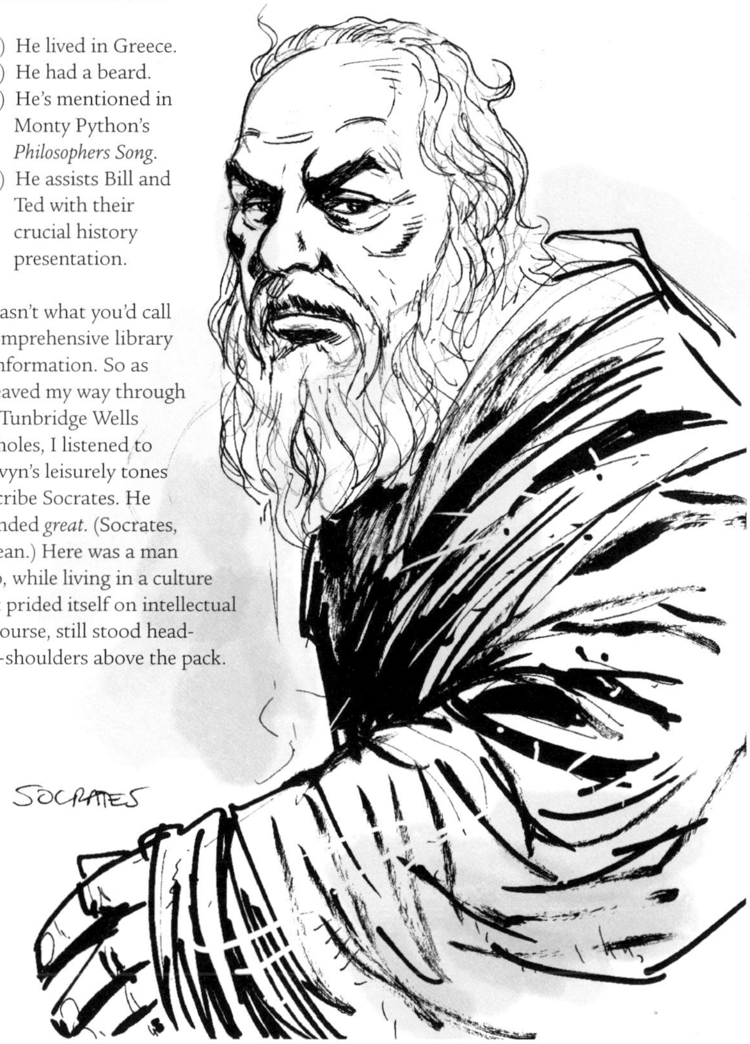
SOCRATES

Left: The first edition of *The Making of Doctor Who*, published in 1972.

Below: Mike Collins' first character sketch of Socrates.

Above: Socrates gets chummy with the Doctor. Pencils by Mike Collins.

Below: A character sketch of the youthful Plato. Pencils and inks by Mike Collins.

thoughts down in the belief that once an idea was put on record it became set in stone, calcified, useless. To Socrates, concepts only came alive when they were being actively discussed, debated and argued. Philosophy was a wrestling match. He didn't believe he possessed any wisdom at all – in fact he insisted that he knew nothing. He felt that to *assume* knowledge meant you had lost the ability to question.

Socrates would go into the Agora, the marketplace in the centre of Athens, and find someone who believed they had expert knowledge of a subject – for example, 'justice'. And he would start to ask them questions. He'd want to know how they defined justice, how they measured it, how it could be tested. Whatever they'd answer would lead Socrates to test their definition with more questions, and eventually it would start to crumble. Pretty soon the 'expert' would be back-tracking, trying to find a new definition – but whatever they came up with would also fall apart under Socrates' cool interrogation.

What Socrates was doing was laying the groundwork for the way scientific procedure developed; how any hypothesis must always be followed by rigorous testing. The 'Socratic Method' also defined medical diagnosis. It also paved the way for cross-examination in the legal system. It's not an exaggeration to say that he guided the evolution of modern-day thinking.

"He's someone the Doctor should meet sometime," I thought to myself, before turning my attention back to the potholes.

Two years whizzed by. After a couple of superb runs of stories from authors Dan McDaid and Jonathan Morris, I found myself itching to try writing the **Doctor Who Magazine** comic strip again. This was something I hadn't done since 2005. I had been co-editing the strip with **DWM** editor Tom Spilsbury for several years, but I hesitated in approaching him. I was worried Tom might not be enthusiastic; it's one thing to get tough with a plot or a script from a freelancer who lives at the other end of the country, and quite another to do it with a bloke who's sitting a few feet away from you in the same office, day after day. That can get, well... awkward. But Tom seemed delighted when I tentatively broached the subject, and immediately promised to increase the strip's regular page-count from 10 pages to 12. Blimey! **DWM**'s assistant editor Peter Ware came on board officially as well (although he had always been offering his thoughts on the strip). We were off and running!

But I was nervous about starting again. I had enjoyed a lengthy and remarkably rosy time on the strip, with reader reaction being very positive – but I was aware that that fact could work against me if people didn't approve of the approach I took this time around. Let's face it; *Doctor Who* fans are never exactly shy about speaking up when they think something's gone downhill. Also, the new audience the magazine had gained since the return of the TV series wouldn't know or care about any past stories I had produced. It was opening night all over again.

I had kept Socrates in mind, and still thought he'd be a good starting-point for a story. I had forgotten how educational a process writing for the **DWM** strip could be. I knew I'd have to familiarise myself not just with Socrates but also his world. My main point of reference was *From Solon to Socrates*, a study of Greek history by Victor Ehrenberg. I found it in a Tunbridge Wells second-hand bookstore, along with *The Classical Age of Greece* by NGL Hammond, *Socrates: A Sourcebook* compiled by John Ferguson, and *Gorgias*, a play by Plato translated by WC Helmbold.

This was going to be a 'celebrity historical'; a type of story that twenty-first-century TV *Doctor Who* clearly enjoys. There seemed to be one obvious ground rule established in them: the celebrity must be the one to save the day, and do so by using some form of personal skill. It's Winston Churchill's battle savvy that clobbers the

But Socrates was no rarefied figure, living a privileged life amongst the fountains and statues, trading platitudes with his peers. Oh, no! He took his ideas to the people, trudging barefoot through the Athens streets, short and feisty, raising hell and stirring up trouble.

He redefined what philosophy was meant to do, to the point that all thinkers who came before him are simply labelled 'Pre-Socratic'. There were great minds, there were geniuses, and there was Socrates. He refused to write his

PLATO

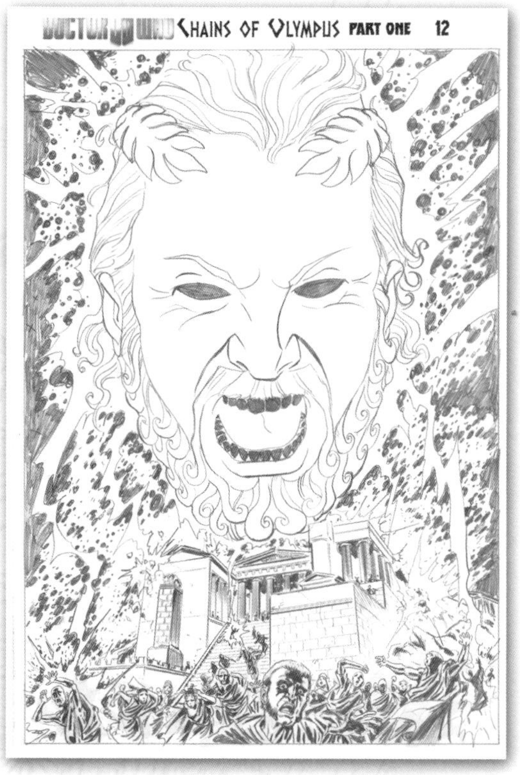
CHAINS OF OLYMPUS PART ONE 12

Left: Zeus is revealed in the climax of Part One. Pencils by Mike Collins.

Daleks in *Victory of the Daleks*. It's William Shakespeare's gift of the gab that destroys the Carrionites in *The Shakespeare Code*. With that in mind, I knew from the start that Socrates would have to use his analytical powers in some way to defeat the enemy. But how? What type of villain could be destroyed by a spirited debate?

The power of belief seemed to be the key. The enemy would need belief as a tool, or even a source of energy. That suggested worship, which suggested gods, and there was the answer: the Greek pantheon of gods, with all their colour and richness of detail. They would need to believe in *themselves* in order to function. Socrates would walk into their midst and, with a few uncomfortable observations, shatter that belief. Yes!

Another starting-point was a fact I discovered in *From Solon to Socrates*: the Athenian authorities, struck by financial hardship during their conflict with Sparta, would sometimes melt down the golden statues of their gods to help pay for the war effort. It seemed like a juicy piece of symbolism to me – the rejection of the spiritual in favour of the practical – and helped kick-start the plot.

Rory made his long-overdue strip début in *The Chains of Olympus*. I had loved him from the start – I think Arthur Darvill turned him into one of the most endearing characters in *Doctor Who*'s history. But Rory's involvement in the comic strip had been a problem: we had been caught in a bit of a continuity trap in our initial run of stories. Rory wasn't an official companion at the start of the Matt Smith era, and was then (temporarily) killed later on. We decided it was best to keep him out of the strip altogether until his position in the series stabilised. Now that it had, I wanted to have some fun with him. Although he can be a fantastic comedic character, Rory is at heart a hero, every bit as thrilled about adventuring in time and space as Amy (he just keeps it a bit better hidden). I was determined to give him a big moment at the story's climax.

We were lucky enough to nail down Mike Collins, an artist who had produced many beautiful **DWM** strip stories in the past, including the first Matt Smith one, *Supernature*. This story had to be bold, expressive and as big as possible, and Mike is a master at that kind of visual. I wanted to start with a huge panoramic shot of Athens with a Cecil B DeMille-sized crowd of extras, all with individual looks and all interacting in a massive marketplace. It was one of those scenes that comics writers cheerfully type out in a few seconds, leaving the artists grinding their teeth for days as they reach for the paracetemol. But Mike turned it into everything I'd hoped for and much more besides, aided so brilliantly by David Roach on inks and James Offredi on colours. It was an astonishing opening, and gave everyone a real boost in confidence. Mike continued to deliver the goods at every turn. I threw everything I could think of at him: the Cyclops, a Griffin, Cerberus, Harpies, the Hydra... He just batted them all back at me with barely a blink! Mike, David and James did a particularly fine job with the gods. I had a specific approach in mind for them: as they were really a manifestation of Calidora's *understanding* of gods, I thought it would be a nice touch to render them in negative, as this was how they were often depicted on pottery and tablets at the time.

All of the monsters, especially the gigantic version of Ares, were inspired by my love of Ray Harryhausen films, most notably *The Golden Voyage of Sinbad*. I saw it at the cinema at the age of nine, and it altered my entire worldview; I realised films *could* look as cool as comics after all! Harryhausen's genius as a stop-motion animator

Below: The first sketch of Calidora by Mike Collins. Mike was asked to 'soften' her features to make her more sympathetic.

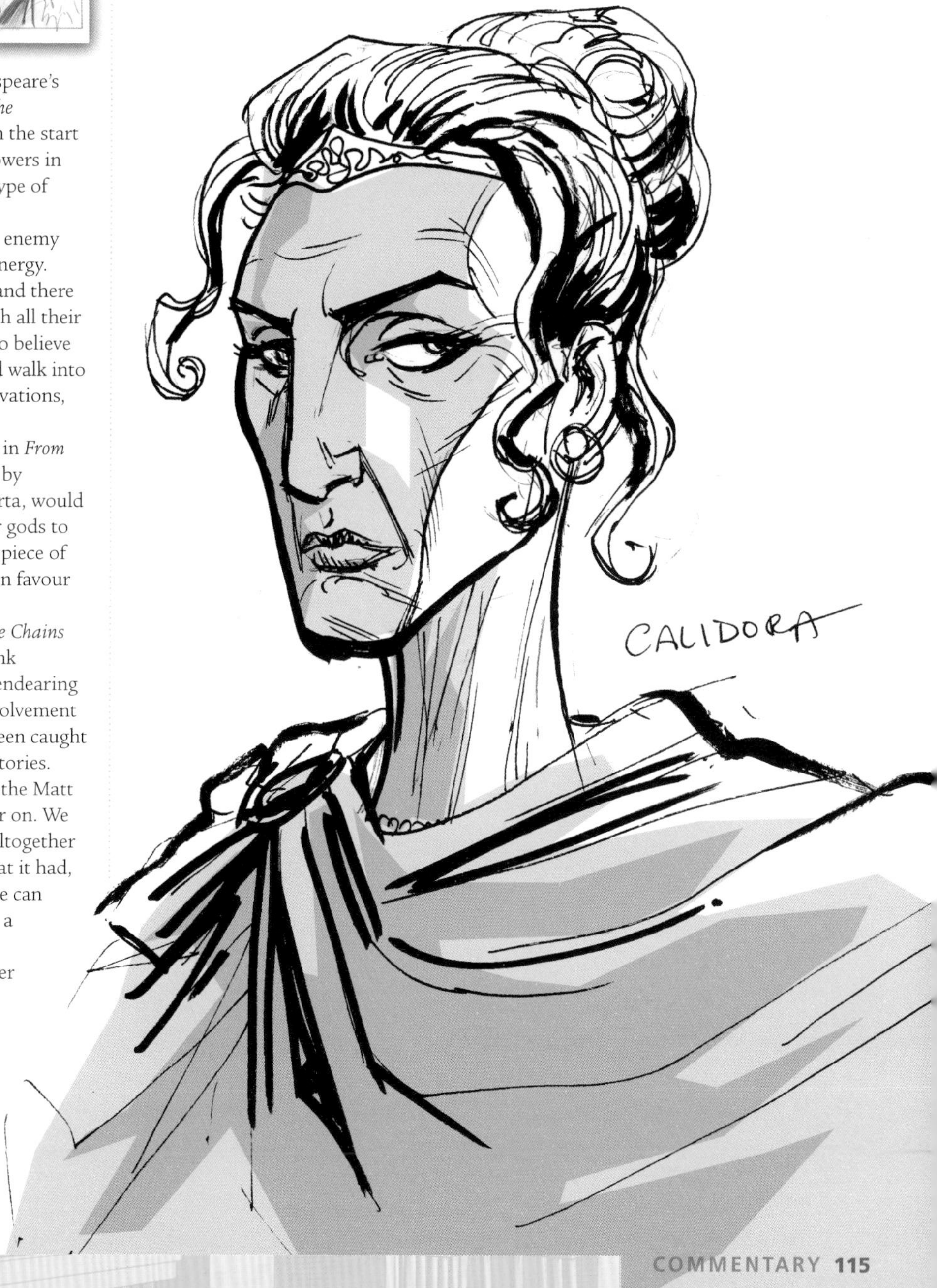
CALIDORA

Right & Opposite Page: Ares is unleashed! The original design rough and finished pencilled page by Mike Collins.

gave us classics like *Jason and the Argonauts, Clash of the Titans* and *The Beast From 20,000 Fathoms*. If you haven't seen them, you've missed some pieces of true movie artistry, so go hunt them down. Computer animation can certainly be beautiful, but there's something truly magical about taking a physical object – a tangible model – and carefully, painstakingly, bringing it to life. Mr Harryhausen was one of the giants.

As I've said, Socrates never wrote anything down, which leaves perhaps the greatest mind in history a tantalising question mark. All we know about Socrates is second-hand information from students like Plato and Xenophon, or from accounts from his contemporaries in Athens. They often contradict each other. He was put into plays like *The Clouds*, turned into a satirical figure, often laughed at. Socrates is in a sense a fictional character who existed in the real world. He refused to be filed and labelled by history and is therefore open to interpretation – which is probably exactly what he intended. He was eventually arrested and tried for 'corrupting the youth of the city'. He had humiliated so many powerful officials in his life that it was perhaps inevitable they would get their revenge in the end. He was convicted in a trial that lasted a day and sentenced to death. By many accounts Socrates was given the chance to escape the city but he refused. As a philosopher he was unafraid of death, and he didn't want anyone to believe otherwise. He drank a cup of hemlock and was dead in minutes.

The thought that Socrates could be the Doctor's *hero* got me excited. It was something I hadn't seen done with the Doctor before, and would give him a more personal involvement in the adventure as a result. That led naturally to the notion that Socrates wouldn't quite be the man the Doctor was expecting to meet: brilliant, sure, but also fallible and in a bad state of mind when the Doctor finds him. As a result, we'd have a disappointed, surly, sarcastic

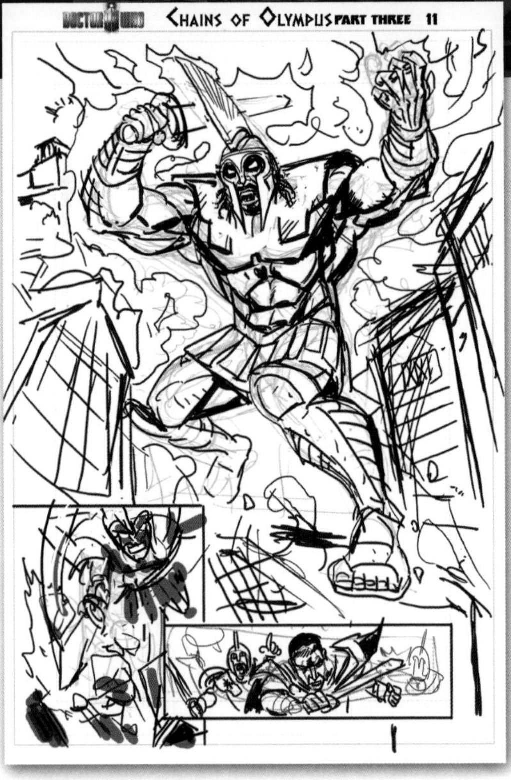
DOCTOR WHO
CHAINS OF OLYMPUS PART THREE 11

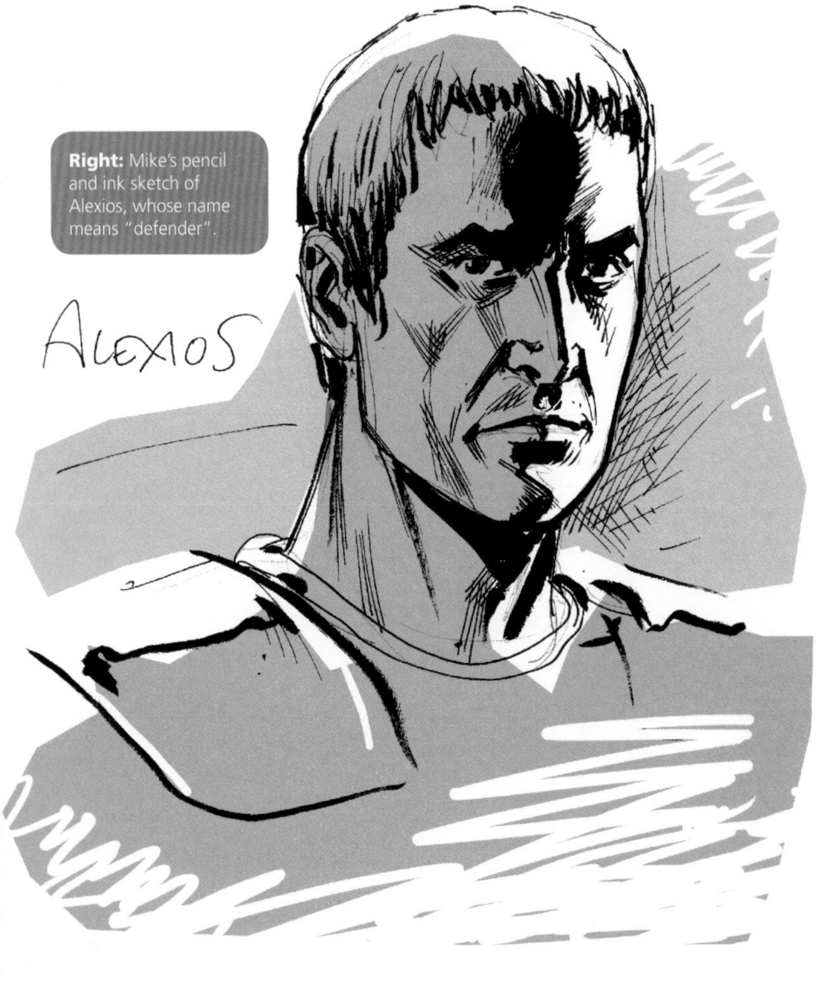
ALEXIOS

Right: Mike's pencil and ink sketch of Alexios, whose name means "defender".

Time Lord on our hands for a while until Amy gave him a much-needed earful. Anything that can throw the Doctor off his game for a bit is like gold dust to a *Doctor Who* writer!

The similarities between Socrates and the Doctor were obvious. Both men are mavericks inside their respective cultures, always happy to stir up trouble and eager to confront authority figures. They make a lot of enemies. They spurn money and material values. They're charismatic and rebellious, easily gaining followers as they challenge the status quo. But there were interesting differences as well; in fact they seemed to be polar opposites in many ways. Socrates stayed in Athens for almost his entire life. He saw no point in travelling; he was on an internal voyage, seeking insight into his own psyche. By contrast, the Doctor couldn't wait to escape his home and go see the universe – but the one thing he always seemed to avoid at all costs was any form of self-examination. Why was that?

Once I had that in mind, I knew that the ultimate conclusion of the entire story arc would involve the Doctor being forced to take a long, hard look at himself. For better or worse, he would have to follow Socrates' advice.

It's only in the last couple of pages of *Chains* that any sense of a larger story to follow is hinted at. It had become a tradition in the **DWM** comic strip to seed some form of mystery through a series of stories that would then grow into a big, climactic adventure. I had done it back in the 1990s with a devious enemy called the Threshold; they had cast a shadow over many of the Eighth Doctor's strip adventures. Dan McDaid had produced a cracking storyline that connected all of his **DWM** strip stories (collected together in *The Crimson Hand* volume), and Jonathan Morris had done the same with his excellent run (available as *The Child of Time*). I wanted to continue the pattern with a view to tying up all the plot threads in time for *Doctor Who*'s 50th anniversary celebration.

Originally I had a very different conclusion for the story arc in mind. At the end of *Chains*, the dying Athena would stare sadly at the Doctor and make an ominous prediction: "You will be trapped within the Box of Eternal Sorrow." The Doctor would mention this to Amy and Rory on the final page but he'd dismiss Athena's warning, believing it to be a reference to the Pandorica (the cuboid prison he's locked inside in the TV episode *The Pandorica Opens*). The Doctor would say, "Tricky thing, trying to predict the future of a time-traveller. Never mind, she meant well." But of course, Athena wouldn't have been referring to the

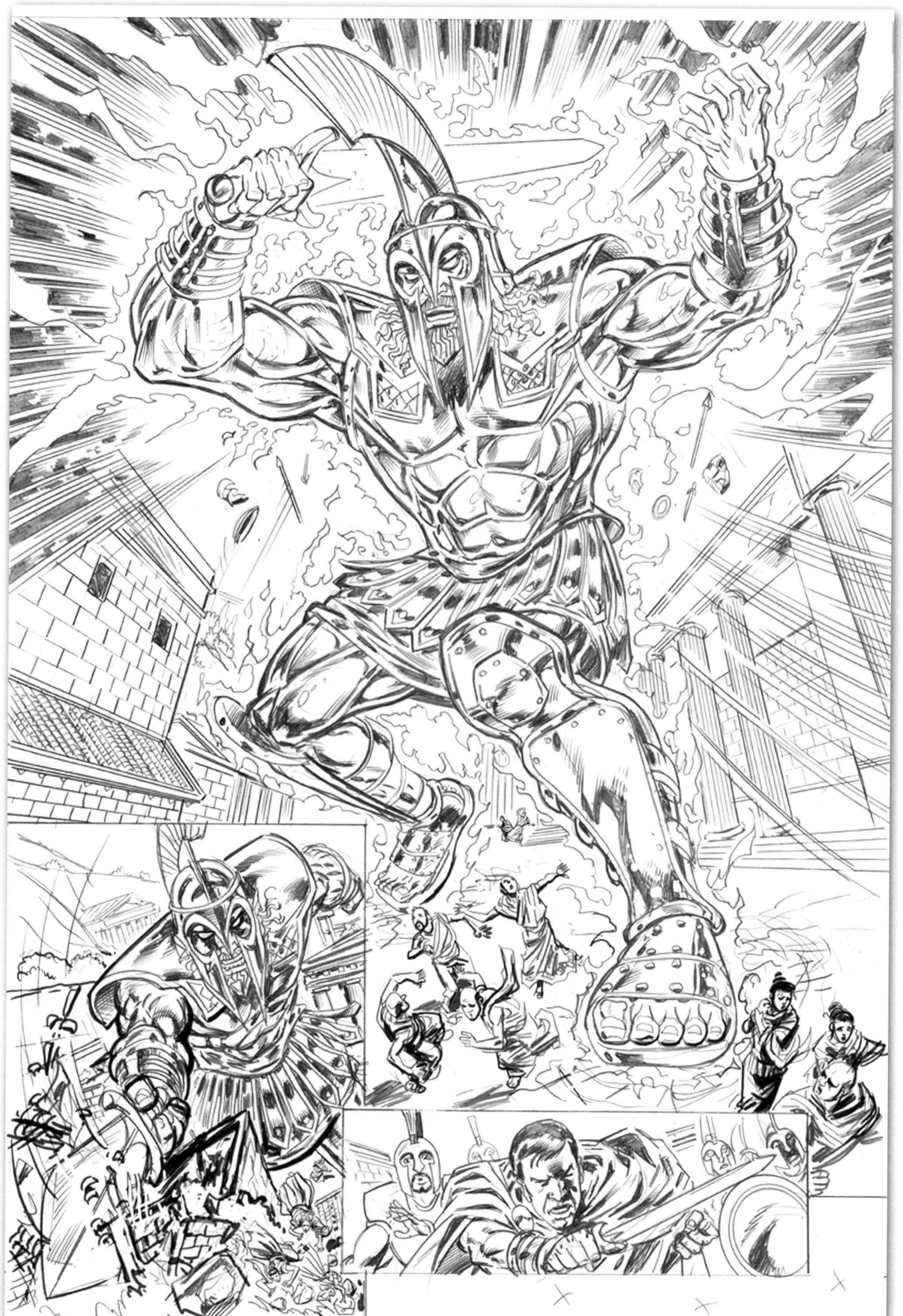

Below & Right: Socrates meets the Doctor, and Rory challenges Ares. Pencils by Mike Collins.

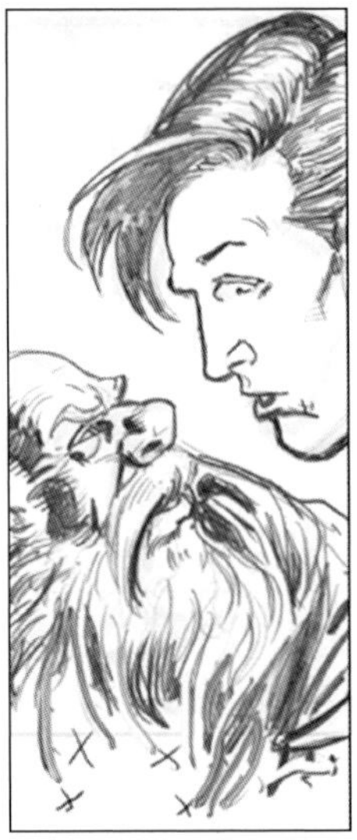

Pandorica at all, and the Doctor would have once again been making the mistake that Socrates warned him of: assuming knowledge that he didn't really possess.

Months later at the climax of the arc, the truth behind Athena's warning would be revealed. The Doctor would suffer some kind of mental attack from his enemies. They would inject his mind with a catalogue of phobias. He'd be turned into an acute agoraphobic, left helpless in his fear, rendered unable to even walk through the doors of the TARDIS into the outside world. Earth would be facing total disaster but the Doctor would be trapped in his ship, curled up in a ball on the floor, unable to help. "The Box of Eternal Sorrow" would turn out to be the TARDIS.

So how would the day be saved? The Doctor would be visited in the TARDIS by his former selves, one after the other, each holding a piece of the truth he'd need to save himself. A furious William Hartnell would offer the Doctor no sympathy, telling him to man up! A sly Sylvester McCoy would fuel his anger at the enemy. An earnest Peter Davison would remind him of his duty. And so it would go until, bit-by-bit, the Doctor would be made whole again. In doing so he would finally have accepted Socrates' challenge to look inside himself, and gain strength from that action. The act of simply stepping through the TARDIS doors would become a triumph for the Doctor – and a sign that the baddies were now in a whole heap of trouble. The true nature of the past Doctors would remain ambiguous. Were they the real thing, pulled out of their individual timelines? Projections

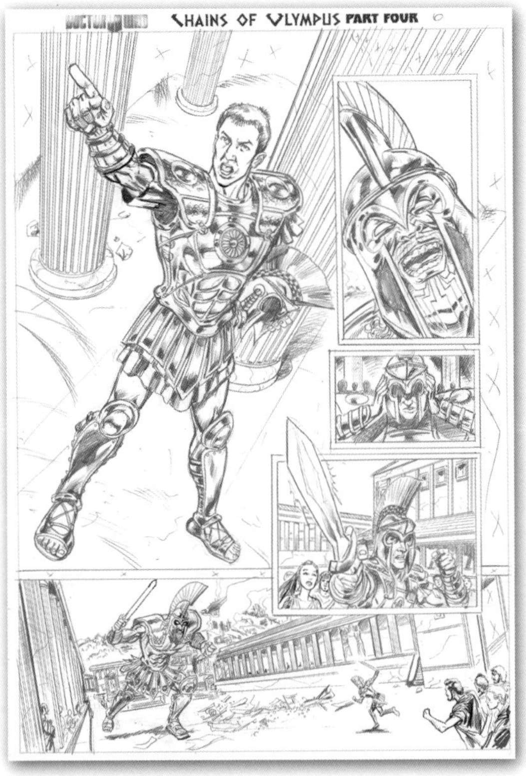
CHAINS OF OLYMPUS PART FOUR

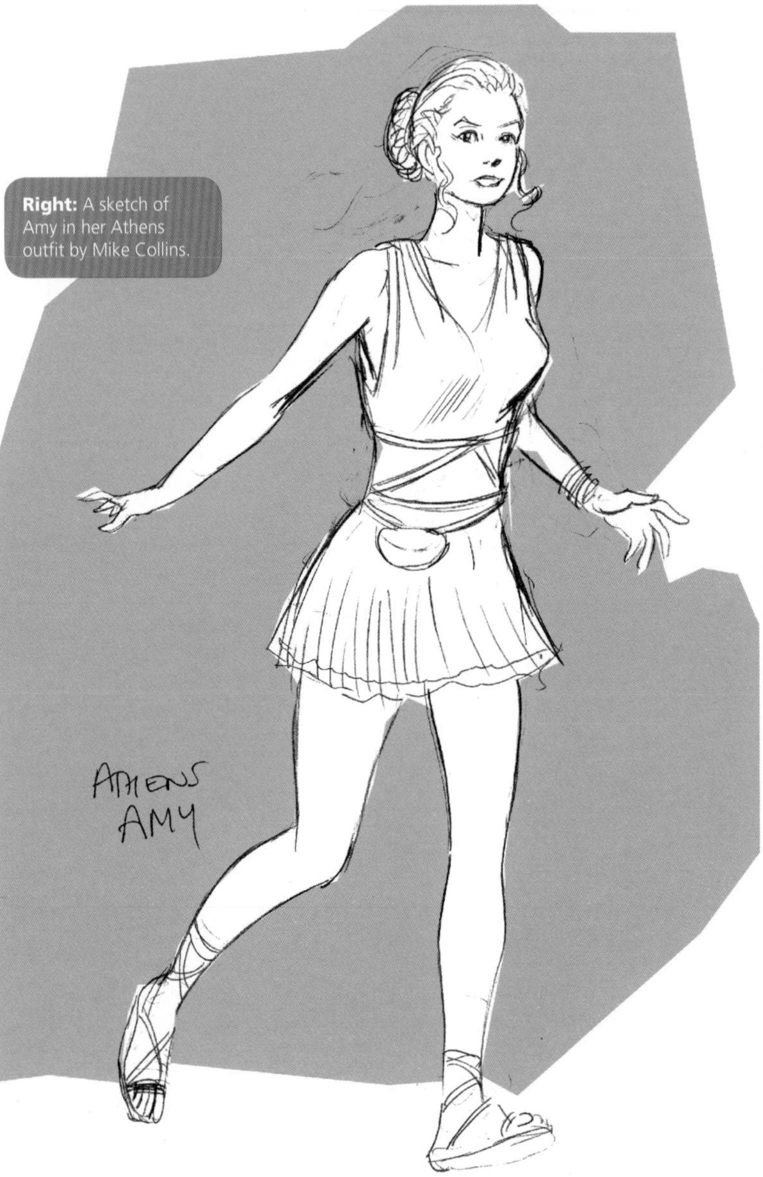
ATHENS
AMY

Right: A sketch of Amy in her Athens outfit by Mike Collins.

created by the TARDIS? Hallucinations from within the Doctor's tortured mind? We'd never know for sure.

I liked the idea a lot, but as I worked my way through *Chains*, I started to have doubts. I assumed there would be some kind of multi-Doctor story planned for the TV series in 2013. That would almost certainly mean I'd have to alter, and possibly even scrap, my story. This type of obstacle had occurred several times in the last few years whenever the comic strip would accidentally veer too close to a future TV plotline. I'd watched Jonathan Morris repeatedly being forced to detour (and often just abandon) his storylines because of this. It was always a painful experience for him and I had no desire to end up on the same road.

There was another concern: even if a multi-Doctor adventure *didn't* happen on TV, I reasoned that other forms of *Doctor Who* – the Big Finish audios or the book series – would probably produce one. There'd be a danger of everyone going to the same well at the same time, and that might look a bit... well, sad. Inevitable comparisons would arise, and that seemed counter-productive to me. It was *Doctor Who*'s 50th birthday – we should all be enjoying each other's company at the party, not competing for attention.

So I started working out another storyline entirely, one that would still involve an inner journey for the Doctor but not have him interacting with his former selves. By the end of scripting *Chains*, I had all the basic beats of the ultimate climax worked out. They led me to Athena's final line. Not a prediction now, but a simple question: "What is buried in man?"

Ah, but if you want the answer to that, you'll have to pick up our companion book, *Hunters of the Burning Stone*. It'll be worth it, trust me...

Mike Collins Artist

David Roach really, *really* hates me. Faced by a request from Scott to show an Ancient Greek marketplace, I took it as a challenge. Just how many people, how much Greek architecture could I fit into the shot – using the **DWM** comic strip mantra: 'DWCCATF' (Draw What Cardiff Can't Afford To Film) – it took me about a week to just draw that opening spread. Then I handed it to David to ink. There may have been tears.

I'm always concerned about giving the *Doctor Who* strips – whether in deep space or ancient history – as much a sense of authenticity as possible. If you can't believe where the story is set before the fantastical things begin happening, you're onto a loser.

This strip was the first where I've extensively used the free online tool Google SketchUp (other free online 3D construction sites are also available, I guess) where someone had actually build a sketchy version of ancient Athens. It wasn't detailed enough to create backgrounds from but it meant I was able to use this virtual Athens to give myself a sense of place through the story. I loaded my bookshelves with tomes on Ancient Greek clothing, architecture, tools and transport (the internet is all well and good, but nothing beats a good book). As ever with historical texts, probably half of them I never opened but they were *there*, so that's what counted.

After going through various reference books, I spotted *Asterix in Greece* on my shelf, and – of course – Albert Uderzo rendered the city in more detail and with greater authenticity than I could ever hope to do.

As to the characters – obviously we had to get Socrates right – he's the lynchpin of the whole story. Scott had suggested Leo McKern, and certainly there are echoes of him in the statues of the philosopher (and the great debater being the image of *Rumpole of the Bailey* has a certain pleasing symmetry about it), but thinking about 'casting' I felt Alun Armstrong (*New Tricks* and *Our Friends in the North*) has a more careworn face... The fact that my version actually looks nothing like either gentleman is part of the process – so long as there's a credible basis to even secondary characters. I felt it important to draw him in a way that made you go from dismissing him as a drunken sot to totally believing him the Smartest Man on the Planet – keeping the mental image of Alun Armstrong (and Leo McKern) in my head while drawing him helped in that regard.

This was to be the first story featuring Rory – now normally, even if you don't nail the likeness exactly, there should be enough clues in the character's clothing to suggest who it is you're drawing – no luck here, as Rory's début is in... a mini skirt toga. Thanks for that, Scott. Of course, Amy is in a mini skirt toga too, so – thanks for that, Scott!

I know Scott has an affection for the character of Rory, and I love how, through the story he goes from potential comic foil to action hero. I loved drawing *The Clash of the*

Titans elements of this – we took to the shorthand of it being '*Doctor Who* directed by George Pal'.

In terms of casting – I used myself as Zeus (the face, anyway – my physique is alarmingly close to that of Socrates), gurning all the time into a mirror, probably unsettling the other members of the studio where I work even more than usual.

Having 12 pages per chapter helped as well in giving us scope to show the scale of the adventure – before, we'd be restricted by telling our tales in an efficient nine, *maybe* ten, pages. I don't think we would have attempted anything as epic as that market scene in an earlier story, as it would have eaten up valuable story time.

The scenes on Olympus, with the simple-yet-effective device of reversing out the art so the 'Gods' looked like vase reliefs are amongst some of my favourites. I had drawn one version of the big reveal of Olympus (Part Three, page eight) but Scott sent it back saying it wasn't epic enough, so I took that as a challenge and kicked it up a gear. David's usual sharp inking and James' astonishing colouring make it a wonder to behold (and definitely a 'DWCCATF' moment).

The Ares metal giant at the end of Part Three gave me and David a chance to channel more of that George Pal/ Ray Harryhausen vibe we'd been putting into the art – with more than a touch of classic Neal Adams *Uncanny X-Men* action.

I loved drawing Rory's rise to hero status in the fourth part, as the Doctor gets sidelined to spectator – Scott's neat inversion of the *Doctor Who* formula.

This is a great – in all senses of the word – *Doctor Who* story, and I think the art team rose to the challenge of Scott's script (though David still has a haunted look in his eyes if you ever ask him about that opening spread).

Above: The story's panoramic opening spread. Pencil art by Mike Collins.

Below: Mike used the Google Sketchup website to help him illustrate Athens.

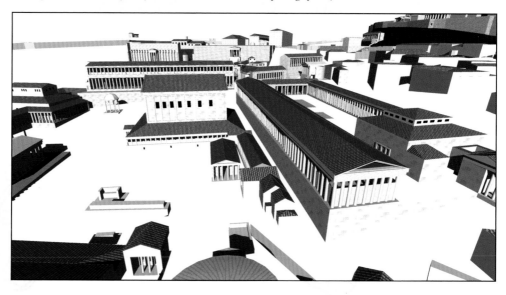

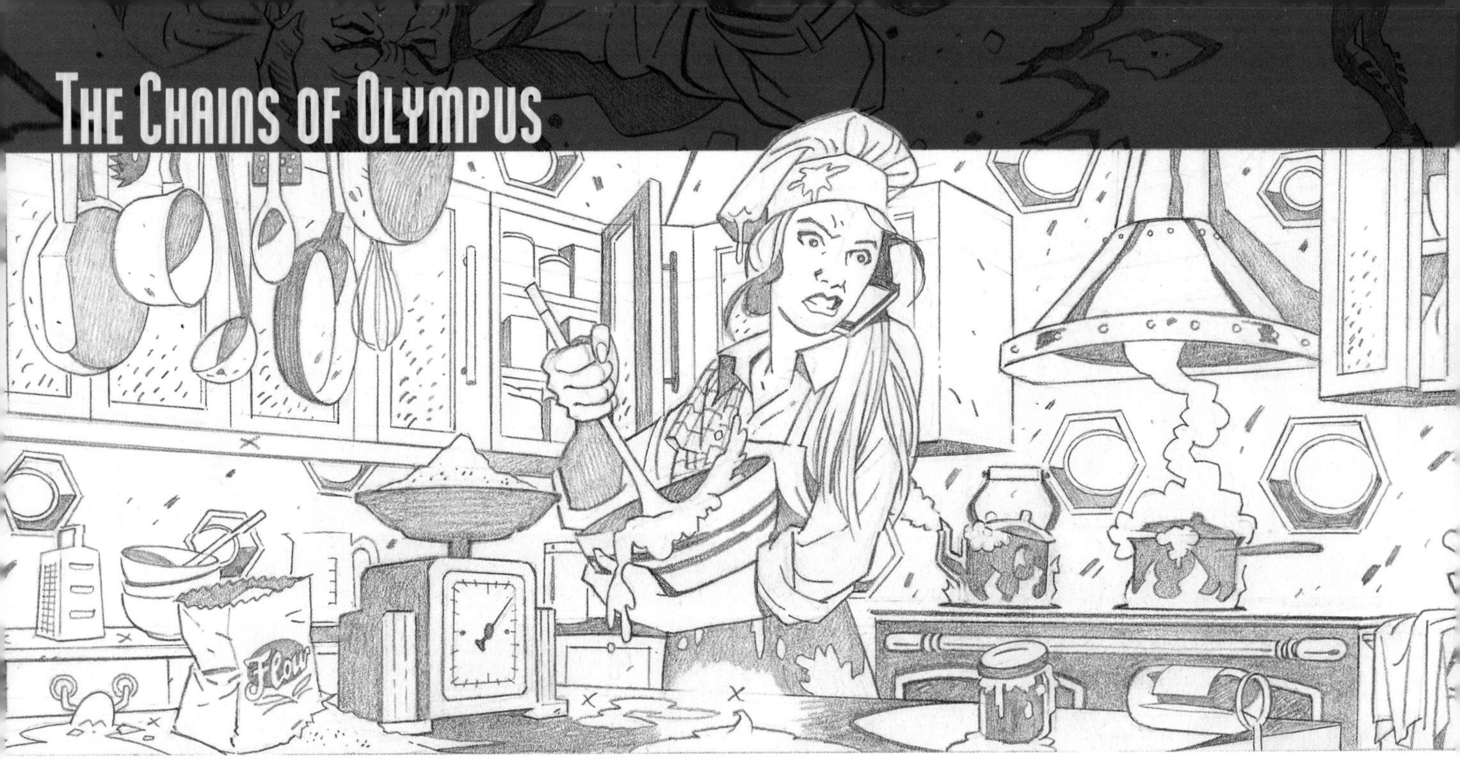
Flour

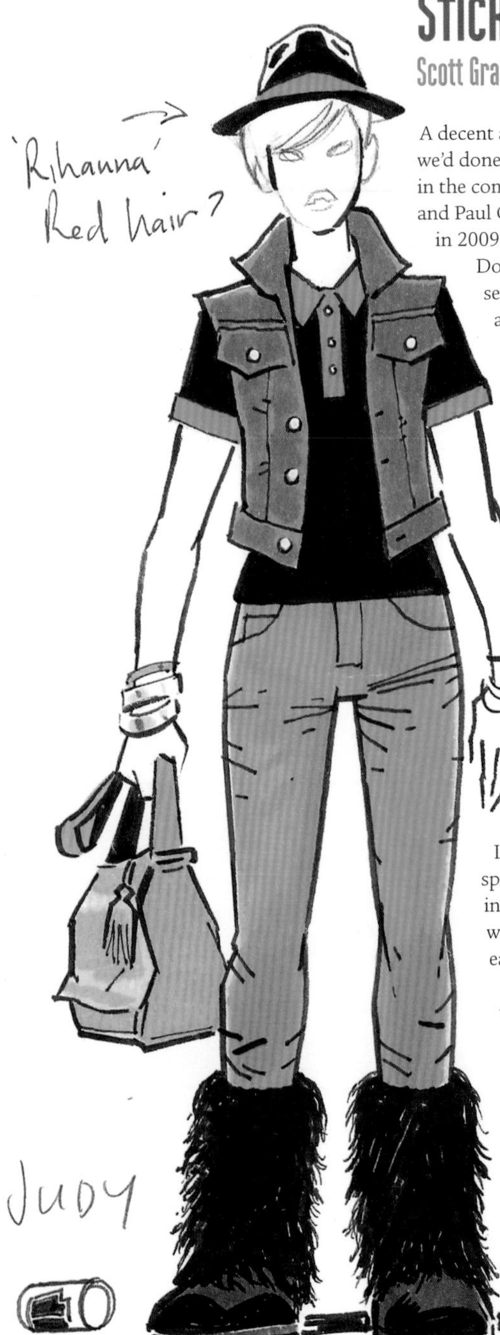
'Rihanna'
Red hair?
JUDY

STICKS & STONES

Scott Gray Writer

A decent amount of time had passed since we'd done a contemporary London story in the comic strip – not since Dan McDaid and Paul Grist's *Ghosts of the Northern Line* in 2009. I thought we should take the Doctor back to his default Earth setting. (I'm sure this had nothing at all to do with the fact that I'd be setting a story in the one place I wouldn't need to diligently research with a big pile of books, oh dear me, no.) And I knew London! I had lived there! Putting the story in such a recognisable place meant that we could hit the ground running – there was no need for a panoramic establishing shot, no need to explain the history of the setting, how the politics worked, what the BBC was, what the local customs were, what the landmarks were called, etc. When we suddenly didn't have to do any of that, I realised just how much page-space that kind of detail eats up in the strip. What I had imagined would be a three-part story was easily boiled down into two.

This one started with an image that will be familiar to any husband in the western world: a frowning man pushing a trolley through a supermarket, clutching a shopping list in one hand and a mobile phone in the other. The thought of that man being Rory, with Amy on the other end of the phone inside the TARDIS kitchen, made me laugh. I'm really surprised they haven't done a supermarket episode on TV yet; it's a fantastic environment for a *Doctor Who* story. Just think of all the props you could play with: not just the food but also the freezers, electronic equipment, kitchenware, toys... Put the Doctor in a supermarket and it'd be like giving him the keys to NORAD. The aliens wouldn't stand a chance.

So anyway, I had a setting: a deathly quiet South London supermarket at three in the morning, a handful of shoppers wandering through it, a lone security guard and a very bored woman on the checkout. What happens next?

I went through my notebook and came across two words I'd scribbled down months earlier: 'Evil Banksy!' I always have a notebook on the go. I'd recommend them to all budding writers – just jot down anything that even remotely resembles a funny idea, because odds are you'll forget it half an hour later, and you never know when it might click into place with something else and form a genuinely interesting thought. So I looked at 'Evil Banksy!' and pondered. A sinister graffiti artist? Maybe creating living graffiti creatures that jump off walls and eat people? Yeah... no, maybe not. But *something* like that. Maybe just his *name* could be a threat...

The thought of a villainous artist reminded me of a story I'd done with Martin Geraghty back in 2001 called *The Way of All Flesh* (reprinted in the *Oblivion* volume). It had featured a baddie called Susini. She was a Necrotist; a member of an alien artistic movement that had decided all acts of creation had to stem from death – in other words, they had to murder people to make art. And their art wasn't even any good – Susini was in fact a pretty rubbish artist. But she did have some badass technology at her fingertips, super-science that looked more like magic, and she had been a good challenge for the Doctor.

I had always been pleased with the idea of the Necrotists. They were villains who didn't belong to any single alien species and weren't out to conquer anything. They were satisfyingly different from the standard *Doctor Who* villain template, but we had only ever seen one of them. Why not bring on another one, with a different look and *modus operandi*, to show how varied they could be?

Silhouettes always look great in comics; they're stark and grab the readers' attention. I had seen an ad in a Marvel comic which featured a black-and-white silhouetted superhero figure composed of words

Above: Amy goes to war inside the TARDIS kitchen! Original pencil art by Martin Geraghty.

Left: A preliminary colour sketch of Judy by Martin Geraghty.

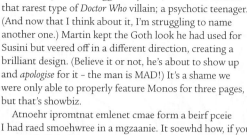

that described him. He wasn't an actual character, it was a symbolic thing. I really liked it – it was a striking image and I mentally filed it away for future use. The Leximorphs came from that.

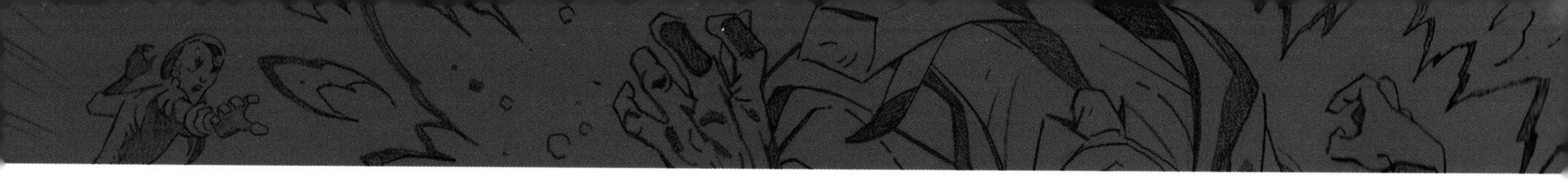

One of the biggest motivations I'd had for returning to the **DWM** strip was the chance to collaborate with Martin Geraghty again. We'd never really stopped working together, of course, as I'd been functioning as the strip's editor for most of the time since I had given up the writing. But Martin and I hadn't been a writer/artist team since *The Flood* in 2005, and I confess I had sometimes watched him work with other writers with a twinge of jealousy. Y'see, the thing is, the guy just kept getting better and better! Martin had been steadily developing his abilities over the years. He'd grown ever more confident as a storyteller while also improving his anatomy, perspective and composition. And just look at his *hands!* I mean it; look at any shot of his characters' hands. They're fluid, expressive, utterly convincing. Hands are the single toughest piece of anatomy for an artist to master. Martin Geraghty draws the best hands in comics. Hands-down!

So with Martin on board, Tom, Peter and I were confident that we'd have something that *looked* great, at least. David Roach was once again supplying his razor-sharp inks, and James Offredi was, as usual, applying some of the most vibrant, well-chosen hues you'll see anywhere in comics.

And as for Roger Langridge, our ever-brilliant letterer... Oh, he had *no idea* what kind of anvil I was about to drop on him.

How many comics have a Harvey and Eisner award-winning writer/artist working as the letterer? I'm guessing just the one. Lettering is a critical part of any comic's visual appeal, and it's essential that it be produced with care, skill and artistry. We are absurdly lucky to have Roger Langridge's phone number. The Leximorphs were essentially walking names, so we knew from the start that Roger would be the man who'd really have to illustrate them. He spent a great deal of time producing many, many incredibly fiddly cut-outs, with no complaint, and did a remarkable job. Thank you, Roger!

The panel where Stringer starts seeing all the familiar high street logos turning into 'Monos' was a real treat. **DWM**'s art editor Richard Atkinson did the honours there, carefully recreating all the logos I had asked for and even adding a couple of his own – his 'M&S' one was just inspired. Thank you, Richard!

I was calling my Necrotist villain 'Zomos' for a while, because the name could be turned into a symmetrical shape in a tag. Then 'Monos' arrived which made far more sense (it simply means 'one'). Graffiti suggested youth, so Monos became that rarest type of *Doctor Who* villain; a psychotic teenager. (And now that I think about it, I'm struggling to name another one.) Martin kept the Goth look he had used for Susini but veered off in a different direction, creating a brilliant design. (Believe it or not, he's about to show up and *apologise* for it – the man is MAD!) It's a shame we were only able to properly feature Monos for three pages, but that's showbiz.

Atnoehr ipromtnat emlenet cmae form a beirf pceie I had raed smoehwree in a mgzaanie. It soewhd how, if you spawepd all the ltreres in a wrod arapt form the fsrit and lsat oens, the biarn cluod slitl tnarltase the wdros as lnog as tehy wree pecald in cxnotet in a stnencee. Taht was a rael eye-oneepr, and I kpet taht fcat in my nbkootek for a few yares. Tihs smeeed lkie the ieadl pcale to use it.

As for that final page – why yes, you're right, that *is* a bit of a puzzler, isn't it? Just who was on that monitor screen? Why did the Doctor look so shocked? And exactly what's "going to hurt"?

I am so very, very sorry, but that's all future story arc stuff. Everything will be explained in our next volume, *Hunters of the Burning Stone*, I promise...

Martin Geraghty Artist

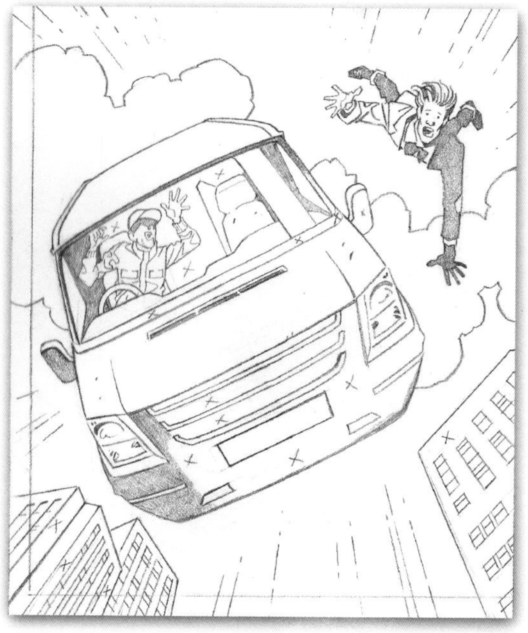

Not so long after this story saw print, The BBC ran a series of trails for Wimbledon 2012 – still easily found on the internet – in which various world-famous ball-clobberers are turned into silhouettes comprised of

Below left: The Doctor and Stringer's team go for a tumble. Pencil art by Martin Geraghty.

Below: Martin's pencil sketch of Detective Inspector Bill Stringer.

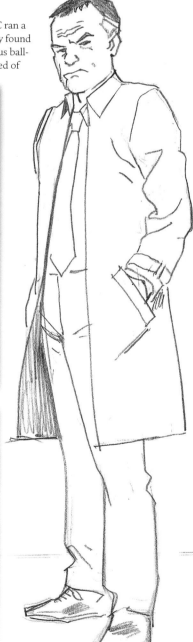

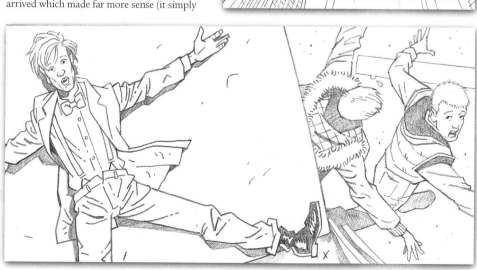

Right: Monos is revealed in Part Two of *Sticks & Stones*. The original rough and finished penciled page by Martin Geraghty.

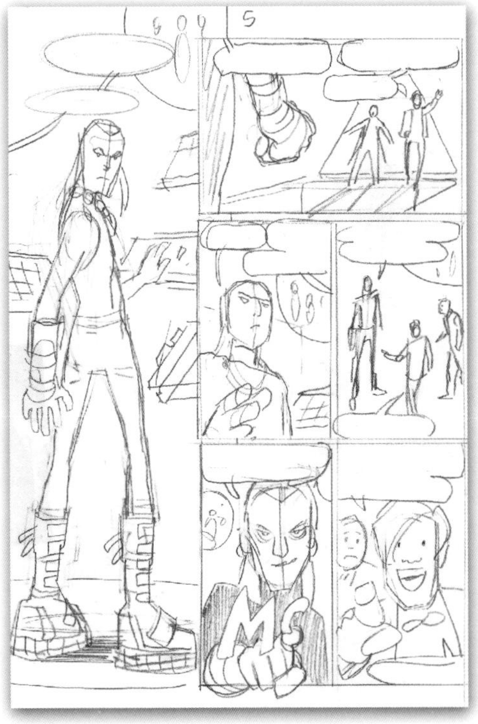

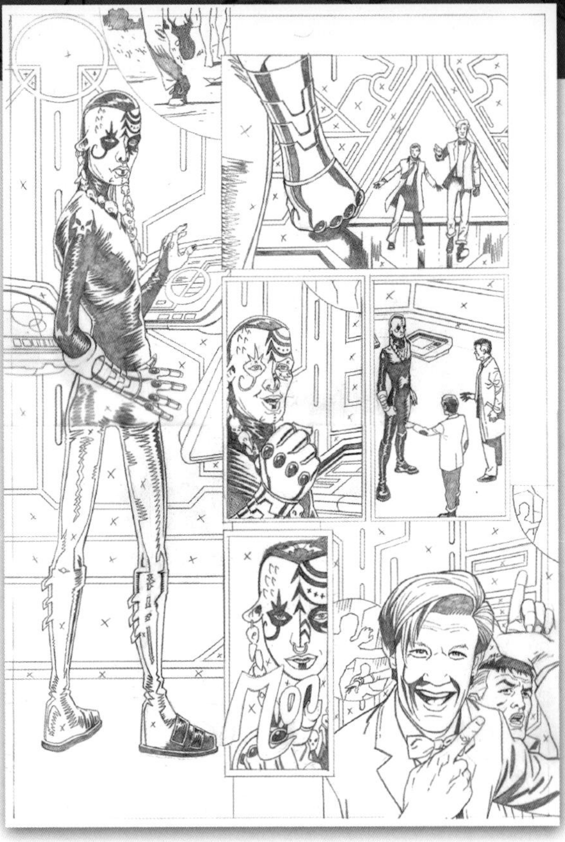

Below: Martin Geraghty's initial colour study of Monos.

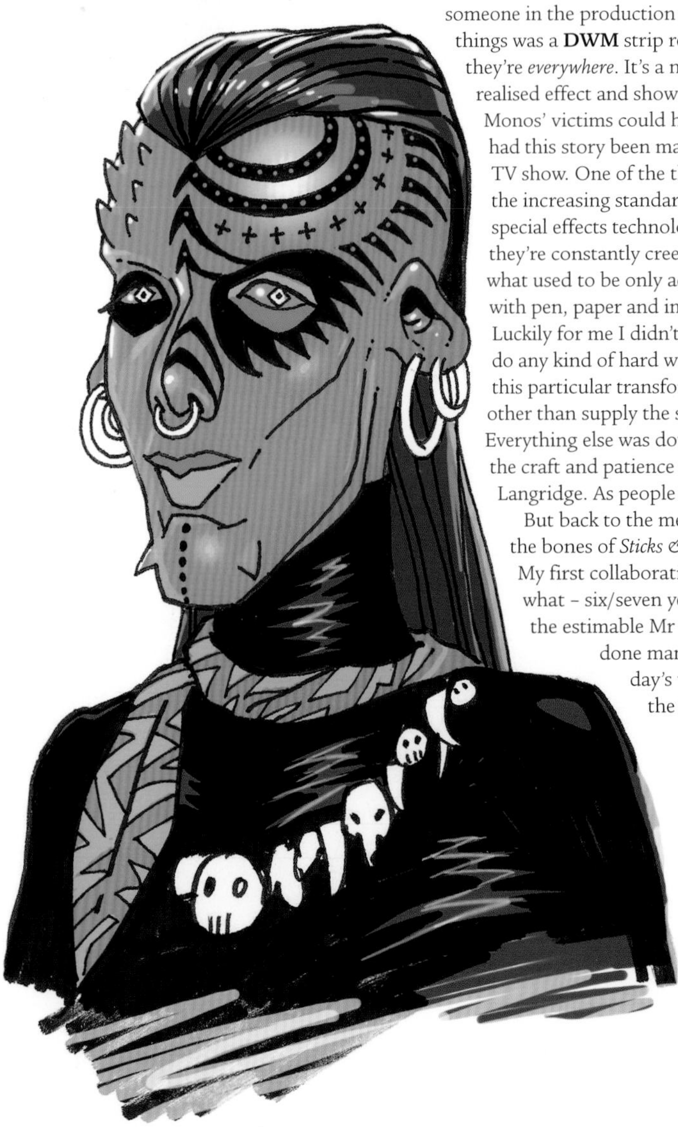

words such as 'Passion', 'Skill', 'Commitment', 'Grunt' and 'Lycra', etc. It's probably sheer coincidence that they fell upon this idea but it's not so much of a stretch to imagine someone in the production side of things was a **DWM** strip reader as they're *everywhere*. It's a nicely-realised effect and shows off how Monos' victims could have looked had this story been made for the TV show. One of the things about the increasing standards in TV special effects technology is that they're constantly creeping up on what used to be only achievable with pen, paper and imagination. Luckily for me I didn't have to do any kind of hard work on this particular transformation other than supply the silhouettes. Everything else was down to the craft and patience of Roger Langridge. As people say, Kudos.

But back to the meat on the bones of *Sticks & Stones*. My first collaboration after what – six/seven years? – with the estimable Mr Gray. I'd done many a decent day's work in the interim under the fine stewardship of Alan Barnes, Rob Davis, Dan McDaid and Jonny Morris but the glory days of *The Flood* still lingered, so the chance to collaborate again with the longest-standing working partnership I have (20 years in summer 2013 since 1993's *Bringer of Darkness*) was to be jumped at. This was a writer who'd reinvented the Master and the Cybermen, created vast new omniverses for our hero to tumble into, defining the era of an entire incarnation of a lost Doctor in the process. What madness was I about to step into?

Open in a supermarket.

I love this. The mundanity of it. It's what *Doctor Who* does better than anything in all its guises: the Krynoid in the lettuce patch. Genuinely, it's a great little two-parter, full of the fine characterisation and plotting we unreservedly expect of the **DWM** strip nowadays. A nicely-paced slice of John Carpenter-style *Who*. Unfortunately it's badly let down by a major element. And that'll be me then.

As a freelance artist I'm always moaning about not having enough time to do a job properly. "That deadline is utterly impossible," I say, then do it anyway. A great man once said on some DVD extra somewhere that comic strip art is never finished, it's just delivered on time, or words to that effect. He should have a statue somewhere for that.

So, having been given an unprecedentedly fantastic lead-in time, I frittered it away doing other assignments until I had to work against the clock to finish it.

Budding Freelancers out there take note: a) Use your time wisely. b) What on earth are you thinking? Get a job.

Anyway, that's why Monos is under-designed and bland. I'm so disappointed in how he turned out, especially given his brief appearance. I've run away from more threatening Emos in Warrington town centre. And one of them was related to me.

And some of the three leads' likenesses are off-colour. As people say, My Bad.

Still, I like all the stuff with the Doctor and the surveillance squad. Page 9 of Part One is actually one of my favourite-ever finished pages, so there's some wheat amongst the chaff. Despite all this artistic shonkiness, Scott's meticulously well-oiled plot mechanism (that will eventually culminate in something truly magnificent) ticks inexorably on...

And the pictures get better.

The Cornucopia Caper

Scott Gray Writer

The previous two stories had progressed quite smoothly, and I was regaining some of my old confidence. Maybe I did know what I was doing after all! Silly me. The next one brought me crashing back to reality with a big *Ka-Boom*.

I had wanted to work with the multi-talented Dan McDaid, and Tom and Peter were kind enough to commission him. So far, so good. I was keen to bring back the Skith, the aliens that Dan and Martin Geraghty had created and used in two stories: *The First* and *The Age of Ice*. The Skith had a really interesting design, a clear motivation and had been a powerful opponent for the Doctor. And Dan had somehow managed to make them genuinely funny without sacrificing any sense of menace. They were great!

The setting would be Cornucopia Multiversity, a massive school floating in a remote region of space. It's populated by students from a wide variety of alien species. They're all very young, wearing uniforms – jerseys and ties, very British in style. The Doctor loves the feel of the place: "Space Hogwarts!" All the teachers are sophisticated robots.

The school is invaded by a Skith spacecraft. The Skithmaster, a large, flamboyant figure (voiced in my head by Stephen Fry), brings with him a group of young Skith: "Skudents". They march in and zap any opposition. The Skithmaster cheerfully announces to the terrified children that Cornucopia has just become part of the Skith academy franchise. However, Cornucopia's purpose is to exchange knowledge between different species, a concept that the Skith find disgusting. The Skudents are all competing to become part of the Mindcore; the Skith hive mind. Only one of them can succeed. All the other Skudents will die in the process – a situation they all accept without any qualms.

The Doctor poses as a professor for a while until his identity is discovered by the Skithmaster. Rory saves him by zooming to the rescue on a flying skateboard he's borrowed from a student. They are aided by Miss Ghost, one of the robot teachers.

Amy gets separated in the chaos and, with a couple of students, explores the area beneath Cornucopia. She finds the Nascian – a huge energy creature – at its heart. She tells Amy that the children are in fact hundreds of years old. They are the survivors of a massive disaster in space caused when the ships they were travelling in accidentally collided with the Nascian. The guilt-ridden creature created the school and has taken care of the children ever since, educating them and healing all their illnesses, even retarding their ageing process.

The Doctor, Rory and Miss Ghost sneak into the Skith ship and learn that the Skithmaster is trying to find the Nascian – he wants to siphon off her power. The Skithmaster orders the Doctor and company to surrender or his Skudents will kill the children. The Doctor has no choice but to fire a telepathic pulse into the Skudents' linked brains. They collapse, apparently dead. The enraged Skithmaster tries to kill the Doctor but is shot by Miss Ghost. The Doctor is surprised to see the robot break her non-violence programming. The Skudents aren't dead, of course, but their minds have been wiped. Now they have a chance to be re-educated at the school in a more positive way. The Doctor points out that there's nothing inherently evil about the Skith – their culture has just evolved in a brutal direction.

Amy convinces the Nascian that she has to let the children go. "I know it's hard... you only want to protect them, keep them safe and happy... But you can't do that forever." A tear falls down Amy's face as she says, "They grow up so fast. Believe me, I know."

After the TARDIS crew departs, we learn that Miss Ghost isn't a robot at all. She's a woman wearing armour who has prior knowledge of the Doctor. More mystery for the future...

I kept pushing the story in every direction I could think of for weeks. *Painful* weeks. It wasn't bad but it wasn't great either. There were a few nice ideas in there, and I loved Amy's bit at the end. I remember describing it to my wife and her responding with an "Ooohhhh!" (Trust me, getting the missus to feel *any* sympathy at all for Amy Pond was quite an achievement. *Not a fan!*) But I wasn't happy. The story lacked any real sense of peril. Actually killing any of the children seemed out

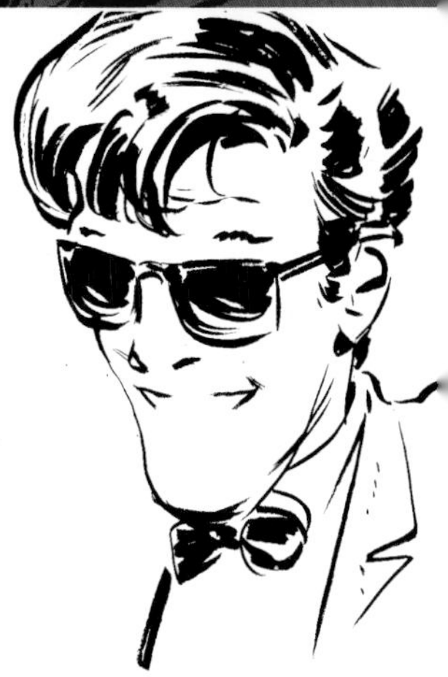

Above & Below: Dan McDaid produced several inked sketches of the Doctor, Amy and Rory before beginning work on *The Cornucopia Caper*.

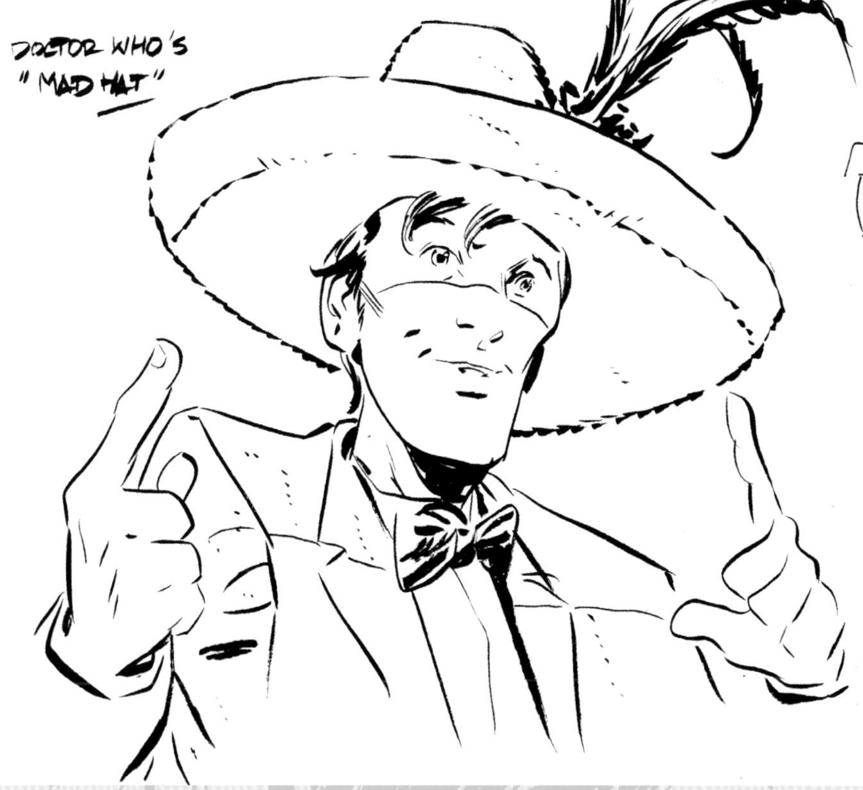
DOCTOR WHO'S
"MAD HAT"

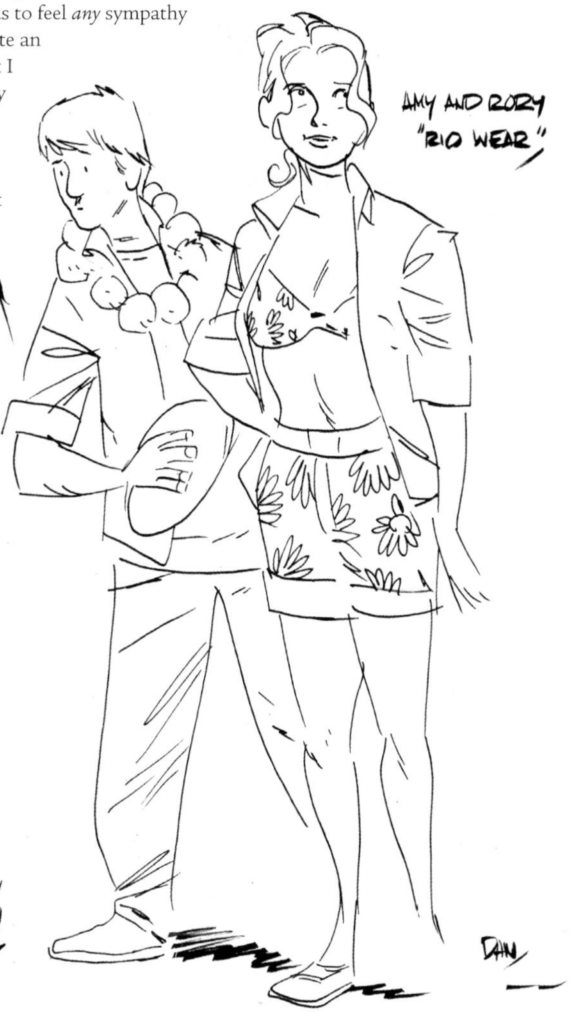
AMY AND RORY
"RIO WEAR"
DAN

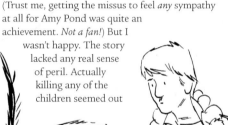

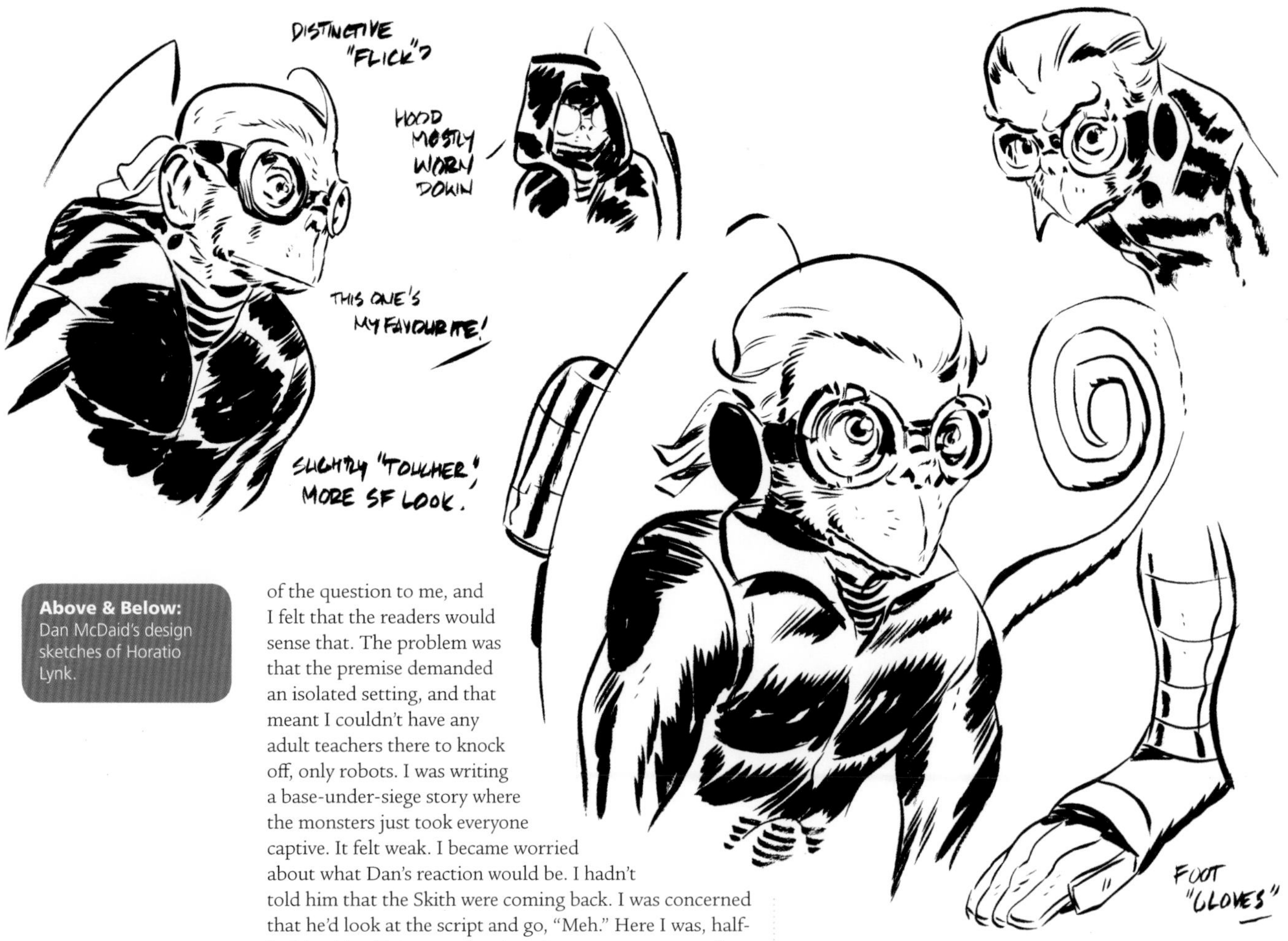
DISTINCTIVE "FLICK"?
HOOD MOSTLY WORN DOWN
THIS ONE'S MY FAVOURITE!
SLIGHTLY "TOUGHER", MORE SF LOOK.
FOOT "GLOVES"

Above & Below: Dan McDaid's design sketches of Horatio Lynk.

of the question to me, and I felt that the readers would sense that. The problem was that the premise demanded an isolated setting, and that meant I couldn't have any adult teachers there to knock off, only robots. I was writing a base-under-siege story where the monsters just took everyone captive. It felt weak. I became worried about what Dan's reaction would be. I hadn't told him that the Skith were coming back. I was concerned that he'd look at the script and go, "Meh." Here I was, half-inching his villains, putting them into a so-so story and then *making him draw it!*

And that realisation – that I had no faith in my own story – made me throw it in the bin. Never even showed it to Tom and Pete. I started again.

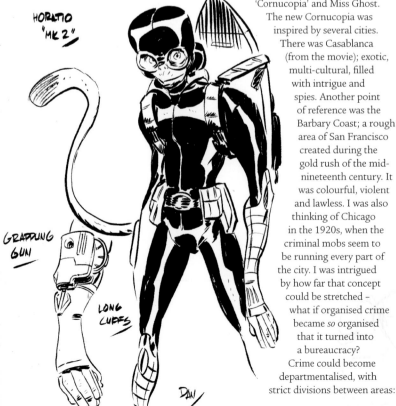

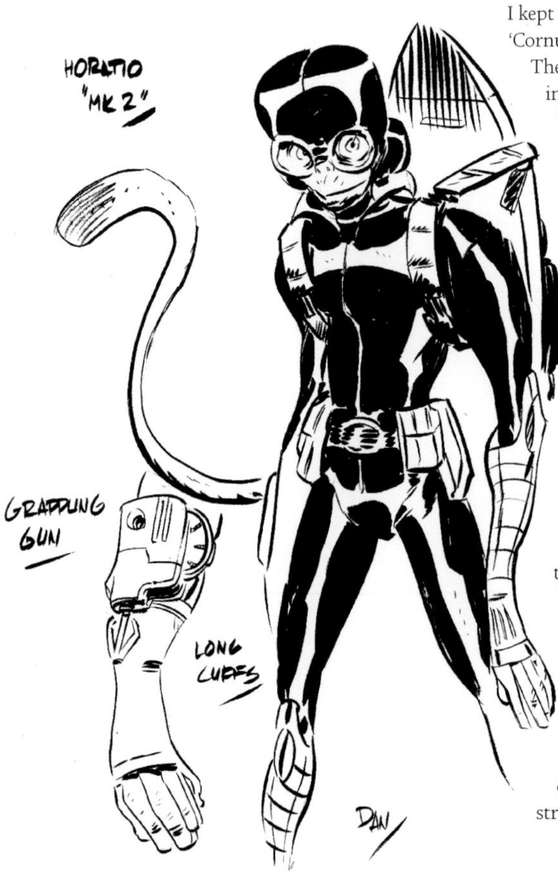
HORATIO "MK 2"
GRAPPLING GUN
LONG CUFFS
DAN

I kept two things: the name 'Cornucopia' and Miss Ghost. The new Cornucopia was inspired by several cities. There was Casablanca (from the movie); exotic, multi-cultural, filled with intrigue and spies. Another point of reference was the Barbary Coast; a rough area of San Francisco created during the gold rush of the mid-nineteenth century. It was colourful, violent and lawless. I was also thinking of Chicago in the 1920s, when the criminal mobs seem to be running every part of the city. I was intrigued by how far that concept could be stretched – what if organised crime became *so* organised that it turned into a bureaucracy? Crime could become departmentalised, with strict divisions between areas: kidnappings could only be carried out by the Kidnappers Union, murders could only be committed by an Assassins Alliance. I thought it was a funny idea and it got me re-energised. I had moved from a base-under-siege tale to another classic *Doctor Who* story template: the Crazy Society.

Some of my favourite TV *Doctor Who* stories are Crazy Society jobs: *The Happiness Patrol*, *The Beast Below* and *Gridlock* all rank very highly with me. They're satirical, colourful and filled with a scary fairy tale charm. But these types of stories can fall flat; there's an inherent danger in the structure of a Crazy Society tale that can easily scupper them. I had never worked it out myself, but luckily Jonathan Morris had given it some thought. I had been reading his excellent blog *Under Three Hundred* (much recommended: you'll find it at *http://underthreehundred.blogspot.co.uk*). In one of his entries, Jonny pointed out that when the villains are in charge of a society, they tend to have no further ambition beyond maintaining the status quo. They don't want to invade the Earth or blow up the universe. Instead, the baddie tends to sit in his control room all day and say things like, "What do you mean, the Doctor has escaped with the rebels? Find him, you fools!" If you're not careful you wind up with a completely static enemy who has no plan, no desires – and no impact on the story.

With that in mind, I set out to give the Crime Lords a proper goal: something huge and omnipresent that they really wanted. A gigantic money box that no-one could break into seemed an obvious choice, and so the Ziggurat was born. I know as Maguffins go it's a pretty blatant one, but sometimes bigger really is better!

There's a strong streak of satire running through *The Cornucopia Caper* and it's very deliberate. It was written when the banking scandal was in the headlines, when the *News of the World* finally slinked off to die in shame, when

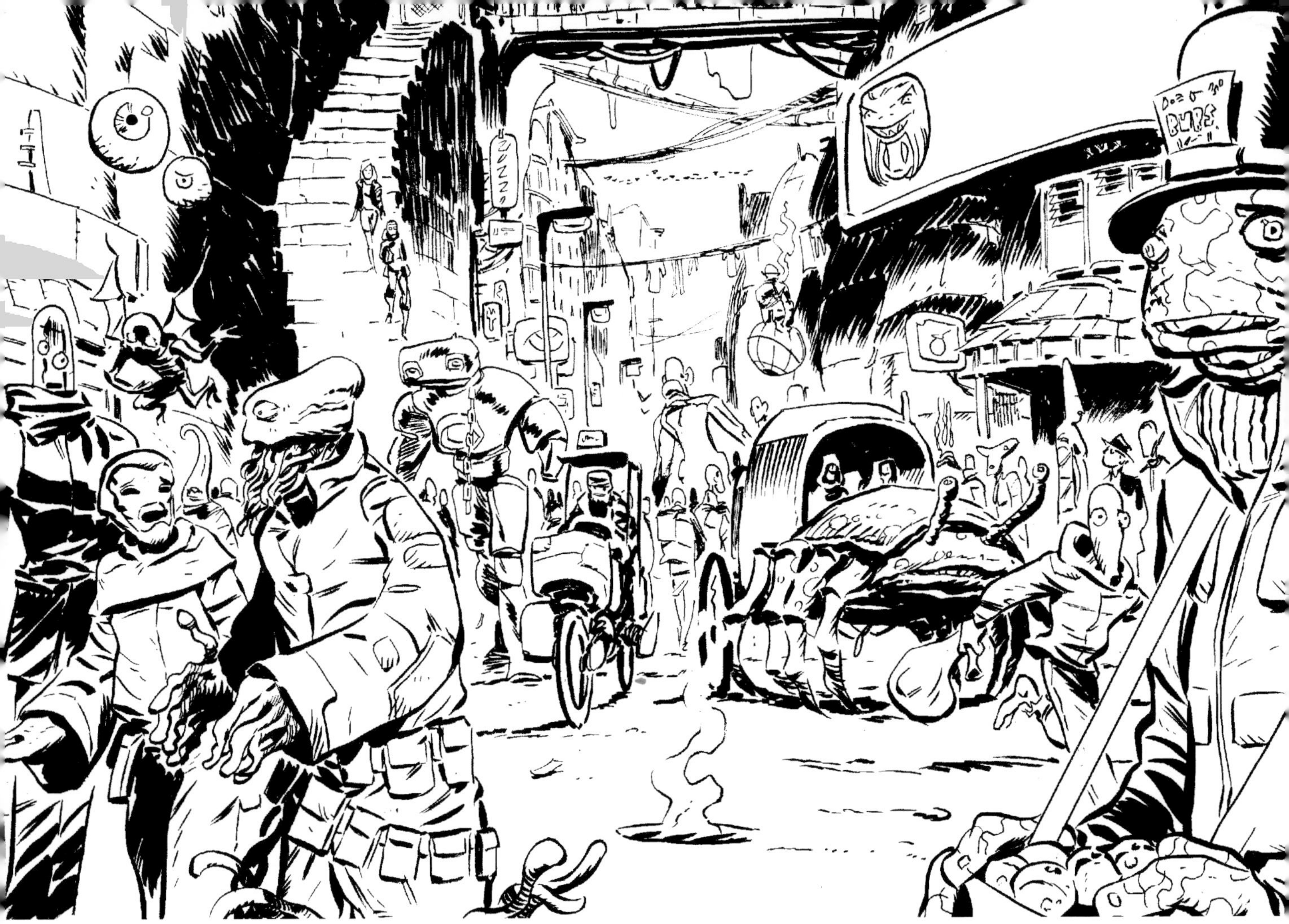

politicians began to blame the recession on the poorest members of society instead of the billionaires who had actually caused it. The system is the system, and the people with the power to change the system are always the ones who benefit from it the most. Politics, banking, media – no part of them ever improves from within, and it's insulting when the people at the top pretend otherwise. The Crime Lords are at least the most honest criminals you'll ever encounter. When they nick your money they put up a billboard to announce it.

I had made the Doctor meet his hero in *The Chains of Olympus*, but now he was faced with something just as challenging: a rival. Horatio Lynk basically hijacks the story in Part One. He narrates the action, steals the Doctor's companion and leads the reader into the world of the story. I knew this was a risky manoeuvre – I wanted readers to like the bloke, and they could have easily taken offence at his spotlight-hogging. But people seemed to enjoy Horatio. When the Doctor meets somebody with a similar set of skills, brains and cunning, he's usually a villain. It was fun to see him wrestling for possession of the story with another hero.

Horatio was quite posh in the outline but by the second page of the script I had turned him into a Cockney. He had several ancestors: there was Monkey from the 80s TV series *Monkey!* – an aggressive, cocky fellow who could fly on his personal cloud. Robin Hood too, of course, plus the Artful Dodger and Spider-Man. I quickly decided on the name 'Lynk' – it felt right somehow. A couple of weeks passed before I realised I'd nicked it from *Lancelot Link: Secret Chimp*, a TV show I'd loved as a kid. It featured real chimpanzees wearing hats and false moustaches, trying to take over the world with overdubbed voices. A classic!

Dan came up with a terrific design for Horatio, and followed suit with the Crime Lords. Granny Solasta was the most important to get right. She was Fagin and the Wicked Witch, with maybe a little pinch of Gollum thrown in. She was always meant to be a proper old school East End villain. (She had Barbara Windsor's voice, by the way.)

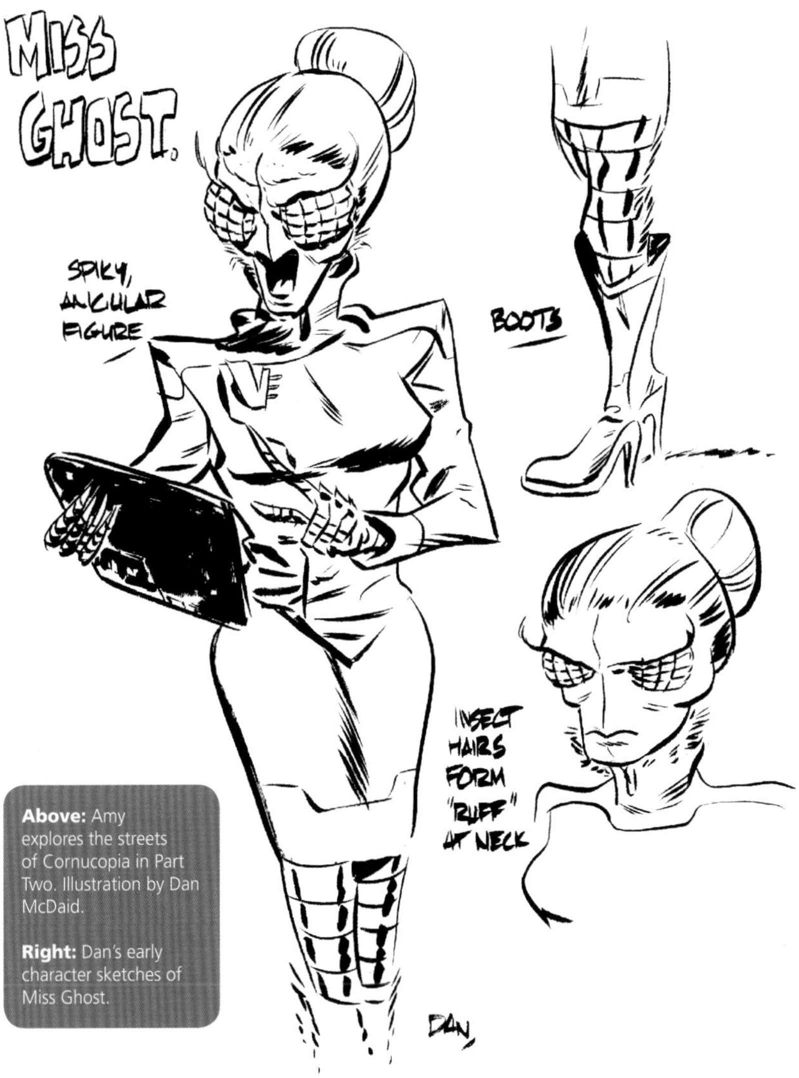
MISS GHOST.
SPIKY, ANGULAR FIGURE
BOOTS
INSECT HAIRS FORM "RUFF" AT NECK
DAN

Above: Amy explores the streets of Cornucopia in Part Two. Illustration by Dan McDaid.

Right: Dan's early character sketches of Miss Ghost.

Above: A design rough from Part Three by Dan McDaid.

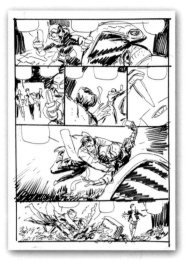

Dan also did an ace job bringing the grimy, textured streets of Cornucopia to life. I wanted it to be ancient, almost medieval in appearance when Amy and Horatio explored its depths. James Offredi aided and abetted with some lush colours – the red sky gave the place a perfectly oppressive atmosphere. Dan draws some of the coolest pyrotechnics in comics, so I made sure to give him a nice big explosion at the end.

It's very easy to fall into narrative traps while writing *Doctor Who*. All its regular elements feel so familiar that the writer can easily forget the characters don't share the same volume of knowledge. Originally I had Granny view the TARDIS on Miss Ghost's digital pad, quickly summon the Crime Lords and announce that the Doctor was going to take them all into the Ziggurat. It was only very late in the day that I twigged: Granny *wouldn't know* the TARDIS was bigger on the inside! Why would she think all the Crime Lords could fit inside it? So I added the scene where she goes into the control room, which led to my favourite line in the whole story: "Yer box steals space!"

As I've said, Miss Ghost was the only character I salvaged from the earlier plot. She was very important: the Last Woman Standing. She seems incidental to the story, just a walk-on character who provides some exposition, but only because that suits her. The Doctor may see through her in the end, but she's giving nothing away apart from a familiar question: "What is buried in man?"

We'll be seeing her again soon, in... yes, you guessed it, *Hunters of the Burning Stone*.

Well, that's it from me. I hope you enjoyed the book. It's been a real privilege to return to the *Doctor Who* writer's seat, and a genuine pleasure to work with everyone on the comic strip team. Happy times and places!

Dan McDaid Artist

I always seem to end up drawing *Doctor Who* in a heatwave. Don't ask me why, I just do. This strip was no exception. Picture me, reader, if you dare, sat only in pants and t-shirt, as the sweltering Dundee sun glints through my living room window, bathing my drawing board in unwelcome natural light and drawing beads of foul sweat from my brow. Outside, there are beautiful girls and loose-limbed boys. Everyone is young. But I bide within, hidden from view. There is toast in my beard. This is what it's like to be a comic book artist. Why am I telling you this? Firstly as a salutary warning to stay in school, but mostly to establish that this strip was bloody hard work, and what passes for a Scottish summer had more or less slipped by by the time I was done. Everything had to be designed from the ground up and (because I live to sail close to the wind) often at the last minute and right there on the final page. Some pages – notably anything with a crowd scene, or that reveal of the Ziggurat interior on page nine of Part Two – took actual days to do. I think I must've drawn thousands of coins. The summer passed.

But I'm getting ahead of myself. At the risk of embarrassing the Most High, I've wanted to work with Scott Gray for bloody *years*. Ever since reading the magnificent *Wormwood* from the heady Paul McGann days (when it was all black-and-white round here) he's been among my favourite comics writers, and certainly my favourite *Doctor Who* writer. Having him as an editor during my own *Who* run was a delight, a challenge, a thrill and a bloody nightmare. But I really wanted to draw one of his scripts, as I knew it would have all the scope and humanity I look for in a good *Doctor Who* story.

I wasn't disappointed. In fact, I was positively overwhelmed, as it turned out Scott had booked me for a widescreen, big-budget fantasy epic, with an entirely alien culture to describe. On the one hand – no reference, yay. On the other hand, I'd have to make everything up from scratch. Then on the other, *other* hand, a chance to indulge my artistic influences – a hint of Moebius in the cityscape,

Below: The developing character sketches for Granny Solasta by Dan McDaid.

ANN WIDDECOMBE STYLE FACE
HUNCHED, BEETLE-LIKE CARAPACE
NECK IS EXPOSED, FOR ADDED HORRIBLENESS.
GRANNY MK3
FLOWING, HANDSOME GOWN, SLIGHTLY GRUBBY...
CAPE?
DAN
DAN

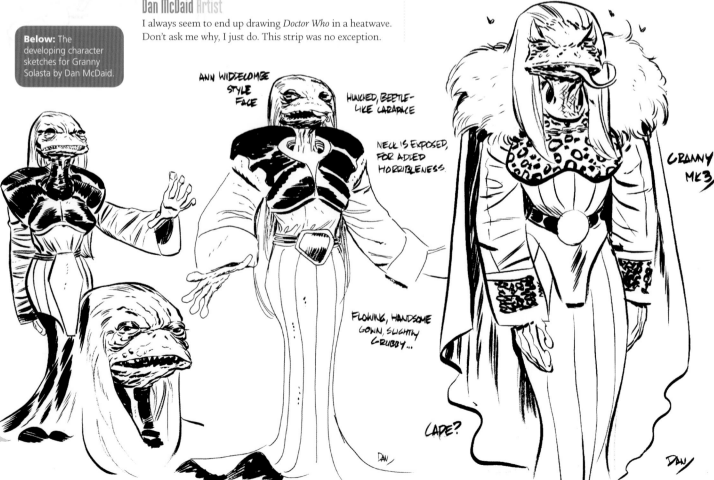

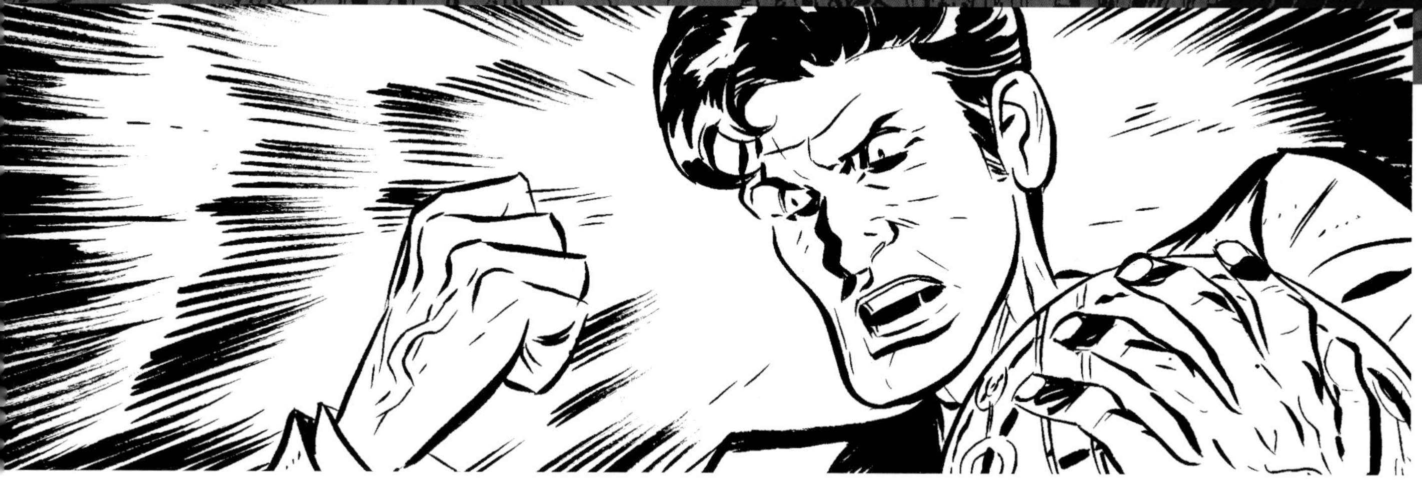

a bit of Walt Simonson in the Ziggurat's inner chamber. And the script specified that guest character Horatio Lynk would have some of the sinewy energy of Steve Ditko's Spider-Man, so I knew he was going to be very, VERY cool to draw.

In fact, the whole strip was heaving with cool things to draw. I think the word is 'toyetic', *ie* designs that are going to make for GREAT action figures. Obviously, there's Horatio himself, a brilliant second lead who pretty much steals the story from the Doctor himself in Part Two, but there's also the various guards, guild members, flying ships and monsters. A huge blast to design and draw, and a potentially lucrative revenue stream. Character Options – call me.

But what I love about Scott's writing is that it's never just cool for cool's sake. There's always an emotional underpinning to everything he writes. While it's easy to be distracted by Horatio's more superficially exciting traits, it's worth noting the small, intimate beats that really bring him to life. My favourite Horatio moments don't see him dodging blaster shots, or zig-zagging his way between flying mines, it's him (rather slyly) guilting Amy into helping him out, or cheekily stealing a kiss at the end. These moments are Manna for comic artists: we like drawing cool made-up stuff, we hate drawing cars, but what we really LOVE is character.

Speaking of Amy... this brings me round to the series regulars, and the endless problems they present. I do love Matt Smith's Doctor, but the challenge of getting him right continues. I think I got as close as I'm ever going to with this strip, and this is partly due to where the show has taken him in the last few years – he's gone from rather a blithe man of action to someone who's seen hurt, horror and heartbreak, and all of these elements allow the artist to bring some nuance to our depiction of the character. I also – on the final page – got to indulge one of my favourite tics from the Dark Doctor, *New Adventures* era of the strip, namely the Sylvester McCoy shadowy brow. That's when you know this sh*t is about to get real.

This was also my second shot at drawing Rory, who has an interesting, regal face, though you do have to be careful not to accidentally draw Nicholas Lyndhurst. I was finally homing in on a reasonable Amy Pond, but alas she's now time-locked in the 1940s, so my efforts are all in vain.

My favourite characters in the whole shebang are the heads of the guilds. The concept of unionised villainy is so rich and literate, I couldn't help but get carried away with it. Granny's my favourite, of course, though it wasn't till I gave her a leopard-print tunic that she really came to life for me. My original sketch showed her adorned with a small cloud of flies, and I do wish I'd kept this detail now as it 'icks' her up a little bit. The rest of the guilds were mostly designed on the page, and what a delightfully baroque shower of bastards they are. And – at last! – a chance to draw one of the mighty Mobox, as Kirbyesque a character as you could wish for. Scott knows me too well.

And then of course, there's the mysterious figure at the story's end. Ah, I loved this bit. A mystery, a threat, a foreboding hint of things to come... The show does this very well these days, but nothing gets it right quite like the comic strip. I had no idea who this character was going to be – that canny Scott had left me in the dark, despite my barrage of inane guesses ("Is it Sharon?") – but I knew she was: a) *probably* female and b) *definitely* going to be eventually designed by Martin and Scott. Fair do's, considering Martin would have to draw him/her more than anyone else. That said, when I turned in my roughs for the strip, I had to make her look like *something*, so I gave her a mask reminiscent of 80s cult comic fave Night Raven, and Scott liked this so much he co-opted it into the final design. Very flattering.

And I'd say... yes, that about covers it. Oh no, wait, there is one more thing: to keep the tedium of coin-drawing down to a minimum, I dotted various silly Easter Eggs around the Ziggurat vault. Can you spot them all? If you can, please bear in mind these are mostly the copyright of other, undoubtedly litigious corporations so... mum's the word, alright? ●

Above: Dan McDaid's original B&W illustration of the angry Doctor.

Below: Dan's design rough for the final confrontation between the Doctor and Miss Ghost.

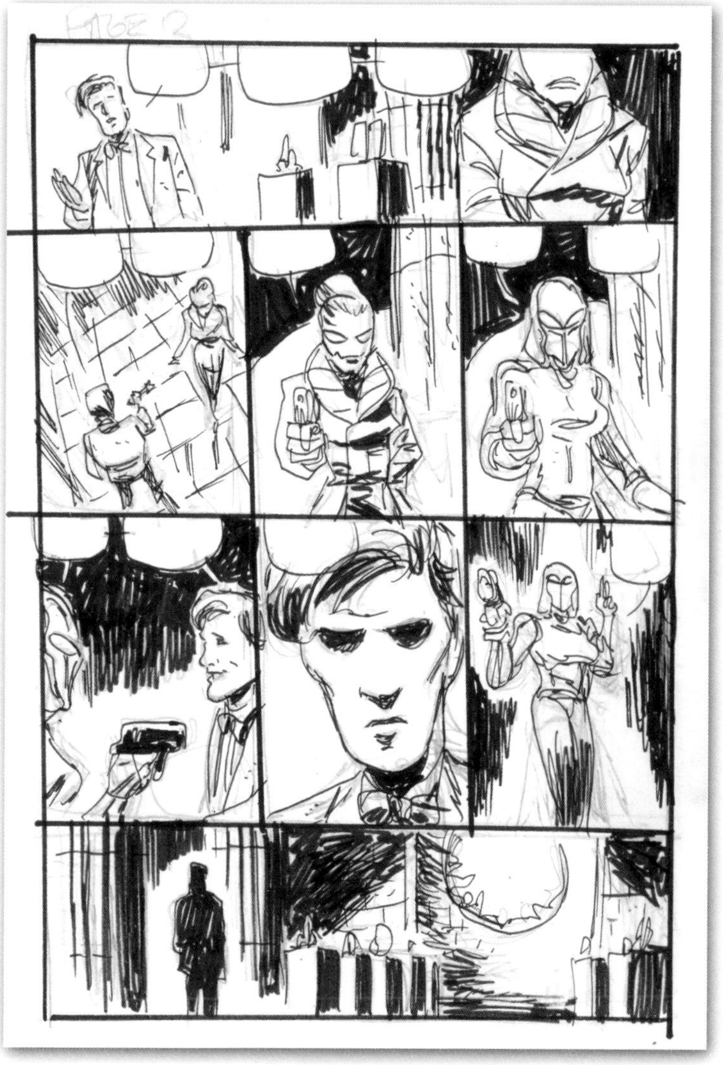

DOCTOR WHO COMIC COLLECTIONS

CLASSIC STRIP ADVENTURES

DAVE GIBBONS
MILLS & WAGNER
STEVE MOORE
DOCTOR WHO
THE IRON LEGION
A PANINI BOOKS GRAPHIC NOVEL

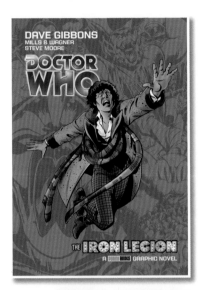

Volume One of the Fourth Doctor's comic strip adventures, containing five digitally restored stories:

THE IRON LEGION, **CITY OF THE DAMNED**, **THE STAR BEAST**, **THE DOGS OF DOOM** and **THE TIME WITCH!**

Featuring work from **Dave Gibbons**, **Pat Mills**, **John Wagner** and **Steve Moore**

164 pages | b&w | softcover
£14.99 | $24.95
ISBN 1-9041 59-37-0

DAVE GIBBONS
STEVE PARKHOUSE
STEVE MOORE
DOCTOR WHO
DRAGON'S CLAW
A PANINI BOOKS GRAPHIC NOVEL

Volume Two of the Fourth Doctor's comic strip adventures, containing 10 digitally restored stories:

DRAGON'S CLAW, **THE COLLECTOR**, **DREAMERS OF DEATH**, **THE LIFE BRINGER**, **WAR OF THE WORDS**, **SPIDER-GOD**, **THE DEAL**, **END OF THE LINE**, **THE FREE-FALL WARRIORS**, **JUNKYARD DEMON** and **THE NEUTRON KNIGHTS**!

164 pages | b&w | softcover
£14.99 | $24.95
ISBN 1-9041 59-81-8

DAVE GIBBONS
STEVE PARKHOUSE
MICK AUSTIN
STEVE DILLON
DOCTOR WHO
THE TIDES OF TIME
A PANINI BOOKS GRAPHIC NOVEL

The Fifth Doctor's complete comic strip run, containing six digitally restored stories:

THE TIDES OF TIME, **STARS FELL ON STOCKBRIDGE**, **THE STOCKBRIDGE HORROR**, **LUNAR LAGOON**, **4-DIMENSIONAL VISTAS** and **THE MODERATOR**!

Featuring art from **Dave Gibbons**

228 pages | b&w | softcover
£14.99 | $24.95
ISBN 1-9041 59-92-3

JOHN RIDGWAY
STEVE PARKHOUSE
ALAN McKENZIE
DOCTOR WHO
VOYAGER
A PANINI BOOKS GRAPHIC NOVEL

Volume One of the Sixth Doctor's comic strip adventures containing seven digitally restored adventures:

THE SHAPE SHIFTER, **VOYAGER**, **POLLY THE GLOT**, **ONCE UPON A TIME LORD**, **WAR-GAME**, **FUNHOUSE** and **KANE'S STORY/ABEL'S STORY/ THE WARRIOR'S STORY/ FROBISHER'S STORY**!

172 pages | b&w softcover
£15.99 | $31.95
ISBN 978-1-905239-71-9

JOHN RIDGWAY
GRANT MORRISON
JAMIE DELANO
DOCTOR WHO
THE WORLD SHAPERS
A PANINI BOOKS GRAPHIC NOVEL

Volume Two of the Sixth Doctor's comic strip adventures containing the following digitally restored adventures:

EXODUS, **REVELATION!**, **GENESIS!**, **NATURE OF THE BEAST**, **TIME BOMB**, **SALAD DAZE**, **CHANGES**, **PROFITS OF DOOM**, **THE GIFT** and **THE WORLD SHAPERS**!

188 pages | b&w | softcover
£15.99 | $31.95
ISBN 978-1-905239-87-0

DOCTOR·WHO
A COLD DAY IN HELL!

Volume One of the Seventh Doctor's comic strip adventures containing 11 digitally restored stories:

A COLD DAY IN HELL!, **REDEMPTION!**, **THE CROSSROADS OF TIME**, **CLAWS OF THE KLATHI!**, **CULTURE SHOCK!**, **KEEPSAKE**, **PLANET OF THE DEAD**, **ECHOES OF THE MOGOR!**, **TIME AND TIDE**, **FOLLOW THAT TARDIS!** and **INVADERS FROM GANTAC!**

PLUS an introduction and commentary by former strip editors **Richard Starkings** and **John Freeman**

188 pages | b&w | softcover
£15.99 | $31.95 | ISBN 978-1-84653-410-2

BBC
DOCTOR WHO
Richard Starkings John Tomlinson Lee Sullivan John Ridgway
NEMESIS OF THE DALEKS

Volume Two of the Seventh Doctor's complete comic strip adventures from the pages of **DWM** and *The Incredible Hulk Presents*. Contains 14 complete stories:

NEMESIS OF THE DALEKS, **STAIRWAY TO HEAVEN**, **ONCE IN A LIFETIME**, **HUNGER FROM THE ENDS OF TIME!**, **WAR WORLD!**, **TECHNICAL HITCH**, **A SWITCH IN TIME!**, **THE SENTINEL!**, **WHO'S THAT GIRL!**, **THE ENLIGHTENMENT OF LI-CHEE THE WISE**, **SLIMMER!**, **NINEVEH!**, **TRAIN-FLIGHT**, **DOCTOR CONKERER!**
and also the adventures of Abslom Daak in **ABSLOM DAAK... DALEK KILLER** and **STAR TIGERS!**

PLUS a massive behind-the-scenes feature, including commentaries from the writers, artists and editors, cut scenes, pencil art, design sketches, and much, much more.

196 pages | b&w | softcover
£16.99 | $24.99 | ISBN 978-1-84653-531-4

These titles are available now from all good bookshops, specialist comic shops and online retailers

Panini COMICS

THE COMPLETE EIGHTH DOCTOR

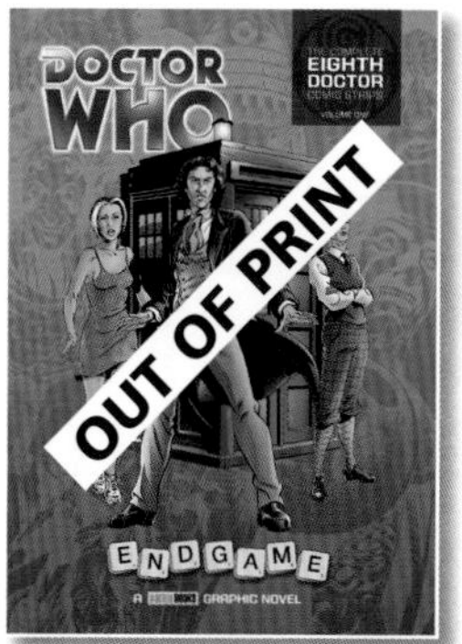
DOCTOR WHO
EIGHTH DOCTOR
OUT OF PRINT
ENDGAME

Volume One of the Eighth Doctor's complete comic strip adventures, containing eight digitally restored stories: **ENDGAME**, **THE KEEP**, **FIRE AND BRIMSTONE**, **TOOTH AND CLAW**, **THE FINAL CHAPTER**, **WORMWOOD**, **A LIFE OF MATTER AND DEATH** and **BY HOOK OR BY CROOK**!

PLUS a 16-page behind-the-scenes feature with unused story ideas, character designs and an authors' commentary on all the strips!

228 pages | b&w | softcover
£14.99 | $24.95 | ISBN 1-9052 39-09-2

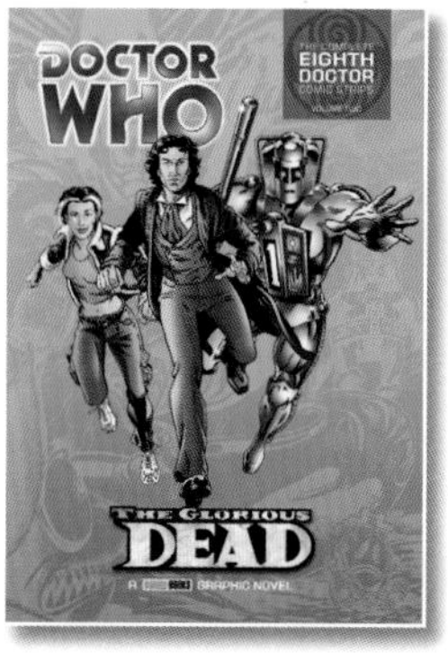
DOCTOR WHO
EIGHTH DOCTOR
THE GLORIOUS DEAD

Volume Two of the Eighth Doctor's complete comic strip adventures, containing eight digitally restored stories: **THE FALLEN, UNNATURAL BORN KILLERS, THE ROAD TO HELL, COMPANY OF THIEVES, THE GLORIOUS DEAD, THE AUTONOMY BUG, HAPPY DEATHDAY** and **TV ACTION**!

PLUS a six-page behind-the-scenes feature and two classic 1980s strips featuring Kroton the Cyberman: **THROWBACK** and **SHIP OF FOOLS**!

244 pages | b&w | softcover
£15.99 | $26.50 | ISBN 1-9052 39-44-0

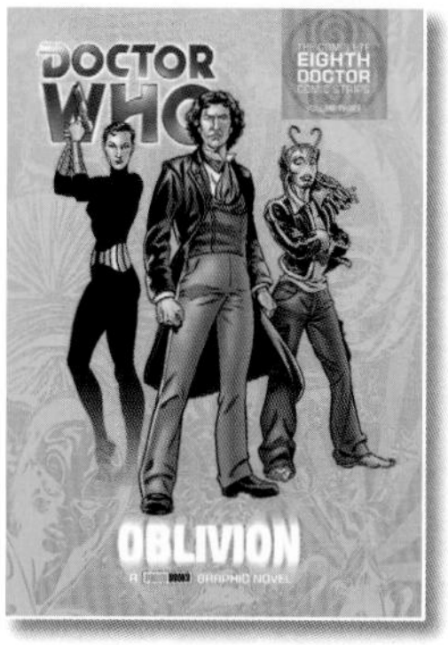
DOCTOR WHO
EIGHTH DOCTOR
OBLIVION

Volume Three of the Eighth Doctor's complete comic strip adventures, containing eight digitally restored stories: **OPHIDIUS, BEAUTIFUL FREAK**, **THE WAY OF ALL FLESH, CHILDREN OF THE REVOLUTION**, **ME AND MY SHADOW**, **UROBOROS** and **OBLIVION**!

PLUS a massive 22-page behind-the-scenes feature, bonus strip **CHARACTER ASSASSIN** and a newly-extended conclusion to Dalek strip **CHILDREN OF THE REVOLUTION**!

228 pages | full colour | softcover
£15.99 | $26.50 | ISBN 1-905239-45-9

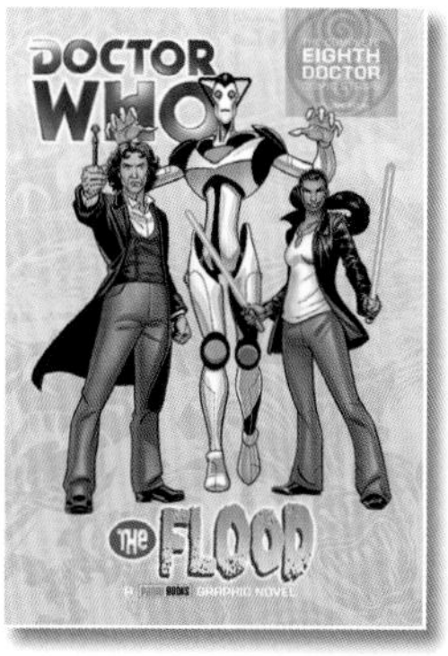
DOCTOR WHO
EIGHTH DOCTOR
THE FLOOD

Volume Four of the Eighth Doctor's complete comic strip adventures, containing eight digitally restored stories: **WHERE NOBODY KNOWS YOUR NAME, THE NIGHTMARE GAME, THE POWER OF THOUERIS!, THE CURIOUS TALE OF SPRING-HEELED JACK, THE LAND OF HAPPY ENDINGS, BAD BLOOD, SINS OF THE FATHERS** and **THE FLOOD**!

PLUS a massive 28-page behind-the-scenes feature, and a newly-extended conclusion to **THE FLOOD!**

228 pages | full colour | softcover
£15.99 | $26.50 | ISBN 978-1-905239-65-8

THE COMPLETE TENTH DOCTOR

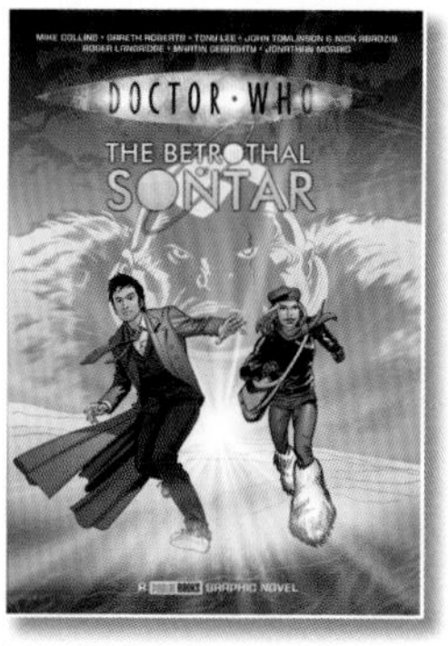
DOCTOR·WHO
THE BETROTHAL OF SONTAR

Volume One of the Tenth Doctor's complete comic strip adventures from the pages of **DWM**, containing eight complete stories:

THE BETROTHAL OF SONTAR, **THE LODGER**, **F.A.Q.**, **THE FUTURISTS**, **INTERSTELLAR OVERDRIVE**, **OPERA OF DOOM!**, **THE GREEN-EYED MONSTER** and **THE WARKEEPER'S CROWN**!

PLUS a massive 15-page behind-the-scenes feature, including commentaries from the writers, artists and editors, cut scenes, pencil art, design sketches, and more.

180 pages | full colour softcover
£15.99 | $31.95
ISBN 978-1-905239-90-0

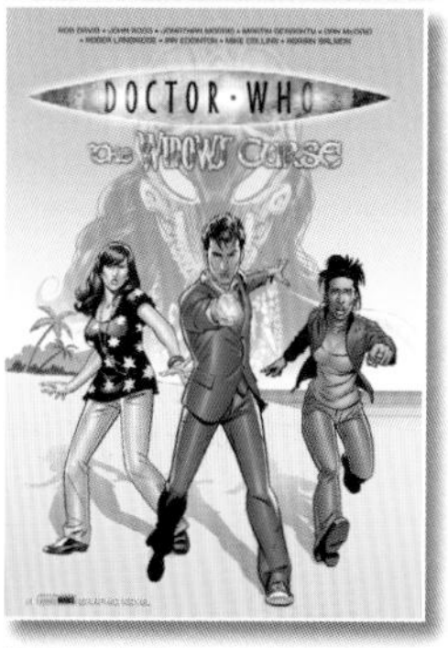
DOCTOR·WHO

Volume Two of the Tenth Doctor's complete comic strip adventures from the pages of **DWM**, containing nine complete stories:

THE WOMAN WHO SOLD THE WORLD, **BUS STOP!**, **THE FIRST**, **SUN SCREEN**, **DEATH TO THE DOCTOR!**, **UNIVERSAL MONSTERS**, **THE WIDOW'S CURSE**, **THE IMMORTAL EMPEROR** and **THE TIME OF MY LIFE**!

PLUS a massive behind-the-scenes feature, including commentaries from the writers and artists, design sketches and more.

220 pages | full colour | softcover
£15.99 | $31.95
ISBN 978-1-84653-429-4

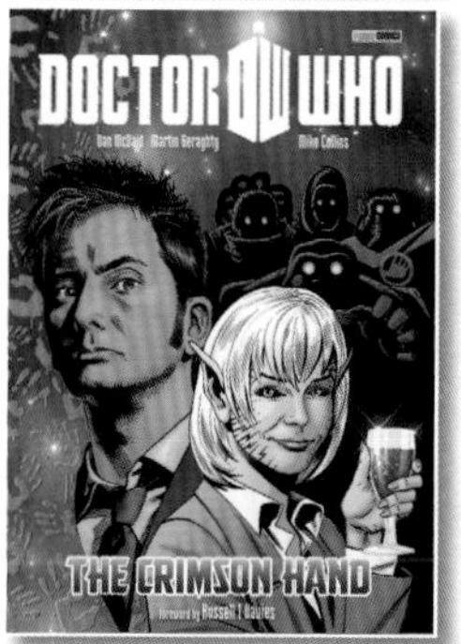
DOCTOR WHO
THE CRIMSON HAND

Volume Three of the Tenth Doctor's complete comic strip adventures from the pages of **DWM**, containing 10 complete stories:

HOTEL HISTORIA, **SPACE VIKINGS!**, **THINKTWICE**, **THE STOCKBRIDGE CHILD**, **MORTAL BELOVED**, **THE AGE OF ICE**, **THE DEEP HEREAFTER**, **ONOMATOPOEIA**, **GHOSTS OF THE NORTHERN LINE** and **THE CRIMSON HAND**!

PLUS a massive behind-the-scenes feature, including commentaries from the writers and artists, design sketches and more.

260 pages | full colour | softcover
£15.99 | $31.95
ISBN 978-1-84653-451-5

THE ELEVENTH DOCTOR

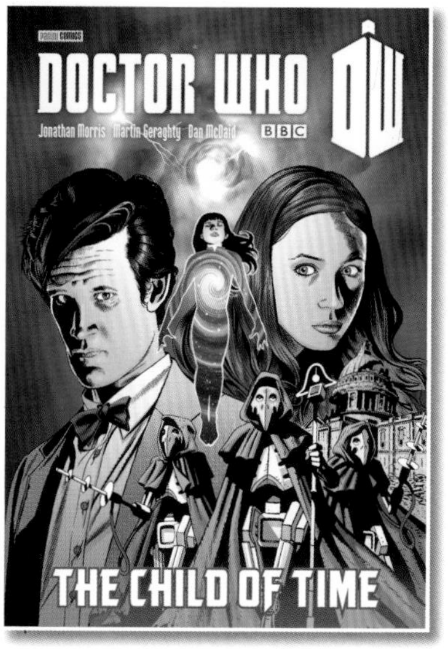
DOCTOR WHO
Jonathan Morris Martin Geraghty Dan McDaid
BBC
THE CHILD OF TIME

Volume One of the Eleventh Doctor's complete comic strip adventures from the pages of **DWM**, containing nine complete stories:

SUPERNATURE, **PLANET BOLLYWOOD!**, **THE GOLDEN ONES**, **THE PROFESSOR, THE QUEEN AND THE BOOKSHOP**, **THE SCREAMS OF DEATH**, **DO NOT GO GENTLE INTO THAT GOOD NIGHT**, **FOREVER DREAMING**, **APOTHEOSIS** and **THE CHILD OF TIME**!

PLUS a massive behind-the-scenes feature, including commentaries from the writers, artists and editors, cut scenes, pencil art, design sketches, and much, much more.

244 pages | full colour | softcover
£16.99 | $24.99
ISBN 978-1-84653-460-7

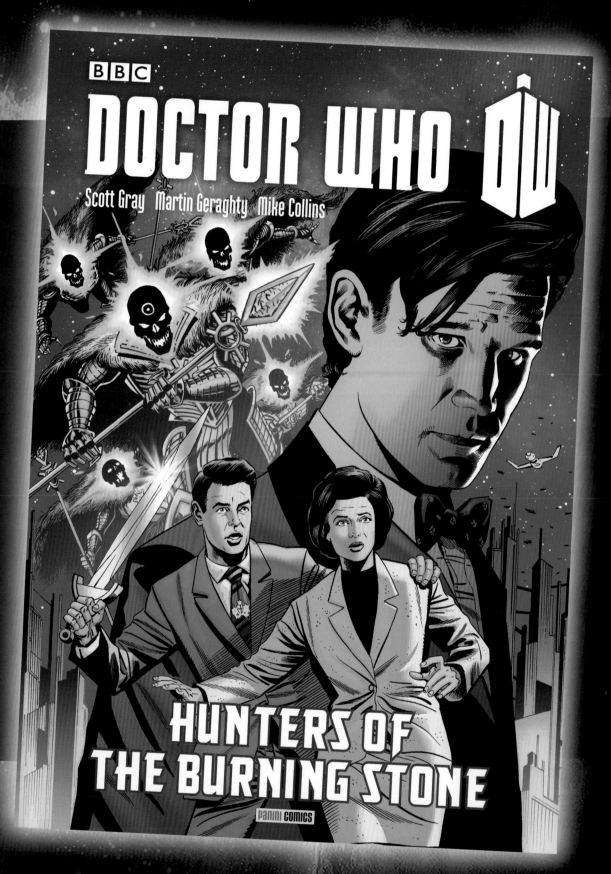